D1199451

FREEDOM AND CONTROL IN MODERN SOCIETY

HM 51
.B44
1964

FREEDOM AND CONTROL IN MODERN SOCIETY

MORROE BERGER

THEODORE ABEL

CHARLES H. PAGE

THIS VOLUME IS WRITTEN IN HONOR OF

ROBERT MORRISON MacIVER

*Francis Lieber Professor Emeritus of Political Philosophy and Sociology
Columbia University*

OCTAGON BOOKS

A DIVISION OF FARRAR, STRAUS AND GIROUX

New York   1978

INDIANA
PURDUE
LIBRARY
JUL 5 1978
FORT WAYNE

Copyright 1954, by Morroe Berger, Theodore Abel and Charles H. Page

Reprinted 1964
by special arrangement with
Morroe Berger, Theodore Abel and Charles H. Page

Second Octagon printing 1978

OCTAGON BOOKS
A DIVISION OF FARRAR, STRAUS & GIROUX, INC.
19 Union Square West
New York, N.Y. 10003

LIBRARY OF CONGRESS CATALOG CARD NUMBER: 64-16378
ISBN 0-374-90608-4

Manufactured by Braun-Brumfield, Inc.
Ann Arbor, Michigan
Printed in the United States of America

CONTENTS

Contents

INTRODUCTION

The chapters of this book have three things in common. They deal with important social and political problems of contemporary life; they have been written by scholars who admire Robert M. MacIver and, as his students or colleagues, have learned from him; and they deal with those subjects of social science that have interested MacIver and which he has illuminated in his books and articles for more than three decades.

In planning this book, the editors aimed to obtain contributions that would likewise illuminate, for the general reader, the student, and the professional social scientist, some of the fundamental and persisting problems which human beings face in our day. The editors and contributors hope that these essays will interest the non-specialist who seeks to understand what is happening in the world, the student who seeks not only knowledge of social life but intellectual stimulation, and the specialist and teacher who will be attracted by the quality of these contributions as well as by their adaptability to the classroom. For the classroom, this book will serve well as collateral reading in social science courses, specifically those on methodology, social control, social change, race relations, contemporary government, social psychology, social and political philosophy, as well as some economics courses.

The chapters in one division of this volume examine the relationship of the individual to the group. In his paper, Gardner Murphy summarizes the state of our knowledge of how each generation of human beings becomes socialized in contact with other human beings, how the ways of the group become the ways of the individual born to it. Describing this process as a mixture of "love-feast and battle royal," Dr. Murphy, from the standpoint of psychology, touches upon the need for external controls beyond those of the superego or the conscience, as well as upon the problem of political obedience itself. Robert Bierstedt approaches the same problem from another side—a sociological treatment of the nature of authority and its inherence in social organization (or what MacIver often calls associations).

Returning to the individual and small group level of analysis, Professors Merton and Lazarsfeld, in an unusual and provocative collaboration, discuss the influence of attitudes toward a social problem (Negro-white relations) upon the patterns of personal friendship. And again, from the standpoint of group analysis, Professor Znaniecki stresses the importance of personal motives, human goals, and social action for the classification of social groups (which he defines, as does MacIver himself, as conscious unities rather than mere aggregates of persons). He finds the most significant basis for classifying these groups not in their size, duration, or complexity, but in their function, which in turn is based upon the desires and actions of human beings.

The persistence of social groupings even when their social position changes is demonstrated in Mr. Glazer's discussion of the transformation of ethnic groups in the United States. He shows how ethnic groups have retained their cohesiveness in general economic and political matters even though they have largely lost their peculiar language and culture (and are but "empty nations"). At this point Dr. Gordon's chapter is complementary, for in it he shows how ethnic quality combines with interests based upon social class, region, and rural-urban differences to form subcultures. This concept of subculture Dr. Gordon analyzes in detail, emphasizing the importance of the ethnic component.

Professor Lipset's chapter on trade unions forms an appropriate transition from this part of the volume on the individual and the group to the second division on the state and society. Professor Lipset is interested in the meaning of the trade union for its members, in terms of their goals; but he also discusses those aspects which the trade union has in common with other forms of human association—that is, the sheer organizational features which, in a bureaucratic society, impede the growth or maintenance of democracy in associational life even where it is most earnestly sought.

Several other chapters likewise touch upon the problem of popular control of popular organizations, including both the state and voluntary associations. Professor Cook adverts to the problem of the relation of the individual and the group, not from the sociological standpoint, as do the writers in the first division, but from the political side of this issue. He finds that man must take moral risks—and this is what makes the human fate essentially tragic. Although Professor Cook sees great promise in the American solution to this perennial problem, he sees in the growth of the welfare state a danger of drift to totalitarianism. And to ward off this danger, he advocates a pluralism that is wider than the old political concept of that name —he calls for "institutional pluralism."

The welfare state and the advent of big business, big government, and big labor, are the subject of Professor Clark's contribution on the interrelations of economic and political forces. He offers the hypothesis, too, that business firms and trade unions have become so large and bureaucratized that they fruitfully may be considered, in economic and political analysis, as political entities. Here again, Professor Lipset's chapter is relevant, for at various points in it he treats the trade union in this way. Thus, nearly all of the contributions in both divisions of the book concern themselves with the place of the individual and the prospects of democracy in a world of large organizations and bureaucracy.

Despite its growing power, however, government, even in the totalitarian states, is not yet all-powerful. Professor Davis shows, in his analysis of the demographic aspects of national power, that the fundamental slow-moving demographic processes are not yet controllable by the state. His discussion of the demographic features of the great powers directs attention to the current bipolar distribution of national power between the United States and Soviet Russia. Professor Catlin examines the ideological aspect of this struggle and suggests the role that political science may play in the development of an "overall strategy of the democratic idea." The social aspects of Soviet Russia's revolutionary history are, in turn, the subject Dr. Inkeles analyzes in his discussion of the internal nature of that regime. Dealing with the government that has exercised more controls over its population and instituted more planned changes than any other in our day, he nevertheless shows how even this virtually omnipotent ruling body has been relatively unsuccessful in its efforts to change the attitudes, values, and sentiments of the Russian people. He shows, also, how far present Soviet society is from the Marxist vision that inspired European socialism. In this, one is reminded of Roberto Michels' prediction (made, incidentally, in a study of the inevitable frustration of democratic ideals in bureaucratic organizations) that "socialists might conquer, but not socialism."

The reader will note, then, that the various chapters of this book revolve around three broad questions: individual freedom in an age of large-scale organization, intergroup relations, and the relation of the individual to his government. These subjects are the ones that have steadily engaged the attention of Robert MacIver. Just how he has treated them the reader will see in the chapters on his contributions to sociological theory and to political theory, written, respectively, by Harry Alpert and David Spitz.

Nor are methodological problems entirely ignored. Of course, the most explicitly methodological chapter is that by Professor Lazarsfeld, in which he gives a formal statement of Professor Merton's substantive analysis of the friendship process and discusses the advantages of such treatment of data. Methodology is discussed also by Professor Znaniecki, who proposes a taxonomy of social groups; by Dr. Gordon, who commends the concept of subculture as an analytical tool; and by Professor Clark, who points to the importance of taking account of political and social forces in purely economic conceptual models.

In the spirit of Robert MacIver's own undogmatic approach to the study of social life, the editors did not seek contributions that would hew to one line as to method or subject matter or interpretation. Nor have they wished to eliminate or even to reduce such disagreements as may be found in these essays. Instead, their aim has been merely to present stimulating discussions of important issues of our time, all of them owing something to the work or inspiration of Robert MacIver. The contributors and the editors, then, have collaborated in this rewarding venture and invite the reader to share in it.

THE EDITORS

SOCIAL CONTROL,
THE GROUP,
AND THE INDIVIDUAL

1

The Internalization
of Social Controls

GARDNER MURPHY

In the difficult task of maintaining its sheer existence on the face of the earth, each species présents some uniformity in behavior. The ecological position achieved in evolution by species (made up of similarly constructed individuals) may be maintained by their progeny insofar as they can respond to environmental demands in the same fashion. When mothers are adequate to the feeding and care of their young, each of the young must be able to respond to this more or less uniform mothering pattern.

Now, these uniformities of behavior are determined in part by structural capacities, but the greater the advance in the phylogenetic scale, the less is guaranteed by structure and the more depends on learning. Much of the uniformity of human behavior results from learning by each individual as he confronts a new external situation, as all babies learn to reach for visually presented objects; but much depends also on learning from other individuals. It is almost entirely with this last problem that the present chapter is concerned.

The problems of (a) socially acquired uniformity in the behavior of human groups and (b) continuity in these behaviors from generation to generation may be formulated as follows: How does each individual learn, in contact with other individuals, to do as others do, to perceive as they perceive, and to value as they value?

THE CREATION OF UNIFORMITY

We begin with the paradox that uniformity depends partly on differentiation. The functional need of the group for uniformity, which we believe to be a need shared by all human groups to some

3

degree, is attended by two other needs which press in the same direction: the need of the strong for followers—that is, the need of the strong for the development of conformity in the weak, and likewise the need of the weak to conform to the strong. We do not raise here the question of the various motives (power, prestige, material gain, etc.), which may be salient in the strong at any given moment; the man of power may need soldiers for defense one day, plowmen for work in the fields on another. Suffice it to say that if there are individual differences in "strength," these play a part in determining the ways in which the weak must walk. And similarly, since the weak are in danger from those outside the system, and from other weak ones a shade stronger than themselves, they cannot function at all unless they conform to the directive of the strong. Animal societies make this clear to us; it is not an artifact of any specific culture, nor is it one of human culture taken collectively. To live together at all, a human group must have uniformities, derived in part from the facts of differentiation within the group in terms of strength and weakness.

But the imposition of uniformity does not mean that all members of the group take on identity of pattern in every respect. Individual differences in structure and in ability to learn limit the degree of such adaptation even when (as in some armies) all are subjected to pressure to develop in one direction. Ordinarily the differentiation goes very much further, not only because of the division of labor but because the strong desire incomplete uniformity. On many issues where power and prerogatives, status and material goods are concerned, they *do not allow* the development of uniformity.

From this follows the fact that there is differentiation down the vertical structural dimension, not only in ways of behaving but in ways of perceiving and in ways of valuing. As Nietzsche put it, there is "master morality" and "slave morality." Veblen [1] gives us a sex and class cleavage, based on the role of the "predatory." All modern societies introduce into the value-transmitting process the secondary processes of defining the behaviors, viewpoints, and values which are appropriate for each subgroup. (In addition, quite aside from vertical position, there are different value-systems to be inculcated in different subcultural groups which enjoy equality of status; and within each neighborhood different families introduce their own individuality into the pattern to which the children are exposed.)

This need of the strong as well as the corresponding need of the weak for a sort of symbiotic differentiation of values is paralleled

---

[1] T. Veblen, *The Theory of the Leisure Class* (New York: The Macmillan Co., 1899).

by the need of adults (for economic, emotional and other reasons) for conformity on some issues and nonconformity on others. The little boy must be a "man," but he must not usurp his father's ways with regard to cigars, bedtime hours, or arguing back. Similarly, the young, quite aside from adult pressures, have an enormous need for uniformity, a clear and consistent pattern which they can grasp and follow; and they have likewise a need for childishness, expressed in a huge area of play and autonomy in which the alien ways of grown-ups can be rejected. One plays pirate, but according to the specialized rules of childhood.

The result of these and other processes of differentiation is a highly specialized system of interchanges between the parents and other surrogates of society on the one hand, and the individual children on the other. The textbooks tell us that the child "takes over the ways of the group." But if the group is complex and differentiated, he cannot possibly do so; as Linton has pointed out, the best he can do is to take over family, neighborhood, and school ways, with the absolute certainty that he will come later if not earlier into grossly conflicting ways. Even the conflict, if I may be permitted this paradox, is part of the integrated system which makes the culture.

Twenty years ago it was my privilege to listen to a committee of alert and representative anthropologists discussing the processes of "acculturation." "How," they asked, "does the individual manage to take over the ways of a second culture, when one has already made one's first culture so fully a part of one's self?" After I had listened a while, I asked: "But how does one acquire one's first culture?" "Oh," they said, "we know the answer to that; one takes over the first culture from one's parents." What a long way we have come from that simple statement today! It sounds in fact so naïve that it is hard to recall how recently we were still allowing ourselves this easy variant upon the tabula rasa theory of the mind; the child was clay in the sculptor's hand; one just "took over" from one's parents.

The most significant clues, I think, in the newer sophistication regarding the actual struggle which the child goes through, have come from psychoanalysis. Whatever errors and false dramatizations the psychoanalytic method may have introduced, it has made clear that three similar and overlapping processes go on continuously in the little child: (1) a demand to be admitted; a yearning for love, acceptance, respect, a place in the group; (2) a protest against exclusion from inferior status and from current social privileges on the grounds of his immaturity; (3) a rebellion against interference with his primitive impulses and having to renounce his own self-expression in the interests of parents' immediate wishes or in the interest of the cultural outlook as a whole.

We come then to the view that any specifiable adult group uses its own way of gentle or forcible coercion to impress upon the young what they should *do, perceive,* and *value.* This is partly in accordance with the pattern expressed in their lives, as they grew up themselves, and partly at variance with it. In turn, the young absorb a great deal of their familial "culture," partly because they want to, partly because they have to. There is no simple osmosis of the prevalent social usages from old to young; there is a mixture of love-feast and battle royal. But for the most part and in the long run they do "take over."

The young are molded into the ways of their elders in three distinct ways: they learn to do as their elders do; they learn to perceive as their elders perceive; they learn to value as their elders value. It is hard to believe that any human group is unaware of facts such as these; but impossible to find any group which understands how this learning occurs. The *goals* of education have usually been reasonably clear (Plato's *Republic* is addressed to men who are explicitly concerned with the redefinition of such goals); the *means* of education are often clear (Locke's confident rationalism and Pestalozzi's warm practicality were well grasped and used). But what of the psychological *process* of learning? It is only in recent years that we have begun vaguely to grasp that we know little about the learning process, whether in relation to doing, to perceiving, or to valuing. And no matter how clearly we may understand the social organizations and educational institutions of a human group, our knowledge of their life is woefully incomplete as long as we do not understand *how* each new generation incorporates, digests, turns into its own substance the ways of doing, perceiving, and valuing which are the ways of life of the group.

THE SELF AND THE SOCIAL CODE

It is customary to introduce our thoughts about the child's assimilation of group norms by referring to those who have defined the modern conception of the child's awareness of himself and of others: notably, J. M. Baldwin,[2] C. H. Cooley,[3] G. H. Mead.[4]

---

[2] J. M. Baldwin, *Mental Development in the Child and the Race* (New York: The Macmillan Co., 1896).

[3] C. H. Cooley, *Human Nature and the Social Order* (New York: Charles Scribner's Sons, 1902).

[4] G. H. Mead, *Mind, Self and Society* (Chicago: The University of Chicago Press, 1934).

Although men such as these are concerned with selfhood, individuality, and the relations of persons to groups rather than with the
assimilation of values and norms, we all must acknowledge their contribution to the understanding of the primary role of the process
of discovery of selves and of others, and the process of introception
of that which is already part of those who are near and dear. Such
hypotheses regarding selves and their assimilation of norms have
become prodigiously rich and complex. This approach (or many
phases of it at least) appears today to be nearing the point where it
can be systematically tested.

Another group of hypotheses about the internalization of social
controls, deriving from cultural anthropology and from the labora-
tory work of Werner,[5] of Sherif,[6] and of Piaget,[7] to be discussed
below, seems today ready to flow into integration with those of the
Baldwin-Cooley-Mead category. A third group of relevant hypotheses comes, as we shall see, from psychoanalysis.[8]

---

[5] H. Werner, *Comparative Psychology of Mental Development* (New York: Harper
and Brothers, Rev. Ed., 1948).

[6] M. Sherif, *The Psychology of Social Norms* (New York: Harper and Brothers, 1936).

[7] J. Piaget, *The Moral Judgment of the Child* (New York: Harcourt, Brace & Co.,
1932.

[8] The hypotheses derived from the interpretation of these three systems of ideas could
be tested by a series of methods outlined somewhat as follows:

I. Comparative
1. Adult responses in different cultures compared.
2. Content and form of the learning processes in different cultures compared.
3. Study of interrelations between learning processes and ultimate personality
characteristics.
II. Genetic
1. Chronological or life-history approaches to the understanding of individuals.
2. Collation of such data from many biographies in the quest for laws.
3. Integration of such statements of laws with laws derived from Method I.
III. Psychoanalytic
1. Probing within the individual personality structure to discover levels of functioning and the dynamic relations between. these levels.
2. Integration of the results with biographical laws derived from II and the
comparative laws derived from I.
IV. Experimental
1. In controllable situations, the experimental verification of the systems of laws
derived from I, II, and III and the systematization of the results into a fresh
consistent theoretical form.
2. Quantification of these laws wherever valid measurements are available.

Although it is not practicable in so short a sketch to use such a classification of
methods systematically, we shall in general proceed in rough accordance with this way
of organizing our concepts and data.

THE SOCIAL MOLDING OF PERCEPTION AND VALUE

The individual learns not only to *do* as others around him do, but to perceive as they perceive, and to value as they value. The dependence of adult patterns of perceiving upon the cultural background is most easily demonstrated by means of the Rorschach test, in which massive group differences appear, for example, when comparisons are made of the Hopi [9] and the Alorese.[10] The white man finds in the trees of the jungle mostly just "foliage"; the South African native finds "game"; but when the same individual is confronted with experimental material it is the white man who discovers the "concealed figures" and the native who sees only a maze of lines. Even without such refined instruments, perceptual selectivity is evident. Moreover, *values* which arise directly in the perceptual situation have often been noted: thus among the Trobrianders a perceived similarity between father and son is accepted as *good;* fathers and sons, everyone knows, look alike. Brothers, however, do not resemble one another, the European who sees them as alike is in one context *rude,* in another context *ridiculous.*[11]

Whether the basic learning process actually varies from culture to culture remains a matter for theoretical discussion. We are impressed by Bateson's conception of deutero-learning;[12] one establishes early in life a *way* to learn; one learns how to learn. For example, one learns through a shock which engenders habits of avoidance; or one learns to analyze into finer and finer detail; or one learns to look for hidden meanings. One then pursues this technique of learning even in areas which appear unlike the one in which such habits were learned. The observations of Bateson and Mead [13] in Bali suggest that despite ultimate human uniformity in the capacity to learn, different combinations of learning techniques are characteristically stressed in different cultural situations. If this line of reasoning is sound, we should expect to find that the personality differences among contrasting cultural groups would ultimately express the fact that in any new situation people "take hold"

---

9 L. Thompson, *Culture in Crisis* (New York: Harper and Brothers, 1950).

10 C. DuBois, *The People of Alor* (Minneapolis: The University of Minnesota Press, 1944).

11 B. Malinowski, *The Father in Primitive Psychology* (New York: W. W. Norton & Co., Inc., 1927).

12 G. Bateson, Social Planning and the Concept of "Deutero-Learning," in T. M. Newcomb and E. L. Hartley, eds., *Readings in Social Psychology* (New York: Henry Holt & Co., 1947).

13 G. Bateson and M. Mead, *Balinese Character* (New York: The New York Academy of Sciences, 1942).

differently. Some things are easy to see and are welcomed; others are hard to see and seem "alien."

The considerations which we have urged document the conception of the "social molding of perception." The phrase still has an odd sound. "For is not perception," says the scholar, "the response of the individual mind; a response contingent upon the physiology of the individual brain?" From Hippocrates to Max Wertheimer and Kurt Goldstein, we have the observations of astute psychologists and physicians tracing the reality-seeking and reality-finding functions of the isolated individual. The whole tradition, however, is partly wrong. It has proved to be just as easy to predetermine perceptual response by social determiners like suggestion, love, hate, and the need for status, as by inner physiological determiners, whether operating at the level of the retina or at the level of the stomach. What is poured into the brain is a fusion of stimulation originating from outside the body and from inside the body. This conception of convergence of outer and inner factors, as developed for example by Sherif,[14] following Koffka, has stood up well under testing. Indeed, it is from this principle of convergence that most of the important modern experiments in perception have been derived.

A glimmer of understanding regarding the determination of the act of perception by the social situation in which the individual finds himself had been achieved in the late nineteenth century; Alfred Binet showed how the hypnotic trance fuses the stimulation derived from a physical stimulus object with the stimulation offered by the words of the hypnotist. It remained, however, for Sherif, working with concepts derived in large part from cultural anthropology, to show in convincing form that the individual in an "incomplete" stimulus situation, structures and stabilizes his perceptual response through use of factors operating within him. Some of these factors may have been planted within him recently by the experimenter; some by other members of the individual's social environment long before. But the fresh perceptual act betrays no line of cleavage or junction between the old elements and the new. It is an integral event; and it is socially shaped.

Since we can actually watch this process taking place, and since we can watch the process almost as easily in the little child whose social development is in considerable measure his progressive "learning to perceive," we find ourselves irrevocably committed to this genetic approach. Not that all psychological problems have to be

---

[14] M. Sherif, *op. cit.*

viewed genetically. But, in the case of perception, we find that each individual develops in his own way. Furthermore, we find, if our logic gives us courage, that social change, whether large or small, can by the same logic be shown to be in large measure the development of new modes of perceiving. Let us proceed then to trace the process of the development of perception, of value-judgment, and of internalization of group controls.

Apparently the objects experienced by infants are as yet dimly defined in regard to their outlines, their position in time and space, and their sensory qualities. The sharp definition and delimitation which we learn to accept and verbalize take a long time to acquire. Moreover, even the distinction between a thing and a feeling about the thing—between fact and feeling, between cognition and affection—is poorly defined, if not indeed completely absent. The first world is therefore not a world of facts, of things, upon which feelings of good and bad, or impulses to approach or retreat are *superimposed,* but rather a world of unresolved wholeness involving a good-or-bad-situation-to-be-coped-with. Werner has proposed that we call this kind of perceiving "physiognomic"—noting how we see a man's character, his intentions toward us directly in the lines and shadows of his expression, rather than first taking note of the contours and then inferring character.

The point seems to be of huge importance for the understanding of our value systems, because it is not hard to show that much of this primitive physiognomic mode of response remains with us through life. The "irrationalities" described by psychiatrists and by anthropologists need not all be the products of rationalization or of any sort of secondary elaboration of material that once was rational; rather, much that we experience is simply the essentially untransformed physiognomic response of the little child.

Differentiation, the learning to select in terms of distinctions, learning to break a thing up into its aspects and to assign it to an appropriate portion of time and space, does of course proceed rapidly. But not on an even front. And as the individual begins to differentiate, the cultural group plays a very large part in determining *which distinctions will be made;* what objects, and *what aspects* of objects, must be separated from their halo of affective-conative context by virtue of the fact that the same thing in different contexts may be "good" or "bad," a thing to be sought or a thing to be avoided: and what objects may very well be left in their primitive physiognomic form.

So far, we are implying that the child clings to his early habits until he is pushed out of them; and this is true up to a point. But

two additional factors are involved.   First, the persons around the
child may in some situations actually *discourage* his attempts to develop a differentiated response.   Insects are not to be lovingly observed; they are simply to be swatted.   Second, after assisting in the
child's completion of the process of differentiation, people may, at
a later time, reintroduce in him the earlier physiognomic attitude.
Thus the direct naïve perception that a person of non-Caucasian
characteristics is an inferior person, or a person of lower physical
type—"anyone can just see they're inferior"—is in general unknown
to the child of two or three; this attitude develops under social
pressures year by year in regions where racial and ethnic prejudices
are rife.   The cognitive clarity of the little child who sees each face
simply as a face, not as "my" kind of face, is progressively blurred
under such conditions.

An even more curious case of the development of a positive physiognomic response, the acquisition of a value and value-judgment
along with its basic percept, is given by Horowitz.[15]   Children of
six years see all or most flags as interesting, pretty, desirable objects.
By ten years of age they see the Stars and Stripes as the prettiest;
just as you and I not only love our national emblem, but directly
see it to be beautiful.

In the light of these two principles we have no great difficulty
in understanding the "self-evident" rightness of the ways of our own
group: (1) Those social ways which we grasp as tiny children, such
as the self-evident lovableness of mothers, remain at the same physiognomic level unless disturbed; such ways are inherently good and
require no justification.   (2) Those objects which we learned to
analyze into objective factors and quasi-independent affective factors may often be resynthesized under social pressure.

Fundamental to this whole process of perceptual organization
is the matter of anchorage, the determination of a region or quality in the total upon which there is emphasis, within which there
is stability, and in terms of which the whole is made coherent.   As
the percept develops from the second to the third stage, it regularly
acquires an anchorage point; indeed the relative intensity, extent,
or other physiological basis for the dominance of one aspect of the
whole pattern tends to give it its position as an anchor, by which it
can be related to other patterns.

Besides such dominance, there appear to be two other grounds
for the assumption of anchorage position by any element in a structure.   The first is its association in past experience with satisfac-

---

[15] E. L. Horowitz, "Some Aspects of the Development of Patriotism in Children,"
Sociometry, 1940, 3, 329–341.

tions experienced by the individual after encountering that particular situation; the situation is followed by "reward": Let any spot of color or tone of voice appear in a context which as a whole is followed by satisfaction but which gives no such satisfaction when this color or tone is missing; thereafter there is anchorage upon that color or tone. This is perhaps a case of the conditioned response; or more likely, it is the basic principle upon which the conditioned response depends.

The second principle is best known by Freud's term *cathexis;* sometimes by the term *canalization.* Let there be in the perceptual pattern something which intrinsically—not because of a subsequent reward—gives satisfaction. Let there be a Titian red in the portrait otherwise not distinguished for beauty, a magnificent oboe in an otherwise pedestrian orchestral piece. Insofar as these give satisfaction, they quickly become anchorage points. "Do you remember that rather pathetic performance at Carnegie Hall?" "Yes; but the oboes saved it." The broad principle exemplified by these two more specific principles may be generalized to read: The satisfaction associated with a percept gives it vitality and the capacity to persist in competition with other perceptual habits.

If now we note that we are constantly rewarded for seeing things as others see them, we find no mystery in the fact that *we learn to see as others see.* If, moreover, we repeatedly see in a manner which leads to distress, we give up the habit. Schafer's [16] principle that we anchor upon what has given us satisfaction is in fact apparently the cue to the widely quoted experiments of Sherif [17] on the auto-kinetic effect: Sherif presented to individual subjects in the dark room a single point of light, requesting estimates of the direction and distance through which it moved. He found each individual characteristically establishing a stable average or norm of estimated distance, with a normal frequency curve of greater and smaller estimates about this norm. He then placed three subjects together in the dark room and required of each a spoken judgment as to the distance the light moved. Here the individual differences between the subjects are at first large; then they converge, as the high-estimate man and the low-estimate man each approach the man at the middle (a "funnel-shaped" pattern). Then when these same individuals are tested alone, they tend to conserve the habits that they acquired in the group.

Much other experimental work of this type has been done, sup-

---

16 R. Schafer and G. Murphy, "The Role of Autism in a Visual Figure-Ground Relationship," *Journal of Experimental Psychology,* 1943, **32,** 335–343.

17 M. Sherif, *op. cit.*

porting clearly the central concept of socially learning to perceive and indicating, of course, that the magnitude of the effect and the rapidity of the learning depend on the looseness, the unstructured quality, of the situation. Since matters of social usage and of moral judgment are often at first indistinct and poorly structured for the child who seeks clear and categorical rules, he is of course easily guided into the perceptual habits standardized in his group. This does not give the group unbridled power over the individual; at any age the individual may perceive under the press of his own needs or his own special clarity of analysis. But most ordinary human beings, sharing essentially the gross and recurrent needs of other human beings in the situation, learn to anchor upon what has been rewarded by social approval and learn to avoid eccentric, bizarre modes of perception which result in their isolation. The individual acquires a trend or set characteristic of his culture and within that of his subculture, or even his family.

The rapidity of such learning depends partly, as the data of Piaget [18] and Lerner [19] show, upon the lack of clear perception by the child of the various individualities and personal needs around him. Egocentrism, the implicit assumption that one is seeing *all there is to see,* and the inability to take into account the role played by one's own selfhood and individuality, result in a readiness to accept as final the good and the bad which are offered as whole indivisible packages by the cultural situation. The statement that the "naughty boy teased the poor cat" conveys to the child not the fact that the boy teased the cat and that this was naughty, but the global reality of naughty-teasing as an attribute of the boy. In other words, moral judgment is physiognomic; Piaget's term for this is "moral realism." Similarly, the ways of those who pattern their lives on a plan different from our own are self-evidently absurd or immoral; the anthropologist's "ethnocentrism" appears to be a direct and necessary derivative from physiognomic perception based on prior perceptual experiences rewarded and punished in one's own group. When norms are not at all clear as to good and bad, we find the child living in a "moral anarchy." Something like this is suggested by DuBois' study of Alor.[20]

The operation of these principles governing anchorage leads of course to the general tendency to perceive and think in terms of wishes; the tendency may be termed "autism." Used not in its tech-

18 J. Piaget, *op. cit.*

19 E. Lerner, *Constraint Areas and the Moral Judgments of Children* (Menasha, Wis.: George Banta, 1937).

20 C. DuBois, *op. cit.*

nical sense in psychopathology, but as a noun derived from Bleuler's phrase "autistic thinking," autism is defined by Chein[21] as the "movement of cognitive processes in the direction of drive satisfaction." Our primary point here is that, in addition to purely personal autisms, society supplies, every day of our lives, forms of social control based on collectively experienced and collectively reinforced autisms.

From this viewpoint it becomes clear that perception (as any student of John Dewey is likely to have suspected all along) is the implementation of a purpose. The sense organs are in large degree turned to catch what we want to catch in order to adapt to the environment; to select those aspects of the environment with which we propose to deal; and to organize what gets through to us from the sense organs in such a way that it helps in the immediate adaptation, exempting us from the boring or threatening task of reconsidering all over again what the ceaseless signals from the outer world might mean.

CONFLICT AND THE RISE OF CONSCIENCE

Reference has already been made to the fact that a limited degree of awareness of oneself facilitates the acceptance of the group outlook. The development of a sharper picture of the self does in fact substantially alter and complicate the subsequent processes by which social norms are understood and internalized. In particular, the self-evident rightness of the norms comes frequently into sharp conflict with what is right from the standpoint of the emerging ego; the personal autisms reject the group autisms. Hence the beginning of the long, complicated process of rejecting group norms to create an area of "immunity" for the ego. The most obvious illustration of this process is the "rationalization" by which we persuade ourselves that the present self-indulgence is not a breach of group norms.

From here on, we find the jungle of the "mechanisms of defense," by which guilt from the infraction of group norms is assuaged by devices for viewing our act through some other spectacles than those issued by the cultural headquarters for daily use.

The escapes are multitudinous and so effective that most societies provide well for the internalization of a secondary system of social controls, over and above those which depend upon the first simple

---

[21] R. Levine, I. Chein, and G. Murphy, "The Relation of the Intensity of a Need to the Amount of Perpetual Distortion," *Journal of Psychology*, 1942, **13**, 283–293.

acceptance of the group outlook. These secondary controls take the form of "conscience." They have traditionally been regarded as immune to rational analysis; the almost supernatural status with which we regard them, as did Kant, has given them a "categorical" quality. The two great inscrutabilities are "the starry heavens and the moral law." With his habit of asking those questions which it is impious to ask, Freud [22] has asked us to look for the answer in the processes of identification with parents. Earlier he had asked us to look at the initial identification with the parent, giver of life and of love. Now he asks us to look for the identification when it emerges in the struggle with the parents. After the age of innocence, the age of naïveté, the process of childish identification becomes involved with the very individual who coerces or threatens the child. This is usually father or mother or both; sometimes big brother or sister; sometimes another source of authority. Identification with the strong, the authoritative, we can see every day as we watch the child; he takes an authoritative attitude toward his doll or his pet; he achieves power by becoming inwardly one with the authority figure. This incorporation within the growing personality of the authority figure is now turned against himself; he is his own disciplinarian. This is the superego. For most children in Western society it is composed largely of images and ideas regarding the father; but there are maternal (and other) elements as well. We may regard the superego, then, for most purposes, as identification with the parental discipline. We find the five-year-old lecturing to himself to be a good boy, developing feelings of guilt when he fails to live up to the superego standard. Conscience is on the way to consolidation. And conscience appears whenever there is conflict between inner impulse and internalized parent-image.

But conscience is seldom fully trusted by those responsible for social codes. If the conflict between impulse and superego is acute and persistent, control of those impulses which are rejected by the social code is likely to break at critical moments. Controls other than those which lie within are therefore typically available to reinforce the power of conscience. The law, the police, the courts, and the penal systems still remain to assist the flagging conscience when much is at stake. As the frustration of impulses accumulates, however, and the tricks of self-justification become more and more complex and more often repeated, external controls must become more and more rigorous. The protection of property and the maintenance of order, in particular, often require much more force than

---

[22] S. Freud, *Inhibitions, Symptoms, and Anxiety* (Stamford, Conn.: The Psychoanalytic Institute, 1927).

the individual conscience can provide. A well-fed populace can function with a weak conscience and a single policeman, but as hunger mounts one finds either more gendarmes or the development of Spartan discipline, or both.

At this point we must remind ourselves that the whole system of internalization depends partly on authority and partly on eager acceptance, as we suggested above. But the balance and interaction of these two must depend both on family structure and on the larger group structure. Thus the conscience which arises in the family may, as in some democracies, extend to all society, making it "wrong" to resist the ways of the group. In some dictatorships, there may be almost no carry-over of conscience to the larger world, and one complies with the despot for no other reason than the fear of his soldiers.

An hypothesis proceeding beyond this point has been engagingly presented by Sherif [23] in a theory of crisis, which specifies that, as internal demands become more and more coercive, the inadequately structured *norms of society are recast;* much which was "wrong" becomes "right" in the face of great need. The old father figures of a patriarchal society are now seen as despots in whom there is no virtue. Sherif is thinking, as do most students of crisis and revolution, in terms of sudden transformation of norms. The principle works as well, however, for slow erosion of the norms, as impulses are gradually more and more frustrated, or as internal and external controls grow weaker.

From a purely external viewpoint, it may appear to make but little difference whether social control is achieved by one means or another. Today one must always ask, however, at what *cost to individual health* and at what *cost to effective group living* the controls are maintained. The anthropologist of yesteryear often implied that men can adapt to almost any social order; today he is much more likely to insist that social orders differ in their capacity to meet the basic demands of humanness in their consequent stability, and in their capacity to provide a good life for those who share in the cultural pattern.

There are, then, *good* and *bad* methods of regulating individual behavior; good and bad ways of changing the norms, and good and bad ways of defining the norms to which a society may aspire to move. All these conceptions of good and bad lie in the intrinsic satisfactions and frustrations of human life; and it is the task of social science to discover not only how norms are developed and how they are internalized by the individual, but also how such

---

23 M. Sherif, *op. cit.*

operations can be conducted in a way providing maximum fulfillment to the individual members of the group.

In American society, for example, we find among children an
ethics of fear and authority side by side with an ethics of love, so
that telling a lie is bad partly because it outrages the father, partly
because it hurts the mother's feelings.[24] There is some evidence,
supported by the work of Burrow [25] and others, that the ethics of
love involves less wear and tear. At this point, objective description
of the internalization of social controls passes over into the ethical
problem of *better* and *worse* ways of maintaining group norms (insofar as we wish to maintain them). But instead of leaving this
problem to ethics alone, psychology can in some measure support
one system of morality as against another, on the grounds that one
meets human needs better than the other can meet them.

---

24 E. Lerner, *op. cit.*
25 T. Burrow, *The Neurosis of Man* (New York: Harcourt, Brace and Co., 1949).

2

FRIENDSHIP AS SOCIAL PROCESS: A SUBSTANTIVE AND METHODOLOGICAL ANALYSIS

PAUL F. LAZARSFELD AND ROBERT K. MERTON

INTRODUCTION

In certain respects, the field of sociology can be aptly described in terms of numerous schools of substantive theory. In a book such as Sorokin's *Contemporary Sociological Theories,* for example, each school is marked off from the others by the substantive class of "factors" which it provisionally takes as the basic determinant of social and cultural patterns; factors such as the geographic or the biological, the demographic, economic, or technological. Increasingly, however, such a description needs to be supplemented by others. Not, of course, that these schools of thought have dropped from sight, but only that they no longer constitute the major forms for organizing the greater part of work now going forward in sociology. Indeed, the major alignments are not so much in terms of schools emphasizing different substantive factors as in terms of what might be called styles of intellectual life.

One such line of division is that between the generalizers and the empiricists, between the sociologists primarily concerned with developing substantive doctrines which go well beyond presently available data and the sociologists primarily concerned with extending the range of certified facts in hand. Another line of division, and the one most in point for this chapter, is that between sociological theories which, comprised of concepts and propositions about social behavior, are substantive in character, and methodology

18

which, comprised of statements about the logic of inquiry, is necessarily formal, rather than substantive, in character. The substantive interest in sociology centers on the assumptions that give rise to hypotheses about social life; the methodological interest, on the assumptions that make for the clarification and empirical testing of those hypotheses. The one is primarily concerned with the *what* of sociological inquiry; the other, with the *how*.

It is readily agreed, in principle, that substantive and methodological analyses of sociological problems are both indispensable; that they are, indeed, complementary. But this ready agreement is relatively uninstructive unless it results in more clearly defining the distinctive role of each type of analysis and the ways in which the two interlock. How, for example, is substantive sociological analysis clarified by being restated in the formal terms of methodology? What, if anything, is lost in the course of this formal re-analysis of substantive propositions? By dealing with questions such as these in the detailed examination of a case in point, this chapter is intended to bring out some of the respects in which substantive and methodological inquiry complement one another.

The substantive case in point is that of the social processes involved in the formation, maintenance, and disruption of friendship; the methodological concern is to identify the logical framework of variables presupposed by a substantive analysis of these processes.

Both parts of the chapter—the substantive and the methodological —have a direct and considerable relation to some of the recorded intellectual interests of the sociologist whose achievements are being celebrated in this book. In several of his works, Professor MacIver has evidenced an abiding interest in the analysis of social processes. Not only does he remind us, for example, that "the social sciences are deeply engrossed in the study of social processes," but, in company with other sociologists, he has singled out for special attention the kinds of social process which are involved in "modes of dynamic relationship, particularly the ways in which people become associated or dissociated." [1]

On the substantive side, Professor MacIver has plainly put the major question with which we are concerned in the special case of the close primary ties involved in intimate friendship. To put it in his own words: "We must . . . consider integration as a social-psychological process operating within the group. How far, under

---

[1] R. M. MacIver, *Social Causation* (Boston: Ginn & Company, 1942), pp. 130–131; *Society* (New York: Rinehart and Company, Inc., 1937), pp. 406ff.

what conditions, and with what limitations does this process actually occur?" [2]

Moreover, Professor MacIver dwells upon the conceptual distinction which is at the heart of the processual analysis of friendship that follows—the distinction between the social and the cultural, between social ties (or interpersonal relations) and a consensus or dissensus of ideas (or values). Among his many statements of this conception, we select one which can serve, almost without the change of a word, to introduce the substantive part of this paper (dealing as it does, with the dynamic interplay of interpersonal attachments and values):

> . . . the principle of integration combines and even confuses two quite different forms of group unity. There is a difference between the subjective harmony of the attitudes of group members toward one another and the harmony of ideas. We can observe in many groups a social unity within which people feel at one though their opinions still differ.[3]

Substantively, then, this chapter may be thought of as dealing with these several observations by Professor MacIver; it is an analysis of certain social-psychological *processes* through which *social relations* interact with *cultural values* to produce diverse patterns of friendship.

On the methodological side, too, there is a bridge between conceptions set forth by Professor MacIver and the concerns of this paper. He has recognized that the empirical study of social process—for example, the persisting or changing patterns of interaction between friends—requires examination of the interplay of *specified variables;* that it is not enough to analyze the process in terms which draw upon an unspecified and, therefore, often changing array of implied variables. He has noted, for example, that in the study of social relationships, conceived as social process, the adjustment of interests and attitudes must be "assessed at every stage of the process." [4]

The methodological part of this paper deals with precisely that problem by attempting to specify analytical research operations appropriate for the study of phases in the social process involved in maintaining or disrupting a social relationship.

This chapter, then, is conceived as an example of the interlocking

---

[2] R. M. MacIver and C. H. Page, *Society: An Introductory Analysis* (New York: Rinehart and Company, Inc., 1949), p. 228; see substantially the same passage in an earlier edition: MacIver, *Society*, p. 243.

[3] MacIver and Page, *op. cit.,* p. 229; cf. MacIver, *Society*, p. 243.

[4] MacIver, *Social Causation*, p. 133.

use of substantive conceptions (both theoretical and empirical) and of methodological or formal conceptions in the analysis of a particular type of sociological problem. It is intended to explore, through detailed illustration, the nature of that triple alliance between theoretical statements, empirical data and methodology which, as Professor MacIver's works indicate, is required to advance disciplined knowledge about social processes.

PART ONE—SUBSTANTIVE ANALYSIS *

This analysis of friendship as social process is drawn from a study,[5] begun some years ago, of social organization and interpersonal relations in two housing communities: Craftown, a project of some seven hundred families in New Jersey, and Hilltown, a bi-racial, low-rent project of about eight hundred families in western Pennsylvania.

Among other things, we sought to identify the networks of intimate social relationships in these communities. As a first step, Hilltowners and Craftowners were asked to designate their "three closest friends, whether they live in Hilltown (Craftown) or not." In both communities, about 10 per cent reported that they did not know as many as three persons whom they could properly describe as really close friends. But the rest had no such difficulty. This resulted in the identification of a cumulative total of almost two thousand friends by Hilltowners and Craftowners, with roughly half of these living in the same community as the informants.[6]

From data of this kind, it was a short further step to search out patterns in the selection of close friends with respect to likeness or difference of attitudes and values or of social status (for example, of sex, race and age, social class, organizational affiliation and standing in the local community). Although this is not the place to present

---

* By Robert K. Merton.
5 The subject of this section will be given fuller treatment in a forthcoming book, *Patterns of Social Life: Explorations in the Sociology and Social Psychology of Housing*, by R. K. Merton, P. S. West, and M. Jahoda of the Columbia University Bureau of Applied Social Research.
6 It should now be plain why we did not adopt the familiar sociometric device of asking residents to designate *only* those intimate friends who happened to live in their own community. Had this been done, we should have had a larger number of "cases for analysis" but these would have included a substantial proportion of persons who were not regarded, in fact, by Hilltowners and Craftowners as their *most intimate* friends. The category of most intimate friends will have thus been diluted by less significant relationships, making it less likely that actual uniformities underlying the structure of these intimate personal ties would be detected. For this reason, the more inclusive sociometric measure was adopted.

these findings in detail, a short general summary is needed as context for our discussion of friendship as social process. Within each community, it was found that the degree of similarity of status-attributes of close friends varied greatly for different attributes, running a gamut from the almost complete limitation of intimate friendships among those of the same race and sex,[7] to entirely negligible selectivity in terms of educational status. We found, further, that for some of the *same* social attributes, the degree of selectivity differed widely between the two communities. There was, for example, a relatively high degree of selectivity in terms of religious affiliation in Hilltown, and relatively little in Craftown. The social and cultural context provided by the community went far toward determining both the general extent of selecting status-similars as close friends and the particular statuses for which such selectivity was most marked. Thus, the more cohesive community of Craftown consistently exhibited a lower degree of selection of status-similars as friends; but when such selectivity did occur, it was as likely to be in terms of *acquired* statuses—those resulting from the individual's own choice or achievement—as in terms of *ascribed* statuses such as nativity and age, which are fixed or predetermined at birth. In Hilltown, on the contrary, selectivity was much more marked in terms of ascribed status, since there was less by way of overarching community purposes to focus the attention of residents on locally achieved or acquired statuses.

From these and comparable findings, it soon became evident that the problem of selection was not adequately formulated by the familiar and egregiously misleading question: When it comes to close friendships, do birds of a feather actually flock together? Rather, it is a more complex problem of determining the degree to which such selectivity varies for different kinds of social attributes, how it varies within different kinds of social structure, and how such selective patterns come about. Our efforts to deal with the first two questions must be left to the complete report of the study; part of the effort to deal with the third question is described in this paper.

Before turning to the analysis of friendship as a social process, however, we must consider a note on terminology.

---

[7] It must be emphasized that such extreme concentration of personal ties within each racial group obtains only for the *most intimate* friendships. (It will be remembered that these data refer to the three *closest* friends of residents.) Short of these most intimate attachments, however, there have developed numerous personal relations across race lines in Hilltown, as will be seen in the complete report, *Patterns of Social Life.*

A Terminological Note. Oddly enough, the English language lacks a word to signify a tendency for friendships to form between people of "the same kind" just as it lacks a word to signify a tendency for friendships to form between those of differing kinds. This is odd because our technical, if not our popular, vocabulary does include words to designate comparable selective tendencies; for example, tendencies for marriage between persons who are alike in one or another respect (this being called *homogamy*) and for the complementary pattern of marriage between persons who are unlike (this being called *heterogamy*).[8] They arrange these matters better among the savage Trobrianders whose native idiom at least distinguishes friendships within one's in-group from friendships outside this social circle.[9] Since our language does not make the appropriate distinction with which we shall be concerned in this chapter, terms must be coined for the purpose (since it would probably be unwise to borrow the exotic Trobriand terminology).

Perhaps we shall be allowed, therefore, to summarize the fifteen-word phrase, "a tendency for friendships to form between those who are alike in some designated respect" by the single word *homophily*, and to summarize the complementary phrase, "a tendency[10] for friendships to form between those who differ in some designated respect," by the correlative word *heterophily* (thus following the comparable terminological practice long since established for types of marriage).

These terms offer more advantages than mere economy of language, although this alone might be enough to justify their coinage. They also help us to escape from the practice, encouraged by loose terminology, of assuming that *either* people of like kind "flock together" *or* they do not, rather than seeing this as a matter of degree. We shall find it possible, and useful, to speak of "degrees of homophily," as measured by indices of positive correlation between the attributes of friends, or of "degrees of heterophily," as measured by indices of negative correlation.

---

8 This has been recognized usage since the writings of Karl Pearson and Havelock Ellis on assortative mating. For one among many recent examples of this usage, see E. W. Burgess and P. Wallin, "Homogamy in Social Characteristics," *American Journal of Sociology*, 1943, **49**, pp. 109–124.

9 As Malinowski reports, "a twofold scheme in the relations between men is clearly defined linguistically by the two words for friend, one meaning 'friend within the barrier,' the other 'friend across the barrier.'" *Sexual Life of Savages* (New York: Harcourt, Brace & Co., 1929), p. 501.

10 In neither of these phrases, does the word "tendency" refer to some propensity assumedly rooted in the individual. It refers, rather, to an observed correlation, positive in the one instance, negative in the other, between designated attributes of friends. In other words, homophily and heterophily are descriptive, not interpretative, concepts.

This terminological usage will also help us to distinguish readily between *types* of assortative friendship, according to the character of the designated resemblances between friends. For example, we draw a distinction between *status-homophily* (observed tendencies for similarity between the group-affiliation of friends or between their positions within a group) and *value-homophily* (observed tendencies toward correspondence in the values of friends). Following the same terminological principle, we can easily register, with brevity and relative precision, even more specific patterns of selection in friendship: comparing the degree of religious status-homophily, say, with the degree of political status-homophily. In short, these terms, brought into being by necessity, may have the virtue of facilitating the analysis of friendship-behavior by suggesting research problems, some of which, we must report, had escaped our notice until the application of these terms had forced them on our attention.[11]

Selective and Adjustive Processes in Value-Homophily. What precedes is by way of prelude. This section will consider selective and adjustive processes in friendship, the discussion being rooted in our empirical materials but branching out to report inferences drawn from these materials.

In this respect, the concern of this discussion differs substantially from that of most empirical studies of patterns of friendship. These deal primarily with the question: who tends to form friendships with whom? But, to the best of my knowledge, empirical studies have not attempted to analyze the processes through which these patterns come about. To be sure, sociologists have never lost sight of the principle that social relations are sustained by social processes, as can be seen, for example, in the "sociological analysis of the

---

11 Since the popular game of criticizing social scientists for their occasional coinage of technical terms continues unabated, Peirce's observation of half a century ago is still timely. ". . . no study can become scientific . . . until it provides itself with a suitable technical nomenclature, whose every term has a single definite meaning universally accepted among students of the subject, and whose vocables have no such sweetness or charms as might tempt loose writers to abuse them—which is a virtue of scientific nomenclature too little appreciated. It is submitted that the experience of those sciences which have conquered the greatest difficulties of terminology, which are unquestionably the taxonomic sciences, chemistry, mineralogy, botany, zoology, has conclusively shown that the one only way in which the requisite unanimity and requisite ruptures with individual habits and preferences can be brought about is so to shape the canons of terminology that they shall gain the support of moral principle. . . ." This is *not* to say that all word-coinages necessarily make for scientific advance; each new term must earn its way. But those who are cowed by the indiscriminate charge that every technical term in social science is merely jargon (i.e., gibberish) would do

dyad" by Howard Becker and Ruth Hill Useem (*American Sociological Review*, 1942, **7**, 13–26).   Nevertheless, the empirical study of friendship has typically been focused on observed patterns of friendship rather than on the processes which give rise to them.   It is clear, however, that the observed patterns can in turn be conceived as the resultants of social interaction, as process rather than product, and it is this conception which is being explored here.

By selective and adjustive processes in friendship we mean patterned sequences of social interaction between friends in which each phase generates and regulates the subsequent phase in such manner as to give rise to the observed patterns of friendship between people of designated kinds.   In principle, one phase is said to "generate" the next when the conditions obtaining at one time prove to be both necessary and sufficient for the relationship obtaining at the next time of observation.   We say that this is so "in principle" because, at the still-primitive stage reached by sociological analyses of social processes, it must be considered adequate if, in actual practice, we can identify the sufficient antecedent conditions without being able to show that they are also necessary.

Throughout our studies of friendship, it has been provisionally assumed that the observed patterns of status-homophily—the positive correlation between the statuses of close friends—are, to some significant but unknown extent, the products of an underlying agreement between the values harbored by friends.   The dynamic role of similarities and differences of these values in forming, maintaining, or disrupting friendships therefore requires notice in its own right.

Racial Attitudes.   As a case in point, we consider the racial attitudes and values of Hilltowners, and their dynamic role in local patterns of friendship.   These values are singled out because in Hilltown, with its equal number of Negro and white families, they have great meaning for residents.   They may therefore affect patterns of intimate association among those who hold these values (just as our studies have found that political values affect personal association in the intensely political atmosphere of Craftown).   These attitudes toward race vary in many, sometimes minute, respects, and no single classification can do justice to their every nuance of detail.   For our present purposes, however, it is enough

---

well to study the rest of the discussion by Charles Sanders Peirce, in *Pragmatism and Pragmaticism,* volume five of his *Collected Papers* (Cambridge: Harvard University Press, 1934), pp. 274–276, 428.

to divide Hilltowners roughly into three types, in terms of their racial values and perceptions.[12]

The first type embraces the Hilltowners who believe that "colored and white people should live together in housing projects" and who support this belief by saying that the two racial groups "get along pretty well" in Hilltown itself. Since their values and their perception of local experience are both consistent with a liberal turn of mind in matters of race relations, these will be called the "liberals." At the other end is the second type, made up of those residents who maintain that the races should be residentially segregated and who justify this view by claiming that, in Hilltown, where the two races do live in the same project, they fail to get along. This kind of consistency between belief and appraisal of the local situation qualifies these residents to be called racial "illiberals." Between these two types is a third, holding an ambivalent position: these residents believe that the races should not be allowed to live in the same project, even though it must be admitted that they have managed to get along in Hilltown. In describing this type as "ambivalent," we mean only that they cannot buttress their opposition to co-residence of Negroes and whites, as the illiberals do, by saying that it inevitably leads to interracial conflict. The logically possible fourth type, comprised by those advocating interracial projects and reporting unsatisfactory race relations in Hilltown, is an empirically empty class and is therefore omitted from further consideration.

With these types before us, we can now ask: do close friends in Hilltown tend to share the same values and further, what is the bearing of similarity or difference of values upon the formation, maintenance and disruption of friendship? Is there, in other words, a pattern of value-homophily and if so, how does it come about?

To answer these questions, it is obviously necessary to devise appropriate indices of homophily and heterophily. We can develop such indices by tracing out the logic of what is ordinarily meant by saying that particular kinds of people usually choose friends of the same kind in their community. This means, presumably, that the

---

[12] These types were identified in terms of their answers to two questions raised during interviews with Hilltowners: "Do you think that colored and white people should live together in housing projects?" and "On the whole, do you think that colored and white people in Hilltown get along pretty well, or not so well?" It was assumed and confirmed in the larger study that intensely-held attitudes would affect the perception of relations between the races in the community and, conversely, that perceptions would, in due course, affect attitudes. In other words, the perceptual and attitudinal components of values are here considered as interdependent.

proportion of their friends having the designated similar characteristic (of social status or, in this instance, of racial values) is appreci-
ably greater than the proportion of people with this characteristic
in the local population. That is to say, they tend to *over-select* sim-
ilars as friends and, at the extreme, to confine their friendships to
individuals of like kind. Thus, if value-homophily does obtain
among Hilltowners, then the proportion of friendships involving
liberals will be significantly larger than the proportion of liberals
in the Hilltown population at large. They will have more liberal
friends than "would be expected" under the hypothesis that they
choose their friends without regard to their racial values (or without regard to the statuses correlated with these values). Correlatively, if heterophily obtains, they will have fewer liberal friends
than would be expected.

By the "expected" proportion, then, we mean nothing other than
the proportion of the local population falling in the designated
category. To find out if over-selection or under-selection occurs,
this expected proportion needs to be compared with the "observed"
proportion of friends in that category. Thus, we can form indices
of homophily and heterophily, expressed in terms of percentages,
by computing the excess of observed over expected frequencies of
designated friendships, divided by the expected frequency, and
multiplied by 100. If there is no homophily at all, this percentage
will of course equal zero. The higher the *positive* percentage (over-
selection) of friends of the same kind, the greater the degree of
homophily and, correlatively, the higher the *negative* percentage
(under-selection) of friends of the same kind, the greater the degree
of heterophily.[13]

Among the white residents of Hilltown,[14] there are definite patterns of friendship in terms of racial values. What is more, these
patterns take the shape to be expected, if the similarity of values
does indeed make for the formation and continuance of close friendships. First of all, we find that the residents having consistent racial
values—the liberals, at one pole, and the illiberals, at the other—
tend to over-select friends among those having the same values.
The liberals over-select other liberals by 43 per cent; the illiberals,

---

[13] It is perhaps needless to add the corollaries of this when detailed analysis seeks
to identify the particular groups which contribute most to the prevailing patterns of
selection: over-selection of friends of differing kind indicates heterophily, just as under-
selection of friends of differing kind may contribute to homophily.

[14] We must here confine our inquiry to white residents, since there are too few
illiberal and ambivalent Negroes with friends in Hilltown to allow comparative analysis. Further detailed statistics will be found in *Patterns of Social Life;* selected sum-
maries of these statistics are sufficient for present purposes.

other illiberals, by 30 per cent. Correlatively, liberals under-select illiberals as close friends by 53 per cent, and illiberals under-select liberals by 39 per cent.

But these patterns of value-homophily contrast notably with the pattern exhibited by white Hilltowners with *ambivalent* racial attitudes. These residents truly reflect their ambivalence in their interpersonal relations: they manifest neither homophily nor heterophily. They simply do not over-select or under-select, as shown by such entirely negligible departures from zero as 2 and 3 per cent. It is as though the ambivalent Hilltowners were expressing their uncertain and inconsistent racial values in a pattern of associating in proportionate measure with all three types of residents: liberals, ambivalents, and illiberals.

These general findings provide a point of departure for discussing the chief problem in hand: What are the dynamic processes through which the similarity or opposition of values shape the formation, maintenance, and disruption of close friendships? On this matter, the very limitations of these data prove instructive. True, we deal here with only one set of values, and, to this extent, we abstract greatly from the many values which find expression in social interaction. But these simplified findings carry further implications: for if some degree of value-homophily—as we call the selection of friends on the basis of common values—occurs when even a single set of values is held in common, then it would presumably be all the greater if several sets of values were held in common. In a sense, we are exploring the limiting case and what holds for it should hold, *a fortiori,* for those cases which better approximate the hypothesis that common values promote the formation or maintenance of close friendship. This study is a first approximation and, manifestly, there is need for extension and further empirical testing of the hypothesis.[15]

The Dynamics of Value-Homophily. Whether one or many values are involved, research findings such as these need to be supplemented by data of quite another kind if we are to acquire an understanding of the role of values in the formation of friendships. These statistical indices simply represent the patterns of friendship as they existed *at a particular moment*—in this case, as they were ob-

---

[15] The great practical difficulties of *empirically* studying the interplay of numerous sets of values and of interpersonal association should not be blinked. The later methodological part of this paper will indicate the complexities that arise as first approximations are followed by successive approximations to the concrete situation under review.

served at the time of our field-interviews. But, of course, these ⌐
friendships are in fact continually in process of change—some being
only in the early stages of formation, others long and firmly estab-   A-4 *
lished, and still others, for one reason or another, being well along
toward dissolution. Static observations, made at a given instant,   ⌋
tempt one to drop this obvious fact from view. Yet we cannot
afford to become imprisoned in the framework of fact that happens
to be at hand, even if breaking out of this narrow framework means
leaving demonstrated fact for acknowledged conjecture.

In other words, we must form a picture or a model of the dynamic processes, both social and psychological, of which the observed patterns of friendship are merely the resultants. And since
our explorations provide scanty and scattered rather than systematic evidence bearing on such processes, this model must remain,
for the time being, largely a matter of supposition. Nevertheless,
it may be useful to report our conjectures, growing out of these
limited materials, since little enough is known about the dynamic
processes that give rise to the observed patterns of an over-repre-
sentation of friends among those with common values, and an
under-representation among those with discordant values.[16]

In picturing the processes leading to value-homophily, let us con- ⌐
sider first the early social contacts between people having identical

---

* Content-units of this section of the chapter have been bracketed and coded for
purposes of the methodological analysis which follows in Part Two. The coding
is of two kinds:

   (a) Each of the content-units has been assigned an identifying *letter*. These will
     be used in our later analysis when we wish to refer to a particular statement
     in this substantive section.

   (b) Each of the content-units has also been assigned one or more *numbers*.
     These designate the analytic operations contained or implied in the state-
     ment. To anticipate the later discussion, four major analytic operations
     will be distinguished in Part Two. These are:
         1—the analysis of sequence rules
         2—the analysis of chains
         3—the elaboration of variables
         4—the elaboration of categories

In addition, lines of the text which contain references to the *mechanisms* by which
the patterns come about have been marked with an asterisk.

The reader need not pay particular attention to this coding at this point; it will,
however, be essential to re-examination of the substantive content in the light of
the methodological analysis in Part Two.

16 We do not, at this point, ask whether the correlation of values among friends
may not be the *result* of close association, as well as a basis for the *choice* of
friends, so that the correlation is spuriously great if it is taken solely to explain
choice. This is probably true and certainly important: and it is considered in due
course in the larger study, *Patterns of Social Life.*

or compatible values. To the extent that these values are given   B-1(a)
expression, first contacts will be mutually gratifying and, in some*
proportion of cases, will motivate persons to seek future contact (or,*
at the least, not to avoid future contact). The racial liberals in
Hilltown, for example, who express their views and find these sec-
onded by like-minded acquaintances have a doubly rewarding ex-*   C-4
perience: they have the satisfaction of voicing deep-seated feelings*
and the further satisfaction of having these opinions endorsed by*
others. In some proportion of cases, this early series of gratifying*
experiences will motivate them to seek continued contact and grad-*
ually result in a strong personal attachment. Particularly if propinquity or social organization facilitate further contact, this proc-   D-3, 4
ess of growing interpersonal attachment and of cumulative rein-*
forcement of values will presumably take place in an appreciable   *
proportion of cases.

It cannot be supposed, of course, that like-minded persons will
invariably express a particular value—for example, their racial
values—during their *early* contacts. In cases where this does not
occur, they will not be motivated to seek one another out, so far   *
as this one value is concerned. Among these residents, however,
some proportion, albeit smaller than in the cases where they have
early discovered their unanimity of opinion, will meet again and,   E-1(a)
sooner or later, although perhaps much later in the history of their   2, 3
relationship, they will have occasion to express this particular value.
By this time, some of these will have formed a personal attachment
on other grounds, and the delayed discovery of their common racial
values will serve to reinforce their relationship, through the process   *
of mutual gratification, as this has been described for the first group   *
of like-minded residents.

For those with similar values, then—whether they both be liberals or illiberals—social contact, because it is rewarding, will moti-   *
vate them to seek further contact. In due course, the proportion   *
of these repeated contacts eventuating in close friendships will be
sufficient to produce a pattern of value-homophily along the lines
observed in our data on the over-selection of like-minded friends.
This sketchy picture of the processes of social interaction between
those with antecedent similar values is consistent with the observed
correlations between the values of friends (insofar as these are not
owing to the mutual accommodation of values after the friendship
has matured).

But if this model accounts roughly for the dominant pattern of
value-homophily, can it also account for the further fact that some
close friendships have developed among Hilltowners having diametrically opposed racial values? Is this provisional model of social

interaction, personal attachment and value reinforcement also con-   F-1(a)
sistent with the double fact that liberals and illiberals *under*-select
one another as friends and, by the same token, that some, though
relatively few, friendships between those with differing racial values
nevertheless do occur? How shall we picture the social interaction
of persons holding contradictory values, significant to each of them?

Again, let us begin by considering those early contacts in which
residents express in words or in behavior a value to which the
others are radically opposed. In a substantial proportion, perhaps
most, of these cases, the fragile beginnings of a social relationship*   G-1(b)
between liberals and illiberals will be broken almost before they   *
have developed. The possible beginnings of friendship are nipped   *
in the bud. Thus, take the case of Mrs. Marsh, a white Hilltowner,
firmly liberal in her racial attitudes, who believes that "here any-
way, Negroes are a lot nicer than the whites. The main thing is
that they are friendlier, and want to be nicer to you." She happens
to express her views to other white residents, living in her own
apartment house. "When I talk to them about it they just call me
an 'old nigger-lover.' It doesn't bother me. I just say to them,
'Well, they're better friends to me than you,' and let it go at that.
That happened once when I had some Negroes to my house for a
supper. Some neighbor said, 'What do you mean having niggers
in your house?' But I don't care what anyone thinks of me, as
long as I know I'm doing right." Mrs. Marsh "may not be bothered" by this exchange of sentiments, but the fact remains that she
has not formed a close personal relationship with any of her neighbors who harbor illiberal attitudes. This episode might stand almost as a prototype of the consequences that follow the expression
of diametrically opposed values by both parties to an incipient
social relationship: each individual provides punitive experience*
for the other and, under such circumstances, it is not strange that
a warm personal attachment does not develop between them. The
expression of conflicting values, even of a single value, motivates
both parties to avoid future contact. In short, if a pair of ac-*   H-1(a), 4
quaintances find themselves at sixes and sevens, they do not long
remain a pair, but become unattached individuals. The incipient
friendship is brought to an early halt. This, then, is one type of   *
process explaining the under-selection of liberal friends by illiberals, and correlatively, the under-selection of illiberals by liberals.

However, it is not always the case that *both* parties to an incipient relationship will express their opposed values. Not infre-
quently, either because of personal timidity, or an ingrained sense   I-3
of courtesy or fear of losing status, one party may respond to the
unpalatable views of the other by preserving an expedient silence.

But to inhibit expressions of one's values, because their expression* would only "irritate" one's associates, is itself a frustrating experience. Under such conditions, further contact with the acquaintance, rather than being rewarding, becomes an occasion for self-defeat and, at times, an occasion for self-contempt. The silent * partner is, to this degree, motivated to avoid further contact, lest* this lead to open conflict. The partner who has freely expressed   J-1(a) his views and has no inkling of the punitive experience he has thus provided for his associate may continue to seek opportunities for further contact which, in an appreciable proportion of cases, will meet with no success, as his timid but aggrieved acquaintance sedulously avoids him. This type of interactive process, generating* motivated avoidance, again results in an under-selection of unlike- * minded associates as friends, in the manner we have found to be the case.

There is, however, a third pattern of interaction between those holding disparate values which does allow close friendships to develop between them. As we noted in the case of social contact between like-minded individuals, it is not at all inevitable that a particular value will be expressed, by one or the other, in the *early* stages of a developing relationship. In some proportion of cases, personal attachments will form in the course of repeated contact long before either partner to the relationship is aware that they are   K-1(a) sharply at odds in this one particular respect—say, with respect to racial values. Once the relationship has become firmly established —which means only that the partners have experienced separate* and mutual gratifications from their repeated interaction—it can, in some instances, tolerate a larger load of disagreement [17] over   L-4 certain values than is possible during the early phases, when the relationship is still fragile. The very same kind of disagreement would threaten or disrupt a developing friendship in its early stages. It would raise doubts about "the kind of person the other fellow really is," since they had not yet come "to know one another" in the short course of their relationship.

The implication of this hypothetical pattern for further research is clear: it means that the degree and kind of value-conflict between friends must be examined within the distinctly different contexts of firm, established friendships, and of tenuous, early friend-   M-1(b) ships. The same degree and kind of divergence in values would,

---

[17] That such personal attachments are sturdy enough to bear the recognition of disagreement on certain values and of occasional hostility is well attested by studies in clinical psychology. For an application of this hypothesis to quite another context of social behavior, see R. K. Merton, M. Fiske, and A. Curtis, *Mass Persuasion* (New York: Harper & Brothers, 1946), pp. 62–63.

on the average, have very different consequences in the two contexts. In any case, this part of our provisional model helps account ⌟
for the minor statistical pattern of a modicum of close friendships
among those holding sharply opposed racial values.

In time, this modicum of intimate personal relations between ⌉
those holding opposed values will be further depleted after friends   N-1(b), 2
make their delayed discovery that they hold these contradictory
values. To say that a strong and undisputed personal attachment ⫤
can safely carry the burden of even serious disagreement about certain values is very different from saying that enduring friendships   O-1(a)
often involve such disagreement. The close attachments which *can* ⌟
tolerate a conflict of values, without acute threat to the relationship,
are probably the very ones least subject to such conflict. For the ⌉
friends, by virtue of their attachment, are strongly motivated to*
modify their values in the service of easing strains on the relation-*   P-1(a)
ship. In the cumulative give-and-take of the friendship, initial divergences of value tend to be reduced. If the friends have an ap- ⫤
proximately equal emotional stake in the relationship, this is likely
to occur through mutual accommodation of their values. If one is   *
more deeply involved in the relationship than the other, his values   Q-4
are more likely to be modified to accord with the values of the less
deeply involved. Presumably, if this self-corrective process did not ⌟
occur, then close friendships would be even harder to come by and
to maintain than they apparently are. As processes of mutual or ⌉
unilateral accommodation of originally conflicting values run their   *
course, these cases also contribute to the pattern of value-homophily
rather than to that of heterophily. This has direct bearing on research, such as ours, which observes patterns of friendship at a particular instant: for some of the cases of close friendship between
liberals and illiberals which turn up in our statistical tables will, at
a later time, appear as cases of friendship between like-minded in-   R-1(a)
dividuals, as one or the other or both revise their values in the   *
interest of preserving the relationship. It is not easy to have a
warm personal attachment where there is an opposition of values.[18]
This gives rise to a motivated tendency toward the formation of   *
common values among fast friends. Not only does intimate social   *
interaction precipitate a deposit of new common values, but it also   *
converts originally disparate values into common values. As a re-* ⌟

---

[18] The capacity to accept disagreement on values among one's friends probably
varies from personality to personality, and presumably, from group to group.
Social norms may induce or even prescribe the toleration of opinions at odds with
one's own, and in groups where such norms obtain, friendships may more often
tolerate a divergence of outlook. But such group-variations, which it would be
instructive to explore, do not affect the central hypothesis, developed in our pro-

sult of these two processes, we should expect value-homophily to increase and value-heterophily to decrease among any given aggregate of friendships observed over an extended period of time.

This conversion of disparate into common values will not, of course, inevitably take place. The original values may be so deep-seated that neither individual finds it possible to modify or to abandon them. Faced with the dilemma of having to choose between their close friend and their basic values, and not wanting to abandon one or the other, the friends may seek the compromise solution of "agreeing to disagree," of placing the particular value under dispute in the category of the "not-to-be discussed." But this would-be solution is essentially unstable. Although they agree not to argue their opposed values, if these values are significant in the life of the group or community, their behavior is bound to betray their opposition. The racial illiberal, for example, joined in friendship with a racial liberal may set such store by the relationship as to forego any effort to convince the other of the error of his ways. But, at best, he can achieve an uneasy toleration, not a stable neutrality or indifference. At one time or another in Hilltown, the liberal-illiberal pair will find themselves in a situation where Negroes are also present. The issue is then inevitably joined. The behavior of each will show whether the individual sides with his friend or with his deep-seated values. Both the relationship and the values are under strain and, in this unstable condition, one or the other or both tend to be modified.[19] When closely interacting* persons have strongly opposed values, continuance of the relationship involves a series of reciprocally induced crises, in which the actions of each often evoke hostility in the other. However, not all such open conflict of values is destructive of the friendship. The kind of conflict which clarifies the sources of previously obscure mutual irritation may actually solidify the relationship, by making*

*

⌐

S-1(a)

⫤

T-1(b)

*
⌋

*
⌐

U-1(a)

visional model, that *some* agreement in basic values is-required to sustain an intimate personal relationship. There is always, so to say, a breaking-point in the relationship, and group-differences in the norm of tolerated opposition of outlook only vary the location of this point; they do not abolish it.

[19] This process seems to have direct bearing on the modification of values and attitudes among those holding a minority-opinion. If lone dissenters enter into close social relations with groups of other-minded persons, they *tend* to accommodate their values to the majority opinion, rather than disrupt these relations. In this way, the values widely held in a community tend to transform the values of initially dissenting individuals, as long as the latter are motivated to maintain personal relationships with "majority-members" of the community. Only if there exist relatively self-contained subgroups, sharing their dissident values, can they continue to maintain acutely opposed values. In either case, there is a structural tendency toward value-homophily. Either the dissidents conform to the majority-opinion, or if they find subgroups which provide a comfortable "home" for their dissident opinions, they conform to the values held by *these* associates.

it clear to both that the relationship means more to them than their clashing values. In any event, we see once again why value-homophily prevails: for if the close relationship remains intact, this phase of unstable compromise will in general give way to accordant, rather than discordant, values.

But it is not always the case, of course, that the friendship does remain intact. When the contradictory values are so deep-rooted as to be unyielding, the social contacts of friends are likely to irritate rather than to satisfy. Continued social interaction then involves progressive alienation from one another. As the friendship cools, the estranged friends look elsewhere for like-minded companions, and these newfound attachments hasten the final dissolution of the relationship. Once more, we see that this model of dynamic interplay between values and friendship anticipates the prevailing pattern of value-homophily among current relationships, because the opposition of deeply-held values tends to disrupt the friendship.

It is now apparent that the static observation of the values of friends at a particular instant too easily loses sight of one class of friendships altogether: the class of disrupted or broken friendships. This oversight is not inherent in the procedure of cross-sectional interviews and is readily overcome by the use of panel-interviews: it would have been possible, for example, to ask Craftowners and Hilltowners to designate their recently broken friendships and to carry on the inquiry from there, much along the lines we followed for current and still viable friendships. But if the oversight is not inherent, it is, surely, prevalent. Few systematic studies of the formation of friendship also incorporate materials on the disruption of friendship. And candor compels us to insist that such materials do not appear in our own quantitative data simply because the need for these materials was not foreseen during our field work. Yet it is the data on broken friendships which may provide the most critical evidence testing this provisional model of the interplay of values and friendship; for these disrupted friendships set a definite analytical task: they should be accounted for by the same model that seeks to account for the prevailing pattern of value-homophily among still-current relationships. Future research on friendship, therefore—whether in housing developments or in the "open community"—will have to take explicit and systematic note of these abandoned friendships and have to study the processes leading to their break-up. We pay our own scanty qualitative data no more than the slight respect owing them when we report that they served, at least, to suggest the necessity of studying terminated friendships, if we are to round out our analysis of the role

V-1(a), 4

W-2

played by common values in the formation and maintenance of friendships.

In spite of these limitations of data, the model we have sketched out does move a certain distance toward a tentative formulation of the processes which give rise to the observed dominant pattern of value-homophily and the observed subsidiary pattern of a few friendships among those with opposed values. At bottom, the model represents merely an extended application to the special case of friendship of the hard-won sociological commonplace that, in noncoerced social relations, common values and strong personal attachments act both as cause and effect, modifying and in turn * being modified by one another. Common values make social inter-*⌐ action a rewarding experience, and the gratifying experience pro-* motes the formation of common values. And just as close associa-* X-1 tion and common values go hand in hand, so do dissociation and alienation from one another's values. For when the partners to the ⊐ friendship develop opposed values, their initial close relations are subjected to strain and some may deteriorate to the final point of* Y-2, 4 dissolution. ⌟

It will be apparent that the conceptions on which this model is based are anything but new, and that they did not originate with any one sociologist.[20] But they take on particular pertinence here by suggesting the dynamic processes which eventuate in the patterns of friendship we have observed statically in Hilltown and Craftown. It may be assumed, finally, that the near future will see the development of a more comprehensive model incorporating,

---

[20] In their main outlines, for example, they are found in the writings of Georg Simmel, *The Sociology of Georg Simmel*, translated and edited by Kurt H. Wolf (Glencoe: The Free Press, 1950), esp. Chapters I and II, and in the discussion of "accommodation" in the first modern textbook of sociology by R. E. Park and E. W. Burgess, *Introduction to the Science of Sociology* (University of Chicago Press, 1921); cf. P. A. Sorokin, *Society, Culture, and Personality* (New York: Harper & Brothers, 1947), esp. Chapter 7. Leopold von Wiese and Howard Becker, *Systematic Sociology* (New York: John Wiley & Sons, Inc., 1932), state some of the germane considerations in Part Two of their book, and in Chapter XXXIX, on the pair or dyad. To our mind one of the most insightful diagnoses of the interaction of pairs—in this case, marriage-partners rather than friends—is provided by Willard Waller, *The Family* (New York: Cordon Co., 1938), esp. Chapters X and XI. In more recent years, these conceptions have been taken up and developed as a distinct focus of empirical research and sociological theorizing. See, for example, the excellent discussion by George C. Homans, *The Human Group* (New York: Harcourt, Brace & Co., 1950), esp. Chapters 5 and 6; and for a discussion of estrangement of social relations and alienation of values, see R. K. Merton and A. S. Kitt, "Contributions to the Theory of Reference Group Behavior," in Merton and Lazarsfeld (eds.) *Continuities in Social Research* (Glencoe: The Free Press, 1950), esp. at pp. 92ff. For the most widely generalized and elaborated formulation of these conceptions, see Talcott Parsons, *The Social System* (Glencoe: The Free Press, 1951), esp. Chapter VII.

into one scheme of analysis, the processes giving rise both to status-homophily—the pattern of friendship prevailing between persons occupying similar statuses—and to value-homophily—the pattern of friendship tending to form between persons holding similar values. When this is achieved, sociologists will at long last have met the challenge implicit in Aristotle's doubts about the adequacy of the adage, ancient by his time, that "birds of a feather flock together."

PART TWO—METHODOLOGICAL ANALYSIS *

The foregoing discussion of value-homophily affords an occasion for examining, specifically and concretely, the interplay between substantive analysis and methodological formalization.

The substantive analysis begins with the finding that friends in Hilltown tend to hold similar values concerning race relations and proceeds to develop a model of social process which might account for this fact. The logical and other analytical operations in this account remain implicit. We can, however, specify the major "operations"—the logical arrangement of data into categories having specified interrelations—implied in the substantive analysis. That is what is meant by "methodological formalization." This formal analysis has two useful purposes. It will bring out, first of all, a logical scheme for the further analysis of processes involved in the formation of friendship. Secondly, it will bring out the respects in which such a scheme of analysis can apply, not only to friendship, but to other studies of social process.

It will be found that each of the major statements in the substantive section presupposes one or more of four basic operations, soon to be discussed. These operations, moreover, can be stated in terms of an existing formalism, so that no new structure of analysis is required. It turns out, also, that the application of this formal analysis does not call for mathematical procedures, nor does it involve quantitative terms other than statements of "greater than," "less than," and characterizations of relationships between variables as "weak" or "strong." [21]

The data supporting the finding of homophily can be presented in a variety of ways. For our purpose a simple schematic presentation will be best. It does not quite conform to the way the data

---

* By P. F. Lazarsfeld. This analysis is one of a series of formalizations developed by Columbia University's project for advanced training in social research. The editorial help of Dr. Patricia Kendall is warmly acknowledged.

[21] In discussing these relationships, we shall use hypothetical figures rather than algebraic or other symbolic terminology.

were originally presented; but it will be seen presently that an adaptation like the one to be introduced is necessary if the interpretations of the main text are to be tested empirically.

Reformulation of the Problem. We will assume that all the members of a community have been classified as liberals or illiberals in terms of their racial attitudes. We will assume, further, that by some kind of chance procedure members of the community have been formed into pairs, which have then been classified as friendship-pairs or as nonfriendship-pairs.[22] This will carry us along for a considerable number of pages. Later on we shall amply rectify this original simplification; provisions will be made for people being neutral in their attitudes, for the existence of one-sided attachments between pairs and for many other more realistic situations.

Our schematic starting point, then, will be a large number of pairs, each of which has been characterized by the two dimensions of agreement-disagreement, on the one hand, and the presence or absence of friendship, on the other. These pairs can be arranged in a fourfold table, so that the relationship between agreement and friendship can be studied. A set of hypothetical figures which reproduce the finding with which the substantive analysis began might look somewhat like the following:

TABLE 1 [23]

	Friends	Not Friends
Agree.........	150	50
Disagree.......	50	150

The empirical finding about value-homophily is of the type represented in these hypothetical figures. Here, as in the actual data, there is definite relationship between the two variables. Among the pairs characterized by the presence of friendship, a majority are also characterized by agreement of values. But among the pairs which have no friendship, a majority are in disagreement.

Table 1 represents the type of result which is obtained in a so-called cross-sectional survey taken at one specific period of time. The purpose of the interpretative analysis was to specify, on a hypo-

---

[22] There are a variety of ways in which the pairing of the community members can be accomplished. The exact way in which this is done is irrelevant for the discussion which follows.

[23] We repeat that numbers are used only for illustrative purposes to indicate the existence or nonexistence of particular kinds of relationships. We might have used algebraic notation instead, but the numerical examples are probably easier to follow.

thetical basis, some of the main processes resulting in an observed correlation between friendship and a similarity of values. But conjectures about processes, of course, require the introduction of a *time dimension.* In order to study the development of a particular pattern one must be able to observe the units of analysis at successive points in time. The first finding is enlarged by the assumption that at some previous period friendship and opinion were not, or not as clearly, related. The static result is replaced by a more complicated one, implying a change; it is this change which then has to be explained. Again we resort to schematic figures. And now an additional element is added to the schematization: in actuality, only one survey was made; but the existence and probable results of an earlier survey are implied in the analysis given in the first part of this paper.

To keep the demonstration as simple as possible, we shall assume that the preceding survey, done at Time I, resulted in the findings of Table 2a; Table 2b repeats the results of the original survey which was carried out at what is now labeled Time II.

TABLE 2

	a Time I		*b* Time II	
	Friends	Not Friends	Friends	Not Friends
Agree..............	100	100	150	50
Disagree..........	100	100	50	150

According to these figures there was no discernible relationship between friendship and agreement at the time of the first observation, when, say, the residents had been in the community for only a short time. But by the time of the second observation, after a six months' interval, the relationship between these variables had become marked. This change in the degree of relationship is exactly of the kind hypothesized in the substantive section.

We shall find it useful to talk of the contact-value combinations which are represented in the 4 cells of each of the tables. The frequencies of these contact-value combinations have changed from Time I to Time II. And to add one final bit of terminology: the "harmonious" combinations have become more frequent. By "harmonious" we shall mean either pairs who are friends and agree, or pairs who are not friends and do not hold the same value. The main issue is now restated in more formal terms: the increasing number of harmonious contact-value combinations through time is to be analyzed.

Now such a formal restatement can be useful only if it contains elements which can be further developed without recourse, at least at first, to additional ideas or assumptions. This is indeed possible in the present case because Table 2 tells only part of the story which would be available to us as a result of observations made at two periods of time with the same set of pairs. The reader is invited to study Table 3, which is sometimes called a sixteen-fold table, with care; it contains all combinations of friendship and agreement at two time periods. Again we introduce hypothetical figures which, as we shall see, reproduce the substantive discussion we are attempting to analyze. They might be of the following sort: [24]

TABLE 3

Time I	Time II				
F A	F A ++	F A +−	F A −+	F A −−	
++	50	20	10	20	100
+−	30	20	0	50	100
−+	50	0	40	10	100
−−	20	10	0	70	100
	150	50	50	150	

(The first symbol in each designation refers to the presence or absence of friendship in the pair; the second to agreement or disagreement.)

Note that the marginals of this sixteen-fold table reproduce the fourfold tables of Table 2. And they indicate the same fact observed previously, namely, that the relationship between agreement and friendship becomes more marked with the passage of time.

It is the purpose of this discussion to show that the proper analysis of this sixteen-fold table, taken in conjunction with other materials

---

[24] Other figures might have been invented. With fixed marginals, a sixteen-fold table has 9 degrees of freedom. But we chose those figures which might have been found had empirical data supporting the several interpretations been available.

which we shall specify, makes it possible to organize profitably all statements about the phenomenon of value-homophily and the processes leading to it contained in the substantive section. It is our contention, in other words, that a sixteen-fold table of this kind provides a formal scheme for statements of process. In order to demonstrate this we must indicate the various analytic operations which can be carried out through use of a sixteen-fold table. We shall then consider whether we have omitted essential parts of the substantive discussion.

The Analysis of Sequence Rules (1). The analysis of what we shall call sequence rules is perhaps the basic operation in this kind of formalization. We mean by a sequence any particular cell in the sixteen-fold table presented above. (We call these cells sequences, because each represents a shift in the state of friendship and agreement from one time to another. Thus, the cell, [(+—) to (——)], represents a change, between the first and second times of observation, from the state of friendship-and-disagreement to that of absence-of-friendship-and-disagreement.) And we mean by a sequence rule any statement about the frequency of a single sequence or the comparative size of two or more sequences.

Clearly, sequence rules will be of varying complexity, depending on the number of sequences involved. The simplest ones are those referring to a single cell in the sixteen-fold table. There are several statements of this kind in the substantive discussion, and each of these statements has been designated by the symbol (1a). Thus the substantive account refers to the "fact that some close friendships have developed among Hilltowners having diametrically opposed racial values." [25] This states, in other words, that, perhaps contrary to expectations, some pairs can be found in the cell char-

---

[25] In this and the remaining examples of the present section, our decision to consider only the presence or absence of friendship, and agreement or disagreement on racial values, means, necessarily, a simplification of the substantive content. Here, for example, the analyst talks of "close friendships"; in other instances, as we shall see, he deals with friendships which are "in the early stages of formation," as opposed to others which are "long and firmly established" and still others which are "well along toward dissolution." Further, he sometimes indicates certain substantive conditions which he considers basic to the process under discussion. For example, he contrasts the processes to be expected when the members of a pair express their values and those which are likely when one or both members remain silent.

In later sections we shall see that our formal structure provides ways of dealing with these refinements of the basic variables and with the consideration of conditions. But these complications must come later, when we have made entirely clear the meaning of formalization on the simplest level.

acterized by the $(--)$ pattern at the time of the first interview, but by the $(+-)$ pattern by the time of the second.

Elsewhere we find the following comment:

To say that a strong and undisputed personal attachment can safely carry the burden of even serious disagreement about certain values is very different from saying that enduring friendships often involve such disagreement.

Restated in the more formal terms which we have introduced here, this statement affirms the relative infrequency of the sequence $[(+-)$ to $(+-)]$. The analyst says that, while it is possible to observe this pattern, it is not common.

In still another part of the substantive discussion we read that:

. . . some of the cases of close friendship between liberals and illiberals which turn up in our statistical tables will, at a later time, appear as cases of friendship between like-minded individuals, as one or the other or both revise their values in the interest of preserving the relationship.

A reformulation of part of this statement indicates that the analyst expects to find a number of pairs characterized by the $[(+-)$ to $(++)]$ sequence.

In general, then, sequence rules involving single cells in the sixteen-fold table are usually concerned with the generality or rarity of particular kinds of shifts. They indicate which patterns of change or stability are expected, and which are unexpected.

A somewhat more complex kind of sequence rule is that involving the comparison of two or more cells in a row of the table. [They are indicated by the symbol (1b).] The usual purpose of this type of comparison is to show that one kind of shift—one sequence—is more frequent than others. For example, we find the following comment in the substantive section:

. . . let us begin by considering those early contacts in which residents express in words or in behavior a value to which the others are radically opposed. In a substantial proportion, perhaps most, of these cases, the fragile beginnings of a social relationship between liberals and illiberals will be broken almost before they have developed. The possible beginnings of friendship are nipped in the bud.

Because this is an extended comment, let us analyze it in some detail. The passage starts out by focusing attention on the pairs of friends who were initially in disagreement. In terms of our sixteen-fold table these are the pairs characterized by a $(+-)$ combination of characteristics at the time of the first interview; they will be found in the second row of the table. The analysis then considers the most likely outcome for ·pairs characterized in this way. It is assumed that "in a substantial proportion, perhaps most, of these cases" the early contacts will not be continued and no firm friendship will develop.[26] It is assumed, in other words, that the sequence [(+ −) to (− −)] is more likely than any others for pairs starting out with this combination of characteristics.

In a later comment, the analyst states a somewhat different sequence rule about the same kinds of pairs. He says that the relationships between friends who are in disagreement is an essentially unstable one, and "both the relationship and the values are under strain and, in this unstable condition, one or the other or both tend to be modified." Again translating this statement into our more formal terms, the analyst assumes that, if one examines the second row in the sixteen-fold table, that in which we find pairs who were initially friendly but in disagreement, two sequences will be relatively more frequent than the others. He states that the most likely sequences for the (+ −) cases are the [(+ −) to (+ +)] or the [(+ −) to (− −)]. This is a corollary, incidentally, of an assumption which he made earlier, namely, that there will be few cases characterized by the [(+ −) to (+ −)] pattern.

It might be asked at this point what is actually accomplished by this kind of formalization. Seemingly, all that we have done is restate the substantive formulations in terms of the symbols which we introduced.

The Heuristic Value of Schematic Presentation. In order to understand the heuristic value of this formal presentation, let us classify all of the sequence rules found in the text. We shall do this by reproducing the sixteen-fold scheme, and inserting in each cell the comments which deal with that particular sequence. To make this scheme as manageable as possible, each statement or content unit in the substantive text has been assigned a distinctive code letter; it is these which are reproduced in the sixteen cells.

		Time II			
		F A + +	F A + −	F A − +	F A − −
Time I	F A + +	B, D, E			
	+ −	N, P, R, T	K, M, O, S, U		G, H, J, M, N, T, V
	− +				
	− −		F		

---

[26] Again we oversimplify the substantive implications of the original passage. The sequence rule developed by the analyst is conditional on the expression of conflicting values by the members of a pair. Again, however, we shall delay for later consideration how these conditional statements can be handled in our formal structure.

What do we learn from this scheme of reformulation? One fact that becomes immediately evident is that all but one of the 18 sequence rules which we have classified deal with pairs of individuals characterized by friendship and that 13 of these 17 statements [27] concern pairs who, at the outset of observation, were friendly, but disagreed on racial values. The corollary of this is that the substantive section was not concerned with pairs which had not established some degree of social contact. There is, in fact, no sequence rule about pairs having like values, but no contact.[28] This does not mean, of course, that such sequence rules cannot be developed. In accord with other hypotheses in the substantive text, we can state a sequence rule of the (1b) type, that in which the frequencies of sequences in a particular row are compared. A relatively probable outcome for the pairs characterized by lack of friendship but agreement in values, it might be suggested, is the $[(-+)$ to $(++)]$ pattern. That is, even though these pairs may not have become friends at the time when they were first observed, we can assume that, through chance or because they were led by their similar values to take part in the same local organizations, some of them will come into contact with one another. Then, as was suggested in the substantive section, they will find the expression of their compatible values mutually gratifying and will be motivated to seek further contact with one another. The end result is that these will become friends in a larger proportion of cases than those with disparate values who are less likely to meet through the same organizations or, if they meet, to establish mutual friendships.

One distinct use of such a formal scheme, then, is that it enables one to bring out specifically and systematically the points which are being stressed in a substantive analysis and, more importantly perhaps, the points which are being disregarded. Another application consists in pointing to alternative options of analysis, to additional ways in which the same material could be analyzed. Our previous distinction between harmonious and disharmonious friendship-value combinations permits us to exemplify such an elaboration.

---

[27] Actually, there are 16, rather than 13, entries in the second row. This results from the fact that three of the coded comments, Statements M, N, and T, each refer to two sequences, held to obtain at different points in the history of the friendship-relation.

[28] Another way of putting this is that the substantive analysis does not concern itself with the problem of the processes through which social contact is first established. That problem is dealt with in another part of the book from which the analysis is drawn, where the role of propinquity and formal organization in making for social contact is considered at some length. The formalization of the text brings out the self-defined limitations of the analysis and goes on to indicate the additional sequence rules which would be involved if this further problem were considered at this point.

Looking at Table 3, we may concentrate on the second and third rows; these contain all the pairs which were disharmonious at the first observation, and indicate what has become of them at the time of the second observation.   As a direct consequence of our definition of the process of homophily, we find that 140 of these 200 pairs had become "harmonious," meaning that they either were now friends in agreement $(++)$, or people holding different values and not friendly $(--)$.   But how has this progress toward homophily been achieved?   Did the value configuration more often determine the fate of friendships, or did friendship more often affect the constancy of attitudes?   The theory under analysis is silent on this point, but our formalization has forced us to make some assumptions, if only because the cells of the sixteen-fold table, Table 3, had to be filled in.   Its most pertinent part is reproduced as Table 4:

TABLE 4

		Time II	
		++	--
Time I	+-	30	50
	-+	50	10

Two kinds of sequences can be distinguished.   In $(+-)$ to $(--)$ and in $(-+)$ to $(++)$ the second sign, designating the values, remains the same, and the first sign, symbolizing friendship, changes; there are 100 such cases.   In the other 40 cases the values at Time II become adjusted to the friendship patterns as they existed at (and persisted from) Time I.   In somewhat loose language we can therefore say that the values are "stronger" than the friendships; if there is disharmony between the two, the social system, represented by our hypothetical community, increases homophily by changing the distribution of attitudes.[29]   This set of figures is probably more in the spirit of the general theory than a different set implying the opposite assumption.   It is important to realize, however, that the homophily result, the shift in marginals, would have remained the same if the entries in Table 4 had been made to read 60 and 20 in the first line and 20 and 40 in the second.   In this case,

---

[29] For the sake of simplicity, we leave out an additional test which has to be applied to the problem of "mutual effect."   Another partial fourfold table would have to be investigated, consisting of the two middle boxes in the first and last rows of Table 3. This is necessary for numerical reasons and does not affect the general trend of the idea.

the implied assumption would have been that friendships are "stronger" than attitudes in their mutual effect.

A second heuristic value of such formalization, then, is to bring out assumptions which have not been made explicit by the original analyst, or those on which he chose not to take a stand. Before pursuing further this relation between general reflections on a topic and its treatment in more systematic forms, we must broaden the whole area under inspection. So far, we have confined ourselves to those rules that can be derived from one sixteen-fold table. This is the simplest scheme relating two variables at two times. Various extensions of this notion result in new, and more complicated, rules. With these elaborations we can begin to restore the complexity of the substantive conceptions which our simplification has necessarily eliminated for the time being.

The Analysis of Chains (2).   A first elaboration to be considered is that of the time dimension. So far we have assumed that we have only two observations of the pairs of individuals. We can now study what develops when these observations are increased to three or more. In order to do this, we shall introduce the notion of "chains," sequences which are extended in time. That is, a pair which, in terms of friendship and agreement, is characterized as $(-+)$ at Time I, $(++)$ at Time II and $(+-)$ at Time III represents one of the many chains which can be distinguished.

The substantive section of this paper does refer to some of these chains. (They are designated by the number 2.) Perhaps the most clearcut of these references is found in Statement Y:

. . . when the partners to the friendship develop opposed values, their initial close relations are subjected to strain and some may deteriorate to the final point of dissolution.

This, as we can see, describes the processes accounting for the chain $[(++) \text{ to } (+-) \text{ to } (--)]$.

The special importance of an extended time dimension is that it permits us to explore new problems. Specifically, we can study whether the future shifts of pairs characterized in a particular way depend on their past history. We note in our original sixteen-fold table, for example, that at the time of the second interview there are 50 pairs characterized by the $(+-)$ combination of friendship and agreement. But these 50 pairs have quite different histories: 20 of them were originally friends sharing similar values; another 20 have a past history, as well as a present pattern, of friendship but disagreement; and the final 10 pairs were characterized at Time I both by the absence of friendship and the absence of agreement. The question is how these past histories will influence future courses of development among these 50 pairs. Operationally, what can we expect from a third observation? Will the 20 pairs characterized by the stable sequence, [(+ −) to (+ −)], manifest a different development in the future than those who have shifted to the (+ −) pattern from either the (+ +) or the (− −) states? That is, will disagreeing friends who have exhibited both friendship and disagreement in the past differ, in their future patterns, from disagreeing friends who previously agreed? There is reason to believe that they will.

The importance of this kind of analysis is that it leads to the development of more refined and specific rules of change, which, in turn, permit more accurate predictions of the ways in which particular types of pairs will behave in the future.[30] One aspect of this deserves special attention.

The Idea of Equilibrium. So far we have dealt with two major elements of a process: (a) an initial distribution of the friendship-value combinations, represented by Table 2a; (b) a set of sequence rules telling how these combinations change over a designated period of time, represented by Table 3.[31]

With the help of these two elements we can describe how the system under study changes from a first to a second stage. And Table 3 tells us what the social theorist has to do: he must make plausible assumptions about the frequencies in each cell; and, in the light of other knowledge, he must state why he makes these assumptions.

But the idea of observations repeated more than twice brings out certain additional matters that have to be considered. One is characteristic for all theory formation: we have to assume that no extraneous factors will disturb the system. Suppose, for example, that as a result of some wave of terror, the community comes to believe that liberal values are dangerous; it might then develop that people who hold liberal values avoid each other, in order to deflect suspicion. This would obviously change the sequence rules exempli-

---

[30] There is some indication in the substantive section that the analyst was aware of the importance of studying past history in order to develop adequate theories about future developments. The most explicit of these is the observation, in Statement W, that it is of strategic importance to study the "class of disrupted or broken friendships." Implicit in this reference is the supposition that pairs who have broken off their friendship may develop differently than do those who have maintained their friendship.

[31] To the statistician, these are known as transition probabilities; but we wish to avoid technical language here. Appendix I gives a more precise formulation.

fied in Table 3, and consequently change the future distribution of the friendship-value combinations.

The present discussion implies, then, that, *ceteris paribus*, the sequence rules remain unaffected by outside influences for a reasonable period of time. But this still leaves two possibilities open: the rules may remain completely constant or may change as a result of intrinsic developments.

Let us first assume that we deal with what is sometimes called a stationary process: the sequence rules controlling the change from one time period to the next remain about the same.

Under these circumstances, it is possible to "compute" the equilibrium position of the system. Our scheme showed that in the first time step, the marginal distribution 100–100–100–100 of Table 2a changed to 150–50–50–150 of Table 2b; as a matter of fact, this shift turned out to be the essence of value-homophily as a process. We now could predict what would happen in another time step by applying the same sequence rules to this new distribution: without elaborating the arithmetic, we should find a Table 2c (not given here) showing frequencies of 145–55–35–165 for the 4 friendship-value combinations, respectively.

A somewhat more complicated computation would tell us that the equilibrium distribution would be 133–57–24–186. This distribution can easily be defined in nonmathematical terms: it is the one which does not change if the sequence rules of Table 3 are applied to it. This kind of equilibrium is well known to social research from many empirical studies. Repeated interviews on such diversified topics as race attitudes, opinions on the role of labor unions, etc., often show the following characteristics: many individual respondents change their positions; but these individual shifts cancel each other out and the so-called marginal distributions for the whole group remain fairly constant over time.

Now let us briefly consider the idea of a process where the sequence rules do not remain constant but are still unaffected by extraneous factors. The sequence rules could depend upon the distribution of friendship-value combinations reached at a certain moment. If, for example, value-homophily has become very strong in a community, a counter-tendency might develop with the view that different kinds of people ought to become associated. The homophily trend described in the text might weaken until a lower degree of correlation between friendship and value has been reached; then the reverse tendency might set in. The result would be an oscillation of the value-friendship distributions around an average. This would be quite different from the introduction of extraneous elements, mentioned above. The whole process would still go on within the system; however, the sequence rules exemplified in Table 3 would not be constant, but would be dependent upon the "marginal" distribution reached at a given moment.

This possibility has been introduced only to show that the formal statement of a process opens up new vistas for substantive speculation. The assumption of a stationary process is probably more in keeping with the spirit of the main analysis than is the assumption of intrinsic oscillations. But even then it can be seen that, for a full understanding of the phenomenon, one more topic needs explication. If one were to apply the notion of homophily loosely, one could ask why the system does not end in complete homogeneity. Why does it not happen that all the people with like values, and only these, are friends? Actually, Table 3 shows that "counter-tendencies" are provided for: there are sequences like [(++) to (−+)] which tell us that, in spite of agreement, friendships will break off and refill the reservoir of "disharmonious" pairs. At least three kinds of speculations can be attached to these counter-sequences. One has to do with extraneous elements, often ascribed to chance: accidental feuds, the conversion of one partner, etc. A second possibility is that other values—those not specifically concerned with racial problems—play a part in the formation and dissolution of friendships. The third possibility is perhaps the most interesting: there could be a phenomenon of satiation, a desire for new challenges when agreement has lasted too long. Whether such tendencies actually play a role can only be discovered by empirical research. We shall have occasion later to speculate on the consequences of such a possibility. At this point, our only purpose has been to indicate what problems derive from the notion of equilibrium, which, in turn, derives from formalization of the idea of an explanatory process.

By now we have gone considerably beyond the intent of the text under discussion, not in order to imply a shortcoming, but in order to exemplify the continuity of questions which can be derived from even the simplest set of repeated observations. It is time to return to the text itself, and to do justice to its own complexity; this forces us to introduce further elements into our "translation."

The Elaboration of Variables (3). So far we have confined ourselves exclusively to the two variables of friendship and agreement. But this represents an oversimplification of the foregoing model of processes leading to value-homophily. At numerous points in the discussion, the analyst indicates that other variables need to be considered if the various processes are to be specified adequately. The introduction of these new variables provides another kind of elaboration.[82]

What kinds of additional variables are brought into the discussion? (The statements are identified in the text by the number 3.) The analyst contrasts the situations which exist when members of a pair express or fail to express their values (Statements B, E, and G). He considers the way in which propinquity or social organization affects the processes with which he is dealing (Statement D). He points to timidity,[83] courtesy, or fear of losing status as variables which might explain why some individuals do not express disagreement (Statement I). He indicates that awareness of agreement or disagreement may affect the development of friendship (Statement K). And he suggests that a "conflict [of values] which clarifies the sources of previously obscure mutual irritation may actually solidify the relationship, by making it clear to both that the relationship means more to them than their clashing values" (Statement U).

The introduction of these new variables has the effect, basically, of increasing the number of patterns with which we deal and of adding to the sequence rules which can be specified. Let us consider how this comes about. Suppose that we start with pairs which are friendly, but in disagreement, the $(+-)$ cases; and suppose that we introduce as our third variable the notion that some of these pairs express their conflicting views while others do not. The first step in analyzing the role of this third variable is to divide the total number of $(+-)$ pairs into those which express their values and those which do not. By then studying the most likely sequences within these two groups, we can determine the influence of such overt expression on friendship. The hypothetical table below indicates that dissolution of friendship is more likely to take place within pairs which give voice to their conflicting values.[84]

---

[82] This form of elaboration is discussed in more general terms, as the procedure of "specification," in P. L. Kendall and P. F. Lazarsfeld, "Problems of Survey Analysis," *Continuities in Social Research*, pp. 154–157, and 163–164.

[83] In other parts of the book, *Patterns of Social Life*, from which the substantive section of this paper is drawn, some of the conditions making for such "timidity" in social contact—for example, timidity induced by differences in social class background—are, in turn, considered. In other words, these additional variables are not purely *ad hoc*, but are derived from sociological analysis of the local social structure.

[84] It will be noted that the introduction of this third variable exactly doubles the number of sequences with which we deal.

TABLE 5

Time I (+ −) cases		Time II				
		F A ++	F A +−	F A −+	F A −−	
Express views		10	5	0	30	45
Do not express views		20	15	0	20	55
		30	20	0	50	

A sequence rule of the (1b) type can be derived from these hypothetical figures. The most frequent sequence for those who express their views is [(+ −) to (− −)]; 30 out of the 45 pairs made this shift. Among those who do not express their conflicting values, however, no single sequence is numerically outstanding.

There are two further points to be noted in connection with this kind of elaboration. The first is that the same variable may have different consequences with different kinds of pairs. That is, the effect of a third variable will depend, in general, on the configuration of the first two variables. For example, as the analyst suggests, the expression of values will, in all probability, serve to reinforce the friendship of individuals who are in agreement to start with. In other words, we assume that this variable, expression of values, has a different effect on the (+ +) pairs than it does on those characterized as (+ −).

A second point is that the substantive contribution made by the introduction of a third variable will depend partly on how that variable is defined. For example, the "expression of values" can mean anything from casual references to those values to incessant discussions of them. Also, the conversations can take place early in the friendship, or at a time when it is well established. The observed effects of these expressions, then, depends partly on how they have been defined and to what stages of the friendship they refer.

The Elaboration of Categories (4). This last point suggests another type of elaboration, namely, a refinement of the variables so that they are no longer simply dichotomous attributes. Throughout our discussion we have dealt with the dichotomies, agreement-disagreement and friends-not friends. It is clear, however, that both of these variables can be defined differently, as was indeed done in the substantive text. Each might be classified as a trichotomy, for example. In that case, agreement might be divided into complete, partial and no agreement. Similarly, the attribute of friendship might be converted into a trichotomy. One might then distinguish pairs involving mutual friendship, those in which only one person claims friendly relations with the other, and those in which neither considers the other a friend.[35] Or, different aspects of the variables might be considered. For example, the substantive formulation refers to different phases of friendships—those which are incipient, those which are firmly established, those which are in one stage or another of dissolution (Statement A, for example). (The references to refined categories of the principal variables are indicated by the code number, 4, in the text.) There are other comments about the intensity of feeling attached to racial attitudes—those which are deep-rooted, those in which the individual has great emotional involvement, and so on.[36]

These refinements of our variables have the same effect, in general, as the addition of a new one—an increase in the number of patterns to be distinguished and a multiplication of possible sequence rules. If our dichotomies are converted into trichotomies, then our original fourfold tables are transformed into ninefold tables, and the original sixteen-fold table, relating the information from two interviews, becomes a somewhat unwieldy table with 81 cells.

We have now reviewed the basic operations involved in this kind of analysis. And, except for one type of statement to be considered presently, the substantive part of the text now seems to have been wholly analyzed in formal terms.

"Mechanism" vs. Sequence Rules. We started out with a sixteen-fold table reporting personal relations and agreement for all pairs of individuals at two points of time. We then introduced three kinds of elaboration: an extension of the time dimension, an increase in the number of variables considered, and finer subdivisions for some of these variables. This permitted us to classify our pairs in an increasingly discriminating way, or, to put it in different terms, the state in which any pair was at a particular moment became progressively more specific. But the propositions with which we dealt were all of the same kind. They were sequence rules indicating the relative frequencies with which transitions from one state to another took place.

It turned out that a considerable number of the pages under ex-

---

[35] It is through these elaborations—of variables or of categories—that we are able to deal formally with statements which previously seemed too complex. These operations free us from the restrictions imposed by our initial simplifications, particularly in presenting the notion of sequence rules.

[36] This is discussed at length in another part of *Patterns of Social Life.*

amination could be translated into such "time-series language." An effort was made to show that such translation clarified the interrelation between different parts of a more discursive language, that it brought out assumptions implied in the original analysis, and that it pointed to further problems—not by adding new questions, but by exploiting systematically the operations introduced by the original author.

This does not mean at all that the reflections under scrutiny were obvious to begin with. As a matter of fact, a formalism highlights a substantive contribution. This can be shown in many ways; but two points deserve special mention. It is possible to develop a theory which assumes that people have a tendency to change friends frequently and are eager for varying intellectual experiences; therefore, they prefer their new friends to have different opinions than did their old ones. Under this assumption we also would find homophily in the sense of increasing correlation of friendship and attitudes from one observation to the next. Appendix II gives an example of a sixteen-fold table where the two marginal value-friendship distributions are exactly the same as in Table 3, while the sequence rules within the table are completely different; the reader is invited to study this table in some detail and to see what its behavioral implications are. The formalism, then, only brings out that one aspect of a process analysis is the existence of certain sequence rules and chains; the actual content of the rules is a theoretical contribution, made in the light of general knowledge and susceptible to further empirical test—a test, incidentally, which is often facilitated by a more formal restatement.

The introduction of additional variables points to a second aspect of the substantive contribution. It obviously makes a difference which specifications are introduced. Under some conditions, changes will come about much more rapidly or frequently than under others; some developments will gather momentum over time, whereas others will stimulate counter-tendencies and be arrested. All this can be put into formal language after someone has thought about such alternatives; and some of these hypotheses will later be corroborated by actual findings, while others will remain stillborn speculations. Behind the formal notion of variables is the hidden hope that those variables which alone can make the formalism productive will be selected.

It would be possible to close our discussion on this note. But there is one final matter to be brought to the fore, even if it must remain in the form of an unanswered question. We have now translated almost all the main passages in the pages under scrutiny

—but only almost. A careful reader will have noticed that certain terms were not covered by our formalization. The language used in our formalization always took the form: often (or seldom) people move from one kind of state (however specified) to another kind. But at a score of points the document described these movements in a specific kind of language. When pairs moved away from a state it was because of a "frustrating, punitive experience," because the individual was "irritated, subject to strain," etc. Conversely, if pairs maintained a state or moved toward it, this state was described as "mutually gratifying," "rewarding," etc. (Lines of the substantive text, in which words of this kind occur, have been marked with an asterisk.)

There are three ways of looking at these comments. They could be stylistic devices, making the sequence rules more vivid by referring to common experiences and observations; in that case, they would be outside the province of the present endeavor. Or they could be short-hand expressions for the introduction of new variables. Earlier sequence rules regarding friends in disagreement, the $(+-)$ pairs, differed according to whether or not they assumed that the members expressed their conflicting views. Similarly, we might distinguish $(+-)$ pairs according to whether or not they experience irritation as a result of their disagreement. Thus, if these comments about reward-frustration refer to additional specifying conditions or to intermediate steps to be covered in additional observations, then we have dealt with them before and they do not offer a new problem. But it could be, finally, that we are faced with an additional notion: mechanisms which are supposed to account for the observed sequence rules in a way not analyzed before.

If this third alternative is the appropriate one, then a whole new area of formal inquiry opens up. Obviously, the introduction of new variables is itself one form of accounting. How does it differ, then, from these proposed mechanisms? Is it that we are moving here to an underlying psychological level, just as, in the field of thermodynamics, we move from consideration of the heat of bodies to consideration of the velocity of their molecules? Or do we have to introduce new concepts, like Lewin's vectors and barriers, operating in the "field" in which we make our observations?

Within the frame of the task which we set for ourselves, these questions cannot be answered. We meet here residual elements in the text which, in their present form, have not been formalized. If we were told a great deal more about at least some of these mechanisms, it might be possible to explicate the role they play in the total analysis. As it stands, our formalization renders its final service by pointing to a next step in the continuity of inquiry.

APPENDIX I

The equilibrium is obviously obtained if the contact-value distribution of the 400 pairs satisfies the following condition:

$$A = .5A + .3B + .5C + .2D$$
$$B = .2A + .2B \qquad + .1D$$
$$C = .1A \qquad + .4C$$
$$D = .2A + .5B + .1C + .7D$$

The coefficients in each of these equations correspond to the columns of Table 3 in the text. The four frequencies add up to $A + B + C + D = 400$. The terminal turnover table is approximately

TABLE 6

		Time II				
		F A	F A	F A	F A	
	F A	++	+−	−+	−−	
	++	66	27	14	26	133
Time I	+−	18	11	0	28	57
	−+	12	0	10	2	24
	−−	37	19	0	130	186
		133	57	24	186	400

For a detailed discussion of the use of transition probabilities in the study of attitude changes, see T. W. Anderson's contribution to the symposium *Mathematical Thinking in the Social Sciences* (Glencoe, Ill.: The Free Press, 1954).

APPENDIX II

A sixteen-fold table which would correspond to the scheme of such a restless and novelty-seeking community is exemplified in Table 7. The reader should interpret both Tables 6 and 7 in terms of the substantive discussion in the text.

TABLE 7

		Time II				
		F A	F A	F A	F A	
	F A	++	+−	−+	−−	
	++	10	20	10	60	100
Time I	+−	60	5	15	20	100
	−+	20	15	5	60	100
	−−	60	10	20	10	100
		150	50	50	150	

EPILOGUE *

The methodological part of this chapter closes on the note that formal analyses like this one may contribute to the continuity and cumulation of sociological inquiry. It may therefore be helpful for the guinea pig who was subjected to this experiment in continuity to report to the experimenter, and to other observers, what benefits, if any, have been gained from the harrowing experience. This short epilogue is intended as such a report.

The formal restatement of the substantive account, it seems to me, has led to at least seven kinds of clarification, each of which will be briefly described and illustrated.

1. *The formal analysis maps the boundaries of the substantive analysis.* Some of these boundaries were set by design, so that certain problems were deliberately omitted. Others, however, were inadvertent and had escaped my notice entirely, until they were highlighted by the formal analysis.

Among the deliberate omissions is any concern with the processes leading to varying rates of social contact between designated kinds of people, as distinct from the processes of subsequent forming of friendships. In other words, the substantive analysis deals only with those cases in which social contact actually has occurred; it does not take such contact to be problematical, as requiring explanation in turn. It advisedly neglects the processes which make for differential probabilities of social contact between persons with similar or discrepant values who live in a sort of enclave (such as a housing development).

Such a problem is considered elsewhere in the study, where it is assumed that persons with similar values, particularly those values salient in the life of the community, will be more often brought into contact, if only because they are more likely to take part in the same organized groups. And this, in turn, would presumably make for value-homophily since at least some of these contacts would eventuate in sustained friendships. For example: although the racial liberals in Hilltown were not formally organized into groups designed to deal with "problems of race relations," they were more likely than illiberals to come into contact through self-selected membership in local organizations which, because of their prevalently interracial composition, were largely boycotted by illiberals. Since this particular problem of forces making for differential social contact happens to be considered in another part of the

---

* By R. K. Merton.

study from which the substantive section of this paper is drawn, I have all the more reason to appreciate the fact that the formal analysis not only identifies the problem but locates the precise points at which it becomes germane to the study of friendship-patterns regarded as social process.

In contrast to such deliberate omissions from the substantive paper, there are other omissions, uncovered by the formal analysis, of which I was wholly unaware. Another way of putting this is that certain analytical problems flow directly from the formal analysis which are not at all evident from the discursive analysis. For example, the "analysis of chains," involving the observation of pairs of categorized people at three or more points in time, brings out with great clarity and with immediate provision for empirical study the problem of the ways in which the past histories of large aggregates of pairs affect the probable future course of their social relationships. It is shown how to distinguish among those who, at a particular time of observation, appear in the same category (for example, as like-minded friends) but who nevertheless differ in terms of their mutual relationships and values at an earlier time of observation. It then becomes possible to connect such past differences to their probable relationship at a third, and still later, time of observation.

Commonplace as this conception would be in the case-study of a particular friendship between this or that pair,[37] it is anything but obvious, as the research literature on friendship testifies, in statistical analyses of large numbers of cases designed to uncover regularities in the formation, maintenance, and dissolution of various types of friendship. The formal analysis thus provides an instructive example of a procedure for linking up the historical or genetic approach to the study of large numbers of interpersonal relations (which deals with the development or biography of such relations)

---

[37] See, for example, Freud's description of the way in which "the development of psycho-analysis cost" him his friendship with Josef Breuer. Sigmund Freud, *An Autobiographical Study* (London: The Hogarth Press, 1935), Chapter II. And for a perceptively detailed account, surely destined to be a classic, of the process of interaction between ideas and personal relations in the friendship between Freud and Wilhelm Fliess which came to an end over a difference of scientific opinion—a friendship which meant much to Freud and remained unmentioned in his autobiographic fragment—see Chapter XIII of Ernest Jones, *Sigmund Freud: Life and Work* (London: The Hogarth Press, 1953), Volume I. If the Freud-Fliess relationship were one of a large number under observation in a study of processes of friendship-formation and disruption, it would be characterized, for immediate purposes, by the sequence-chain: $(--)$ $(-+)(++)(+-)(--)$. But, of course, a detailed study, such as Jones', of the dynamics of this friendship in particular would consider much else that was involved in the history of the friendship.

and the functional approach (which deals with the consequences of these relations for those directly involved in them and for the larger group at particular times). It shows how to combine what have been called diachronic and synchronic perspectives on interpersonal relations.

2. *The formal analysis brings out and systematizes assumptions hidden in the substantive analysis.* From the formal restatement, it becomes evident that the substantive account deals with friendship-formation as immanent process. In other words, the process resulting in various patterns of friendship is provisionally regarded as taking place in a closed system. But as the formal analysis goes on to show, this immanent process may be either of two kinds. It may be a stationary process in which the sequence-rules are comparatively constant, that is, in which the turnover of cases is such that the distribution of various kinds of interpersonal relations and values remains relatively unchanged. Or it may be an oscillatory process in which the sequence-rules depend on the total distribution at each particular time, thus producing successive distributions which vary about an average. Even under the most charitable interpretation, it cannot be said that these types of immanent process were recognized in the substantive account. But once stated, these distinctive types of process suggest further problems, as I shall report later in this epilogue.

3. *The formal analysis clarifies concepts by giving them operational meaning.* In the course of the formal restatement, certain concepts which were loosely embodied in my own account become operationally defined, without loss of meaning, with net gain in clarity, and in terms that enable them to be more readily utilized in empirical study. As an example of this we can take the concept of an "unstable condition" (which I took to characterize cases in which the opposition between deep-seated values of friends put both the relationship and the values under stress so that one or the other or both tend to become modified). In the more exacting symbolism of the formal analysis, this refers to the sequence-rule in which the number of cases of friends with conflicting values $(+-)$ is being depleted at a comparatively rapid rate, losing cases, at each new time of observation, either to the $(--)$ or the $(++)$ category. An unstable condition can be said to obtain, then, for cells in such an analytic tabulation which lose cases at a relatively rapid rate. Although this statement apparently says no more than the statement which it replaces, it says it better—better in the sense that it facilitates analytic operations by the sociologist who would study this process empirically, and better in the further sense that it raises

productive questions. Here, for example, the more rigorous formulation directs our attention at once to the circumstances under which this unstable condition is more likely to result in one or in another of the alternative outcomes.

In much the same way, the formal analysis takes a general observation in the substantive analysis and converts it into a problem amenable to further research. Thus, I had suggested at several places that values and personal attachments are *interdependent,* that they "act both as cause and effect, modifying and in turn being modified by one another," and that this tends to result in value-homophily. The formal review leads us not to reject this notion of interdependence, but to clarify it. It provides a procedure for discovering which of the interacting elements preponderate; more specifically, for ascertaining whether discrepant values of friends are more often modified to produce accord or whether these values are more often maintained intact at the expense of the relationship. It will be agreed, I suppose, that such provision for discovering which outcomes predominate under specified conditions moves an appreciate step beyond the mere assertion of interdependence. And by providing a means of obtaining empirical findings, the procedure provides a further basis for theoretical elaboration of the problem.

4. *The formal analysis presses for clarification of the logical status of concepts.* In the last part of the methodological analysis, it is observed that one class of terms seems to resist systematic incorporation into the formal framework of analysis. These are the terms that apparently attribute the movement of pairs from one state to another to certain dynamic processes: persons are motivated to seek or to avoid contact, they find the relationship gratifying or punitive, they are subject to strain. Granting that these terms are something more than mere rhetoric, there still remains the troublesome question of their logical status, an obscure question which I am willing to discuss but find myself unable to answer.

It is suggested in the methodological section that these terms may be *either* additional intervening variables of the same order as those already covered by other sequence-rules, *or* that they are explanatory mechanisms, possibly requiring a new mode of analysis. Although I am far from clear on the matter, I suspect that the alternatives are overlapping, rather than mutually exclusive. It seems to me that these are interpolated variables which can be formalized by sequence-rules but that they are nevertheless mechanisms of an explanatory rather than a depictive character. Such classes of mechanisms are explanatory in the sense that they comprise relationships between variables which have been found, with great regularity, to have observable consequences for designated systems (in principle, the systems may vary greatly: a respiratory system, the organism, the self, partners in a social relationship, a social organization or a complex of related organizations or institutions). When they are applied to phenomena which are regarded as a special case in point, as another specimen of this regularity, they are said to explain.

In the present case, the mechanisms refer to sequential relationships between variables which are caught up in one or another version of the "law of effect" (a principle which seems to be found in otherwise most varied schools of psychology). By this is meant, in the present context, some version of the principle that patterns of interaction among individuals are sustained or modified by the punitive or gratifying consequences of such interaction.[38] Together with many others, I have assumed that the law of effect is one of the dynamic principles underlying functional and processual analysis in sociology.

From the formal analysis, we can see just where this principle enters into the interpretation. The social and cultural structure, as I shall presently suggest, goes far toward determining what will ordinarily be experienced as punitive or gratifying as well as the circumstances under which such experiences are likely to occur in interpersonal relations; the principle itself provides a basis for anticipating the probable outcomes of this experience. In short, these mechanisms involve sequence-rules which, having been found to hold in otherwise diverse situations, are being provisionally applied to see if they "fit" this particular type of situation.

5. *The formal analysis brings out the operational character of the method of successive approximations.* As is well known, successive approximations constitute a procedure through which analysis comes progressively closer to the complexities of actuality by the gradual introduction of more variables. It is also widely recognized that this method is useful and even essential to disciplined analysis. Nevertheless, discursive writing in particular runs the risk of violating this precept in practice although asserting it in principle. Such writing often moves back and forth between first rough approximations, using a few variables, and better approximations, using more

---

[38] This is not a latter-day version of psychological hedonism which, through the years, has been repeatedly found to be an inadequate and unreliable conception. For this principle still leaves open the important question of what makes certain experiences punitive and others gratifying, and it is precisely recognition of this that abandons the naïve hedonistic view that diverse social patterns can be *derived* from the same psychological equipment of individuals.

variables, without the author being aware of what is taking place.

It is true that some awareness of all this is expressed in the substantive portion of this paper; the reader is reminded that "we deal here with only one set of values and, to this extent, we abstract greatly from the many values which find expression in social interaction." But this remark is made once and for all, without identifying the precise points at which further approximations to the concrete actuality are being successively introduced.

In the formal analysis, on the other hand, the strategy of successive approximations is under more thorough control because the procedures of analysis require each consecutive step to be specified. Analysis is carried forward a certain distance before it is complicated by new variables, and each of these transitions to further complexity is described in terms of new analytic operations. From the beginning, it is shown how far the analysis of the process can go by considering the interrelations of only two variables at two times of observation, "without recourse to additional ideas or assumptions." Somewhat later (in notes 25 and 26), the reader is informed of certain other variables which are being advisedly neglected for the time being. Still later, it is shown how four additional variables, incorporated in the substantive account, would be systematically utilized in the formal analysis of the process.

Even those who do not deny the necessity for such step-by-step analysis in principle may find it useful to have a procedure which requires this mode of analysis, thus seeing to it that practice conforms to principle. Each consecutive step in the deductive analysis can then be checked with the results of observation before going on to the next. This avoids the danger of constructing shaky though towering edifices of deduction in the shape of long sorites in which each component is a product exclusively of reason rather than of observation organized by reason.

The step-by-step procedure in the formal analysis has the further merit of stipulating the most important restrictions upon the abstract analysis, rather than avoiding this task by assuming "all other possibly relevant things to be equal." By indicating *which* presumably significant variables are being provisionally taken as constant at each stage, the formal analysis provides direction: it points to the next step in the series of approximations.

In this way, the procedure acts as a prophylaxis against the fallacy of misplaced concreteness, in which conclusions are dubious because one has failed to acknowledge what is being left out of account in the analysis and assumes that the conclusions apply to the complex situation as it actually is, rather than to the relations of a few elements within it. In this case, for example, it precludes the fallacy of regarding the degree of homophily in particular groups as the outcome of *nothing but* the few variables here taken into account.

The procedure guards also against a sister-fallacy, what might be called the "and-also" fallacy. This is the misconstruction, common among those who are aware of the dangers of misplaced concreteness, which in effect makes an abstract analysis immune to criticism or disproof, by simply attributing all discrepancies between the hypothetical scheme and actual observations to "other factors" in the situation. At times, there are passing allusions to these factors, without serious regard to the complex problems of really incorporating these many additional variables into a disciplined analysis. The nothing-but fallacy is apparently most often exemplified by those who do precise work but implicitly assume that the few factors taken into account tell the whole story; the and-also fallacy by those who allude to a long list of additionally relevant variables without accepting the responsibility of actually incorporating these into the analysis.

It seems to me that the type of formal analysis in this paper goes far toward preventing both kinds of fallacy: it avoids the first, by periodically indicating certain variables which are being eliminated from the analysis for the time being and avoids the second, not by merely listing these additional variables but by showing *how* they can be brought into the analysis.

6. *The formal analysis stimulates the formulation of additional substantive problems.* Not only does the formal analysis serve to clarify problems raised in the substantive account, and to raise new problems of its own, but it leads also to the statement of further problems which neither the substantive nor the formal analysis had stated in so many words.

As we have seen, the formal analysis shows that homophily, provisionally conceived as a self-contained process, may be either a stationary process—in which the distribution of values-and-personal-associations remains fairly constant—or as a process oscillating around an average, in response to self-induced tendencies and counter-tendencies. Departing from these conceptions of stationary and oscillating processes, the study of friendship can move onto still another conceptual plane, where it deals with the processes through which patterns of homophily and heterophily take on functional significance for the environing social structure. On this plane, the central problem is no longer the familiar one of ascertaining the extent to which friendships are confined to persons of similar social status or with similar values; a problem which, important as it is, tends to be detached from the context of designated variations in social structure.[39] Nor is it the correlative problem, with which this chapter has been primarily concerned, of tracing the processes through which such selective patterns come about. Instead, on this plane of functional sociology, it is the problem of discovering the processes through which different degrees of homophily become functionally appropriate or inappropriate for different types of environing social structure. This perspective on interpersonal relations involves questions such as these: Do various types of social structure have distinctive equilibrium positions for homophily? What are the functions and dysfunctions of various kinds and degrees of homophily—how do these consequences affect the workings of the more inclusive social structure? Through which mechanisms do the consequences of homophily for the social structure operate so as to maintain such equilibria? And correlatively, what leads to the failure of such mechanisms to appear, or to operate effectively?

That the degree of homophily varies greatly among social organizations and communities is a matter of common observation; as we have seen in the introductory pages of Part I, for example, it differed materially in the two housing developments under study. Status for status, there was a higher degree of homophily in Hilltown than in Craftown—a far greater proportion of friendships was confined to those of the same age, religion, nativity, occupational status, and so forth. But it now seems that such empirically observed variations in the degree of homophily can be regarded as problematical, as a beginning for further inquiry. Each type of local social structure can be thought of as having its functionally

---

[39] It is singularly appropriate that the sociologist to whom this volume is dedicated should have called attention, some time ago, to the need for relating processes of interpersonal association to the social structure. As Professor MacIver put it (in his *Social Causation,* 130–131): "The social sciences are deeply engrossed in the study of social processes. . . . One familiar type [of study] is that which centers attention on particular modes of dynamic relationship, particular ways in which people become associated or dissociated, singling each out for characterization either in general or as it manifests itself in localized instances. In sociology this procedure recalls such names as Simmel and von Wiese, and among Americans E. A. Ross, R. E. Park, and E. W. Burgess. These writers treat of competition, conflict, domination, submission, assimilation, amalgamation, indoctrination, and so forth, as distinctive forms of social process. . . . One difficulty inherent in the work of all these writers is that social processes, if studied in this manner, are apt to be detached from the social structures that give them definition and specific quality. This detachment sometimes makes the treatment of processes arid or abstract or unconvincing, and from our point of view has the disadvantage that, by its lack of definite reference to structure, it makes causal investigation difficult except in general socio-psychological terms that do not go much beyond mere classification and description."

appropriate degree of homophily (corresponding, presumably, to its position of equilibrium). The task then becomes that of discovering whether, in accord with the hypothesis, marked departures from this level of homophily produces dysfunctional consequences for the social structure which tend to return the system of interpersonal relations to the previous level.

Such a conception is not, of course, far removed from what is already known about social organization. It is not difficult to conceive of a type of organization in which "too great" a degree of value-homophily would be dysfunctional to the workings of that organization: "excessive" value-homophily in a bureaucratic organization, for example, might mean that the recruitment and promotion of personnel are based, in large part, upon friendships of this kind so that major positions become increasingly staffed by men having the same values and outlook. Beyond a certain point, this could result in rigidities and lack of adaptability of the organization which, in due course, lead to marked reactions against such disruptive "cliques." Or again: "too high" a degree of status-homophily might reduce the amount of informal communication between subgroups below the point which is functionally required for the organization or the community, with deterioration in its effective operation, and a consequent reaction against homophily.[40]

Analytically distinct from the social structure as a context for homophily is the related context of culture. As the formal analysis in effect states, marked increases of status-homophily within a community in which the subculture emphasizes the norm of minimizing status-differences (for example, of class, nativity, or occupation) would be expected to precipitate a sense of threat to this norm among members of the community. Local communities disturbed by what is often described as "snobbery" can be taken to exemplify the type-case in which a degree of status-homophily culturally de-

---

[40] A counterpart to this type of situation was found in Craftown, which had been confronted with a great variety of community-wide stresses: epidemics, "floods," inadequate facilities for schooling, etc. As is observed in another part of *Patterns of Social Life:* "The patterns of inter-status friendships came about, not as the consequence of a planned integration of subgroups within the community, but as the consequence of a series of actions aimed to meet immediate difficulties confronting the community. . . . It is probably true that if differences of nativity, religion, occupation, etc., had been allowed to loom large in Craftown and to preclude or to minimize interpersonal relations between those of different social status, the community would have been relatively ineffectual in meeting its problems. Specific problems would more often have been variously evaluated by the separate subgroups in the community and, to this extent, would probably have intensified group cleavage within the community. . . . A deterioration of community effort and a deterioration of interpersonal relations would have reinforced one another to form a vicious circle of progressive ineffectiveness."

fined as "excessive" releases social forces which may affect the frequency and character of friendships. Such counterreactions are often observed in the direct and expressive form of arranging for "get-togethers" among those of differing status. It is in contexts such as these, perhaps, that we can locate the patterns of stationary and oscillatory process to which the formal analysis directs our attention.

In this sense, the formal analysis leads us to strike out on directions of inquiry which supplement, not supplant, studies in which the major problem is characteristically that of identifying the types of people most likely to enter into close friendships. The major concern would be that of tracing the processes through which different degrees of homophily within designated types of social structure and culture produce functional and dysfunctional consequences which in turn react to affect the patterns of friendship.

7. *The formal analysis clearly illustrates the reciprocal relations of methodological and substantive inquiry.* In spite of caveats to the contrary, the foregoing remarks might seem to imply that the analysis of procedure is *preferable* to the analysis of substance. This is of course very far from my intention. As a matter of fact, the formal analysis has shown that the very complexity of social systems puts a special premium on the theoretical basis for selecting significant or appropriate elements for analysis. Thus, far from minimizing the importance of a substantive conceptual scheme, the methodological analysis underscores its importance and does so by focusing attention on the distinctive place of each conceptual element in the total analysis. All this is made quite explicit in the methodological section: "The formalism . . . only brings out that one aspect of a process analysis is the existence of certain sequence rules and chains; the actual content of the rules is a theoretical contribution. . . ." And again: "It obviously makes a difference which specifications are introduced. . . . All this can be put into formal language after someone has thought about such alternatives. . . . Behind the formal notion of variables is the hidden hope that those variables which alone can make the formalism productive will be selected."

In these terms, the entire formal analysis bears out the interlocking and mutually supporting character of methodological and substantive study. This one example suggests that other such re-analyses might usefully take the place of the occasional polemics that would set methodologist and theorist in what must be only mock opposition to one another.

As I now see it in the light of this experience, the formal re-analysis of a substantive interpretation offers a number of devices for thinking through the implications of what has been said, beyond the point which more discursive analysis ordinarily encourages or even permits. It can show that some implications have not been fully drawn, that they lead further than was supposed, and that other implications have not been drawn at all. As an example of the first kind I cite the notion of the interdependence of values and personal relationships which was extended to include the question of preponderating forces in such interdependence under diverse conditions; as an example of the second kind, the range of problems which emerges when homophily is thought of in terms of stationary or dynamic equilibrium.

These few retrospective comments should be seen in context. They are not intended to give credit where credit is due, however laudable such a purpose may be in another connection. They are intended only to single out, as best I can, the various specific uses of this formal re-analysis of a substantive conception, with a view to identifying some of the functions of this re-analysis for social theory and research. If these remarks also imply a tribute to the author of the formal analysis, that cannot be helped.

3

THE PROBLEM OF AUTHORITY

ROBERT BIERSTEDT

In the vast complexity which is a human society the exercise of authority is a constant and pervasive phenomenon. Society indeed is impossible without order—in a larger sense society is synonymous with order [1]—and it is authority which serves as the foundation of much of the order which society exhibits. Every day thousands of persons interact with thousands of others in relationships which involve superordination and subordination, the issuance of commands and obedience to them, the announcements of decisions by some and the acceptance of these decisions by others. Here we have a phenomenon of considerable significance and one which requires serious sociological analysis. What is it, in short, that confers upon some men the right to command, upon others the obligation to obey? Why should anyone exercise this right, anyone owe this duty? How does authority contribute to the order which all of the members of a society desire, those who obey as well as those who exact obedience?

If we seek examples of the exercise of authority we shall find them in every sector of society. It is authority which enables the jailor to hand to Socrates the cup of hemlock with the rueful but reasonable expectation that he will drink it; authority which enables the elders of the synagogue to execrate, curse, and cast out Spinoza with all the maledictions written in the book of the law; authority which confers upon an American president the right to remove an imperious general from his commands. On less exalted levels it is authority which enables a vice-president to dictate to his secretary, a sales-manager to assign territories to his salesmen, a personnel manager to employ and discharge workers, an umpire to

---

[1] On the problem of order in general, see Florian Znaniecki, *Cultural Sciences: Their Origin and Development* (Urbana: University of Illinois Press, 1952), Introduction and Chapters 1, 2, and 6.

banish a player from a baseball game, a policeman to arrest a citizen, and so on through innumerable situations. All these can serve to illustrate the ubiquitous character of the phenomenon we are about to analyze.

In inaugurating an inquiry into the nature of authority, however, it is advisable to exercise several cautions. In the first place the sociological literature on this subject, astonishingly enough, is somewhat scanty. Indeed, Florian Znaniecki remarked as late as 1935 that he was unacquainted with any sociological monograph on authority, although he conceded that the historical and political literature was "very rich." [2] In the second place, Roberto Michels, in an article specifically devoted to this problem, an article rich in insights, says nevertheless that "It is futile to discuss the *raison d'être* of authority." [3] Observations like these suggest at least some of the difficulties which an analysis will encounter.

A second caution concerns the fact that the problem of authority is susceptible to treatment on several different levels. One of these levels might be called the philosophic. Here the problem is the apparent opposition between liberty and authority. The literature here, of course, is voluminous, and it embraces in an important sense the entire history of political philosophy from Plato to MacIver. It is an issue, in fact, which is of continuing concern to philosopher and citizen alike. It is not, however, the problem we wish to pursue in this place. Another level might be called the political, that is, the level on which the competence of the political scientist is most relevant. Here we should meet, for example, problems of political obligation, of the particular kind of authority represented by the law, of the delegation of powers, of political power in general, and of public administration. On problems of this kind too there is a large literature and one which it would not be possible to examine in the space at our disposal. There is, however, a third level on which a discussion might proceed, and this level we shall call the sociological. It is less abstract than the first of the levels mentioned and less restricted in scope than the second. On this level we shall be interested in authority wherever we meet it and not only in the political organization of society.

One should not have to contend that the problem of authority in this last sense belongs to sociology. It is indeed obvious that the problem of authority rests at the very bottom of an adequate theory of the social structure. When MacIver, for example, seeks "the au-

---

[2] *Social Actions* (New York: Farrar and Rinehart, 1936), p. 673.

[3] "Authority," *Encyclopedia of the Social Sciences*, Vol. II, pp. 319–321.

thority beyond the authority of government" he knows that even government, in a sense, is not merely a political phenomenon but primarily and fundamentally a social phenomenon, and that the matrix from which government springs itself possesses an order and a structure. If anarchy is the contrary of government so anomy is the contrary of society. Authority, in other words, is by no means a purely political phenomenon in the narrow sense of the word. For it is not only in the political organization of society, but in all of its organization, that authority appears. Each association in society, no matter how small or how temporary it might be, has its own structure of authority.[4]

Before discussing the nature of authority proper it will be convenient if we first distinguish it from two other phenomena with which it is sometimes confused. The first of these is competence. Thus, we commonly speak of a given person as "an authority" on a given subject. Branch Rickey, for example, is an authority on baseball, Lou Little on football, Emily Post on etiquette, Arturo Toscanini on music, Charles H. Goren on bridge, and every professor on the subject he teaches. In this sense authority is related to influence but not to power, and in this sense it has nothing to do with legitimacy and nothing with obligation. It is recognition of competence which encourages us to accept the opinions of those who have achieved prominence and prestige in their special fields of endeavor. There is nothing compulsory about this acceptance, and if we accede at all to opinions of this kind it is as a tribute to eminence rather than as an obeisance to authority. We voluntarily respect the competence of others, but authority requires our submission. When the situation involves competence, furthermore, one may choose one "authority" rather than another, Casey Stengel rather than Branch Rickey, for example, or Herman Hickman rather than Lou Little, and so on. Competence, in other words, exerts influence; authority exacts obedience.[5]

It is interesting to note in this connection that our language tricks us into error. When we speak of an order or a command having been issued by "competent authority," we do not, curiously enough, mean competence at all. We mean not that the authority is com-

---

[4] The word "association," throughout this paper, is exactly synonymous with "organized group."

[5] This distinction has more recondite consequences of a political character than can be considered in this place. Ernest Barker has suggested, for example, that the authority of science can be used to perfect the science of authority. *Reflections on Government* (London: Oxford University Press, 1942), p. 232. See his discussion of this issue, pp. 231–234, and especially the note to p. 232.

petent, but that it is legitimate. In an inferior position, for example, we may obey the command of a superior whose authority we
recognize even when it seems unreasonable, and disobey a command which seems reasonable if we question the authority of the
alleged superior to issue it. Superior knowledge, superior skill,
and superior competence need not be involved in the exercise of
"competent" authority. As Talcott Parsons points out, the treasurer of a corporation may have the authority to sign checks dis-
bursing the corporation's funds, but this does not imply that the
treasurer is a better "check-signer" than any one of hundreds of
others.[6] The authority to sign checks, in short, has little relation
to the capacities of individuals and much less to the caliber of their
calligraphy. Robert MacIver, similarly, has said that "The man
who commands may be no wiser, no abler, may be in no sense
better than the average of his fellows; sometimes, by any intrinsic
standard, he is inferior to them." [7]

In view of considerations like these it is difficult to determine
why Roberto Michels should begin his discussion with the statement
that "Authority is the capacity, innate or acquired, for exercising
ascendancy over a group." [8] We shall contend, on the contrary,
that there is no clear sense in which authority is a capacity, that it
is certainly not innate, and that it is never acquired except in the
process of social organization. We shall further contend that it
always has an institutional and never, except indirectly, a personal
origin.[9]

The second phenomenon with which authority is sometimes confused is the phenomenon of leadership. Here again, for reasons
which have considerable cogency, it seems desirable to maintain a
distinction. It cannot be said that Max Weber, who otherwise
contributed so many penetrating observations on this problem,
maintained complete clarity on this point. It is the introduction

---

6 Note 4 to p. 58 in Max Weber, *The Theory of Social and Economic Organization,*
edited by Talcott Parsons (New York: Oxford University Press, 1947).

7 *The Web of Government* (New York: The Macmillan Co., 1947), p. 13.

8 *Loc. cit.*

9 In one sphere, however, it is especially difficult to dissociate the authority of competence from the authority of legitimacy. This is the sphere of religious authority.
It is clear that the authority of a philosopher, for example, is the authority of competence and that the authority of the praetor, on the contrary, is the authority of power.
But what shall we say about the authority of the pontiff? What supports the decretal
issued by a religious hierarch? Is it his competence, the unique capacity imputed to
him of direct communication with the deity? Or is it his authority which stems from
his superior administrative position in the hierarchy? This situation introduces difficulties of a special and interesting kind and requires, unfortunately, a more elaborate
analysis than we can give it here.

of charismatic authority into his treatment which prompts this reservation. Weber, as is well known, distinguished charismatic authority from traditional authority on the one hand and from rational-legal authority on the other. Charisma, of course, is a gift of grace which, imputed to a leader by his followers, gives a divine sanction, encouragement, and even justification to his actions. A charismatic leader is believed to be different from other men; he rises above them because he is touched with divinity; there is something of the celestial afflatus about him. It is interesting to notice that persons whose achievements are so impressive that they distinguish them from the multitude are frequently suspected of charisma,[10] and indeed it is of significance for the sociologist of religion that the attribution of charisma seems to be the initial stage in apotheosis.

But leadership is not authority. As in the case of competence, no one is required to follow a leader and no one involuntarily satisfies a leader's desire or grants a leader's wish. The fiat of the leader lacks legitimacy. One may follow or not and no sanction except possibly the informal sanction of being regarded as odd by other followers is applied to those who abstain. The situation is different with respect to authority. A leader can only request, an authority can require. The person subjected to an order by "competent authority" has no alternative but to obey.[11] The examination must be taken at the appointed time, taxes must be paid, the draft induction notice must be observed.[12] Obedience to an authoritative command is not a matter of a subordinate's arbitrary decision. Leadership depends upon the personal qualities of the leader in the situations in which he leads. In the case of authority, however, the relationship ceases to be personal and, if the legitimacy

---

10 The biographer of John Maynard Keynes, for example, permits himself to speculate as follows: "In making a final appraisement of Keynes' influence, some may seek to attribute it to a gift or special power that lies outside the range of normal human qualities; they may seek for some mysterious aptitude, some nameless gift, bestowed on him from the unseen world." From R. F. Harrod, *The Life of John Maynard Keynes* (New York: Harcourt, Brace & Co., 1951), p. 646. This suggestion is immediately rejected, but if sophisticated scholars can allude, however lightly, to such a possibility, it is easy to see how the multitude, in any society, might concede charisma to those whose extraordinary achievements win them extraordinary devotion.

11 Unless, as we shall subsequently observe, the situation is rearranged in such a manner that the subordinate is able to withdraw from it.

12 An amusing story comes from England concerning the Londoner who, upon receiving his draft induction notice, replied, "See Luke 14:20." ("I have married a wife and therefore I cannot come.") To which the War Office answered, "Your attention is drawn to Luke 7:8." ("For I also am a man set under authority, having under me soldiers, and I say unto one, Go, and he goeth; and to another, Come, and he cometh.")

of the authority is recognized, the subordinate must obey the command even when he is unacquainted with the person who issues it. In a leadership relation the person is basic; in an authority relation the person is merely a symbol.

We may summarize these observations by noting that an authority relationship is one of superordination and subordination; the leadership relationship, on the contrary, is one of dominance and submission. These are independent variables. Superordinates may or may not be dominant individuals in a psychological sense; subordinates may or may not be submissive.[13] The exercise of authority does not necessarily involve a personal relationship of any kind. As suggested immediately above, those who exercise authority, especially in the large-scale associations of complex societies, are frequently unaware of the individual identities of the persons over whom the authority is exercised and, conversely, the latter may be unaware of the personal identity of the former. In a military establishment, for example, thousands of men are sent to the far corners of the earth by an official whom they have never seen and whose name they may even fail to recognize. This official, in turn, is unacquainted with the men thus subjected to his command and he may not see or even sign the paper which dispatches them to their destinations. It would be inappropriate to contend that there is any leadership in this situation or that this kind of authority, as Michels has suggested, marks some kind of capacity, "innate or acquired," for ascendancy. Leadership, in short, like competence, is a species of influence; authority is a function of power.

Once we have distinguished authority from competence and from leadership we are prepared to indulge in some statements of a more positive character. Our first observation is perhaps the obvious one that authority is always a property of social organization. Where there is no organization there is no authority. Authority appears only in the organized groups—the associations—of society, never in unorganized groups or in the unorganized community. An absence of organization implies an absence of authority. There is authority only within an association, never in the interstices between associations. The exercise of authority, furthermore, never extends beyond the limits of the association in which it is institutionalized and which gives it support and sanction. The dean of women, for exam-

---

[13] Leadership qualities, of course, are frequently involved in a man's rising to a position of authority, but this is another process. Frequency is not necessity, as can be seen in countless illustrations, from the monarch to the sheriff, where no test of leadership—or of competence—is imposed.

ple, may require all women students to be in their domiciles at a certain hour in the evening, but such an order can have no effect upon the young women of the community who are not students at the university. The collector of internal revenue may not examine a candidate for the degree of doctor of philosophy, a policeman may not decide a close play at second base, and so on through all the situations of society.[14] This observation, of course, contributes nothing to the analysis of the phenomenon; it merely gives it a locus. But the locus is significant. If we ask where in society authority obtains, we shall reply in associations, and never anywhere else.

If authority is created in the organization of an association it is necessary, accordingly, to examine the process in which an unorganized group is transformed into an organized one. In this process several things happen. In the first place, informal procedures and patterns of interaction come to be standardized as norms. In the second place, roles come to be standardized as statuses. It is the institutionalization of procedures into norms and roles into statuses which results in the formal organization of the association. Norms and statuses then constitute the structure of the association; they are its organization. More particularly, the role of leader, which one or several members of the group have been playing, comes to be institutionalized in one or several statuses to which authority is now attached in accordance with the norms. These roles become statuses in order that the stability of the association may be assured and its continuity guaranteed.

It is apparent that no association of any size or degree of complexity can maintain a constant membership. The inexorable process of life itself determines that the personnel of the association will change over the course of time. Some associations, of course, cannot survive the individual departures of the people who comprise them because they have no method of recruitment.[15] Any association whose members wish it to survive and to gain an independence of particular personnel must institutionalize its roles into statuses and must create authority where initially there was only leadership. The leader who has been instrumental in organizing the association

---

[14] An instance of error in this respect concerns the late General Patton. On a tour of inspection at an army post he became annoyed at a telephone lineman who paid no attention to his passing and who continued to work at the top of the pole. The lineman refused in addition to obey the general's peremptory command to come down from the pole and stand at attention. At this point the general, near apoplexy as the story goes, demanded to know the man's name and company. The name is unimportant; the company was the Bell Telephone Company.

[15] This is Simmel's "broken-plate" pattern.

may subsequently be indisposed or withdraw from the circle of his followers. Unless his role has been institutionalized such a contingency would jeopardize the association's existence. After it has been institutionalized the leader may even be deposed from whatever position of authority he may occupy without damage to the group. A structure is thus necessary if associations are to survive the flow of individuals in and out of membership. The supreme test of the organization of an association, in fact, is satisfied when it can sustain a total turnover in personnel.

The formal organization of an association, in short, is constituted of norms and statuses. The norms are attached to the statuses and not to the persons who occupy them. The norms involve rights, duties, privileges, obligations, prerogatives, and responsibilities as they are attached to particular statuses in the structure of the association. The right to exercise authority, that is, the right to make decisions and to enforce them, is now attached to certain statuses, and this right receives the support of all those who belong to the association and who conform to its norms. But the exercise of authority is not only a right; it is also a duty. The occupation of certain statuses implies the obligation to make decisions in the name of the association and the obligation to enforce them.

It is important to recognize that authority is never exercised except in a status relationship. As a right and as a duty it is always attached to a status and is never a matter of purely personal privilege. When an individual issues a command in his own name rather than in the name of the status or position which he occupies, we have a sure indication that it is leadership, not authority, which is being exercised. Sometimes, of course, there is a penumbra of uncertainty with respect to the authority vested in a status, and the right to make a decision, as in jurisdictional disputes, may be more hotly contested than the policy which the decision involves. Similarly, the authority of one status is always exercised over another status and never over an individual as such. It is not the case that Mr. Jones, the vice-president, issues orders to Mr. Jackson, the cashier of a bank. It is the vice-president who issues orders to the cashier in independence of the identity of the individuals who occupy these statuses. Authority is thus a function of the formal organization of an association, and it is exercised in accordance with specific and usually statutory norms and statuses. It makes no appearance in the informal organization. The superordination and subordination of associational statuses is characteristic of all formal social organization and it is this hierarchical arrangement, this stratification of statuses, which permits and indeed makes possible the exercise of authority.

That authority involves a status and not a personal relationship can be illustrated in addition by some interesting cases of status reversal which alter the superordination and subordination of two individuals. One factory-worker may be subordinate to another in the status hierarchy of the factory. In the union local to which they both belong, on the other hand, the latter may be subordinate to the former. In the Navy a commander of the line exercises military authority over all lieutenant commanders, both line and staff, but when he occupies the status of patient he is subject to the orders of a lieutenant commander of the medical corps who occupies the status of doctor. On a civic committee an employer may occupy a status subordinate to that of one of his own employees. For that matter, the President of the United States, superior in several hierarchies, takes orders from the officers of the Secret Service who are charged with the protection of his person. It is obvious that examples of this kind could be multiplied.

In spite of this important distinction it would be improvident to ignore the fact that personal factors do enter into status relationships and that the latter are seldom "pure" except in cases where the two individuals involved are wholly unaware of each other's identity. It is a fact that persons evaluate each other "intrinsically" in terms of their personalities and not only "extrinsically" in terms of their conformity to the norms which their statuses impose upon them. It is an additional fact that the informal organization of an association sometimes takes precedence over its formal organization. Subordinates in these situations frequently exhibit capacities as leaders and begin to play leadership roles; superordinates, on the other hand, frequently withdraw informally from the responsibilities of their statuses and exercise only a nominal authority.[16] Nor can we ignore the familiar phenomenon by which the possession of a status involving authority exerts an influence upon personality. Otherwise submissive individuals, "dress'd in a little brief authority," sometimes assume an authoritarian air, and otherwise dominant individuals, stripped of the perquisites of status, sometimes exhibit a new humility. Recognition of the intrusion of psychological factors does not alter the fact, however, that authority is exer-

---

[16] On the intrinsic and extrinsic evaluation of persons see E. T. Hiller, *Social Relations and Structures* (New York: Harper & Brothers, 1947), Chapters 13, 14, and 38. For an illuminating article on formal and informal organization see Charles H. Page, "Bureaucracy's Other Face," *Social Forces*, Vol. 25, October, 1946, pp. 88–94.

cised in a status relationship and not in a personal relationship, and that the relationship becomes increasingly impersonal with increase in associational size.

What, now, sustains the authority exercised by some people over others? Why should a subordinate obey a superordinate when he disapproves of the command? Why, in fact, does subordination not imply agreement, insubordination dissent? Why does an inferior obey a superior whom he may obviously dislike, whom he may never have met, or to whom in other relations he may be totally indifferent? A preliminary answer to these questions has already been suggested: both the superior and the inferior recognize that they are operating in a status relationship and not a personal relationship and that personal sentiments are irrelevant to the exercise of authority in the situation. Indeed, a person is expected and even required to exercise the same kind of authority over friends and intimates that he does over enemies and strangers. In the ideal case the exercise of authority is wholly objective, impartial, impersonal, and disinterested. The judge who has violated a traffic regulation is expected to fine himself.[17]

This observation, however, does not answer the more general question. The reasons people submit to authority, in the larger focus, are the reasons which encourage them to obey the law, to practice the customs of their society, and to conform to the norms of the particular associations to which they belong. This question has received a comprehensive discussion in the literature of political philosophy and sociology and the treatment which Robert M. MacIver has given to it in several of his works is unexcelled.[18] This treatment requires no recital or repetition here. But the reason why men in general conform to the norms does not always explain why particular men accept particular authority especially in situations where the person who exercises authority introduces new norms, when he exercises, in effect, a legislative function. What supports the authority in these instances?

---

[17] The writer is indebted to Talcott Parsons for the suggestion that in the ideal case authority is as impersonal as a traffic light.

[18] See particularly the section entitled "How and Why Men Obey," *The Web of Government*, pp. 73–81, *et passim;* and *Society: An Introductory Analysis* (with Charles H. Page) (New York: Rinehart & Co., Inc., 1949), pp. 142–146 and the whole of Chapter 9, pp. 189–209. For an interesting recent discussion, one which depends to some extent upon MacIver's, see F. Lyman Windolph, *Leviathan and Natural Law* (Princeton: Princeton University Press, 1951), Chapter 2. This problem ultimately becomes a problem in moral philosophy, the problem of the proper relationship between the individual and his society.

The only possible answer to this question is that authority in these, as in all other cases, is supported, sanctioned, and sustained by the association itself. The person who exercises it is recognized as an agent of the group. He represents the group. He acts not in his own but in the group's name. Insubordination now is a threat not to a personal relationship but to the continued existence of the group. It is an assault upon the group, a denial of the validity of its norms, and, even more significantly, an attack by an individual upon a majority. Since authority is attached to a status, in a system of statuses supported by the majority of the members, and since this system of statuses is synonymous with the organization of an association, it is apparent that any disinclination to accept the status arrangement and the exercise of authority involved in it implies a disinclination to accept the group itself. It is the majority of the members of an association who support its structure and who sustain the authority exercised in particular statuses in accordance with particular norms. If we seek the rationale of authority, therefore, we find it in the very factors which induce men to form associations in the first place, to band together in organized groups, and to perpetuate these associations. It is the desire for stability and continuity which guarantees that the exercise of legitimate authority will be maintained in the statuses of the association, not as an underwriting of particular decisions, but as a bulwark behind the organization of the association itself. An individual who rejects this authority is jeopardizing the continued existence of the association.[19] The ultimate answer therefore to the question of what sustains the authority exercised in an association of any kind is that this authority is sustained by a majority of the association's own members.[20]

We have finally to inquire whether authority is a phenomenon exercised by coercion or by consent. Does the person who accepts a command from superior authority do so, in short, because he has to or because he wants to? Both Barnard and MacIver seem to accept the latter alternative. Barnard, for example, speaking primarily of the nonpolitical associations of society (but including

---

[19] Chester I. Barnard has noted in this connection that: "If objective authority is flouted for arbitrary or merely temperamental reasons, if, in other words, there is deliberate attempt to twist an organization requirement to personal advantage . . . then there is a deliberate attack on the organization itself." *The Functions of the Executive* (Cambridge: Harvard University Press, 1938), p. 171.

[20] For an elaboration of the role of majorities in organized groups see Robert Bierstedt, "The Sociology of Majorities," *American Sociological Review*, Vol. XIII, December, 1948, pp. 700–710.

the army), says, "The existence of net inducement is the only reason for accepting *any* order as having authority," and, even more strongly, "The decision as to whether an order has authority or not lies with the persons to whom it is addressed, and does not reside in 'persons of authority' or those who issue these orders." [21] His discussion emphasizes the view that the direction of authority proceeds from the bottom up rather than from the top down in any associational hierarchy.   MacIver, similarly, speaking of political authority and the governmental associations of society, says that the identification of authority with power is "inept" and further that "The accent is primarily on right, not power.   Power alone has no legitimacy, no mandate, no office." [22]   Kingsley Davis, on the other hand, refers to authority as "a system of normatively sanctioned power;" [23] Horace Kallen calls authority "the sanctioned exercise of indirect coercion;" [24] for Lasswell and Kaplan authority is synonymous with "formal power;" [25] and the present writer has defined it as "institutionalized power." [26]   Finally, Michels, meeting the dilemma head-on as it were, insists that "Even when authority rests on mere physical coercion it is accepted by those ruled, although the acceptance may be due to a fear of force." [27]

A possible solution to this apparent contrariety of opinions rests in a distinction between two kinds of associations, voluntary and involuntary.   In a voluntary association membership is a matter of consent, and people voluntarily give their allegiance to it.   They conform to the norms of the association for the same reason, let us say, that they conform to the rules of the games which they play; that is, they conform because the desire to play exceeds the desire to win.   Similarly, they accept the authority of others in voluntary associations because the desire to belong exceeds the desire to make independent decisions on matters of associational concern.   This is doubtless what Barnard means above by "net inducement."   The candidate for the degree of doctor of philosophy, for example, accepts the authority of his examiners to ask him questions, a student accepts the authority of the instructor to evaluate his academic

21 *The Functions of the Executive*, pp. 166, 163.
22 *The Web of Government*, pp. 85, 83.
23 *Human Society* (New York: The Macmillan Co., 1949), p. 48.
24 "Coercion," *Encyclopedia of the Social Sciences, op. cit.*, Vol. III, p. 618.
25 Harold D. Lasswell and Abraham Kaplan, *Power and Society* (New Haven: Yale University Press, 1950), p. 133.
26 "An Analysis of Social Power," *American Sociological Review*, Vol. XV, December, 1950, pp. 733ff.
27 "Authority," *Encyclopedia of the Social Sciences, op. cit.*, Vol. II, p. 319.

work, and an employee accepts the authority of his employer to assign his duties. In voluntary associations, in short, authority rests upon consent, and it might be appropriate in these circumstances to define authority as institutionalized leadership.

In involuntary associations, however, the situation is somewhat different. A soldier may not defy the order of a superior officer, a citizen may not ignore the demands of the tax-collector, and a prisoner certainly may not refuse to accept the authority of his guards. In certain associations, in other words, voluntary withdrawal is impossible, and these are what we should be inclined to call involuntary associations. In associations like these it would be somewhat unrealistic to deny that coercion is present in the exercise of authority. It is in these situations that authority becomes a power phenomenon, and it is in these that we can define authority as institutionalized power. In voluntary associations, then, we could say that authority is institutionalized leadership; in involuntary associations that it is institutionalized power. In the former authority rests upon consent; in the latter, upon coercion.

This solution, however, is not quite satisfactory. In the first place it is not always easy to distinguish between voluntary and involuntary associations. The distinction is one of degree. There are many associations, in addition, which one may voluntarily join but from which one may not voluntarily withdraw. In the second place, and possibly more important, authority which may or may not be accepted hardly qualifies as authority in accordance with the ordinary connotation of the term. There is something mandatory, not merely arbitrary, about the acceptance of authority and no analysis can quite rationalize this mandatory element away and retain the full significance of the phenomenon. Furthermore, even in what we have called voluntary associations a member who refuses to submit to constituted authority is ordinarily required, in an exercise of authority, to resign. If he refuses to resign there must be still another exercise of authority to compel his withdrawal from the association and to repel the threat to the group as a whole which his insubordination entails. In view of these considerations it would seem as if our problem requires yet another answer.

In order to find this answer we have to dare an apparent disagreement with MacIver. In order to retain the central connotation of the concept we are examining it seems desirable to assert that authority is always a power phenomenon. It is power which confers authority upon a command. But it is sanctioned power, institutionalized power. The power resides in the majority of the members. It is the majority which supports and sustains the association and its norms. This observation enables us to say that authority is always delegated. Its ultimate source is the power of the majority. The formation of an association, its stability and its continuity, involves the formal delegation of the power which resides in the majority to one or several of the group's members as agents of the whole. It is true, of course, that an individual's membership in an association may be a matter of consent and he may similarly be free to withdraw. But so long as he remains a member, the authority exercised by his superordinates, supported by the majority of the members, is mandatory and not a matter of voluntary determination. The consent in these cases applies to membership in the association and not to the acceptance of the particular commands of constituted authority. Membership may be voluntary, but acceptance of authority is mandatory. It is one of the conditions of membership. Stated alternatively, an individual may be free to belong or not to belong to a particular association, but as a member he is not free to question or to reject the authority exercised by other individuals in accordance with the norms of the association. Considerations like these encourage us to conclude that when consent is involved, as it is in voluntary associations, it applies to the fact of membership and not to the acceptance of authority.

The disagreement with MacIver, however, is only apparent and stems from a slightly different conception of power. We can agree that "power alone has no legitimacy, no mandate, no office," and that authority is not simple power in this sense. But when we say that authority is institutionalized power we attribute a legitimacy, a mandate, and an office to its exercise, and with this proposition there is every indication that MacIver would agree.[28] We have attempted in this chapter to discover how this institutionalization occurs and how it characterizes every association, every organized group, in society. We have suggested in addition that the institutionalization of power is a process which occurs in the formal organization of groups and that it is institutionalized in them as authority. Without the support of the power which resides in the majority of the members of associations there would be no such phenomenon as authority. MacIver's definition of authority as "the established *right,* within any social order, to determine policies, to pronounce

---

[28] Although it involves an additional issue, and one which we have no space to discuss, authority is distinguishable from force in that it always makes some appeal to rationality. An act of authority is not susceptible to argument but it does, in contrast to an act of force, attempt to satisfy the criterion of reason.

judgments on relevant issues, and to settle controversies," [29] is therefore quite in accord with the argument of this chapter. We have
merely attempted to show how this right becomes established and
how it is sustained. We should maintain, in conclusion, that it is
difficult to explain these processes without recourse to the concept
of power.

---

[29] *The Web of Government,* p. 83. See also *Society,* pp. 146–147.

4

THE POLITICAL PROCESS
IN TRADE UNIONS:
A THEORETICAL STATEMENT

SEYMOUR MARTIN LIPSET

Observers have called attention to the fact that in their internal organization and operation, most labor unions more closely resemble one-party states than they do democratic organizations with legitimate and organized oppositions and turnover in office. This pattern is so common in the labor movement that one defender of the Soviet Union has pointed to it as a justification of the one-party regime in that country. At the 1947 convention of the International Longshoremen's and Warehousemen's Union, Harry Bridges stated:

What is totalitarianism? *A country that has a totalitarian government operates like our union operates.* There are no political parties. People are elected to govern the country based upon their records. . . . That is totalitarianism . . . if we started to divide up and run a Republican set of officers, a Democratic set, a Communist set and something else. We would have one hell of a time. . . . (Emphasis by the writer.) [1]

---

[1] Quoted in *Proceedings of the Seventh Biennial Convention, I.L.W.U., April 7–11, 1947* (San Francisco, 1947), p. 178.

Bridges' frankness is matched by an earlier statement of John L. Lewis made at the 1933 convention of the A.F. of L. in reply to an attack on him, as being a "dictator," by Daniel Tobin, then president of the Teamsters' Union. Lewis stated, "The United Mine Workers are not apologizing for the provisions of their constitution. . . . *We give Tobin the right to interpret his own constitution in the Teamsters' Union and to run his organization any way he wants to run it—and we understand he runs it. Frankly and confidentially we do the same."* Quoted in Eric Hass, *John L. Lewis Exposed* (New York Labor News Company, 1937), p. 50.

Philip Taft, in a study of union political systems, has pointed out that, "opposition

In large part, however, the literature which deals with the problem of bureaucracy and oligarchy in trade unions either simply documents this fact in one or more unions, or reworks Michels' classic analysis of the conditions which breed oligarchy or dictatorship in parties and unions.[2] Little work in this field is aimed at developing a set of propositions which can be tested by research.

This chapter represents an attempt to specify at least some of the factors which must be considered in any attempt to develop a theoretical framework for the analysis of one aspect of trade union behavior, that of internal political organization. Each of these sections below contains a number of hypotheses about the functional relationship between different aspects of the social structure and the conditions for democracy or dictatorship in trade unions. It will be evident to any student of the trade union movement that this list of hypotheses or variables is not exhaustive.

Hypotheses that bear on the probabilities of oligarchy in trade unions can be drawn from analyses (a) of factors endemic in the structure of large-scale organization, (b) of attributes of the members of trade unions, and (c) of the necessary functional adaptations to other structures and groups that trade unions must make to achieve organizational stability.

The Need for Bureaucracy. Unions, like all other large-scale organizations, are constrained to develop bureaucratic structures, that is, a system of rational (predictable) organization. The strains toward bureaucracy derive from both internal and external sources. In dealing with their members or locals, unions must set up administrative systems with defined patterns of responsibility and authority. Subordinate officials and administrators must operate within the given rules for dealing with repetitive situations. The larger the size of a local union, or an international, the greater the need to establish a bureaucratic hierarchy. A large local, for example, may be involved in handling workmen's compensation, apprentice schools, pension plans, hospitalization, insurance, assignment of workers to jobs, besides the usual trade union tasks of

---

in union elections is the exception, rather than the rule." "Opposition to Union Officials in Elections," *Quarterly Journal of Economics*, Vol. 58, p. 247.

2 Robert Michels, *Political Parties* (Glencoe: The Free Press, 1949). Two books which summarize and illustrate Michels in terms of the American labor movement are: Sylvia Kopald, *Rebellion in Labor Unions* (New York: Boni and Liveright, 1924); and James Burnham, *The Machiavellians* (New York: The John Day Co., Inc., 1943). An excellent general discussion of the problem of union government will be found in A. J. Muste, "Factional Fights in Trade Unions," in J. B. S. Hardman, ed., *American Labor Dynamics* (New York: Harcourt, Brace & Co., 1928), pp. 332–348.

collective bargaining, handling of worker's grievances, and keeping basic records on all members.

On the international level, these problems are often magnified by the increased size and complexity of operations. These tasks require the creation of a specialized staff which is appointed by and under the control of the officials. The knowledge and skill of union operation gradually become available only to members of the administrative elite.

In addition to the need for bureaucracy which is inherent in the sheer problem of administration—a determinant largely related to the size of the structure—the degree of bureaucratic centralization of unions is influenced by the extent of centralization in the structures of outside groups with which they must deal. We would suggest as a research hypothesis that the more centralized an industry, the more need for a union to be bureaucratic. A union such as the steelworkers', which bargains with a few gigantic corporations, must set up a union authority structure which parallels that of the corporations. Grievance procedures, or wage rates, will be comparable in every part of the industry. The union cannot permit a local leader in one plant to reach an agreement that may be used as a precedent for the handling of grievances in other parts of the country.[3]

Management bureaucracies will usually demand "responsible union leadership" as the price for recognizing the legitimate positions of unions. "Quickie" or wildcat strikes over grievances, jurisdictional or factional fights, militant demands by a membership in excess of those agreed upon by the union officials and all other kinds of actions outside the control of the union officers tend to upset the rationalized routine of production or profit making, and management will demand their elimination. This insistent demand by management for union "responsibility" often leads to undemocratic unionism since it sometimes becomes a demand that unions coerce their members.

It is worth noting here that there is a basic conflict between the value of democratic unionism and "responsible" unionism which many conservatives and business leaders do not recognize, at least in their public pronouncements. The dictatorial mechanisms found in many unions may be regarded as a functional adaptation to management's demand that their yielding on union security issues must be followed by union responsibility.

---

[3] See Joseph Shister, "The Locus of Union Control in Collective Bargaining," *Quarterly Journal of Economics*, Vol. 60, August, 1946, pp. 513–545.

At least one major industrial union has openly acknowledged this problem. Golden and Ruttenberg, writing as officials of the United Steelworkers, have pointed out that the union has consciously developed a number of mechanisms, partly educational and ideological, and partly formal control devices, to prevent variations in local practices. In *The Dynamics of Industrial Democracy,* they describe a case in which a militant and loyal local union officer was expelled from the union because he refused to recognize that he could not set local policies which violated national agreements. The problem of the local leader under a national bureaucracy is well put by this expelled leader: "Being a good union man is agitating— that's what I always knew as a union man—and I got fired for agitating. . . . The company has had it in for me since 1933. I'm a thorn in the flesh to it. Now the union sides with the company and I am out." [4]

It should be recognized that adaptations to the need to adjust to bureaucratic industry which serve the need of union organizational stability also serve the interests of the leaders of trade unions by reducing the hazards to their permanent tenure of office. By increasing the power of the administration over local units, the officials reduce the sources of organized opposition. The United Automobile Workers recently gave its international executive board the right to suspend the officials of local unions for violating international policies. This modification in the union's constitution was defended as necessary for contract negotiations, but it also served the function of enabling the international officials to eliminate potential oppositionists. In both their conciliatory tone—as when they call for intra-union discipline and responsibility—and in their militant tone—as when they call for union solidarity in a dispute with management—union leaders strengthen their own hands and justify their monopolization of internal power in the course of articulating organizational needs and purposes.

However, unions which are small or which do not deal with large centralized industries may permit local units a great deal of auton-

---

4 See Clinton S. Golden and Harold J. Ruttenberg, *The Dynamics of Industrial Democracy* (New York: Harper & Brothers, 1942), pp. 60–61. Recently in one major industry, management officials complained to the union heads about the propaganda against monopolies and large profits that the union was sponsoring. These industrial executives pointed out that the continued union criticism which charged management with lack of good faith and legitimate functions stimulated attitudes among the members that made them responsive to agitation for wildcat strikes, and encouraged them to refuse to cooperate with management production objectives. Union officers, who were themselves sympathetic to socialist objectives, were forced to agree that a long-term contract and continued stimulation of antagonistic attitudes toward large-scale capitalism were incompatible.

omy. The International Typographical Union, for example, permits its locals considerable freedom in negotiations. It is, however, operating in an industry which does not have large national companies and which is in part noncompetitive from one section of the country to another. Even this union, however, limits the freedom of its locals to strike or to make concessions to management on issues involving union security, or jurisdiction over various mechanical processes. The I.T.U., like many other unions, is faced with the problem that a prolonged series of strikes in different parts of the country may bankrupt the union's strike funds.

A somewhat different situation giving rise to increased bureaucratization may also be found in the case of industries that are highly competitive. In such industries, the pressure for bureaucratization may come from the union; large unions are often unable to stabilize their own position unless the industry becomes less competitive, and therefore more predictable, in character. Unions such as the garment unions have developed highly centralized structures so as to be able to force employers to develop similar collective bargaining practices. In some cases, the unions have been able to force bureaucratic structures on employers by forcing them to join industrial associations and to set up codes of business practice. In such highly competitive industries, unions are as constrained to prevent their local units from violating standard policy as are unions operating within highly bureaucratized industries.

The increased participation of government boards in collective bargaining may be introducing a new strain toward increased trade union bureaucracy. Increasingly, local unions are yielding powers which they once possessed to their international, as the locus of decision shifts from a local to a national governmental level. This phenomenon is an illustration of the functional interrelationship between patterns of social organization. The reaction to increased bureaucracy in one institutional area, in this case government, increases the need for bureaucratization of other institutions such as trade unions, which interact with it.

As control over decisions shifts away from the local levels, there is a decrease of membership participation, and interest in local affairs as they lose importance. Similarly, disagreements over policy are increasingly limited to conflicts over national policies, knowledge about which is limited to members of the bureaucracy itself. Thus, conflicts occur more and more as administrative fights at international headquarters and less as political struggles between groups in the locals. The implications of this shift were once graphically expressed to a friend of this writer's by a steelworker when he said, in explaining his lack of interest in the local union: "We don't have a union anymore, we have a contract. The economists and statisticians negotiate contracts—all we can do is vote yes or no to them."

Increased bureaucratization of trade unions and industrial relations not only fulfills organizational imperatives for efficiency, predictability, and "responsibility," and the leadership's needs for stability and control, but also contributes to specific goals and purposes of the ordinary worker. Insofar as unions operate to protect their members from management arbitrariness and caprice in hiring and promotion, they emphasize rational and impersonal norms and standards such as seniority and "equal pay for equal work." Such impersonal standards, systematized, standardized, and administered are a bulwark of worker security, but are also grist for the bureaucratic mill.

Bureaucracy as an organizational pattern which effectively meets so many and varied needs—of the organization, of leadership, of the members—has deep roots in the trade union movement. It may be stated as a general proposition, however, that the greater the bureaucratization of an organization, the less the potential within it for membership influence over policy formation.

Communication. One major source of administrative power which is exclusively available to the incumbent bureaucratic hierarchy is control over the formal means of communication within the organization. The formal right of free speech of individual members means little as an effective check on administrative power if the union leaders have control over all public statements made by members of the administrative or field staff, the union newspaper, and the expense account, which enables officials to travel around the country to see and talk to local members and leaders. Merton and Lazarsfeld have noted that the monopolization of the channels of communication, and the consequent absence of counter-propaganda, is one of the basic conditions for effectiveness of propaganda in shaping attitudes and behavior.[5] This condition, as they note, is indigenous to the structure of totalitarian states; it is also characteristic of the one-party structure of most labor unions.

This particular form of control has a number of consequences for the power structure of a union. The only viewpoints about union

[5] R. K. Merton and P. F. Lazarsfeld, "Mass Communications, Popular Taste and Organized Social Action," in Lyman Bryson, ed., *The Communication of Ideas* (New York: Harper & Brothers, 1948), pp. 95–118.

matters that are widely available to the membership under such conditions are those of the administration. Official policy is justified, opposing proposals or programs discredited if mentioned at all, and the only information concerning union affairs which reaches the general membership is that which officialdom wishes them to acquire. Secondly, this control of communications performs the function of obstructing the possibility of crystallization and organization of opposition. Even if the membership is not thoroughly convinced of the correctness and efficiency of administration policies and there is widespread discontent, organizing active opposition presupposes a means of "getting together," of communicating. The reduction of "collective ignorance" is impossible without widespread contact and information.

No administration group can exercise a total control over the flow of communications within its organization. Different organizations vary in the degree to which the administration "party" approaches a monopoly over communications. Any attempt to analyze the factors which differentiate democratic from nondemocratic organizations must consider the determinants of such variations. A few are suggested in the following comments.

Communications reaching the membership from sources outside of the organization may weaken administrative control. Political parties, for example, do not, in the United States at least, control the newspapers which their members read. Such newspapers by criticizing acts of party leaders can help create the basis for factional opposition. It is interesting to note that in the labor and socialist parties of Europe the party usually owns or controls the newspapers which support the party. This control over the party press facilitates continued domination by party leaders.

Trade unions are not usually exposed in the press to treatment of their internal structure or political processes. There have, however, been a number of cases in which outside media have attempted to reach trade union members. In New York, the Yiddish press, especially the *Forward*, a socialist paper, played a major role in the life of the garment unions for a long period. This paper, which was widely read by immigrant Jewish garment workers, criticized union policies and often acted as the organ of groups within the union. As might be expected, the union leadership in the garment unions resented the independence of the *Forward*. In many unions today, the press of the Catholic Church reaches Catholic workers with propaganda about internal union issues, and it has played an important role in factional situations. Radical political groupings have played a role similar to that of the Catholic organizations in furnishing union members with information and propaganda about their union.

Certain occupational groups have supported newspapers or magazines that are devoted to news of the trade but which may be independent of union control. This has been true for occupations such as entertainment and printing, whose unions have significantly more internal democracy than most trade unions.

It may be suggested that where the means of communicating with the bulk of the membership is not monopolized by the administration, the potentialities for internal political conflict are greater than when they are so controlled. In small union locals, interpersonal or oratorical communication may be effective in reaching the members, and control of the organizational machinery is not an important communications asset. In larger one-party organizations, however, the effective monopolization of communications will vary inversely with the extent to which communications media stemming from extra-organizational sources are directed to the members of the organization. Such independent organs which concern themselves with internal union problems can be based on an ethnic community which overlaps with an occupation, on a religious group which similarly overlaps, on political groups that are concerned with the internal policies of trade unions, and, in a few special cases, on interest in occupational affairs.

The Distribution of Leadership Skills and Its Relevance for Organizational Politics. In most unions, one of the principal factors which operates to perpetuate incumbent power is the administration's almost complete monopoly of the chances for learning political skills. One of the few roles open to a manual worker in which he can learn such skills is that of union leader. In the political life of the nation as a whole, political leaders are recruited mainly from those occupations whose members must learn political skills in order to carry out their occupational role. These skills are largely ones of organization and communication. The legal profession is, of course, the one which best trains its members in such skills. Many business executive positions also require political skills—the successful executive must be able to make speeches, secure assent, mediate conflict, and so forth. Executives who have been concerned with public relations work must learn these skills. The leaders of mass organizations, trade unions, farm groups, professional societies, and many other groups are necessarily men who possess political skills. In large measure, the existence in the society at large of many and diverse "political" leadership roles means that almost every group can find politically trained people to present and organize support for its viewpoints.

If one examines the structure of the trade union movement, and raises the question of the sources of political leadership within unions, it is apparent that the principal source of leadership training is the union administrative and political structure itself. Union officers, if they are to maintain their position, must become adept in political skills. The average worker, on the other hand, has little opportunity or need to learn such skills. He is rarely, if ever, called upon to make a speech before a large group, to put his thoughts down in writing, or to organize a group's activities. The officers' monopoly of political skills within the union may therefore be suggested as one of the major factors which prevents the effective organization of opposition sentiment in labor organizations, and which enables an incumbent administration to use its superior communicative skills to subdue or divert discontent.

The one-party union organization may offer mobile, office-seeking union members the opportunity to learn organizational skills through formal educational programs or through participation in unpaid voluntary positions. Such aspiring members, however, are usually subjected to a barrage of administration views on economics, politics, and union organization. Mobility within the union structure requires that the aspirant take over the norms and orientations dominant in the organization—that is, those held by the leaders. Moreover, one would expect that active members—potential leaders— will be receptive to the viewpoint—broad or narrow—afforded by the administration and will tend to develop a loyalty to it as the source of a more interesting and rewarding pattern of life activity than formerly experienced. In this sense a union organization may provide ambitious workers, who are confined to their occupation, opportunities that few other agencies in society do.

Aside from sheer education or indoctrination, the individual aspiring leader has literally one place to go if he is to go anywhere, and that is into the administration. Unless some opposition group exists, his political activity has to be within the bounds set by the administration. Union officers, who are often faced with a paucity of skilled and capable prospective subordinate officials, given the lack of any means to train them, are usually willing and even anxious to co-opt capable union activists into the administrative structure.

The major advantage accruing to union officers from their possession of the skills of politics may, however, be lessened and even eliminated if the members of their union have other extra-organizational sources of developing these skills. Members of a trade union may learn political skills as a consequence of their occupational roles or through participation in some other organization in which they are given the opportunity or are required to learn political skills. For example, actors must learn to deliver speeches effectively, and observers of the membership meetings of Actor's Equity report that there is a high degree of membership participation in discussion, as well as a long history of diverse internal political tendencies.

The average manual worker who belongs to a union, however, does not gain these abilities through his job, and research studies clearly indicate that he does not tend to belong to formal organizations outside of the union. Ordinarily his opportunities for learning organizational skills are few. There are, however, at least two organizations which have contributed to the training of workers in political skills, churches, and radical political parties. In the United States and Great Britain many workers belong to churches whose membership is predominantly working class and whose lay leaders or ministers are themselves workers. Various observers of the British labor movement have pointed to the fact that many of the early leaders of British trade unions and labor political groups were men who first served as officers or Sunday School teachers in the Methodist or other nonconformist churches.⁶ In the United States, many of the early leaders of the United Automobile Workers, which had a large membership from the South, were men who had been active in Southern sects. Today, the Catholic Church, through the Association of Catholic Trade Unionists and Catholic Labor Schools, seeks to train Catholic workers in the skills of oratory, parliamentary procedure, organization, and administration. In situations in which Catholics as a group wish to fight the incumbent leadership, Catholics trained in these church groups often form the active core of opposition groups.

On the other side, left-wing political parties, such as Communists and Socialists, have contributed a large number of the labor leaders of America. Workers who join such parties are trained, formally or informally, in the skills of organization and communication and

---

⁶ "The training in self-expression and in the filling of offices and the control of public affairs which these [Methodist] Societies provided for a great host of working men and women was invaluable as a preparation for industrial combination and for the future work of Trade-Unionism. The Dissenting Chapel and the Methodist Society were the pioneer forms of the latter self-governing labour organizations, and they became the nurseries of popular aspirations after place and power in civic and national government." A. D. Belden, *George Whitefield the Awakener* (London: S. Low, Marston and Co., Ltd., 1930), pp. 247ff.

become potential union leaders. During the late thirties, John L. Lewis, though a political conservative, was forced to hire many Socialists and Communists as C.I.O. organizers because these parties were the only reservoirs of organizing talent and skill that were friendly to the labor movement. One of the assets which has enabled Communists to gain support from non-Communists within the labor movement is the fact that in many unions Communists, although they are a small minority, are the only persons not in the union administration who know how to organize an effective opposition.

One key, then, to the potential for an active internal political life of any organization is the availability of trained political participants within the organization. This in turn will vary with the status of the occupation, with the extent to which union membership overlaps with membership in other groups which may provide independent sources of leadership training, and with the opportunities for gaining leadership skills as a consequence of the occupational role.

Status of Leaders. It has been noted frequently that labor union officials tend to become set apart from the rank and file of their union both in their styles of life and in their perspectives and modes of thought. This cleavage is most clearly visible in the upper rungs of union administrative hierarchies, where the income differential between union officials and working members is sizable, and where the more or less permanent tenure of most national officials makes their higher income more secure and more regular than many workers can ordinarily expect. This higher, more secure income, together with the different range of experience that is involved in being a union official—desk-work, travel, association with business, government, and other union leaders—provides the basis and the substance for styles of life markedly different from that of the men in the shop. At the local level there is not generally a large difference between the official's income and the worker's pay, but the local officer still has a big stake in the security of his income, the greater chances which he has to rise within the union structure, and (by no means least important) the fact that the union job gets him out of the shop into a much pleasanter, more varied, and more rewarding type of work.

The special interests and kinds of activity and experience of the union official, both on and off the job, appear to create bonds of sentiments, common orientations and perspectives, which, while sharpening the cleavage between officials and rank and file, serve as important cohesive elements within the leadership group. The members of a union officialdom, who share far more in common with each other than they do with the rank and file, appear to develop a self-consciousness regarding their common interests which finds expression in their use of the organization machinery for the defense of their individual tenures and group retention of power.

If a trade union structure is further viewed as part of the total system of social stratification, other factors which contribute to the tendency for oligarchy and undemocratic behavior on the part of labor officials become clear. Status, the honor and deference accorded individuals by (specified) others, has no meaning except as it locates an individual, group, or stratum, on a status hierarchy relative to others in the same frame of reference. Psychiatrists and social psychologists have indicated the tremendous importance to an individual of the status accorded him by those from whom he claims a given status. In American society, an individual's status is most closely correlated with his occupation, but it is also influenced in some contexts by such attributes of the individual or group as kinship, power, length of residence, and other factors. If we look now at the status of the working members of a union as compared with the status of the officers of the same union, it may suggest how these relative statuses affect the degree and nature of the participation of both in union affairs.

In general, the officers of local and international unions do not appear to be accorded status by virtue of their association with their particular trade or industry, but rather are accorded a status that accrues to the quite different roles they play in their occupation of "trade-union official." That this status is very much higher, both in the eyes of the general public and their own rank and file than is the status of almost all working class occupations, can hardly be doubted. North and Hatt's study of the relative job prestige of different occupations as ranked by a national cross-section of the population indicated that "official of an international union" ranks about the same as "proprietors, managers, and officials," considerably higher than any manual occupation.[7] The following comment by Howe and Widdick exemplifies the strong impressionistic evidence that workers themselves generally accord higher status to their officers than to their fellow workers.

The status of the union official can be very high; . . . he is usually highly respected by the workers for his presumed superior knowledge

---

[7] Cecil C. North and Paul K. Hatt, "Jobs and Occupations: A Popular Evaluation," in Logan Wilson and William A. Kolb, eds., *Sociological Analysis* (New York: Harcourt, Brace & Co., 1949), pp. 464–473.

and greater articulateness; he earns a larger and more steady income than they do; he does not have to submit to factory discipline and can keep comparatively flexible hours; and he enjoys what is for most Americans a very great privilege and mark of social authority: he can wear "white collar" clothes rather than work clothes.[8]

Each of the grounds on which this deference is accorded the leader —knowledge, skills, income, job control, head instead of hand work —not only has its own tendency to separate the official from the ranks in terms of style of life, perspectives and so forth, but also taken together support a status differential which works autonomously to *justify* the leader's monopolization of union functions and important activities which his position in the union hierarchy only makes *possible*. He not only wields his power and makes his decisions by virtue of his office but, equally important, the high status accorded him by the members serves to legitimate his authority, in a familiar self-reinforcing pattern of power and status: union office carries with it power, develops skills, supports a middle-class style of life, and is in fact a middle-class occupation. All of these factors, together with the position itself, are accorded relatively high status by the rank and file, which status serves to legitimate the entire role and the actions of its incumbent.

There is a basic strain between the democratic values of the trade union movement and this system of status placement inherent in the structure of most trade unions. With few significant exceptions, every trade union official has moved up in the status hierarchy through his own achievements. The occupation is one of the few high status ones in which status is secured almost completely by achievement rather than ascription. Most high status positions necessarily carry with them some security of tenure once a given position is reached. Democracy, however, implies permanent insecurity for those in governing positions—the more truly democratic the governing system, the greater the insecurity. Turnover in office is inherent in the democratic value that demands equal access by all members of the system to positions of power, and a certain amount of instability of high-status position is implied in majority rule. Thus, every incumbent of a high-status position of power within a democratic system must, of necessity, anticipate a loss of position if democratic values are accepted.

It is not in harmony with what is known of psychological needs of individuals to expect persons in such positions to accept this insecurity with equanimity. Once high status is achieved, there is

---

[8] Irving Howe and B. J. Widdick, *The U.A.W. and Walter Reuther* (New York: Random House, 1949), p. 257.

usually a pressing need to at least retain and protect it. This is particularly true if the discrepancy between the status and the position that one is apt to be relegated to upon losing the status is very great. In other words, if the social distance between the trade union leader's position as an official and his position as an ordinary member is great, his need to retain the former will be correlatively the greater.

It is quite true that this insecurity is faced by holders of public office in any democratic society, but there are important differences. Politicians in the larger society are more than likely to be drawn from what Max Weber so perceptively termed the "dispensable" occupations such as that of lawyer or journalist.[9] These occupations are dispensable in the sense that the practitioner is able to leave them for extended periods and enter politics without any loss of skill during his period of absence (perhaps the opposite is true in the case of the lawyer!) and return to the practice of his profession without too great a financial loss or dislocation. Actually, former public officials, whether lawyers or not, are usually able to capitalize on the skills and informal relations established while in office. A defeated politician is often in a better financial and status position after leaving office than while he was a public official. And, significantly, for the democratic process, he may continue to play the role of political leader outside of office and be of use to his party in opposition.

The trade union leader, on the other hand, if he is one of the relatively few who are defeated after serving in high union office, cannot find a position which will enable him both to maintain his high-status position *and continue to take part in the union's political system.* The differences in the style of life and status of the union leader as over against that of the rank and file are among the factors that might explain why so many union leaders who lose office for one reason or another do not return to the shops, but leave the occupation entirely, or secure an appointive office in some other union hierarchy. Instead of returning to the shops to attempt to regain popular support for themselves and their programs, they seek positions that will enable them to maintain the styles of life and status positions they enjoyed while in office. The absence of an experienced trained cadre of leaders in the ranks, which defeated office holders could provide, makes very much more difficult, if not impossible, the maintenance of an active opposition in the ranks which

---

[9] Max Weber, *From Max Weber: Essays in Sociology,* translated and edited by H. H. Gerth and C. Wright Mills (New York: Oxford University Press, 1946), p. 85.

could present alternative sets of leaders and policies at union elections. When all the men of experience in union affairs are either in the administration or out of the union, there is no nucleus of skills, ideas, and reputations around which an opposition can crystallize. The history of the United Automobile Workers is a good example of this phenomenon. Their three former presidents, and former international secretary-treasurer, as well as a number of past vice-presidents and other high officials, have left the union for jobs in private industry or other unions.

The alternative for a defeated leader to leaving the union is a return to the assembly line or the mine pit, with all that such a return implies in loss of status, income, and power. It is impossible to imagine John L. Lewis digging coal after defeat by the Miners' convention.[10]   Return to the shop, even by local leaders, in addition to making for a sharp reduction in style of life, is often experienced by the former officer as humiliation and failure. There is evidence that it is also perceived in this way by his fellow workers.

The strenuous efforts on the part of many trade union leaders to eliminate democracy (the possibility of their defeat) from their unions, are, for them, necessary adaptive mechanisms. The insecurity of leadership status endemic in democracy, the pressures on leaders to retain their achieved high status, and the fact that devices are readily at hand in their control over the organizational structure and the differential skills that leaders possess vis-a-vis other union members, are strong factors in the creation of dictatorial oligarchies.

The relation of a leader's status to his efforts to minimize democracy in a union are, as we have seen, quite direct. The hold of a union machine on officials does not simply lie in the fact that lower and middle level leaders retain their jobs at the pleasure of the top administrative leaders. This is so clear in most unions that it tends to obscure the fact that it is primarily the attractiveness and status of these positions as compared with work in the shops that gives the union office holders their huge stake in their positions and, correlatively, depending on their rank makes them dictatorial (if they hold high rank) or subservient to their union superiors (if they hold a low or intermediate position).

The effect of high but insecure achieved status becomes clear if we examine the consequences for the union structure of an occupation which gives status to the worker equivalent to or superior to that of union official. Under these conditions, union machines

---

10 See Bernard Barber, "Participation and Mass Apathy in Associations," in A. W. Gouldner, *Studies in Leadership* (New York: Harper & Brothers, 1950), pp. 493–494; and A. J. Muste, *op. cit.*, p. 341.

cannot be as strong and cohesive, nor demand and receive complete devotion and obedience from subordinate officials. The lack of a clear and significant differential of privilege (and style of life) between the officers and the rank and file will mean that the elected leader is not under as great a strain to eliminate democratic procedures and the possibility of turnover while the top leaders will not possess the sanctions—the withdrawal of significant privileges— the implicit threat of which is in most cases sufficient to enforce discipline within the administration machine.

Wide differentials of status, income and other privileges between union officers and the rank and file have clearly dysfunctional consequences for a lively internal political life. They make for a bifurcation of interest and sentiment between leaders and led and a fierce defense by the former of their special privileges, through their creation of tight administrative machines based on the patronage these privileges provide, machines which are staffed by dependent officials controlled by the "threat" of being returned to the ranks. These patterns may be avoided in unions in which there is comparatively little distance or gap in privileges between leaders and rank and file. No one has attempted to systematically gather data to test this hypothesis, although it obviously can be done. For want of such data, one can simply point to the fact that some of the most democratic unions in the country come closer to meeting these conditions than the overwhelming majority of trade unions.

Actor's Equity and the American Newspaper Guild are trade unions whose members may aspire to achieve higher income and status than the officials of the union. Far from suffering from entrenched oligarchies, these two unions have faced difficulty in recruiting union members to serve as full-time officials. Their solution to the problem has been to create a number of unpaid policy-making positions, so that members might continue their occupational careers while serving as union officials. In Actor's Equity, few of the members of the Executive Council ever run for re-election. In the Guild, many of the officers come from the lower status nonjournalist occupations which the union has organized. Recently, the highest full-time official of the Guild, who previously had not been a journalist, resigned to become editor of a labor newspaper. This latter action conforms to the value system of the craft, which ranks the occupation of journalist higher than that of union officer. Another union which has a history of continuous opposition to administrations and frequent turnover in officialdom is the International Typographical Union. The members of this union are among the best paid, highest status groups of American workers. This may help account for the fact that in the I.T.U. defeated union leaders return to the printshop after losing office. Interviews with members and leaders of this union suggest that they have a strong attachment to their craft, and also look upon it as an important high-status job.[11] The fact that defeated union leaders in the Typographical Union and the Newspaper Guild find it possible to return to their trade after leaving office without loss of status or radical change in their style of life may be one of the facilitating factors in maintaining an institutionalized opposition system in these unions.

Participation. Participation by members in the activities of an organization is neither a necessary nor sufficient condition for the existence of membership influence on organizational policy. On one hand, there may be a low level of political participation in an organization or society, and yet, through the existence of different bureaucracies competing for power, the membership or electorate, though passive in the day-to-day political activities, may affect policy through their ability to withdraw or contribute support to one or another of the competing bureaucracies during elections. On the other hand, a membership or citizenry may be active through regular attendance at meetings, belong in large numbers to various organizations with political functions, and yet have little or no influence on policy. This is the situation in totalitarian states and in some one-party trade unions. The totalitarian leader is concerned with having his followers attend meetings, read political literature, listen to broadcasts, and engage in other similar activities, since this means that he can reach them with his point of view and attempt to indoctrinate them. If the members or citizens are not "politically" active, they are also removed from the influence of the controlling power. Some totalitarian states have undertaken large-scale literacy drives with the explicit purpose of increasing the probability that the citizenry would absorb the prescribed ideology. Similarly, some trade unions, especially those under Communist control, have made strenuous efforts, including making attendance at meetings compulsory, to increase participation by their members. It is fairly obvious that Communist labor leaders are not anxious to encourage and deepen internal democracy in their unions, but rather recognize that by multiplying the controlled activities of the members they are increasing their own chances to reach and indoctrinate them, and so reduce the possibility that the

---

11 For an analysis of this and other factors which are related to the high level of democracy in the I.T.U., see the forthcoming book on this union by S. M. Lipset, Martin Trow, and James Coleman.

membership will develop hostile attitudes. As a general hypothesis, one might suggest that the greater the changes in the structure of society that a governing group is attempting to introduce, or the greater the changes in the traditional functions of unions that a union leadership is attempting to effect, the more likely a leadership is to desire and even require a high level of participation by their citizens or members. The radical changes that accompany social revolution, or on a smaller scale, the transformation of a trade union into a political weapon, put severe strains on group loyalties and create the potential for strong membership hostility toward the leadership. A high level of controlled and manipulated rank-and-file participation is perhaps the only effective way, given the leadership's purposes, of draining off or redirecting the discontent which violent changes in traditional patterns and relationships engender.

Nevertheless, it would appear that a situation which normally results in high participation by members of a group has higher potentialities for democracy—that is, for the maintenance of an effective opposition—than one in which few people show interest in, or participate in, the political process. An opposition faced with the problem of communicating with and activating an uninterested and passive membership is under great handicaps compared to the incumbents. Contributing greatly to the existence of one-party oligarchy in the trade union movement is the fact that normally few members show any interest in the political process of the union. The factors which are conducive to this apathy, therefore, are part of the general cluster with which we are concerned in this chapter.

Various sociologists have pointed out that roles in American society are necessarily segmentalized. The American workers, especially, but members of other social classes as well, do not have the integrative participation that individuals in nonindustrial societies experience. In our society, work, leisure, family relations, politics, and many other aspects of life are organized or insulated institutional orders within the social structure. The two roles that are defined by our society as most salient and significant are the occupational role and the kinship role. All others, for example, the role an individual plays as a member of a voluntary association, are more or less subsidiary and peripheral.[12] Although there is a great proliferation of voluntary associations in the United States, a large proportion of the population, especially the manual workers, is not involved in such organizations, and a much greater proportion do

---

12 See Bernard Barber, *op. cit.*, pp. 477–504.

not actively participate in them. As has been indicated earlier, most of these organizations are essentially one-party systems with an active controlling elite and an inactive mass membership. Most of these organizations exist to serve social needs which are segregated from the occupational and kinship roles, and these needs are socially defined as of secondary importance. When the membership of such political, fraternal, charitable, or other leisure-time organizations show a lack of interest in their internal operation or control, this is called "apathy" and is ritually deplored. Even in trade unions and professional associations which affect the individual's occupational role vitally, such membership "apathy" is the usual state of affairs in the absence of severe organizational crisis.

When members are not impelled to action by organizational crisis, the outcome of which may directly affect them, various socially-structured forces away from active participation are decisive. It seems to be generally true that large numbers of men in a union cannot be organized for any considerable length of time solely on the issues of political struggles for organizational power. A naked struggle for power in a union is apparently too corrosive of personal relations, too removed from the deepest, most enduring concerns of the members, and holds too little promise of ultimate reward to those not anticipating jobs, to be able to sustain mass interest for a prolonged period. Of course, factional fights are rarely presented as naked power struggles but are almost always focused around contracts or other union issues, and sometimes, as in the early period of the U.A.W., these economic struggles for union recognition and security are sufficiently moving to sustain widespread, although intermittent, interest in factional fights for periods of several years. But sooner or later, as external conditions become stabilized, the deep and enduring concerns of job, family, recreation, and friends pull the ordinary member out of the disputations and time-consuming arena of factional struggle back to the normal and routine rhythms of life. Only a small minority find the rewards for participation in union affairs and politics great enough to sustain a high level of interests and activity.

Against this background of general membership apathy in most voluntary associations including trade unions, the fact remains that there is considerable variation as between individuals, groups, and organizations in the extent of membership participation. The standard sociological analysis which has been re-specified above does not account for such variations, nor does it identify additional variables which might help explain the differences. Since we are concerned with variations in the level of membership participation and its consequences for the possibilities of democracy in private organizations, it is important to explore some of the sources of such variation.

Participation in any organization appears to be related to the number and saliency of functions which an organization performs for its members, and to the extent to which any or all of these functions require personal involvement. In most cases, trade unions perform only one major function for their members, that of economic collective bargaining. This function can be performed by a more or less efficient union administration without requiring any membership participation, except during major conflicts. In such unions, one would not expect continuous participation by more than the comparative handful of the union's members who are involved in administration.

There are, however, a number of important exceptions to the usual situation in which the mass of inactive union members are serviced, more or less adequately, by a small staff of contract negotiators and administrators. In some occupations and unions, participation in union affairs affords additional rewards to members in the form of higher status, improved job opportunities, or valued social relations. Under certain conditions, unions do not merely perform for their members the protective and acquisitive functions of collective bargaining, but operate, within and as part of an "occupational community," a network of social relations among members of a union which involve them with each other in most or all of their social roles. Participation in the occupational community is not focused exclusively on the union's economic functions, or internal politics, but is sustained by just that wide variety of motives and interests that are not involved in membership in the average union. As we shall see, the existence of an occupational community has very great consequences for the political life of the union itself.

One source of an occupational community is the geographical isolation of a given job. In the small mining towns of the United States, workers interact with each other constantly in all their social roles, in their religious, leisure, and informal organizations as well as in their union. Similar conditions appear to exist for sailors and longshoremen. This frequency of interaction of union members in all spheres of life appears to make for a high level of interest in the affairs of their unions, which translates itself into high participation in local organizations and in a high level of democracy and membership influence on the local level. It is true, of course, that most of the unions in this category are oligarchic and dictatorial on the international level, but the high level of membership involvement may be one of the major factors which accounts for the militant tactics pursued by the oligarchs in these unions. It is also true that these unions appear to have more frequent rank-and-file upheavals than other similar low-status, oligarchic unions.

An occupational community may, however, also occur in large communities in which members are not physically isolated from interaction with other workers. These occur most frequently under conditions of "deviant" work schedules, that is, in occupations which require their members to work nights, and/or weekends. Such deviant work schedules cut the workers off from normal social interaction with their neighbors, friends, or relatives, who have their leisure time in the evening. As a result, persons on "deviant" shifts apparently interact socially much more frequently with their fellow workers. One would expect that policemen, printers, actors, and other groups would reveal a much higher pattern of leisure-time relations with workers in the same occupation than would other groups of workers. Such leisure relationships often result in the formation of formal organizations such as sports clubs, veterans posts, religious organizations, and others, whose members are limited to those working in one of these occupations.

A related factor to the above which may operate independently in a similar way is the extent to which the reference group of occupational members is, in terms of other workers in the same occupation, or groups or individuals in the larger community. One would expect that the more involved people are in an occupational community, the more likely they are to use other members of the community as their significant others, and, consequently, are more likely to participate in many activities linked to the community, and to adhere to its norms. In addition, however, certain occupations, such as journalism or acting, are occupations in which the workers view the judgment of their co-workers as the principal measure of professional esteem. These occupations are, of course, atypical for the trade union movement, but they appear to illustrate the relationship between participation in a group and its function as status reference group.

At the core of these hypotheses regarding membership participation in unions is the observation that the work patterns and environmental conditions of an occupation will largely determine the number and variety of relations that members of the occupation will have with one another. In the majority of manual occupations, workers relate to each other almost exclusively in their occupational roles. But in some occupations, work schedules, geographical isolation, or certain aspects of the work itself will make for a greater frequency of interaction among the workers, off the job as well. Where such "occupational communities" exist, the union becomes an institution which organizes relations among its members in a variety of their social roles. This has direct consequences for union politics. The component groups of the occupational community, especially if they are independent of union leadership control, serve to keep union issues alive. In providing regular opportunities for union members to meet frequently outside of working hours, these organizations and groups also provide opportunities for informal discussion of current union controversies and of the relative merits of candidates; thus they serve as auxiliary sources of information and opinion which are not under the control of the incumbent administration. Moreover, it is in the occupational community that prospective opposition leaders can learn the skills of politics and find independent sources of status and power on which to base a challenge to the incumbents. A genuine "occupational community" such as exists among the printers, actors, journalists, miners, and sailors, may make not only for greater membership participation in union affairs but may also provide one of the bases for the creation of organized opposition to the incumbent leaders, thus operating to increase the influence of the rank and file on union behavior.

A number of "progressive" trade unions have attempted to increase participation among their members by using their educational departments to create leisure-time organizations for their membership. One may note that the attempts of union organizations to impose extra-vocational activities artificially upon their members usually fail. Unions such as the International Ladies Garment Workers and the United Automobile Workers have made valiant efforts in these directions with comparatively little success. The workers in these industries apparently have other sources of leisure activities, and the opportunity to use union facilities does not affect their behavior. In the I.L.G.W.U., studies of participants in such organizations have revealed that the activists are mostly women who, for a variety of reasons, have been forced to search out formal leisure groups. These women are, disproportionately, widows, divorcees, or unmarried women, who have reached an age when most of their friends are married, plus another group of married women whose children have grown up. Unless there are specific conditions which tie a union or occupation to nonoccupational needs of workers, as through the occupational community, the attempt to meet these needs through union-sponsored organizations apparently fails.

There are a number of factors which appear to be correlated with the status level of given occupations that affect the level of participation in a union. In general, one might expect that the degree to which workers identify with a given occupation and its union will be related to the status of the occupation. One would expect, therefore, a higher level of union participation among high-status workers whose status derives from their craft.

In addition, studies of participation in politics and in other voluntary associations have shown that the higher the status of the group in question, the more likely they are to be active in such activities. One would suggest, therefore, that the closer a working-class group approximates a middle-class way of life and orientation the more likely it is to show a high level of union participation. This may be, as was suggested earlier, partly the result of the fact that, in a high-status occupation, the narrower gap in status between the rank and file and the leadership reduces the pressures on the latter to keep a tight oligarchic grip on union affairs. But, in addition, the higher education and occupation-linked status aspirations of workers in "middle-class" occupations such as journalism, the entertainment fields, and printing, apparently lead them to use their unions more freely, for more purposes, and participate in them more widely than do workers in low-status occupations. Some work has been done on the connections between social class and participation in voluntary associations other than trade unions.[13] Similar investigations can be carried through between and within given trade unions which would shed light on this question of the relationship between social class, especially in its subjective and reference-group dimensions, and participation in trade unions. A start has been made in this direction in such pilot studies as those of Gouldner, Chinoy, and Shepard.[14]

---

13 See Herbert Goldhamer, "Some Factors Affecting Participation in Voluntary Associations," Ph.D. thesis, University of Chicago, 1943. Mirra Komarovsky, "The Voluntary Associations of Urban Dwellers," *American Sociological Review*, December, 1946, pp. 686–698. Bernard Barber, "Mass Apathy and Voluntary Social Participation in the United States," Ph.D. thesis, Harvard University, 1949.

14 A. W. Gouldner, "The Attitudes of 'Progressive' Trade Union Leaders," *American Journal of Sociology*, March, 1947, p. 389. Ely Chinoy, "Local Union Leadership," in A. W. Gouldner, *Studies in Leadership* (New York: Harper & Brothers, 1950). Herbert A. Shepard, "Democratic Control in a Labor Union," *The American Journal of Sociology*, Vol. 54, January, 1949, pp. 311–316. It should be emphasized, however, that the sheer increase in the income of workers in a given occupation may actually have the opposite effect of reducing participation in union affairs. If the higher income permits workers to approach middle-class income status, while the occupation itself remains low status, they may attempt to disassociate themselves from the occupation. For example, a study of the members of the San Francisco Longshoremen's Union indicated that many unionized longshoremen moved away from the waterfront after receiving large

Time-Line Factors. The preceding sections have discussed the consequences of different aspects of trade union structure and of attributes of their members derived from their position in the larger social structure for the possibilities for democratic government in trade unions. Each of these factors was discussed as a continuous variable with one end making for greater democratic potential and the other for oligarchy and dictatorship. There are, however, a number of other conditions which can influence the degree of democracy in organizations. These we may call "time-line factors," since they are in large measure related to conditions which occur only at specific periods in the history of organizations.

Patterns of Organization. The variation in historical origins of different trade unions and other voluntary organizations may determine subsequent temporary or long-term variations in their organizational structures. It is possible to distinguish two ideal-type patterns through which organizations are created. One is organization from the top down, where the group which originally starts the association organizes other individuals or branches into a larger structure. In such a situation, we may expect the existence, from the start, of a formal bureaucratic structure with the new subordinate officials deriving their authority from the summits of the organization.

On the other hand, a large national organization may come into existence as a federation either through the successive but autonomous formation of one group after another with some sectors leading the way from the time standpoint, or by the comparatively simultaneous formation of a number of unconnected groups, which later unite. In both cases a ready-made opposition is built into the organization. In such federations, the creation of a "one-party" bureaucratic hierarchy would require the reduction of once independent groups or leaders to subordinate status and power positions. Moves in this direction often meet strong resistance from the autonomous leaders of component units. Instead of a clear hierarchy of leadership, there is considerable competition for leadership among those who were at the top of comparatively independent units before real amalgamation occurred.

The varying political histories of different unions may be related to the different ways in which they were first organized. The United Steel Workers of America, for example, was originally formed

---

wage increases, and became less active in the union. It is only when high status is linked to the occupation that we should expect to find greater participation. The study referred to above is an unpublished one by Joseph Aymes, a graduate student in the Department of Psychology at the University of California.

by the Steel Workers Organizing Committee under Philip Murray. With few exceptions, almost every local of this union was created after the initial power structure was established. From its inception until two years ago, when the problem of succession of leadership first arose, there have been no serious factional disputes in the union. Any local center of disturbance was eliminated by Murray. On the other hand, the United Automobile Workers, which parallels the Steelworkers in age, size, and centralization of industry, was formed out of an amalgamation of a number of existing automobile unions, and a number of its other local units were organized independently of national control and with relatively little help from the national body. The subsequent bitter factional fights in this union are in part a consequence of the attempt of various national administrations to set up a single bureaucratic hierarchy. Most of the factional leaders in the U.A.W. were leaders in the early organizing period of the union, and the different factions have largely been coalitions of the groups headed by these different leaders jointly resisting attempts to subordinate them to the national organization. In spite of the fact that the structural conditions in a large industrial union like the U.A.W. are not favorable to internal democracy and large-scale rank-and-file participation, it has taken close to two decades to approach a one-party structure, and the process is still not completed.

It may be stated as a general hypothesis that the greater the number of independent sources of power and status in an organization, the greater the possibility that alternative factions or parties will be established to oppose the incumbent party. As we have seen, whether or not there are such independent sources of power and status in an organization is related among other things to the pattern of initial organization and the extent to which an organization is structurally constrained to form a large administrative bureaucracy.

The Problem of Succession. In any control structure which does not have a democratic system for replacing leaders or in which there is no formally prescribed system of promotion or selection, the problem of succession often precipitates a crisis. The death of the leader of a one-party structure necessarily upsets the power equilibrium. The more the power structure was organized around personal allegiance to the "leader" the more likely his death or retirement will result in major internal conflict.[15]

---

[15] See Alvin W. Gouldner, *Bureaucracy and Industry* (Glencoe: The Free Press, 1954), for an excellent empirical study of the consequences of a succession crisis in a factory.

In large measure, the passing of a dictatorial union leader creates or re-creates the situation that exists in a union which has been formed from a merger of existing autonomous groups. With the elimination of the person at the top of the pyramid, the leaders immediately below him may each claim equal rights of succession. Such a situation carries within it the potentialities of factional cleavage. As in the earlier case, the union may be faced with the problem of creating a power hierarchy out of equals. Each of the claimants has the resources of control of a segment of the organization, reputation, and skills in union politics.

A recent situation which illustrates this pattern has been occurring in the United Steel Workers. Philip Murray became seriously ill during 1950 and was not expected to live. During his long stay in the hospital, several members of the International Executive Board began preparing for the struggle to succeed him. The apparent monolithic character of the organization, to which attention was called above, broke down. Murray, upon recovering, learned of this struggle and, according to reports, attempted to rearrange the internal power hierarchy in the union so as to prevent a succession conflict. It is clear that Murray died before he was able to complete his internal rearrangements. No open conflict developed, however, as David McDonald, the secretary-treasurer, immediately stepped into the presidency, before his opponents could successfully organize against him. It is clear, however, that a number of top Steelworker leaders resent McDonald's succession, and close observers of the union would not be surprised if open factional conflict developed within the union.[16] There is an interesting similarity between the succession problem of the Steelworkers and that in the Soviet Union which developed in 1923–1924 around the illness and subsequent death of Lenin. Like Murray, Lenin took ill, and several members of the Central Committee began immediately to struggle over succession. Lenin was aware of this and attempted to eliminate Stalin as a candidate, but, as history has recorded, failed. Lenin's death brought about a bitter internal fight for succession in which at least five members of the Central Committee attempted to succeed to his mantle.

Within the trade union movement, there have been situations in which the death of a strong dictatorial leader did not result in a succession crisis. The death of Sidney Hillman, the president of the Amalgamated Clothing Workers, for example, was not followed

---

16 See Daniel Bell, "The Next American Labor Movement," *Fortune*, April, 1953, pp. 120–123, 201–206; and "Labor's New Men of Power," *Fortune*, June, 1953, pp. 148–152, 155–162, for analysis of problems of succession in Steelworkers' and other unions.

by any open internal cleavage. This seeming exception to the succession crisis, however, was not due to a lack of conflict among Hillman's lieutenants. Two major groupings exist within the union led by Hyman Blumberg and Frank Rosenblum. Each, however, is very powerful in his own right, based largely on different regions of the country. Blumberg's power rests in the East, while Rosenblum's is in the Midwest and other sections of the country. Instead of an open conflict developing over control of the entire union, the previous secretary-treasurer, Jacob Potofsky, was made president, even though he has little backing of his own. It is significant to note that in this union, in which a strong leader did not succeed a powerful president, the old leader, Hillman, has been deified. The union constantly erects monuments of various kinds to Hillman, and his name is used to legitimate all present actions. Here the existence of regional blocs may lead to a permanent division of power, as has occurred at times in nations. Such a regional distribution of power contains within it the seeds of a secession movement.

Max Weber, in dealing with the succession problem in one specific context, has pointed out that the death of a charismatic leader (one to whom his followers impute extraordinary personal qualities) may cause his staff and followers, whose power does not rest on any traditional or legitimate basis, to experience tremendous insecurity about the consequences of succession.[17] He stated that one solution to the anxiety of the followers and the weakness of their position was the bureaucratization of the structure. Weber's formulation of the problem did not clearly indicate the manner in which succession brought about increased bureaucratization. More recent investigators have extended his analysis, pointing out that resistance to the authority of a new leader by the remaining staff of the old one leads him to institute allegiance to rationalized rules—that is, to increased bureaucratization. One might hypothesize on the basis of this analysis that when a trade union leader with charismatic attributes is succeeded without conflict, as in the case of Hillman, the union will become more bureaucratic. There is impressionistic evidence to suggest that this has been the case in the Amalgamated Clothing Workers. In this latter situation, the potentialities for democracy will be reduced rather than increased. There is as yet, however, little definitive evidence for this hypothesis.

There do, however, appear to be trade unions in which the process of bureaucratization has reduced the problem of succession to

---

[17] Max Weber, *The Theory of Social and Economic Organization*, trans. by A. M. Henderson and Talcott Parsons (New York: Oxford University Press, 1947), pp. 363–373.

one of moving up a recognized ladder. It is possible to raise, if not answer on the basis of existing evidence, a number of questions which relate aspects of organizational structure to the process of leadership succession. Under what conditions will succession crises occur so as to give the membership some voice in the choice of a new leader? Under what conditions do the leaders of a union hierarchy feel constrained to keep the struggle within the hierarchy itself? When does a succession crisis open the door for new and independent groups to contest for union leadership? Under what conditions does the process become one of moving up within the hierarchy?

The succession crisis actually may give students of union organizations the opportunity to test many of the hypotheses contained in this chapter. The conditions which determine variations in patterns of succession should be the same ones that have been suggested here as determining variations in union political structures. A study of a large number of cases of succession should enable us not only to shed more light on the process of succession itself but may be the best way to test hypotheses bearing on the factors making for differential degrees of leadership control and oligarchy.

Crisis Situations. Unions, like most human groupings, occasionally undergo changes or meet threats that disturb the stability of the going structure. Such crisis situations often upset some of the sources of control of union administrations, and open the way to the organization of political differences. It is impossible to list all the sources of crisis which may upset a union's stability but some of the most important are: the succession crisis, already touched on; shifts in the business cycle resulting in a reduction in the wages of the members, and weakening the organization through the unemployment of many members; strikes or lockouts, especially prolonged and defeated ones; new technological devices which result in a reduced need for the skills of the members; changes in legislation which weaken the bargaining position of a union; jurisdictional rivalry with another union.

Any of the situations listed above may require a union leadership to make major policy decisions and reverse traditional practices. The consequence of the crisis may be the loss of relative position or privilege by one section of the union as compared with another, or perhaps a loss in economic position for the entire union. A major shift in policy may upset the support for a given leader among the rank and file, or among sections of the union officialdom.

Any disruption of stable internal relations and of the basis for membership support may give subordinate leaders the hope that they can take over the organization and solve the crisis through new methods.   Such factional fights, the most common form of organized intra-union opposition, are the characteristic mode of conflict when leaders and groups of leaders, who have arisen out of the power sources opened up during crisis situations, challenge the incumbent administration or each other.   Their sources of power and status, based on the rank and file rather than on organizational machinery, while strong and spontaneous, are linked to the specific crisis situation, and are transient.   If a would-be leader is not able to institutionalize his power and status by hooking it to the one enduring source of power and status in the union, the administrative hierarchy itself, he is likely to find that his strength in the ranks does not outlive the crisis in which it was born.

The specific effects of crisis on trade unions or other organizations, however, cannot be predicted simply from the knowledge that a given equilibrium has been upset.   A crisis may result in a major split among the top leaders of an organization, or it may appear to have the exact opposite consequence by giving a leader the opportunity to tighten his control.   An anxious membership faced with grave and vital problems, and wanting to get things "done and done fast," may agree to give considerable power to the man or group who appear ready and able to do the job.   Union leaderships have often secured consent to the growth of secrecy in policy formation, or in dispersal of funds, as a means of strengthening the union against the employer during crises.   Measures adopted to maintain unity and secrecy against employers may become a means of strengthening the internal power of the incumbent administration.

The specific determinants of different responses by trade unions to organizational crises can be identified only through an analysis of variations in organizational structures and types of crises.   Although we cannot undertake this type of analysis here, it is important to recognize that for any specific case external factors may modify the pattern of behavior expected on the basis of the internal analysis.

Calling.   So far in this analysis the characteristics and values of the leaders themselves have not been considered.   Although the personal attributes of the men who guide and control trade unions are not the major causal factors in union activities and structure that some observers would make them out to be, they can still be examined fruitfully without subscribing to the "great man" theory of history.   In examining the behavior of different trade union leaders who are in roughly the same structural position, there seems to be considerable variation in their behavior in terms of their personal integrity and commitment to democratic values. Persons familiar with the personal characteristics of large numbers of labor leaders have pointed to men like Philip Murray, David Dubinsky, and Walter Reuther as individuals who have made special efforts to minimize the more obvious negative consequences of bureaucratization and oligarchy in their unions. It is difficult to specify clearly the differences between these leaders and other groups of leaders, but the distinction which appears most appropriate is between those officials to whom the occupation of union leader has some component of a "calling" and those for whom union activity is primarily a livelihood and a means for the achievement of personal goals. The former is the leader who sees in the union something to which he can dedicate himself. His motivation in this direction usually stems from some ideological base, although it need not have any particular salient political content: the union itself and the welfare of the workers may be his main concern, rather than a more far-reaching political goal. For this type of man, initially at least, the material rewards of the position are overshadowed by his idealism. Such men are characterized by strong convictions and a sense of responsibility.

At the other extreme is the leader who looks upon his union office as a job with mobility potential. In the extreme case, he is an individual who may have had other avenues of mobility blocked to him, and who has planned to enter the union hierarchy with the express intention of raising his status and standard of living. This latter group of "career" or bureaucratic leaders may include what one observer of the trade union movement has called the "accidental" leader. He is often a man who is fairly fluent and personable, who speaks up at meetings or is chosen by his work-mates for some minor position in the shop, is recognized by the union leadership as a potential asset, and is co-opted into office. An apprenticeship in the lower rungs of the union hierarchy may not be felt as rewarding by many such individuals, but those who find it so may soon be in the position of the consciously-motivated union "careerist." For these men, the rewards that go with status and office within the union create a continuing motivation to retain and increase these rewards.

Several points may be made with regard to this classification of leaders. It is, of course, an abstraction from a far more complex reality, as all conceptualizations are. Although no one leader completely exemplifies any one type, the supposition is that any given leader can be located on the continuum of "committed-careerist" orientation.[18]

This classification is not suggested with the intent of introducing idiosyncratic variations in personal motivation as factors explaining variations in union behaviors. Rather, it is proposed in the context of raising the questions: Under what conditions is one or the other type more likely to be found, and what are the consequences for union behavior when such variation exists? These conditions seem to be related to time-line factors, somewhat similarly to the situations discussed above. Leaders who are characterized by a "calling" are usually men who have helped to organize their union from the start, have come to power as a result of taking part in an internal "revolution" against an entrenched dictatorial oligarchy, or have entered the labor movement as a result of a commitment to a political ideology which views the labor movement as an instrument to be used to gain a desired social goal. In the formation of a new union or participation in a 'revolt" against entrenched leadership, active and leading individuals have historically faced great difficulties. The organizers of new unions have often faced the dangers of loss of job and blacklisting in their industry, and sometimes imprisonment and physical injury. The monetary rewards have usually been slight or nothing at the beginning. The new leader may be accorded status by his fellow workers but, if he is organizing a new group, may be subject to personal attacks on his character and is frowned upon by those with status in the larger community and in the industry. Men who are willing to take such risks must be motivated by more than a desire to make a higher salary or gain a white-collar position. In many initial organizing situations there is little assurance that these rewards will be forthcoming even if organizational success is attained. Participation in a revolt against an entrenched oligarchy often carried with it the same risks as in an initial organizing situation.

The leaders of new unions or internal political groups, therefore, are often men who have a "calling" to build a labor movement to further some important social ideal. Without such men, revolutionary movements (and union organization often resembles revolutionary activity) could not be started. Only a strong commitment can outweigh the sanctions attendant on activity in such a group. There is evidence for this proposition in the disproportionate role which radicals have played in the creation of many if not most

---

[18] The "committed" orientation probably plays a part in the motivation of all union leaders. To carry out their role of workers' leader effectively they must to some extent believe that they are serving the workers' interests. See Ely Chinoy, *op. cit.*

American trade unions. As mentioned earlier, John L. Lewis was forced to employ many young Communists as organizers for the C.I.O., when it first started, because they were the only people with the necessary skills who were willing to take the risks involved for low pay. In large measure, two of the three major unions in the C.I.O., the U.A.W. and the United Electrical Workers, as well as most of the smaller ones, were organized by Communists or democratic leftists. The one major exception, the United Steelworkers, was organized by professional organizers from the Mineworkers Union, but even there Lewis employed many who had been in the left-wing opposition to him in the U.M.W. The opposition to Joseph Ryan's control over the Longshoremen's Union, which eventually culminated in the formation of an independent West Coast union, was led in large part by Communists. Men like Samuel Gompers, Sidney Hillman, David Dubinsky, John Mitchell, and many others, all had some relation to the Socialist movement when they helped form their unions.

The strong commitment which presumably many of these men had when they first become union leaders was in large measure vitiated under the pressures of office. Reference to actions of such once-committed union leaders which seem to demonstrate that they no longer operate in terms of original value goals may obscure the fact that, for the leader himself, the commitment and calling may still exist. It must be stressed that it is far less the personal weakness of the individual or his conscious rejection of past commitments that is involved, but rather the constraints of the structure within which he operates which bring about actions that to the analyst appear to be oriented to the simple maintenance of office, or which may be undemocratic and at odds with what can be objectively described as the goals of the union. As Michels has pointed out, in a great number of cases, regardless of the leader's original commitment or sense of "calling," there are pressures—some of which we have been attempting to examine—which result in the leader equating the security of his own position with the best means of achieving union goals.

The "career" union leader is more likely to be found in long established unions. As we indicated earlier, union office has become an important avenue of social mobility for manual workers. Entering the hierarchy of a stabilized bureaucratic union carries with it many advantages and few liabilities. Persons with ideological commitments are likely to be at a disadvantage rather than at an advantage in seeking office in a stable organization. Their adherence to utopian or ideologically prescribed ends will bring them into conflict with the day-to-day pragmatic policies of the union, even of those still led by men who formerly adhered to these values. Ideologues, men with a "calling," are likely to be viewed as irresponsible by the heads of bureaucracies. They are more likely to select men who will fit into a bureaucratic framework, men who will work within the framework of the organization's goals as defined by the leaders. Weber's discussion of the bureaucratization of charisma is relevant to the situation in the trade union movement, as men with a "calling" are replaced by "bureaucrats."

The change from "calling" to "bureaucracy" is not a direct time relationship. Holding all other factors constant, one would expect that the older a union is, the more likely its leaders will be persons who have come up the bureaucratic route to power. This process may, however, be reversed or slowed by crises in which an incumbent leadership is overthrown. It may also be affected if the union leadship remains organizationally affiliated to an outside grouping, such as the Communist or Socialist parties, and recruits its successors from the external organization. Continued affiliation with such groups in the context of the American labor movement, however, has meant the continual creation of elements of strain for the union leader. The policies of such external groups and parties have been considerably at variance with those prescribed by the trade union situation. The leaders, therefore, have been under pressure to leave the parties when the parties demanded that the trade unions follow policies which might disrupt the internal equilibrium or stability of their unions or affect their chances for re-election. The Communist Party has, in part, been able to prevent this situation from occurring in some unions where it has maintained union factions whose loyalty was to the party and not to the particular union leaders.

Another factor which enters into the difference in behavior between the originally "committed" leader and the "bureaucratic" leader is the possible variation in their reference groups, that is, the groups of "significant others" whose esteem they value.[19] While, as was indicated earlier, individuals who become union leaders consequently change their status and slough off many of their old friends and associates, few men can escape completely from their past. Men who entered the union movement to serve a cause are more likely than persons who moved up a bureaucratic hierarchy

---

[19] For a fuller discussion of the relationship between trade union behavior and the reference groups of members and leaders, see S. M. Lipset and Martin Trow, "Reference Group Analysis and Trade Union Wage Policy," in Mirra Komarovsky, ed., *Interdisciplinary Frontiers in the Social Sciences* (forthcoming).

to have as a frame of reference for their own achievements the judgments of other persons who also believed in the cause. Many former Socialists who are now trade union leaders still attempt to explain and justify many of their actions as being consistent with a socialist or left-democratic goal, and this orientation does influence their behavior in ways that cannot be understood solely by reference to the objective situations of their unions.

It may be suggested that some of the differences between seemingly similar large oligarchic and bureaucratized unions lie in the fact that some are led by men who still view their positions in terms of a "calling," whereas others are led by "careerists." The first group may be no more democratic in practice, but they are often more accessible to the membership, more aggressive in their tactics, more concerned with violations of a union ethic of service to the membership, and have greater personal integrity. A Socialist or other radical past is obviously more likely to be related to such behavior than a Communist past. The "called" leader whose values involve concern with democracy is also more likely to be concerned with the forms of democracy than is the "bureaucratic" leader.

It is, again, difficult to posit hypotheses about the relationship between "calling" as a leadership orientation and the conditions making for significant internal democracy within a trade union. It is probable that the different "calls" that have led people into the labor movement will be related to significantly different types of behavior. A former Communist, for example, may continue to operate an effective dictatorial machine after leaving the party, and while his behavior may differ in terms of more militancy and integrity as compared with leaders who have come up the "bureaucratic" path to office, he may be far more ruthless in using the organizational machinery to maintain power. A "calling" may also be related to ruthlessness in the maintenance of power by "democratic" labor leaders. The sense of righteousness and devotion to a "cause" that usually is associated with a political or religious calling may for the labor leaders who have such a sense of "calling" serve to legitimate actions which might strike observers as being at considerable variance with their presumed values and goals. Given the fact that the "committed" leader "knows" that he is serving the "right" cause, opponents may be seen as witting or unwitting agents of the enemy, whether the enemy is defined as the employers, the capitalist system, or the Communist Party.

On the other hand, "committed" leaders, although often ruthless in dealing with opposition, appear to have a need, flowing from their commitments, to believe that the membership actually approve their actions, and they attempt to convert as many as possible to their approach. Concern with the "education" of the rank and file is more likely to be found in unions led by "calling" leaders than in those led by "careerists." Such efforts often help to give the appearance of greater democracy as evidenced by greater "participation." Moreover, the effort to build a trade union machine on a consistent ideology, as well as the more typical basis of mutual reward and obligation, often turns out to be dysfunctional to the stability of the bureaucracy. New situations which require the establishment of new policies may lead men who take their ideologies seriously to disagree. The fairly common pattern of factional disagreements and cleavages in leftist political groups would appear to reflect the greater sense of serving the righteous cause that these movements require from their leaders and members, as compared with more conservative groups. Unions in which leftists have held power in the United States appear to have had more frequent internal differences than those which followed the Gompers nonpartisan policies.

Value Systems. In its concern with structural and time-line factors as they relate to structure, this analysis has thus far ignored in large part the effect on union organization of the value system of the total society, and more specifically, the value systems of the different strata of workers who belong to unions, as well as the manifest goals of different unions.

One would expect that (holding structural and time-line factors constant) trade unionists, whether leaders or members, will behave differently within the significantly different value systems which characterize different social structures. An American trade union operating within the American social structure with its emphasis on individual achievement, the rights of each individual to equality with others, and the norm of democracy, should behave differently from a German union working within the context of a more rigid status system, with greater emphasis on ascription than achievement, with greater legitimation of the leadership role, with less concern for the right of the individual compared with the collectivity, and with presumed less emphasis on the norm of democratic control. Similarly, the behavior of two American trade unions should vary with the composition of their memberships, insofar as the difference in membership is reflected in different weights and distributions of these crucial norms regarding authority and democracy.

The more a given group holds a democratic, anti-elitist value system, the more difficult it should be to institutionalize oligarchy. On a comparative social structure basis, it is clear, therefore, that the German union leaders can maintain an oligarchic structure with less strain deriving from membership values than leaders of American unions can. German workers might be expected to accept more easily the permanent tenure of leadership, the lack of discussion of policies, and the absence of opposition. American workers, on the other hand, all other things being equal, would presumably be more likely to resist hierarchical control. Given the assumption that leaders in both countries would seek to make their tenure secure, we would expect that American labor leaders would be under greater pressure to formalize dictatorial mechanisms so as to prevent the possibility of their being overthrown. Or, to put it another way, since the values inherent in American society operate to make American union officers more vulnerable than, say, their German counterparts, they would be obliged to act more vigorously and decisively and dictatorially to stabilize their status.

Within the American labor movement somewhat similar variations exist. Some American unions have memberships which strongly hold the value of rank-and-file participation and control; other memberships hold these values less strongly. It has often been observed that participation in national politics varies with position in the society; it may similarly be suggested that the higher the status of the worker, the more likely he is to claim a right in decision-making. Such high-status values, combined with the greater resources of high-status workers for political participation, would, if our assumptions are empirically valid, add to the possibilities for democracy in a union. There are two distinguishable organizational responses to this condition. One is the pattern of institutionalized democracy as found in the I.T.U., Actor's Equity, and similar unions. The other pattern is a more rigorous use of dictatorial mechanisms by leaders whose position is vulnerable, given the followers' democratic values.

One would, therefore, expect to find among the unions in which the conditions for the maintenance of oligarchy are not stable, a greater proportion of the two extremes, democratic institutions and dictatorial mechanisms. One union which illustrates both of these tendencies within the same international is the Musician's Union, some locals of which are as democratic as Equity, while other locals and the International itself are dictatorially oligarchic.

Another adaptive mechanism which operates to make oligarchy and American democratic values compatible is an ideology that emphasizes the specificity of the functions of a trade union. The more narrowly an organization defines its functions, as fulfilling limited and specific needs, the less likely a member will feel the need to participate in and influence the policies of the organization. People may belong to many organizations, such as the American Automobile Association, a local consumer's cooperative, a medical plan, a bowling group, a national stamp club, and many others, without feeling any obligation to participate actively in the internal operation of the group and without feeling coerced by the fact that decisions are made without their having been consulted. In large measure, each of the various voluntary associations to which people may belong is judged on the basis of the ability to satisfy a limited need of its individual members. Conversely, the more diffuse the functions of a group or organization, the more likely an individual is to find sources of disagreement with and desire to participate actively in its operation.

Applying the above analysis to trade unions, the union which simply operates as a "business union" may be placed in the category of specific, one-function organizations. Outside of the shop organization where there is normally the largest participation by workers, the single major task of the "business union," collective bargaining, does not take place more often than once a year, and in many unions only once every two or three years. The day-to-day administration of union affairs need not concern the average member any more than do the day-to-day activities that go into running a veterans' group, or a medical plan. It is of course true that a union deals with the individual in his occupational role, and we might expect it to call forth more of his interest and concern than other voluntary organizations to which the individual relates through his less important roles. But the generalization would still hold on a comparative basis—that is, the more specific the functions of the union, the less involvement by members; and the more diffuse its functions, the more the membership involvement. Such unions as the I.T.U. and Actor's Equity, which fulfill many functions related to the status and leisure time of their members, are organizations in which we might expect to find high membership participation and involvement.

Thus, the ideology most appropriate for a union seeking to limit its functions is that of business unionism, the most common ideology in American unions. By stating that a union should not be concerned with other than the traditional trade union activities of collective bargaining, worker defense, and membership welfare, union leaders are also stating that they do not want other values derivative from various extra-union interests to affect them.

"Business unionism," as a set of ideas justifying the narrowest definitions of a union's role in society and area of service to its members, thus discourages widespread membership participation and legitimates oligarchic leadership. The congruence of business unionism as an ideology with oligarchy as a power structure by no means fully explains the widespread adoption of business unionism rather than any other definition of union goals and purposes. The point here is that whatever other factors may be related to the acceptance of the ideology of "business unionism," one of its consequences is to reduce some of the strains inherent in perpetuating an oligarchy in an organization whose membership holds democratic values.

No one has attempted either a qualitative or quantitative analysis of the relationship between diffuse political or specific "business union" ideologies and the presence or absence of political conflict within trade unions. The general proposition may be suggested, however, that the more diffuse the ideology of a trade union, the greater the likelihood of internal factionalism. European trade unions, which are much more politicized than American ones, have been more prone to internal cleavage. American observers of European unionism, however, have called attention to the fact that a secular tendency in the direction of business unionism exists in Europe. This fact has been used as validation for the hypothesis that the normal function of trade unions is business unionism, that is, collective bargaining, and that labor unions tend to shed the superfluous and organizationally dysfunctional political ideologies. Selig Perlman has presented the case for this thesis most brilliantly in his *Theory of the Labor Movement*.

Such analysis, however, which treats trade unions as collective bodies, and does not differentiate between the needs of the bureaucracy and those of the membership, tends to ignore the possibility that the drive to limit the functions and goals of unions may be primarily adaptive mechanisms of a security-seeking leadership, rather than (as Perlman suggests) stemming from the social situation of workers. The commitment, for example, to support a socialist party, or general socialist objectives, necessarily involves acceptance of discussion of differences in politics. Many British trade union conventions at present must spend considerable time discussing the split between Aneurin Bevan and the leadership of the Labor Party and the Trades Union Congress.

To suggest that limiting the functions of trade unions is functional to the stability of the bureaucracy does not imply that the members of most or any trade unions are prone to support broad definitions of union goals. In fact, as much of the earlier analysis suggests, the majority of union members are apathetic and probably more conservative than their union officers. This fact, however, does not negate the generalization that any factor such as a "business union" ideology, which serves to reduce the possibility for internal cleavage, also operates to lower the potential influence which a membership may have on the policies of the organization.

Conclusions. The analysis developed in this chapter obviously implies some pessimistic conclusions about the long-term chances for democracy in trade unions. To recapitulate the major points in this analysis:

1. The structure of large-scale organization inherently requires the development of bureaucratic patterns of behavior. The conditions making for the institutionalization of bureaucracy and those making for democratic turnover in office are, as we have seen, largely incompatible; and the degree of incompatibility will vary with the degree of bureaucratization as imposed by the need to come to stable terms with other bureaucratized institutions in the union's environment.

2. The structure of large-scale organization gives an incumbent administration very great power and advantage over the rank and file, or even as compared with an organized opposition. This advantage takes such forms as control over financial resources and internal communications, a large permanently organized political machine, a claim to legitimacy and a monopoly of political skills.

3. The ease with which an oligarchy can control a large organization will vary with the degree to which the members are involved in the organization. The more important organizational membership is considered, and the more participation in it there is as part of multiple social roles, the more difficult it will be for an oligarchy to enforce policies and actions which conflict with the values or defined needs of the members. The concept of "business unionism," which assumes that a union performs only the one major function for its members of securing the best possible contracts, may be viewed as a functionally adaptive ideology to prevent internal politics and conflict and to promote limited participation on the part of the members. Any conception of trade union functions which

serves to increase the involvement of the members in the organization increases the potentialities for democratic conflict.

4. The inherent instability of democracy in trade unions can be deduced from an analysis of the implications of a trade union as a status-placing mechanism.

a. A functional requirement of the leadership role is that it be assigned higher status, that is, be a higher achievement than the follower role.

b. A dominant value of achievement implies that upward mobility, achieving high status, is a cultural goal.

c. One key attribute of a democratic political structure is the existence of the possibility for the circulation or rotation of leadership. This means that oligarchy can be avoided only if a mechanism exists by which leaders can be retired from office.

d. In society at large, political leaders may leave office and assume positions of equivalent or higher status. In the trade union movement, however, institutionalized democracy generally requires that the leader move from a high-status to a low-status position if he is still to remain within the union.

e. The institutionalization of movement from high to low status, which is what democracy in trade unions means for the leaders, would involve the institutionalization of a major deviation from the dominant value of achievement.

f. Fulfillment of these contradictory norms would result in anomy for the leaders and is a psychologically impossible situation.

The obvious conclusions of this analysis are that the functional requirements for democracy cannot be met most of the time in most unions. For example, the conflict between democratic and achievement norms means that democracy can exist as a stable system in unions only where the status differentiation between leaders and followers is very small. This may help account for the fact that democracy is found mostly in high-status unions and in local unions. Instead of suggesting that power corrupts in all situations, this analysis suggests that such "corruption" is a consequence of specific social structures, *where conformity to one norm necessarily involves violation of another norm.*

The emphasis in this chapter on the undemocratic character of most labor unions is not designed to negate the general proposition of the political pluralists that trade unions, like many other internally oligarchic organizations, serve to sustain political democracy in the larger body politic. As Franz Neumann, among others, has made clear, many internally dictatorial associations operate to protect the interests of their members by checking the encroachments of other groups.[20] Even the most dictatorial union is a better protector of workers' economic interests and of political democracy within the larger society, than no union, provided that the union is not a tool either of the state or of the employer. In large measure, the chance that the collectivist society which is developing in most countries will be democratic rests in the possibility that trade unions, although supporters of socialist objectives, will maintain their independence of the state. The behavior of the trade unions of the Commonwealth and the Scandinavian countries furnishes real evidence that such a pattern is possible.

It is also necessary to remember that even the most dictatorial trade union leaders must be somewhat responsive to the economic needs of their members. A union oligarchy which does not defend the economic interests of the rank and file may find its membership disappearing, as John L. Lewis did in the twenties. Lewis, then a trade union as well as a political conservative, almost lost the United Mine Workers. Only after adopting the militant tactics for which he is now famous was Lewis able to rebuild the union. A trade union which is not an economic defense organization has no function, and will not long remain on the scene. The fact that most unions do represent their members' interests must, however, not be confused with the problem of internal democracy, for as Howe and Widick have pointed out:

> There is one decisive proof of democracy in a union (or any other institution): oppositionists have the right to organize freely into "parties," to set up factional machines, to circulate publicity and to propagandize among the members. . . . The presence of an opposition . . . is the best way of insuring that a union's democratic structure will be preserved. . . . To defend the right of factions to exist is not at all to applaud this or that faction. But this is the overhead (well worth paying!) of democracy: groups one considers detrimental to the union's interest will be formed. The alternative is dictatorship.[21]

METHODOLOGICAL APPENDIX

Students of the labor movement will be able to point to major exceptions to each proposition suggested in this chapter. Clearly, it is impossible in the case of given organizations or individuals to abstract any one variable and make it the sole or even primary determinant of a given behavior pattern. The problem of how to deal with multi-factored determinants of specific behavior patterns is a basic one in the social sci-

---

[20] Franz L. Neumann, "Approaches to the Study of Political Power," *Political Science Quarterly*, June, 1950, pp. 161–180.
[21] Irving Howe and B. J. Widick, *op. cit.*, pp. 262–263.

ences. When dealing with individuals, analysts may partially escape this difficulty by collecting data on a large number of cases, so that they can isolate the influence of specific factors through use of quantitative techniques. The analysis of organizations is hampered, however, by the fact that comparable data are rarely collected for more than a few cases. The cost of studying intensively even one large organization may be as much as that of gathering survey data from a large sample of individuals.

The usual procedure followed by most analysts in searching out the determinants of a given pattern of behavior, such as oligarchy or rank and file militancy within a given labor union, is to cite those factors present in the organization which seem to be related to the behavioral item in question. Such a procedure is essentially *post factum,* however, if the only case in which the given pattern of significant variables is observed is the one under observation. The analyst rarely has the opportunity to establish any controls or comparisons. Often an attempt is made to escape this dilemma by citing illustrative materials from other cases, which appear to validate the hypothesis. Such illustrative data do not solve the methodological problem of validation, and usually only serve to give the reader a false sense of the general validity of the interpretation.

It is of crucial importance, therefore, that students of organizational behavior address themselves to the problem of verification of hypotheses. At the present time, one may spend a great deal of time examining the large number of studies of individual trade unions or other large-scale organizations without being able to validate a single proposition about organizational behavior. The data collected in such case studies do not lend themselves to re-analysis to test hypotheses, since the researchers rarely focused their observations in terms of any set of explicit hypotheses.

Three methods may be tentatively suggested as ways through which greater progress can be made in this area: the gathering of quantitative data from a large number of organizations, clinical case studies, and deviant case analyses. The following example illustrates the first method, quantification. In order to test the proposition that the greater the status differentiation between the officers and members of a trade union the more likely such an organization is to have a dictatorial political structure, data could be collected from a large number of international and local unions. Such research would be difficult, but might be accomplished by devising rough indices of status which would allow an observer to develop some measure of the size of the status differential between members and officers of different groups. Hypotheses about the relation of the product market to union structures could be similarly tested.

Another method that could be used in this field is analogous to the clinical procedure employed in the biological sciences, in which prognoses are made on the basis of a theoretical analysis. One could make predictions about the behavior of organizations in future critical situations that require changes. One optimum situation for such research is the succession crisis, which every organization must confront. The succession crisis has an additional advantage for study since it is a repetitive event. There have been literally thousands of cases of succession in the labor movement, as leaders have died or retired. Studies of variations in the consequences of succession would permit the testing of hypotheses dealing with factors that operate to stimulate or repress internal conflict within organizations.

A third possible solution to the methodological difficulty is the analysis of *deviant cases*—in the labor movement, specifically those organizations which are characterized by a high level of democratic procedures, membership participation, or both. If one knows that a given behavior pattern, such as oligarchy, is common to almost all large unions, then the repeated study of oligarchic groups will yield few new insights in the possible variations which may affect internal political structures.[22] Paul Lazarsfeld has pointed out that "deviant case analysis can and should play a *positive* role in empirical research, rather than being merely the 'tidying-up' process through which exceptions to the empirical rule are given some plausibility and thus disposed of." The existence of a deviant case (for example, the highly democratic political system of the International Typographical Union) always implies that the theoretical structure—in this case, the theory subsumed in Michels' "iron law of oligarchy"—is oversimplified and suggests "the need for incorporating further variables into . . . [the] predictive scheme." [23]

---

[22] See Joseph Goldstein, *The Government of British Trade Unions* (London: Allen and Unwin, 1952), for an excellent description of oligarchic control in a British union. This study, however, adds little except more facts to Michels' classic analysis.

[23] See Patricia Kendall and Katherine M. Wolf, "The Analysis of Deviant Cases in Communications Research," in Paul F. Lazarsfeld and Frank Stanton, eds., *Communications Research 1948–1949* (New York: Harper & Brothers, 1949), pp. 153–154.

5

SOCIAL GROUPS
IN THE MODERN WORLD

FLORIAN ZNANIECKI

Since the first decade of this century, the study of human groups has been increasingly considered one of the most important tasks of sociology. In 1932, Eubank, after a thorough comparative survey of the various conceptual frameworks used by sociologists, came to the conclusion that the concept of group would become the main foundation of systematic sociology.

Inasmuch as sociology is now recognized as a generalizing science, we should expect a steady progress of scientific generalizations about human groups, based on comparative research. But, because of the vast diversity of those complexes to which the term "group" has been applied, their logically consistent classification, or "taxonomy," is a necessary foundation on which all other generalizations about them depend, just as the taxonomy of living organisms formed a basis for causal, functional, ontogenetic, and phylogenetic generalizations.

Yet, in 1945, Logan Wilson summarized the results of his survey of various theories of human groups as follows:

the lack of an adequate classificatory scheme precludes the full view of group interaction. . . . Most of the makeshift empirical schemes of classification and analyis have logical inconsistencies, but the logically consistent schemes tend to have the shortcoming of limited applicability.[1]

In 1951, Robert J. Dubois (at Wayne University) wrote a Master's thesis in which he compared the classification of groups included in American textbooks of sociology from 1932 to 1949, under the

---

[1] "Sociography of Groups," in *Twentieth Century Sociology*, eds. George Gurvitch and Wilbert E. Moore (New York: The Philosophical Library, 1945).

assumption that textbooks are intended to communicate to students the main results of research recognized by scientists. Out of forty-eight textbooks surveyed, eleven had no classification of groups whatsoever; the other thirty-seven differed so much that not a single logical class was included in all of them.

Why this astonishing lack of agreement among sociologists concerning the classification of human groups? I believe that it is mainly due to the fact that most sociologists underestimate the importance and difficulty of reaching taxonomic generalizations. Like all scientific generalizations, they can be reached only by inductive methods, that is, by comparative analysis of particular cases. Every classification should be viewed as a hypothesis which must be tested by further factual evidence and, if necessary, supplemented, modified, or supplanted by another hypothesis. This explains why it took more than twenty centuries to develop an adequate classification of living organisms. But some sociologists consider classifications as merely ways of pigeonholing data for some special purposes of their own,[2] or as typological generalizations, each of which overlaps many others.

Now, taxonomic generalizations in the natural sciences, especially in biology and chemistry, are classifications of limited, united *systems* of interdependent components. The primary task in such classification is to discover, by analyzing those systems, what are the similarities and differences in their composition and how these components are integrated. Twenty years ago, I postulated that the same heuristic principle can be applied to the investigation of human groups. In other words, I assumed hypothetically that there is a distinct logical category of limited systems which are composed of interdependent human individuals, and I applied to such a system the term "social group." Since then, numerous students have collaborated with me in the investigation of social groups in this sense. They analyzed widely diverse groups and compared the results of their analyses.

Our taxonomy of all kinds of social groups has not yet been completed; nevertheless, we have reached a methodological approach which makes it possible to include most of the social groups found in the modern world under definite logical classes, not merely types.

---

[2] See, for instance, George Lundberg: "It is not our purpose to insist on one definition rather than another of certain plurels. ['Plurel' is more or less equal to 'group.' F. Z.] That is the task which should be performed to suit the needs of empirical research as they arise. . . . It is our contention that definitions are not dictated by the nature of data but by our adjustment needs." *Foundations of Sociology* (New York: The Macmillan Co., 1939), p. 362.

On this basis, we can draw generalizations about their changes under definite influences: generalizations about functional relationships between the groups of certain logical classes, and phylogenetic generalizations about the emergence of new classes. When we compared the results of our studies with the theories of human groups previously developed, we found that they approach most closely MacIver's theory of "associations," [8] although we used a somewhat different conceptual framework.

We had to define, first of all, the term "social group." Our chief difficulty came from the wide and indiscriminate use of the general term "group." The common denotation of this term is a plurality (or "plurel") of objects, whether these objects are interconnected or not. Thus, an agglomeration of objects within a limited spatial area—inanimate things, plants, animals, or human individuals—has been called a group, merely because of their spatial proximity. Statisticians use the term "group" to denote a plurality of individuals selected from a "population," according to certain indices, and summed together, even when such a group is nothing but an arbitrary construct without any factual connection among its units. A number of sociologists apply the term "group" to a "social class," usually under the assumption that the people who, according to certain standards, are considered as belonging to such a class must be somehow united. This assumption conflicts with historical evidence that the development of class solidarity has usually been a slow process, the result of many efforts of ideologists and social leaders. Of course, we cannot eliminate this indiscriminate use of the term, but we may exclude from our study of the groups which we call *social* all plurels of individuals who cannot be proved to be united.

The next problem which we had to solve before starting to draw comparative generalizations about social groups concerned their composition and the relationship between their components on which their unity is based. Here we were facing the old naturalistic doctrine, according to which human groups are essentially like animal groups, in that they are composed of individual organisms which are interdependent in the symbiotic sense, that is, in that their differentiated behavior in response to stimuli enables them together to survive in adaptation to their natural environment. They differ from animal groups merely because of the distinctive biological nature of the human genus. Within the human genus, however, there are specific biological variations; consequently, some sociologists classify human groups according to ra-

---

[8] Cf. Robert M. MacIver, *Society* (New York: Farrar & Rinehart, 1937).

cial differences or ecological differences, due to their geographic environments, and according to such secondary differences as sex and age.

This ontological doctrine of human beings as components of human groups is supported by an epistemological dogma, according to which the only valid scientific knowledge is knowledge based on that kind of empirical evidence on which the natural sciences (astronomy, physics, chemistry, biology, etc.) are based. Thus, all we can truly know about a human group is what a scientist discovers when investigating the organisms of its members and observing their outward behavior accessible to his sensory experience.

We had to reject this naturalistic doctrine as inapplicable to the groups which we studied, in view of the overwhelming historical evidence that such groups were *cultural products*, for example, churches, scientific associations, literary academies, philharmonic orchestras, industrial and commercial corporations, bureaucratic governmental groups. Like all cultural products—language, literature, art, religion—they must be investigated with what I call the "humanistic coefficient." The investigator cannot rely upon his own experiences and conceptions of them, but must ascertain how they are experienced, conceived, and evaluated by those conscious human agents who actively deal with them.

An investigator who uses the humanistic coefficient in studying social groups of human individuals finds one characteristic common to all, which enables him to distinguish each of them from a mere plurel of units as well as from a combination of organisms. Within every social group which we studied, we found some kind of conscious, intentional *cooperation* among its participants.[4] Such is, for instance, the difference between a mere crowd gathered in a city square and a group of people who form a religious procession under the leadership of priests, or who march in a parade to the tune of music, expressing thus symbolically their admiration for a military hero. This is how a labor union or a socialist party differs from the working class, or how an association of peasants cooperating in order to raise their socio-economic status differs from the peasants as a class.

Before we speak further about cooperation, we had better define this rather vague term more exactly. Cooperation implies positive functional interdependence among the actions of several agents. This means that the realization of the purpose of each contributes

---

[4] MacIver also considers cooperation as an essential common characteristic of social groups: an "association" is a cooperating group which is organized (*op. cit.*, p. 11).

to the realization of the purposes of the others. Such is most obviously the case when a number of craftsmen build a house, or a number of musicians play a symphony. In both of these cases, interdependence between the actions of particular craftsmen or musicians results from the fact that all of them together seek to realize a common purpose.

The individuals who compose a social group may cease to cooperate as soon as a particular purpose has been realized and never resume their cooperation, or they may continue to cooperate for the realization of other common purposes. In any case, the social group exists so long as its members continue to cooperate. A group of craftsmen building a house may dissolve as soon as the particular house is completed or continue to exist and build more houses. A symphony orchestra lasts as long as it repeatedly plays symphonies. A number of acquaintances and friends living in a community and taking turns as hosts in arranging parties form a rather long-lasting companionate group.

We may call the total sequence of cooperative activities which members of a group perform, so long as the group lasts, the *function* of the group. The examples we have just mentioned show that the functions of social groups can differ considerably. And this raises the question: What is the connection between the function of a group and its composition?

A comparative survey of the membership of social groups performing definite functions conclusively invalidates the naturalistic doctrine that human groups must be conceived as being composed of human organisms (or "human beings" as biopsychological entities). The same individual can and usually does belong to several separate groups with different functions, and his membership in any of them does not depend upon how he is defined by biologists or psychologists, but on the way he is perceived and evaluated by the other members of his group.

We find in every social group certain cultural standards by which its members are defined and judged. An individual is a group member not as a "human being," but—to use a well-known term—as a *person* who is supposed to perform a specific *social role* within the group. And his roles in different groups may differ greatly. Every social role involves definite "duties" toward others and definite "rights" on which the fulfillment of those duties depends. His role as a group member requires that he cooperate with other members to further the function of the group; only when he does so, is he granted the rights of a member.

To make mutual understanding possible, a group member must

be acquainted with the basic components of the culture which the members share—usually language, certain ideas and beliefs, some elementary material values and techniques, etc. He must also accept those cultural patterns by which mutual personal valuation and interaction between members are guided, and conform to these patterns; if he does not, he may be expelled from the group. And if the group regularly performs specific collective activities, for example, religious rites, industrial production, music, sport, scientific research, etc., he must learn how to contribute to them.

These requirements are most clearly manifested by social groups when, in the course of their duration, they admit new members. To be admitted, an individual must be judged fit for the performance of his role as a member; and the standards of admission are more or less exacting, depending on the presumed importance of his role. When a group wants new members and those available are not yet considered fit for participation, active members must prepare them by the well-known cultural process called *education*.

When a social group is, as a matter of fact, composed of individuals with common and distinctive biological characteristics, such as race, sex, or age, this is obviously due to the cultural conditioned conviction that only people who have such characteristics are fit to perform the social roles which members are required to perform. And, as we know, such convictions differ considerably and change in the course of history.

This general survey of the ways in which individuals become active members of social groups led me to the hypothetical conclusion that social groups constitute a distinct category of systems composed of culturally patterned social roles which individual members perform.[5]

Having thus eliminated the naturalistic doctrine of social groups, we encountered another problem, mainly methodological: Where shall we begin our comparative analysis of social groups so as to make its results most productive scientifically?

We might have started, as Comte and Spencer did and as some sociologists do today, with the analysis of a territorial "society," politically united and institutionally "structured," under the assumption that such a society constitutes a system and that all the social groups to which inhabitants of its territory belong are components of this system. This assumption, however, has already been invalidated by empirical research. Consequently, we decided to

---

[5] Cf. "Social Groups as Products of Cooperating Individuals," *American Journal of Sociology*, May, 1939.

proceed in another way: to investigate and compare limited social groups, abstracted from territorial "societies," and then try to ascertain the relationships among them and to discover which of them are really integrated.

Next, the question rose: Ought we to begin by studying small social groups, composed of individuals who are in frequent face-to-face contact with each other, or larger, more complex social groups? According to some theorists, those small, face-to-face groups provide a key to the understanding of all social groups. This was the assumption underlying Cooley's theory of "primary groups," and it is explicitly or implicitly accepted by many sociologists and social psychologists who investigate parental families, neighborhoods, companionate groups, boys' gangs, coteries, factions, "informal" groups within large "formal" groups, experimental groups formed in schools on all levels, sociometric and sociatric groups, etc.

There are serious arguments in favor of this assumption. Such groups, according to anthropological evidence, are primary in the sense that they were the earliest social groups in the course of human history; all other social groups must have evolved from them. Furthermore, sociopsychological evidence shows that they are also primary from the point of view of individual life-histories; for the socialization of every individual begins within them.

Nevertheless, we came to the conclusion that the study of contemporary primary groups should not be separated from the study of larger, more complex social groups. The mere fact that the members of primary groups are in face-to-face contact is not a sufficient reason for including all such groups in one distinct logical class. How can we include in the same logical class a parental family, a rural neighborhood, a companionate upper-class group in a city, a rebellious boys' gang, a football team, a group of musicians, the French Academy of "forty immortals," and a score of scientists working on a common problem? Are not the two latter groups more like certain larger complex associations than like primary groups? Moreover, many specific face-to-face groups are integral components of larger groups,[6] for example, a student seminar in a university, a nominating committee of an association, a platoon of soldiers, a small specialized group of workers in a section of a factory?

We decided, therefore, that it would be more productive scientifically to concentrate our comparative analysis on relatively large

[6] Cf. MacIver, *op. cit.*, pp. 236–237.

social groups which are not reducible to face-to-face groups.   In selecting these groups for study, we proceeded as follows.

First, we chose groups which obviously differed widely in certain respects, and only later we compared each of them with some apparently similar group or groups.

Then, we gave preference to groups which performed complex collective activities requiring considerable specialization among cooperating agents.   And, although we did not ignore short-lived groups, we investigated mainly more enduring groups, especially those which continue to exist even when their membership gradually changes.

Finally, whenever factual evidence was available, we tried to investigate these groups from the time of their formation throughout their existence.

Thus, we studied the initial stages in the formation of many diverse social groups: local subgroups of large churches, missions, certain modern sects; colleges and universities; volunteer military groups struggling for national independence; several revolutionary class groups; labor unions; racial groups; fraternal groups; industrial and commercial groups; professional associations, charitable societies; reform groups; immigrant groups in the United States; some literary, artistic, musical, scientific, and philosophical associations.

We found that the formation of nearly every one of these groups started with a small set of ideologists who shared a common culture and became aware of some practical problem concerning a particular value, a class of values, or a system of values which was important to them.   Such was, for instance, the problem of how to convert and save heathens; how to make people accept a new divine revelation and follow the prophet who announced it; how to improve and spread education of the young within a certain area; how to liberate "our nationality" from foreign oppression; how to free all workers from capitalistic exploitation; how to raise the status of workers in particular factories; how to preserve white supremacy; how to promote the advancement of Negroes; how to gain wealth; how to help the poor; how to multiply the production of certain technical objects or to stimulate the demand for them; how to maintain high ethical standards and the functional efficiency of professional physicians, lawyers, teachers, or engineers; how to promote the development of a certain branch of knowledge or literature in a certain language, or the plastic arts, or music.

Awareness of such a problem was not necessarily followed by active efforts to solve it; sometimes nothing was done.   In those cases in which a solution was attempted, a social group was formed, usually at the initiative of one individual (sometimes of several individuals) who assumed the role of social leader and gained an increasing number of active followers willing to cooperate for the common goal. Sooner or later, the group became planfully organized, and its leader, with the help of auxiliary leaders, functioned as coordinator of the activities of its members. Sometimes, indeed, the original problem was differently defined by several leaders, or different ways of solving it were planned; then, several separate groups might be organized. This is well exemplified by the emergence during the nineteenth century of various revolutionary groups, each functioning differently with respect to the working class.

In comparing the development of these planfully organized groups, we discovered considerable differences in their size and in the complexity of their organization. Certain groups were from the very outset intended to remain rather small, others to increase vastly in membership. Some sociologists, in classifying groups, consider these differences in size as basic. However, when we study groups in the course of their duration, we find that their size obviously depends on their function. The function of playing musical symphonies can be performed only by rather small groups of musicians; but the function of protecting the economic status of musicians in the United States can be performed most effectively by a group which includes all American musicians. When the function of a literary academy is to maintain high standards of literary productivity, only a selected minority of men-of-letters, whose own works fully conform with these standards, is supposed to be capable of performing this function. But if the group is a political party intended to gain and maintain control of the government of a modern state, it attempts to recruit the largest possible membership, since this is essential for the efficient performance of its function.

The complexity of the organization of a social group depends partly on its size and partly on specialization of the functions which its members perform and which together constitute the social function of the group. When the group is too large for all its members to be in direct contact with each other while performing their individual functions, it must be divided into smaller subgroups; then, the total integration of its activities requires a gradation of coordinators. Thus, a political party has many local subdivisions, each with a leader and auxiliary leaders. But its organization is less complex than that of an automobile factory, since the functions of its subgroups are basically alike, whereas the total function of the factory requires considerable specialization of its subgroups.

But, whatever the origin, composition, size, and organization of the social groups we studied, at a certain stage of their development we had to take into consideration another sociological problem: What does a particular social group mean to its members? Is it only "we," a solidary grouping of "us," in the sense of individuals cooperating for a common purpose? Such seems to be, indeed, the meaning of most primary groups, and also of organized groups whose members expect to solve their common problem in the near future, for example, a group of workers on strike, a group of capitalists trying to gain control of some industrial or commercial enterprise, a group trying to introduce a specific change into the legal system of a state. But an organized group whose function is intended to last for a long time acquires a different meaning for its members. A church, a university, a labor union, a professional association, an academy of sciences or letters, a political party, a legislature, an administrative governmental bureau, or a military or naval department which functions in peace as well as in war is conceived by its members as a superindividual entity having an existence of its own. It is identified as the same, even though, in the course of time, older members leave or die and new members take their places. Such an identification is manifested by the use of a proper name, often also by some other symbol designating this particular group. This is not a new phenomenon: a clan, a Chinese ancestral family, or an aristocratic European patrilineal family was also identified as a superindividual entity which continued to exist through centuries.

The old controversy as to whether social groups in this sense have a real existence or whether only individual members really exist, is scientifically irrelevant, as irrelevant as the controversy whether gods have a real existence. They do exist as *cultural* data, experienced and identified by numerous individuals; and they continue to exist in this sense as long as they are so experienced and identified. What is essential is whether and how these experiences affect the actions of the people who share them, for these actions are indubitably real. Thus, what is essential from the point of a comparative science of religion is that the believers in a god regularly participate in worship, make sacred implements, build temples, uphold the social roles of priests who attempt to control the actions of laymen. What is essential for the scientific study of social groups is that, if a social group is a superindividual entity from the point of view of its members, these members (often also outsiders) do act as if such an entity existed.

How is this entity conceived by its members? According to the predominant conception, it is both a social value and a social agent, analogous to an individual person. Like an individual person, it has definite rights and duties. It continues to exist and to function because its members act in conformity with the norms which these rights and duties imply.

The primary and universal right of every enduring social group is to be protected by its members against any dangers which threaten its existence, its solidarity, its prestige, its power. All loyal members are in duty bound to defend it against enemies and against disloyal members whose conduct has a disorganizing effect upon its function. Besides this, every group has possessive rights to certain values, material and ideational, which its members are supposed to recognize and support.

Thus, almost every group has possessive claims to certain portions of space, though it may partly share them with some other group. For instance, the claim of a state government to control a certain territory, partly shared with regional and local governments; the possessive claim of an industrial group to the area which its factory occupies; the claim of a university to its campus. Every group which regularly meets has permanent or temporary rights to its meeting place. The economic rights of social groups are also well known. Thus, a financial corporation as a group owns the capital it uses; although some members of the group have shares in this ownership, it is the group as a whole which has the supreme possessive right.

The rights of social groups to ideational values vary considerably. Thus, many a religious group claims exclusive rights to its deity; it is the one and only group that truly represents its deity and can propitiate it. Many a social group has a secret lore which outsiders cannot share. With the development of cultural creativeness in literature, art, music, philosophy, and science, all creative works of members of a group come to be considered exclusive possessions of the group, whether the group is a special association or the solidary intellectual nucleus of a modern nationality united by a common culture.

A comparative survey of these various rights indicates that they are considered essential for the continual functioning of the group.

But how can a social group—an administrative governmental bureau, a financial corporation, an industrial group, a university, a labor union, a professional association—regularly function as a superindividual agent, performing duties which are not reducible to the performances of individual agents? It can because those members of the group who coordinate the activities of other members function as representatives of the group as a whole. A member who performs such a role is in duty bound to act on behalf of the group as if the group acted through him, and he has the right to expect that other members will react to his actions as if they were actions of the group. And these duties and rights are subjected to collective sanctions.

Inasmuch as such a role is considered essential for the continued functioning of the group, it becomes *institutionalized.*[7] This means that there must always be somebody who performs this kind of role; if one individual ceases to do so, another individual must take his place. The rights and duties which it includes, as well as the sanctions to which they are subjected, remain the same whoever performs the role. Such is the institutional role of the priest in a religious congregation, of the mayor in a city government, of the manager of an industrial group, of the president of a university, of the colonel of a regiment. Since in large and complex groups no single individual can perform all the coordinating functions, a number of institutional roles graded in rights and differentiated in duties are necessary, for example, assistant managers, secretaries, and planning engineers in a factory; a provost, a secretary, a recorder, and deans of colleges in a university.

Because of this relative permanence of standards and norms which regulate the institutional roles of members of enduring groups in relation to other members, many sociologists devote their attention to what they call the "structure" of these groups, implying that they have a static inner order.[8] Actually, such standards and norms are only conceptual constructs, ideological systems (typically so, when formulated in a constitution) which do not become realized unless and until actively applied. The group remains a dynamic system, existing as long as it functions, whether its function changes or does not change. Institutionalization of the roles of coordinators frequently represents only that stage of its development when its formation has been completed, its function has been well defined,

---

[7] Cf. Florian Znaniecki, "Social Organization and Institutions," in *Twentieth Century Sociology*.

[8] Some sociologists, even though aware that social groups include a dynamic process of interconnected human actions, are inclined to interpret it as a psychological process. Such is, for instance, the approach to "group dynamics" of Kurt Lewin and his disciples.

and it is expected to last indefinitely; and when, consequently, it requires a permanent type of social organization with authority substituted for leadership. Many instances show how slowly this stage is sometimes reached in the history of social groups. Therefore, we prefer the term "institutional organization" rather than "structure"; especially since, as we shall see, whenever the function of the group changes in the course of time, its organization must also change.

Thus, after a comparative study of many different groups we came to the conclusion that all the other characteristics which sociologists have used in classifying them—composition, size, duration, complexity, collective possessions, and social institutions—depend upon their functions. Consequently, the essential condition for developing an adequate taxonomy of social groups is the possibility of classifying their functions. And since the functions of social groups consist of the actions which their members individually and collectively perform, the classification of these functions must be based on a classification of human actions.

My attempt to classify human actions is based on the fact that they are culturally patterned, tend to conform with definite standards, by which their main objects are defined and evaluated, and with norms, by which the ways of dealing with these objects are regulated.[9] Thus, technical actions, dealing with material objects, constitute a general class which differs from actions of religious worship, where the main objects are deities; actions dealing with language, literature, music, the plastic arts, philosophy, and science form distinct classes which differ from each other and from the first two classes. Many different subclasses may be found within each class.

For the study of social groups, the most important class is composed of *social* actions, whose main objects are human individuals and groups. As we have seen, whatever the purposes for which group members cooperate, they also perform social actions of which other members or the group as a whole are the main objects; and, if the group is to endure, these actions must conform with definite standards and norms. Moreover, the specific function of many groups, for example, hospitals, groups of social workers, pro-' fessional societies, some administrative groups, is cooperatively to perform social actions intended to benefit individuals who are not members. Such a function is obviously social and quite distinct

---

9 Cf. Florian Znaniecki, *Cultural Sciences: Their Origin and Development* (Urbana: University of Illinois Press, 1952), Chapter XI.

from the functions of technical production, religious worship, playing symphonies, carrying on scientific research, etc.

A different classifactory scheme was introduced by MacIver. He classified actions primarily by "interests." The term "interest," as defined by him, denotes the objects with which agents deal and which are evaluated by them; he emphasizes, however, the influence which men's experiences and valuations of these objects have upon them, rather than the cultural standards by which they are defined and evaluated.

Notwithstanding this difference in approach, most of the logical classes of associations in MacIver's taxonomy [10] were included in ours. Thus, we fully agree as to the objective existence of such general classes of associations as industrial, financial, professional, aesthetic, as well as schools and learned societies, each with functionally differentiated subclasses. Our classifications did not always agree with his, but such disagreement can be settled by further research. And we have postponed the problem of "the state" (which he includes under the general category of "association"), for we preferred to investigate functionally specialized governmental groups and the relationships between them and the other groups with which they interact before drawing any generalizations about states.

There are also methodological difficulties in classifying certain groups which perform several different functions, for it is not always easy to discover which of these functions are basic and which are only auxiliary. Nonetheless, our classification of the groups whose basic functions have already been ascertained enables us to reach certain hypothetical generalizations about their changes under definite external influences, about the evolution of new varieties, and about connections between groups. I can only briefly mention some of these generalizations.

We did not attempt to study changes due to natural factors. We studied many cases when a group is subjected to the aggressive expansion of another group which interferes with its function; for this is the main origin of active conflicts between groups. The effects of such interference seem to depend partly on the relative power of the interfering group and the methods it uses, but also—perhaps even more—on the function of the group subjected to this interference. Our tentative hypothesis is that groups which deal mainly with material values—technical or economic—are rather eas-

---

10 MacIver, *op. cit.*, p. 262.

ily disorganized or even completely dissolved, whereas groups functioning on behalf of ideational culture, especially religious or
national, often become more solidary and better integrated in defense against aggression.

We have not yet reached any systematic theory about the historical evolution of social groups in general, only a heuristic hypothesis,
according to which new varieties of groups evolve in consequence
of cultural innovations. Such new groups frequently remain functionally differentiated divisions within an older, larger group.
Thus, within the Roman Catholic Church (a group whose main
permanent function is religious), such groups evolved as monastical
orders performing technical, artistic, intellectual, and sometimes
even military functions; maintaining schools on all levels, mis-
sionary groups, hospitals, charitable groups, recreational groups,
and recently, political parties. Within the government of a modern state, numerous specialized administrative groups are evolving,
which divide old functions or assume new ones. Often, however, a
new functional group, evolving from an older group, becomes separated; this is how many specialized independent scientific associations evolved in modern times from older, more inclusive "learned
societies." Important technical inventions frequently lead to the
organization of separate industrial groups. New literary, musical,
and artistic styles result in the formation of separate independent
aesthetic associations.

In investigating connections between social groups, we concentrated on two main modern trends. We studied the process of unification of separate social groups with similar functions, as exemplified
by the American Federation of Labor and the Congress of Industrial
Organizations, the Chamber of Commerce, the International League
of Red Cross Societies, international federations of national scientific associations, etc.

On the other hand, we investigated the partial integration of
diverse, but mutually supplementary, functions which specialized
associations perform. Such an integration of the functions of various industrial, agricultural, commercial, and financial associations
is already well known.[11] Less known, but perhaps even more significant, is the partial integration of the functions of such widely
different and separate social groups as literary, artistic, ideological,
scientific, technological, and educational associations which are mutually supplementary, in that each of them makes a distinct con-

---

[11] Cf. MacIver, *op. cit.*, Chapter XVI.

tribution to the creative growth and preservation of some modern national culture.

In consequence of such studies of the differentiation and the integration of social groups, we have redefined the general concept of "society"; but this leads to difficult problems beyond the range of this chapter.

6

SOCIAL STRUCTURE AND GOALS
IN GROUP RELATIONS

MILTON M. GORDON

In the voluminous literature on racial and cultural group relations in American life, two basic related considerations appear to
have received a minimum of attention, both in terms of theory and
research. These considerations, in brief, are (1) the outlines of
American social structure within which attitudinal and behavioral
relationships between persons of varied ethnic backgrounds occur,[1]
and (2) the various possible goals in the area of reduction of group
tensions articulated with reference to the kind of social structure
they respectively imply.

The minimal attention given to these topics, both demanding
close attention to social structure, can hardly be justified on theoretical grounds, since relevant description and causational theory alike
logically demand their articulation. An intermediate explanation,
which itself merits further investigation, is that societal analysis in
the science of sociology has long been institution-centered, with secondary focus on social processes, and (apart from the elementary
age and sex categories) tertiary and residual attention relegated to
social structure. Interestingly enough, the beginnings of a change
in this emphasis emerge not from ethnic group analysis, from which
they might be expected, but from the community studies in social
stratification. The yet prevailing dominance of the institutional
approach, however, may be quickly ascertained from an examina-

---

[1] E. Franklin Frazier, in his Presidential Address before the American Sociological
Society in December, 1948, called attention to this fundamental omission. See "Race
Contacts and The Social Structure," *American Sociological Review*, Vol. 14, February,
1949, pp. 1–11.

tion of current textbooks in the various fields of sociology and is strikingly confirmed in the contents of a recent volume designed as an overall survey of American society by one of the most careful and nonidiosyncratic of American sociologists.[2] This dominance is regrettable, since social structure is the basic framework within which institutions function and social processes take place; it is not merely a casual addendum to them.

An adequate theory of social structure for modern complex societies must go far beyond age and sex categories to ascertain the broad social units within the national culture, each of which may allow for the unfolding of the life-cycle within its invisible but operationally functioning borders. Such analysis must carefully investigate clique and associational memberships, ecological concentration, occupational relationships, courtship and marriage practices, and psychological orientations with respect to the degree of their delimitation within broad social categories. Such investigation, moreover, cannot afford to rest with one-category analysis. It is not enough to know, for instance, that X per cent of marriages in American Town is ethnically endogamous and Y per cent is endogamous with respect to social class. An equally important question for the student of social structure is the distribution of endogamous marriages within each "social box" set up by combining the ethnic and class categories.[3] If other social factors prove relevant, their addition to the correlational structure is indicated. Such analysis extended along the entire gamut of institutional and associational life would eventually provide a relatively precise outline of American social structure, the varied effectiveness of its dividing lines, and finally a sociological setting for the analysis of the problems of persons who are marginal or mobile with regard to the various internal structures.

As a name for these internal structures, made up of a combination of social categories and usually providing for the unfolding of the life-cycle, the term *subculture* is appropriate. Although this term has found casual and not infrequent usage heretofore, it appears to have stood, usually, for discrete units (that is, ethnic group alone, social class alone, etc.), occasionally for temporary groupings touching only one phase of the life-cycle, such as play groups and gangs,

---

2 Robin M. Williams, Jr., *American Society, A Sociological Interpretation* (New York: Alfred A. Knopf, Inc., 1951).

8 For an empirical study which shows awareness of the need for such analysis, see August B. Hollingshead, "Cultural Factors in the Selection of Marriage Mates," *American Sociological Review*, Vol. 15, October, 1950, pp. 619–627.

and sometimes for area-localized groups.[4]   The present writer offered in a paper several years ago a systematic presentation of a theory of subcultural structure which has specific articulation and delineation.[5]   The paradigm presented there, with minor modification, is as follows: a subculture is a social division of a national culture made up by a combination of ethnic group (used here as a generic term covering race, religion, or national origin [6]), social class, region (North-East, Mid-West, South-East, etc.), and rural or urban residence.   Examples of a specific subculture would be the following: Negro, upper-class, North-East, urban; white Protestant, lower-class, South-East, rural; Jewish, upper-middle class, Mid-West, urban; and so on.

The theory of subcultural structure posits that, in "ideal type" terms, the four major factors listed above form in their combination a functioning unity which has an integrated impact on the participating individuals, in relation to both social structure and psychological orientation.   With respect to social structure, they constitute the social setting within which the socialization process and the majority of later primary contacts take place.   Psychologically, they provide the "social field" with which subnational identification and "consciousness of kind" constellations are joined.

The evidence which lends support to the subcultural theory varies widely in the preciseness of its focus in subcultural terms but is impressive in its cumulation when examined with this focus.   It

---

[4] An early use of the term is that of Ralph Linton in *The Study of Man* (New York: D. Appleton-Century Co., 1936), pp. 275ff.   Linton's analysis is focused largely on area-localized groups within a tribal culture.   Alfred McClung Lee, in several papers, has used the term to refer to subgroups within a national culture and has related the analysis to norms and behavior patterns.   See his "Levels of Culture as Levels of Social Generalization," *American Sociological Review*, Vol. 10, August, 1945, pp. 485–495; "Social Determinants of Public Opinions," *International Journal of Opinion and Attitude Research*, Vol. 1, March, 1947, pp. 12–29; and "A Sociological Discussion of Consistency and Inconsistency in Intergroup Relations," *Journal of Social Issues*, Vol. V, No. 3, pp. 12–18.   A completely different meaning of the term "subcultural" is Joseph K. Folsom's.   Folsom uses it to refer to behavior patterns which are below the level of cultural choice and are the inevitable products of human bodily structure and a given environment.   See his *The Family* (New York: John Wiley & Sons, Inc., 1934), pp. 46ff.
    This list is by no means exhaustive.
[5] Milton M. Gordon, "The Concept of The Sub-Culture and Its Application," *Social Forces*, Vol. 26, October, 1947, pp. 40–42.
[6] Some writers use "ethnic group" to refer specifically to a national origin group. However, there is a need for a generic term to embody the common grouping principle involved in race, religion, and national origin divisions.   Since "national origin," while a bit cumbersome, is already available for its specific, a "neutral" term such as "ethnic group" seems appropriate for generic usage.   This usage is in accord with that of E. K. Francis in "The Nature of The Ethnic Group," *American Journal of Sociology*, Vol. LII, March, 1947, pp. 393–400.   (This article is particularly noteworthy for its cogent theoretical analysis of structural and psychological aspects of the "ethnic group.")

consists in large part of the monographs detailing community studies in social stratification and/or ethnic group life.[7] On the whole, the most cogent studies, as far as the combination of a class-ethnic approach is concerned, are those dealing with the Negro group. Here, the historical separation from the white social system has been so apparent that investigators have been able to concentrate structurally on class divisions within the Negro group. Most studies of non-Negro ethnic groups, or those dealing with social class in the white community generally, have been less satisfactory in this respect (the work of Hollingshead and Myers, noted in footnote 7, constitutes a notable exception) largely because of the lack of a theoretical apparatus which could suggest the right questions for research, such as: What is the nature of the class divisions within the ethnic subsystem? To what extent do members of a particular class within an ethnic subsystem (for instance, the Jewish) have clique and institutional contacts with members of the same class but a different ethnic subsystem (for instance, the white Protestant)? To what extent do members of a particular class in a particular ethnic group have social contacts with members of the same ethnic groups but of a lower or a higher class? The need for answers to such queries as these becomes strikingly apparent when, leaving the simpler descriptions of the immigrant colonies, we ask ourselves: What are the social structural and psychological orientations, in the double dimensions of ethnic group and class, of the children of immigrants (and *their* children) who are described so patly and uniformly as "rising in the class structure"? Trying to shake out of the existing literature a focused and even a roughly quantitative answer to this question is a frustrating experience.

---

[7] Some examples are: W. Lloyd Warner and Leo Srole, *The Social Systems of American Ethnic Groups* (New Haven: Yale University Press, 1945); Allison Davis, Burleigh B. Gardner, and Mary R. Gardner, *Deep South* (Chicago: University of Chicago Press, 1941); St. Clair Drake and Horace R. Cayton, *Black Metropolis* (New York: Harcourt, Brace & Co., 1945); Elin L. Anderson, *We Americans* (Cambridge: Harvard University Press, 1937); Irvin L. Child, *Italian or American* (New Haven: Yale University Press, 1943); Ruth D. Tuck, *Not With the Fist* (New York: Harcourt, Brace & Co., 1946). For an analytical survey of the social stratification studies, see the writer's Ph.D. dissertation, *Social Class in Modern American Sociology* (Columbia University, 1950); microfilm publication by University Microfilms, Ann Arbor, Michigan, 1950.

The studies of August B. Hollingshead and Jerome K. Myers at Yale, dealing with the social structure of New Haven, show a clear awareness of the relevance of the combined class-ethnic approach and offer some data to sustain it. See August B. Hollingshead, "Trends In Social Stratification: A Case Study," *American Sociological Review,* Vol. 17, No. 6, December, 1952, pp. 679–686. Hollingshead declares (p. 686): "In short, a major trend in the social structure of the New Haven community during the last half-century has been the development of *parallel class structures* within the limits of race, ethnic origin, and religion."

The inclusion of the regional and the rural-urban categories in the subcultural construct suggests itself because of the well-known variations in mores which they occasion. Undoubtedly, they are of considerably less importance than the ethnic and the class categories. To round out the outlines of the subcultural social system, however, their inclusion seems justified. A three-way breakdown along the rural-urban continuum is also suggested, as follows: rural —small city—large city. It should be pointed out that spatial separation, in itself, is not an indication of subcultural separation. A lower-middle class white Protestant from Detroit is not to be distinguished subculturally from his counterpart in Chicago. They merely live in different spatial units of the same subculture.

Social structure, psychological orientations, and overt behavior patterns constitute a major segment of interrelated variables. Subcultural analysis provides a theoretical framework for studying different cultural behaviors not simply from the point of view of class differences, or of ethnic group differences, or the regional or rural-urban categories, in artificial isolation from one another, but from the standpoint of their functional integration. After all, no person is *just* an ethnic group member, or *just* a social class member, *just* a Southerner, etc. His social background is a complex, not the solitary category which happens to be the particular enthusiasm of the investigator. Using the subcultural apparatus we can begin to assign behavioral frequencies to the social configurations which provide meaningful comparisons of group cultures within a national society.[8] We can also begin to answer with more cogency such questions as: Which category is more important for predicting specific behavior differences, ethnic group or social class? This is achieved by setting up a comparative causal analysis for ascertaining the relative efficacy of each subcultural component *at different points along each of the other continua.* For instance, behavioral differences in recreation patterns between two ethnic groups may be minimal at the upper-middle-class level, let us say, and considerable at the lower-class level. A statement simply in terms of ethnic group and social class, each unfactored, would cover up these varied relationships. On the other hand, if the differences proved to be minimal at all parts of the class continuum, then such

---

[8] For an empirical study which combines the ethnic and class categories in the manner here suggested, see Allison Davis and Robert J. Havighurst, "Social Class and Color Differences In Child Rearing," *American Sociological Review*, Vol. 11, December, 1946, pp. 698–710. From this study we can quantitatively compare behavior frequencies in 4 groups: middle-class white, lower-class white, middle-class Negro, and lower-class Negro. The regional and rural-urban factors were held constant, all respondents being residents of Chicago.

a finding, obtained by subcultural analysis, cannot be attacked on the grounds of a skewing occasioned by a hypothetically possible differential class structure in the two ethnic groups.

Adequate theoretical attention to social structure in the terms here suggested would also place many behavioral phenomena in a research setting which gives them more illumination and social meaning.   Take, for instance, the already cited phenomenon of ethnic intermarriage.   Once the incidence and certain social characteristics of the partners are ascertained, subcultural analysis suggests the third fundamental (and up to now virtually ignored) question of what happens to the intermarried couples and their children with reference to their placement and psychological orientation in the American social structure.[9]   Do they identify with one or the other of the ethnic groups of the partners, do they remain marginal, or is some third alternative taking place, such as the gradual building up of an intermediate social structure consisting precisely of "intermarrieds" and other "marginals"?   Without such analytical inquiry, intermarriage frequencies actually tell us more, by implication, about those who do not intermarry than about those who do.[10]

The matter of psychological orientations, that is, group identification and patterns of "in-grouping" and "out-grouping," is complicated by the fact that we are dealing here with more than one dimension.   Although a person may participate largely in a social field circumscribed by both ethnic group and social class borders, the attribution of ethnic group membership *by itself* is a powerful pattern in our culture—a pattern generated both by pressure from within the ethnic group and from without.   Rare is the Negro, or

---

[9] A study by Judson T. Landis deals with selected consequences (divorce, religious training of children, and marriage partner change of faith) of Protestant-Catholic marriages which produced children. See "Marriages of Mixed and Non-Mixed Religious Faith," *American Sociological Review,* Vol. 14, June, 1949, pp. 401–407.

[10] Cf. Frazier's statement with regard to Negro-white intermarriage: "What I wish to emphasize is that if studies of intermarriage are to have sociological significance, they must analyze intermarriage within the frame of reference of two social worlds or the social organization of the white and Negro communities. Outside of this frame of reference, the extent and trend of intermarriage as measured by statistics becomes a meaningless abstraction and no extrapolation of statistical trends on intermarriage will provide any key to the future course of this relationship. If intermarriage were studied within the frame of reference of the changing nature of the contacts which are occurring between the social world of the whites and the social world of the Negroes, both the extent and trend of intermarriage would acquire meaning and provide a basis for prediction." *Loc. cit.,* pp. 4–5.

See also Milton L. Barron's article "Research on Intermarriage: A Survey of Accomplishments and Prospects," *The American Journal of Sociology,* Vol. LVII, November, 1951, pp. 249–255.

the Jew, for instance, who can fail to respond affectively to events or to evaluative allegations which concern respectively Negroes or Jews as a group. Nevertheless, the participation field and the field of close behavioral similarities are likely to be class-confined, as well as ethnic-confined. Thus we may distinguish two types of psychological constellations corresponding to these respective experience patterns. "I am ultimately bound up with the fate of these people" is the type of constellation attached to the ethnic group as a whole.[11] We may call this *historical identification* since it is a function of the unfolding of past and current historic events. On the other hand, "These are the people I feel at home with and can relax with" is the type of constellation attached to those persons with whom one participates frequently and shares close behavioral similarities. According to the subcultural hypothesis, these persons are likely to be of the same ethnic group *and* social class (and regional and rural-urban categories). This constellation we may call *participational identification*. To sum up: in terms of psychological orientations, the ethnic group is likely to be the group of historical identification, whereas the subculture will be, in the majority of cases, the group of participational identification. It should be pointed out that identification with larger units—that is, American society as a whole, "Western society," "all humanity," are likely to be present at different levels of structuring.

Substructural theory is not advanced here as a set of propositions that are completely demonstrated and whose quantitative outlines are completely known. The appropriate vocal motto for large orders of generalization abstracted from evidence of wide divergency and degree of focus is not "How true I am," but "How true *am* I?" The available evidence certainly suggests a high degree of probability that these internal social structures, made up of the combination of social categories specified do exist within American society and that a large proportion of the population participates predominantly within them (respectively), with the aforementioned results behaviorally and psychologically. The *degree* to which these propositions are valid is a matter for further empirical inquiry structured by the outlines of the theory itself. A major virtue of the theory is that it can be precisely articulated for such inquiry. Community researches which studied the combined social categories of residents against social participation (home visiting, clique-membership, institutional affiliation, courtship, marriage, etc.), ecol-

---

11 See, in his discussion of the Jewish group, Kurt Lewin's concept of "interdependence of fate" as the major functional criterion of group belongingness: Chapters 10, 11, and 12 of *Resolving Social Conflicts* (New York: Harper & Brothers, 1948).

ogical concentration, behavior patterns, and psychological orientations would give us quantitative and qualitative expression of the degree of validity of the theory. Problems and adjustments of "marginals" would become illuminated by attention to the kinds of structures they are marginal *to*. The important question of to what extent occupational and "interest" groups (for instance, intellectuals) cut across the subcultural categories and form social structures of their own poses itself for analysis by the same criteria which underlie the induction of subcultural existence. The phenomenon of social mobility becomes related to the types of structures left and those entered. In this connection we may distinguish between the *subculture of origin,* into which one is born, and the *subculture of achievement,* which one may enter later if he is mobile. Certainly movement from one social class to another involves subcultural change. Changes of ethnic identification or participation, while patently more difficult, call for similar analysis. The oversimplification often attendant on one-category analysis is avoided, and internal outlines of American social structure usually overlooked present themselves for study. To take one such overlooked area: What are the structural relationships of upper-class white Catholics to upper-class white Protestants in the large metropolitan areas where there are at least numerical possibilities for the existence of parallel structures? Do these parallel structures in fact exist? Or does integration take place? Until we ask such a question in these terms, we will not know the answer.

Further use of subcultural theory is indicated in the study of the causes of group prejudice. Granted that some prejudiced persons will be found in all strata of society, there is the task of allocation of frequencies so that we ultimately may know whether some subgroups furnish larger proportions of bigots than others and are associated quantitatively with particular kinds of prejudice. "Personality" theories of prejudice, currently the subject of intensive investigation, should be based on a foundation of subcultural analysis in order that more and more layers of the causational background may be uncovered. Such inquiry would concern itself not only with specifying the subcultures (if any) most significantly related to bigoted attitudes but with discovering the *kinds* of social-structural background which are attached to both the bigot himself and the context of his previous relationships with members of minority groups. Has the bigot been marginal or mobile himself? Has he experienced contacts (if any) with minority individuals who are marginal, or have his contacts always taken place in situations where subcultural division was paramount? Have his contacts been across class lines, and, if so, in what direction? Questions such as these are a necessary part of inquiry into the causes of prejudice if a fuller picture is to be secured.

Thus far we have been concerned with the outlines of American social structure as they exist in the present. Subcultural analysis is also an indispensable tool for clarifying the whole area of social structural formulations *implicit* in the various end-product attitudinal goals of "better group relations," "the reduction of intergroup tensions," "intergroup harmony," etc. This is a subject (social-structural goals) which, in view of its fundamental importance both to the question of the desirability of alternative termini in themselves, and the strategic considerations respectively attendant upon them, has received far from commensurate attention.[12]

Such discussion of structural goals as may be found is usually placed in the framework of the basic alternatives of assimilation and cultural pluralism. In the typology which this writer proposes, (in addition to assimilation) two types of cultural pluralism are distinguished, an additional integrative type of social structure is delineated, and attention is called to a fifth alternative, combining certain aspects of cultural pluralism and social integration.[13] Certain preliminary remarks, however, are in order. Subcultural analysis points to the need for examining in detail institutional and associational affiliations, the structure of cliques and home-visiting patterns, the kinds of psychological orientations, and other previously mentioned components of cultural-pluralistic living, in order that its functioning and its problems may be delineated. Without such investigation the term "cultural pluralism" is a vague and boneless abstraction. Secondly, adequate analytical theory requires that a distinction be made between structure and behavior in discussions of ethnic group adjustments in American society. It is, for instance, usually assumed that a plurality of groups formed on the ethnic principle assures a corresponding plurality of behaviors. Such need not be the case at all since the persistence of multiple social organization may be the result of psychological pressures continuing to stem from both within and without the group long after major differences in behavior patterns have vanished as a result of common exposure to the mass stimuli of modern industrial society.

---

[12] Two of the more cogent discussions are found in Arnold and Caroline Rose, *America Divided* (New York: Alfred A. Knopf, Inc., 1948), pp. 166–177; and Robin M. Williams, Jr., *The Reduction of Intergroup Tensions* (New York: Social Science Research Council, 1947), pp. 11–12. It is, perhaps, indicative, however, that the latter monograph, an overall survey of research considerations in the intergroup relations field, devotes only one and one-half pages to this problem of social-structure goals.

[13] Cf. the typologies of the Roses, and of Williams, in the places cited.

Third, subcultural focus illuminates the fact that cultural pluralism (in both the structural and behavioral sense) of a certain kind exists regardless of the ethnic factor in modern society in the presence of social class differences. Cultural pluralism in the ethnic sense thus usually adds to—"enriches," if one wishes—the sources of cultural stimuli but is not an exclusive alternative to "a dead level of uniformity," as some of its proponents suggest. On the other hand, the claim of the assimilationists that, except for ethnic divergences, we would have in America a completely unified society with the virtual absence of cultural differences and social divisiveness is thus seen to be specious. And, finally, in this connection, it must be understood that discussions of cultural pluralism in the usual context in terms of its desirability or undesirability deal with the ethnic factor alone; such discussion concerns the desirability or undesirability of the existence of a plurality of *ethnic cultures,* apart from social class, regional, and rural-urban considerations. This procedure is, of course, permissible and even necessary for conceptual focus on the problem at hand as long as one knows what he is holding constant and can bring it back in for consideration when the need arises. It is, then, in the sense of *ethnic cultures* (as distinct from subcultures, which include more than the ethnic factor) that the ensuing typology of alternatives in American social structure with regard to ethnic group relations is offered.[14]

Assimilation. The assimilationist goal calls for the complete acculturation of immigrants, or at least their children and succeeding generations, to "American ways and customs." As a number of observers have noted, these "ways and customs" on further inspection turn out to be those of the white Protestant Anglo-Saxon middle class.[15] The assimilationist proposal is sometimes phrased in terms of the "melting pot," but whatever the early proponents of the phrase meant by it, it is clear that in the assimilationist process most of the "melting" is to be done by the immigrants and their descendants, who are to melt into the dominant ethnic culture

---

[14] The alternatives distinguished here all fall within the framework of attempts to achieve a nondiscriminatory society. Patterns of segregation involving discrimination and second-class status as, for instance, white-Negro relations in the South, are deliberately excluded.

[15] Although distribution along the whole class ladder except, perhaps, the very top, is implicitly expected. See, in this connection, Robert K. Merton's stimulating essay which deals, in part, wiith some of the inconsistencies of this position: "The Self-Fulfilling Prophecy," *The Antioch Review,* Vol. 8, Summer, 1948, pp. 193–210; reprinted in Arnold M. Rose (ed.), *Race Prejudice and Discrimination* (New York: Alfred A. Knopf, Inc., 1951), as "A Social Psychological Factor."

(white Protestant) rather than contribute to a new amalgam composed of equal or proportionate contributions from each group. Viewed from this standpoint, the invitation to assimilate is an invitation not to pool one's ethnic background into a common "American culture" but, rather, to submerge its identity into that of another ethnic group.

Further light on the assimilationist goal is shed by keeping in mind the crucial distinction between behavior and social structure, which may be phrased in this connection as a distinction between *behavioral assimilation* and *structural assimilation.* As far as behavior is concerned, by and large the assimilation process has taken place, regardless of theoretical considerations. With large-scale immigration to the United States curtailed in the middle nineteen twenties, ethnic problems increasingly center around the native-born. With few exceptions the descendants of immigrants have enthusiastically adopted "American ways." Indeed, in the vast majority of cases, as a result of their exposure to the larger environment, they have been socialized into them so that these behavior patterns are as indigenous to them as to the children of Anglo-white Protestants. Differences in religious worship still remain, of course, but it is doubtful if these, apart from their social implications, can be considered a major source of tension.[16] Segmental interest in ancestral folk music, dance, literature, etc., when it exists is hardly a threat to the dominance of American patterns. Minor differences in speech patterns are sometimes apparent, particularly at the lower- and lower-middle-class levels, as a result of inflections received from exposure to the parental language. But even these will probably disappear in successive generations. In short, present conditions, even though characterized by *some* cultural variation, display the essential triumph of behavioral assimilation [17] and the promise of its increasing success. It is in the realm of social structure that the assimilation process has floundered, for reasons that can be analyzed sociologically.

Structural assimilation has not taken place, in the large, for two overall reasons: a sufficient number of members of the majority group have not wanted it; and a sufficient number of members of

---

[16] Cf. R. M. MacIver's statement: "But we do not find sufficient reason to regard religion *by itself* as of crucial importance in provoking the tensions and cleavages manifested in the everyday relationships of American society." *The More Perfect Union* (New York: The Macmillan Co., 1948), p. 12.

[17] There are differences of degree, of course, depending particularly on factors of spatial isolation and degree of discrimination. The American Indian on reservations and the poverty-stricken "folk" Negro of the rural South are patently still some distance away from Anglo-Saxon middle-class patterns.

most of the minority groups have not wanted it. These reasons, to be sure, require further analysis. Either one, by itself, would be sufficient to retard structural assimilation. The combination of the two has been all the more effective. To illustrate the first, consider the Negro. Far from being encouraged to assimilate structurally, the American Negro has been carefully and systematically excluded, with minor exceptions, from white Anglo-Saxon Protestant social structure (cliques, home-visiting patterns, churches, fraternal societies, neighborhoods, etc.). To lesser and varying degrees this exclusion has been leveled at other minorities, falling with least force on Catholics from Northern and Western Europe.

The attitudes of minority group members themselves toward structural assimilation vary both *among* groups and *within* groups. There is reason to believe that the Negro group has one of the largest proportions of persons who, at least, theoretically, desire complete structural assimilation.[18] There are logical reasons for this: the vast majority of Negroes are Protestants, and their relationship to an ancestral African heritage is hardly focused enough to interfere with such a goal. The religious minorities, Catholics and Jews, are in a somewhat different position. Religious differences presuppose religious organization and a certain amount of communal life. Thus there are internal pressures to maintain this communal life and particularly to discourage intermarriage. In the case of the Jews, this communal identification and organization was given added impetus by the virulent anti-Semitism (and its consequences) of the Nazis. Nationality background groups have similar, although often less powerful, internal stimuli to maintain ethnic identity and communal organization. When seen from the point of view of the alternative of merging not into some neutral overall American social structure but specifically into the social structure of white Anglo-Saxon Protestants, somewhat reluctant themselves to enable the merger, the choice of ethnic identity and social organization becomes more understandable. This is not to say that there is not a considerable number of Catholics and Jews (and white Protestants) who, in all probability, would favor virtually complete structural assimilation even in these terms. But, analyzed in this fashion, the logic of parallel social structures should become clearer.

In short, although there are some community associations and activities which are in their very nature community-wide and not specifically white Anglo-Saxon Protestant (professional organiza-

---

18 See Goodwin Watson, *Action for Unity* (New York and London, Harper & Brothers, 1947), p. 96. Nevertheless, Watson points out necessary qualifications to the assumption that all elements of the Negro community are so inclined.

tions, labor unions, and political parties are some of the examples which come to mind), the assimilationist viewpoint has overestimated the degree to which an overall "neutral" American social structure actually exists for minority groups to be assimilated into; it has underestimated the indigenous drive for separate communal organization present in the minority groups themselves, and the essential logic of this position, given certain premises; and it has overestimated the willingness of members of the majority group to encourage minority entrance into those aspects of its social structure which imply intimate social intercourse.[19]   For these reasons, structural assimilation has not taken place in any quantitatively significant sense, nor does this analysis suggest that it is likely to do so in the near future.

Cultural Pluralism: General Considerations.   The goal of cultural pluralism, broadly speaking, envisages a society where ethnic groups would be encouraged to maintain their own communal social structure and identity, and preserve certain of their values and behavioral patterns which are not in conflict with broader values, patterns, and legal norms common to the entire society.   The nature of this social subsystem is seen to be a pattern of intimate social relationships and institutional affiliations which allows for the unfolding of the major aspects of the life-cycle within its borders. Those social class differences and consequent second series of social subsystems which would ordinarily develop would be confined respectively within each of the ethnic systems.   Two types of cultural pluralism may be distinguished, hinging on the degree of contact existing across ethnic lines and the nature of the contact—that is, whether *primary,* involving intimate, family or clique-oriented association; or *secondary,* involving relatively impersonal and non-intimate association.

Cultural Pluralism A—The Tolerance Level.   At the "tolerance level" of group relations, ethnic groups would maintain such a high degree of social isolation from each other that virtually all primary contacts would be within the ethnic group and most secondary contacts would be either correspondingly confined or, if across ethnic lines, completely accommodative.   The various ethnic

---

[19] There are, of course, numerous intimate friendships in American life between persons of different ethnic backgrounds, and some intermarriages.   But they are not encouraged by the nature of the dominant outlines of American social structure.   They are, so to speak, marginal to it.   Limitations of space prevent further development of this point.

groups would be encouraged to have tolerant attitudes toward one another and to maintain such relationships as would be necessary to meet the demands of a common legal system and allegiance to a common government. This type of cultural pluralism is difficult to maintain without considerable spatial separation and is sociologically unsuited to a culture-complex consisting of urban industrial society and democratic norms, which requires considerable interchangeability of individuals and frequent communication and contact. Nevertheless, certain of the social-structural features of this level (as distinct from the psychological) may be seen to characterize Negro-white relationships in the South. The chief value of distinguishing this level here, however, is to throw a clearer focus on the next level of cultural pluralism.

Cultural Pluralism B—The Good Group Relations Level. The "good group relations" level envisages a society where ethnic groups maintain their social subsystems, but where the degree of contact across ethnic lines is substantially greater than that existing at the "tolerance level" and where secondary contacts are considerable in number and primary contacts take place in limited frequency. This societal goal implies employment integration, common use of public accommodations, inter-ethnic composition of civic organizations, and frequent symbolic demonstrations of intergroup harmony which emphasize common goals and values. It encourages such degree and frequency of primary relationships as does not threaten the existence of the respective ethnic group's subsystem and identity, support of in-group institutions, and endogamous marriage patterns. Readers will recognize in this description considerable similarity to the outlines of American social structure as it exists, ethnically speaking, at the present time. Attainment of those "secondary" integrative aspects now partially lacking plus the psychological attitudes which will facilitate the harmonious operation of such a social structure emerges as the explicit or implicit goal of many, if not most, agencies and individuals currently working in the "intercultural" field.

The Community Integration Level. This level is presented as an "ideal type" construct outlining a theoretically attainable goal for those persons who wish to bring people of diverse ethnic backgrounds into a common intimate social structure and who reject assimilation as previously delineated. Precisely in the structural realm it envisages multiple primary contacts across ethnic lines to the point of complete lack of emphasis on ethnic background as a factor in social relationships (except as an "interest" factor). It differs from the "assimilation" goal in that it is not predicated on other ethnic groups merging into the white Protestant Anglo-Saxon, but on common recognition of the fundamental equality of validity of all backgrounds. This requires both appropriate psychological orientations (on this level there are no "hosts" and no "guests") on the part of participating individuals and, in many cases, the refashioning of institutions to proclaim symbolically this equality and the common values which embrace the diversity. It involves no need for renunciation of ethnic background since the common values attest to its co-validity, but allows individuals to make as much of it or as little as they wish. It does, of course, imply emphasis upon the basic value of all-inclusiveness ("the brotherhood of man"), which is probably to be found somewhere in the value-hierarchy of every specific ethnic group in America.

The community integration level may sound strangely similar to what early proponents of the "melting pot" may have had in mind. But it differs from this goal in several respects. First of all, it focuses on social structure rather than on cultural behavior. Its "dynamic" is the bringing of people together in social participation, not the amalgamation of cultural patterns. Secondly, like cultural pluralism, it emphasizes legitimate and continued pride in ethnic and cultural background and puts positive values on the variety of cultural behaviors, allowing the give and take of current interaction to sort out the patterns of the future. Thirdly, it recognizes the undesirable nature of many aspects of renunciation of ethnic identification, and provides for its retention and positive evaluation, interpreting participation at the community integration level as, in part, a further implementation of specific ethnic values. And finally, it "faces up" to problems of social structure and institutional life implicit in the goal of interethnic social relationships which may be sustained through the life-cycle.

A Mixed Type: The Pluralistic-Integration Level. The rationale of any set of structural goals in interethnic relations must deal with the question of whether these goals are to be achieved by authoritarian pressure or by voluntary choice. Certainly proponents of cultural pluralism have indicated their belief that ethnic groups should be free to develop important features of their special heritage and to maintain respective social structures. As both Rose [20] and

[20] *Op. cit.,* pp. 173–174.

Schermerhorn [21] have noted, by the same principle such choice should also be available to individuals, who should be free to cultivate whatever degree of their ethnic heritage they wish to and to participate socially on the basis of their individual interests. Or, in the words of MacIver, "Only when differences are free to stay apart or to merge or to breed new variations of the community theme can human personality have fulfillment and creative power, drawing its sustenance where it finds its proper nourishment, neither clinging to likeness nor worshiping difference." [22] The assimilationist goal does not meet either of the above criteria. Cultural pluralism by itself meets the criterion of "group choice" but not that of individual choice, since under even the most favorable conditions the "deviating" individual is forced into the position of either some type of ethnic "conversion" or marginality. The community integration goal is similarly authoritarian if made a compulsory norm. The only structural goal which would seem to meet both criteria of democratic choice is one which envisages a "mixed" social structure in which ethnic subsystems would exist alongside a subsystem composed of persons who wished to live at the "community integration" level, and which allowed easy passage from one subsystem to another at the wish of the individual. Such a mixed type of social structure may be called "the pluralistic-integration" level. The implementation of this level requires the conscious effort of those individuals who wish to participate interethnically in significant fashion in providing institutional arrangements which will bring into being the "community integration" social structure as one of the existing array. Such arrangements will include interethnic neighborhoods, cliques, summer resorts, places of worship, fraternal and social organizations, and not least, attitudinal recognition. Since the persons who would be attracted to this task would very likely be persons who are presently on the margins of the existing ethnic structures and/or who are motivated by goals which are not normative in the present society, they might well recruit with the paraphrased call: "Marginals of the world, unite!"

It is not intended to give the impression here that choices in social participation need be definitive or all-embracing. Even in present society persons have the opportunity to select friends from, and to a certain extent participate socially in more than one ethnic subsystem at the same time. Such opportunities would be increased and facilitated at the pluralistic-integration level.

---

[21] R. A. Schermerhorn, *These Our People* (Boston: D. C. Heath & Company, 1949), p. 443.

[22] *Op. cit.*, p. 10.

To summarize briefly, this paper has called attention to the need for more than minimal attention to social structure in the group relations area, and has outlined a system of social-structural analysis whose theoretical propositions have partial verification and are articulated for further research.   It has used this system to crystallize and formulate alternative structural goals implicit in the desire for "better group relations."   Such analysis may be useful in a field where, as one authority has put it, "our crucial need is not so much for isolated 'new data' as for studies whose significance is mutually reinforced by being placed in a framework of interrelated theory." [23]

---

[23] Williams, *The Reduction of Intergroup Tensions*, p. 26.

7

ETHNIC GROUPS IN AMERICA: FROM NATIONAL CULTURE TO IDEOLOGY

NATHAN GLAZER

For many years now there has been little discussion of the problems of creating an English-speaking nation, with a common nationality and a single loyalty, out of a population at least half of which stems from non-English-speaking peoples. The fact that Americans are also—and in some cases, and some respects, primarily —Germans, Italians, Poles, Jews, and so on, is taken deadly seriously by the politicians and quite as seriously by the general mass of Americans, but tends to be ignored by academicians. There are certainly enough discussions of the colored minorities but hardly enough of the Italians, the Poles, the Jews, and others as such.

Two quite contradictory concepts have dominated the consideration of this problem: that of the "melting pot," and that of "cultural pluralism," or, more dramatically put, of "a nation of nations." (The latter two terms denote the same thing, and while we use all three terms we will continue to speak of only two concepts.) All three terms were introduced by immigrants themselves, or by those who spoke for them. The first term was coined by Israel Zangwill in his 1906 play, which bore it as a title. Other writers had used the phrase "smelting pot" before him, but it was in the form of "melting pot" that the idea it embodied—that in America all nations were to be quite shorn of their original characteristics and were to emerge as a new and higher nation combining the best of the old—became popular. The idea of "cultural pluralism" was introduced in a series of articles by Horace M. Kallen which began to appear in 1915 and were ultimately collected in his book, *Assimilation and Democracy*. The term "a nation of nations," which is in effect "cultural pluralism" revived for the 1940's, was introduced into this context of discussion by Louis Adamic in his 1944 book of that title.

Paradoxically, it was when the tide of immigration was at the full, and poured immigrants into this country at the rate of a million a year, that the idea of the melting pot, asserting that these diverse peoples would form a single nation, was put forward. At that time they were more diverse than ever before, for, besides the Southern and East European immigration that had become dominant toward the end of the century, the Eastern Mediterranean, that museum of variety, had also begun to make up a large part of the stream of immigration. It was at this moment that it was suggested that there was no serious problem of blending all these millions into a single people.

Also paradoxically, it was twenty years after this great stream was cut off by law, and after we had lived through the longest period in the nation's history during which, without having to contend with new millions, we could attempt to mold these elements of many nations into one, that Louis Adamic proposed, in a series of books, that we should consciously maintain the individuality of each of these peoples, even though they had received no recruits for twenty years, and even though he himself (like everyone else, liberal or conservative, in the 1930's) was against changing the law to permit letting in any more.

To add one more paradox: both concepts, one proposing complete assimilation, the other insisting on even artificial measures to preserve diversity, were propagated by the non-Anglo-Saxon immigrant groups themselves, and particularly by Jews, the most active adherents of a free immigration policy throughout the debate over the issue (Zangwill and Kallen were both Jews). But if we were merely to list paradoxes, we would never get beyond them, for a problem that has had a brief period of glory as a subject for polemic and then has dropped from sight before any successful intellectual resolution of its dilemmas has been put forward, is sure to produce paradoxes. Still, it is worth unraveling the few with which we have begun before considering the real dimensions and significance of this problem.

Both concepts were propaganda directed toward the older groups of the American population by the newer. The "melting pot" argued that, despite their apparent exoticism, the new immigrants would soon be such complete Americans that they would be indistinguishable from anyone else. Consequently, they should be allowed to enter freely, and there need be no fear of division caused by them. But during World War I, the new groups, acting with no apparent concern for this argument, began to take up the causes of their respective homelands with some vigor. And twenty-five years later, they again reacted to the conflict in Europe with more heat than Americans established here somewhat longer. And, in addition, they continued to show a remarkable persistence in maintaining formal and informal organization that kept them, to some extent, apart from the rest of American society (of course, the older Americans were doing the same thing). To speak in these circumstances of the "melting pot" was in effect only to criticize the newer immigrants and their children for not having fulfilled the promise of their earlier slogan. The new slogans of "cultural pluralism" and "a nation of nations" now offered them the right to be different —or to be themselves. These terms proposed an image of America in which difference was not only permissible, but was conceived of as a source of strength. Since the Jews were unique in that throughout this period they were in desperate need of places to which to emigrate, it is not surprising to find that they introduced two of these terms and were perhaps the most active propagators of all three.

But if we were to conclude that the first concept, since it argued as to what the shape of the future would be, was pure ideology and had no relation to fact; and that the second, since it represented a modification based on actual history, was a true reflection of the situation that came into being, we should be wrong. Both concepts contained roughly equal measures of truth and ideology. Both, although introduced or applied by popular writers, serve well as the sociologist's "ideal types" or "polar concepts," marking out the limits of what might have happened, although neither one exactly described what did happen.

What, then, did happen? What was the result of the greatest migration in history? To what extent did the migrants merge into a single great community, and to what extent did they preserve their individuality? What parts of their lives and interests did they sacrifice to the new nation, and what did they retain for their original groupings?

It would be simple if the two concepts of the "melting pot" and the "nation of nations" could be assigned to different periods, if we could believe, as so many do, that the earlier immigrants (Germans, Irish, Norwegians, Swedes, English) did indeed assimilate rapidly, and that for them the "melting pot" worked, and appropriately described their history here; while the later immigrants—Italians, Jews, Poles, Slovaks, South Slavs, Greeks, and so on—did not assimilate as rapidly, and that to them the "nation of nations" concept was applicable.

On the basis of the facts, one could more easily argue the opposite. An important section of the major ethnic element in the earlier migration, the Germans, came with just the idea of creating a nation of their countrymen in America. In the 1830's there was considerable agitation among disappointed German liberals for the creation of a new, and free, German homeland in America, and a sizable number of Germans emigrated to Missouri and southern Illinois to carry out such plans. In the 1840's, large tracts of land were bought in Texas by German noblemen, and many thousands of German settlers were sent there with the intention of creating a German nation in Texas or even transforming Texas into a German state. A little later, a tremendous German migration took place into Wisconsin. The most perceptive writer on the Germans in America argues that at least some of those involved in fostering it were very likely motivated by the idea of making Wisconsin a German state— and they very nearly succeeded.[1] But the effect of this German effort at nation-building in America was only a few all-German schools, a few all-German towns, which by the third and fourth generation were speaking English and were demanding that the sermons be delivered in English.

The Germans in Europe were a nation before they became a state. Here in America, great numbers of German immigrants came only with the intention of fostering the development of the German nation-state in Europe, or, as we have seen, of creating it directly here, amidst conditions of freedom. The Irish, the second most important element in the earlier immigration, were also a nation before they were a state and, like the Germans, many came here with the intention of assisting the creation of an Irish state in Europe. On one occasion they did not hesitate to organize armies in America to attack Canada. But they did not, as did the Germans, make any serious efforts to create an Irish nation in the full sense of the word in America. In 1818, Irish associations in New York and Philadelphia did petition Congress for a large tract of land on which to settle Irish poor from the Eastern cities; but there seems to have

---

[1] John A. Hawgood, *The Tragedy of German-America* (New York: G. P. Putnam's Sons, 1940), pp. 216–217. The best account of these attempts to create "New Germanies" in America is in Hawgood, pp. 93–224.

been no national intention involved.[2] The decision of the U. S. Congress on this occasion ended once and for all the possibility of highly conscious European nations re-creating themselves in America. It refused to sell land in blocks for such purposes, insisting on individual sales and individual settlement. And this was certainly one of the most important decisions made in the first half-century of our national existence. In any case, it is highly questionable whether national homogeneity, even had Congress approved the Irish request, could have been maintained. Individual motives kept on asserting themselves, among the self-conscious Germans and others, and again and again caused the destruction of homogeneous colonies or led the immigrants who had come to settle on the land, with its conservative influences, to desert it for the city, with its powerful assimilative effects. The decision, on the national level, in favor of individual settlement, together with the tendency of individual settlers to strike out without the formal assistance of colonies and settlement companies (with their inevitable authority over the settlers), made it impossible, despite the ideology of the Germans and perhaps of some Irishmen, to create new nations in America.

A third factor was equally important, and that is the division of labor which took place on the frontier, where English-speaking elements, everywhere, were the first settlers, with all the prerogatives and power of such status. If, like the Mormons, the Germans had struck out into unsettled territory, they would have a state or states for themselves, with all the power—for example, to determine the official state language—that the constitution grants to states. But they never, not even in Wisconsin, had the power to mold a state in the way that the Mormons had in Utah. Everywhere the first-comers were Anglo-Saxons. Centuries in the new world had created the highly specialized breed of the frontiersman, who could do the initial clearing of wilderness while feeding himself with the aid of his rifle. Influential guidebooks written for German and other prospective immigrants warned the farmers of the Old World to avoid the frontier—it was not for them.[3] After the initial clearing the immigrant generally made a better farmer than the Anglo-Saxon. After all, the worst farmers in the country are the descendants of this pioneering stock in our Southern and border states; the

---

[2] See M. L. Hansen, *The Immigrant in American History* (Cambridge: Harvard University Press, 1940), p. 132.

[3] See, for example, Hawgood, *op. cit.,* p. 24.

best are the immigrants and their children.[4] But this economic prosperity attendant upon the superior techniques of the immigrants did not give them the power to mold the cultural and political life of the state. Again and again, we see how the first few thousand settlers in an area had far more influence in this respect than the hundreds of thousands who came later. The early settlers set up the school system and the legal system; they wrote the state constitution; they had the most political experience; they had the prestige which led the later more numerous groups—or at least their children—to conform to their standards, rather than vice versa.[5]

So, although many Germans, and some Irish, came with the intention of creating "a nation of nations," sizable numbers of them became leading ingredients of the "melting pot."

Perhaps more successful in creating nations, at least for a while, were what we might call the "intermediate" immigration—the Norwegians and Swedes. If the Irish and the Germans came from nations that were not yet states, the Norwegians and Swedes came from states that were not yet nations. The upper classes in all countries are aware of their existence as a nation; it is they who create national literature, a national language, a national culture. But, although these stages in the creation of a nation were completed quite early in England, France, and Germany and national consciousness had percolated down to the lower orders in those countries by the nineteenth century, in Norway and Sweden the creation of a nation in this sense was largely a product of the nineteenth century and did not seriously affect the peasantry until then. The peasants who came to this country from Scandinavia thought of themselves less as members of nations than as coming from a certain family and village and as belonging to a certain church.

Despite this, more of them were successful in creating a national existence in America than were the Germans; that is, they lived in homogeneous colonies using the native language, had newspapers, books, and publishing houses in their own language, a church conducting its activities in the native language, and schools to main-

---

[4] In 1920, the census showed that immigrant farmers, who constituted one tenth of all white farmers, owned one seventh of all white farm property. See E. S. de Brunner, *Immigrant Farmers and their Children* (Garden City: Doubleday, Doran & Company, Inc., 1929), p. 43.

[5] See, for the best account of this kind of development, a series of articles in the *Wisconsin Magazine of History*, by J. Schaefer, "The Yankee and The Teuton in Wisconsin," 1922–23, Volumes VI and VII; and for the general point, Hawgood, *op. cit.*, pp. 201–202.

tain the knowledge of the language and culture in succeeding generations—all this, which at best characterized only a limited portion of the Germans in America, held true for a much larger portion of the Norwegians and a sizable proportion of the Swedes. And this was accomplished without the aid of the ideology which moved the Germans. It was accomplished solely by the conditions of their settlement in America.

Although there was no need for the Norwegian or Swedish peasant to think of himself as a Norwegian or Swede in the home country—and indeed, he did not—he was immediately faced with the need for establishing his own identity here. He had to consider whether he should send his children to the English school or set up his own school; whether to attend the English-speaking church or build branches of the established church of the old country. The natural course for rural settlers—and the vast majority of Norwegians and Swedes, in the first years of their immigration, became farmers—was to seek out the regions where friends and countrymen had settled earlier. In this way, dense concentrations of settlement were established, marked off from the surrounding countryside, and these were inevitably described, by those living within them and those outside, as "Norwegian" and "Swedish." The conditions of settlement gave the answer to the question of what kind of cultural and religious life to lead. Although they arrived with no ideology and with no strong concern for, or knowledge of, Norwegian or Swedish culture, the segregation of Norwegian and Swedish farmers into homogeneous colonies inevitably led to the rise of an ideology and the growth of a concern for the old culture and religion, which concern was maintained for three generations.[6]

Insofar as the Germans settled under the same circumstances, they showed the same history; but the Germans were much more widely distributed, occupationally and geographically, than were the Norwegians and the Swedes. The Irish were more limited geographically, but they were concentrated in the cities, in which such an isolated folk existence was impossible, and they were even more dispersed occupationally than were the Germans.[7]

---

[6] For good accounts of the Scandinavian immigrants see Hansen, *ibid.;* and T. C. Blegen, *Norwegian Migration to America,* 2 volumes (Northfield, Minnesota: The Norwegian-American Historical Foundation, 1931 and 1940).

[7] For the evidence on these points of distribution (which is not nearly so full as one would wish, but sufficient to support the points made), see *Occupations of the First and Second Generation of Immigrants in the United States,* Reports of the Immigration Commission, 28 (which is based on the 1900 census); and Niles Carpenter, *Immigrants and Their Children,* 1920 (Washington, D. C.: Government Printing Office, 1927) (based on the 1920 census).

As long as these homogeneous colonies on the great plains could be maintained, such "nations within nations" could also continue; but the growth of the cities, the rise of greater attractions there than in farming, and the actual decline of the farming population were the means by which these colonies, too, were reduced, and these elements, too, in sizable measure, entered the melting pot. But in the isolated areas, they remained nations.

It is consequently rather simple-minded to think of the Germans, Irish, Norwegians, and Swedes as groups that easily assimilated to the Anglo-Saxons who had been primarily responsible for the creation of American culture. The Germans in particular had a strong feeling against assimilation. They felt that they had brought culture to a relatively benighted country—as indeed, in certain respects they had; they opposed intermarriage; they felt very strongly about the maintenance of Germanism. One might argue all this was sentiment, because they never succeeded in giving really strong institutional form to their feeling for German life and culture, and when World War I came, they buried their opposition and quite disappointed the German government with their American patriotism. And yet, as late as 1940, when President Franklin D. Roosevelt, who did not conceal his anti-Nazi feelings, was running against a candidate of German descent (Wendell Willkie), the old American Germandom showed itself in full force. German-language newspapers called openly for the support of the "German" candidate.[8] Counties indistinguishable, on census returns, from their neighbors, turned strongly against Roosevelt: these counties would have been distinguishable in the census returns of 1890, when they would have shown a high proportion of German-born from the great German migrations during the middle of the century. This close correlation between Roosevelt's losses and counties with a strong proportion of German descent was pointed out by Samuel Lubell, who further pointed out that this loss was most severe in those counties with the smallest proportion attending high school, those, in other words, most removed from the active centers of American culture.[9]

We can, I think, conclude that where these early immigrants were isolated and remained rural, they showed an amazing persistence in maintaining the old language, religion, and culture (to be more exact, we should say that variants of each developed in response to American conditions, for nothing was transplanted un-

[8] Louis Adamic, *Two-Way Passage* (New York: Harper & Brothers, 1941), pp. 216–218.

[9] Samuel Lubell, *The Future of American Politics* (New York: Harper & Brothers, 1952), pp. 131–132, 148.

changed). For those who settled in cities, as did the Irish, many of the Germans, and the later Norwegians and Swedes, a shorter time sufficed to remove the language and culture they had brought with them.

But in the cities another factor came into play to maintain cohesion, which also had the same effect on the farms; that was ideology. The urban Irish did not live under circumstances that permitted them to construct in America the amazing replicas of the old country that rural settlers were able to create in many places. They became culturally indistinguishable from their surroundings much faster than if they had become farmers; but they continued to be distinguished by their strong concern for the fate of the old country.

We can thus point to two very distinct sources in the complex of factors preventing the full assimilation of the early immigrant groups: one arose from the conditions of settlement (isolation and concentration); one arose from ideological commitment. The Germans were strengthened in their apartness by both; the Irish by the latter; the Norwegians and Swedes, with no country to free from a foreign yoke, only by the former.

The newer immigrants showed the same range of variability, with the same, as well as different, factors at work. They also came from nations struggling to become states (Poles, Lithuanians, Slovaks, Croats, Slovenes), and states struggling to become nations (Italy and Turkey and Greece) as well as areas quite outside these Western concepts of state and nation (Syrians); and they included, as their second most numerous element, a people (the Jews) who fall into none of these categories easily. But, reflecting the far more backward conditions of Eastern and Southern Europe, almost all these groups were, unlike the earlier immigrants, so completely cut off from the political life of the areas from which they came—which, in almost every case, was the monopoly not only of a different class, but of a different people—that an ideology brought from Europe could have little to do with preventing their assimilation.

However, the newcomers became nations in America. As Max Ascoli writes of the Italians (we must remember that the great mass of Italian immigrants, who rank first in the new immigration, as the Germans rank first in the old, come from the depressed South): "They became Americans before they ever were Italians." [10] Indeed,

---

[10] In *Group Relations and Group Antagonisms*, edited by R. M. MacIver (New York: Harper & Brothers, 1944), p. 32.

the effort of creating a national language, a task which the Western European nations had accomplished centuries before, was considerably facilitated for these Eastern peoples by American emigration. The coming together in American cities of people of various villages speaking various dialects required the creation of a common language, understood by all. The first newspaper in the Lithuanian language was published in this country, not in Lithuania.[11] The urbanization of many East European peoples occurred in America, not in Europe, and the effects of urbanization, its breaking down of local variation, its creation of some common denominator of nationality, its replacement of the subideological feelings of villagers with a variety of modern ideologies—these effects, all significant in making the East European peoples nations, were in large measure first displayed among them here in America. The Erse revival began in Boston,[12] and the nation of Czechoslovakia was launched at a meeting in Pittsburgh. And all this should not surprise us too much when we realize that some European areas were so depopulated that the numbers of immigrants and their descendants in America sometimes equaled or surpassed those who were left behind.

If nations like Czechoslovakia were in large measure created here in America, other immigrants were to discover in coming to America that they had left nations behind—nations in which they had had no part at home. Thus, the American relatives of Southern Italians (to whom, as Ignazio Silone and Carlo Levi describe them, the Ethiopian war meant nothing more than another affliction visited upon them by the alien government of the North) became Italian patriots in America, supporting here the war to which they would have been indifferent at home.

The backwardness of these newer peoples had one other major consequence related to the problem of their continuance as distinct groups in America. It was among these groups that the violent turning away of the second generation from the life of the first—that intense passion for Americanization which so often characterizes children of immigrants, as well as large numbers of immigrants proper—became an important phenomenon. Thorstein Veblen, son of a Norwegian immigrant, was raised speaking his father's language and going to his father's church. If he ever had a passion for assimilation, it could be countered by the pull of an ancient culture

---

[11] Robert E. Park, *The Immigrant Press and Its Control* (New York: Harper & Brothers, 1922), p. 50.

[12] Park, *op. cit.,* p. 50.

which the Anglo-Saxon world respected: he could translate Icelandic sagas.

Similarly, one can understand how it was possible for German culture to maintain itself among such large numbers in the second and third generation; had it not been for the trauma of World War I, it would undoubtedly have been much stronger among the fourth generation than it is today. For not only could the Germans boast a connection with one of the strongest and most advanced nations in the world; the Americans themselves, up until World War I, sent their most promising students to study in German universities.

How much sadder was the condition of Slovaks and Ruthenians and Croats! If some intellectuals in these groups were creating a national language and culture, their own peasants—let alone the rest of the world—knew nothing of it. They could not even answer the common American question, "What are you?" They are listed in immigration and census statistics indiscriminately as natives of "Austria-Hungary," and they themselves often lacked any clearer notion of who they were than the Americans who dubbed them "bohunks." [18] On the one hand, the conditions of existence in a strange land led them to come together to found newspapers and beneficial societies, and eventually to determine to take pride in their ancestry and some interest in their homelands. But at the same time, the fact that they came from nations of peasants, caste nations without an aristocracy or a middle class, and with only the beginnings of an intelligentsia, meant that large numbers of them were unable to define themselves, as the earlier immigrants had done, as members of ancient and honorable peoples.

In all this, the Italians were somewhat more fortunate. For while they were really in the same position, the accidents of history had tied them up with the advanced nation of North Italy; and while they may never have heard of Michelangelo or Dante at home, here they and their children, reading the new Italian press created for their guidance, could learn of them and take pride in them. The Jews, as usual, were in an ambiguous position, being the most despised and the most praised among nations at the same time; and they showed a complete range from those who rejected their parents and culture most completely, to those most fierce in their attachment to them, thus paralleling the feelings of anti-Semites and philo-Semites outside their ranks.

The tragedy of these nationless and past-less immigrants has no-

---

[18] The earlier Lithuanian immigrants called themselves Poles. See Park, *op. cit.*, p. 51.

where been better told than in a book by Louis Adamic.[14] Adamic, himself an immigrant from one of those relatively history-less peoples of the Balkans, was an indefatigable and passionate seeker after knowledge of the history of these groups in America. He traveled around the country; he spoke before and with groups of second generation Poles, Ukrainians, South Slavs, and others. He wrote more on this problem than anyone else, and he was as perplexed after he had written his fifth book on the subject as he was before he had written the first. He was deeply worried about the second generation arising from people in whom they felt they could take no pride. He met this second generation all over the country, and he found them changing their names and becoming more Americanized in their attachments to fads and surface mannerisms than the "Americans" themselves. Since they were people who had rejected their past, whose lives had apparently begun only yesterday, they seemed, to themselves and others, rootless and unreal. In *What's Your Name?* Adamic tells at great length the story of the son of a Lemko coal miner, who had come to hear Adamic lecture once in Cleveland. The Lemkoes are one of those small peoples of the Carpathians related to the Slovaks and the Ruthenians and who, one guesses, ended up a separate people rather than a subgroup or a dialect simply through accident. In the town where the father was a coal miner, there were a number of Lemkoes, but even there the matter of self-definition arose. One could choose to go to a variety of churches. One could assimilate to one of the dominant ethnic groups among the coal miners, or continue to assert one's identity as a Lemko, or become an American. The man who told Adamic his story decided to change his name and become an "American," without further identification. The difficulties and miseries that began to plague him as he got a job as a history teacher, married, and had a child, are utterly convincing; but the solution of his problems—his return to his original name, and his acceptance of his illiterate father—is not.

And yet, while psychologically unconvincing, the story of the acceptance of his origins by this son of a Lemko immigrant incorporates an important sociological truth: that is, that the course of immigrant assimilation in America (and presumably many similar social processes) is not linear; while there is a period of rejection of one's past and of passionate acceptance of the new culture, it is often succeeded by a return, in some sense, to the original culture. Of course, the culture one returns to is not the culture one left:

---

14 *What's Your Name?* (New York: Harper & Brothers, 1942).

thus, the nature of the interest of some young Jews today in their East European background is perhaps more remote from the real character of East European Jewish life than their fathers' rebellion against that life, for at least the rebellion arose from direct contact with it. Yet, on an ideological level, if not on the level of culture, the third generation shows a tendency to return to the first. (We use the terms first, second, and third generations not only to refer literally to immigrants, their children, and their grandchildren; very often the antagonistic reaction of the "second generation" is found among the immigrants themselves, the "returning" reaction of the third generation among their children. What we speak of are three phases that may be condensed into the history of a single individual, or expanded to cover the history of four.)

This important phenomenon was first discussed, to my knowledge, by our greatest student of immigration, Marcus L. Hansen, in a talk given to the Augustana Historical Society ("The Problem of the Third Generation Immigrant," Rock Island, 1938). His perception was all the more remarkable in that he discovered this third-generation reaction among those groups in whom, to my mind, it was mildest and least impressive: the earlier immigrant groups of Scotch-Irish, Germans, and Scandinavians. Among these groups, the steady disintegration of the culture brought by the immigrants themselves proceeded evenly. There were no important shocks, such as later immigrants received in the form of quota acts, alien registration acts, and anti-immigrant agitation, for despite the presence of this type of sentiment throughout American history, it was never so strong against the Northern and Western European immigrants as it was against those from Eastern and Southern Europe. The one great shock the even development of this earlier element suffered was World War I, which served rather to hasten the abandonment of German culture and to short-circuit a fully developed third-generation reaction.

I think it was just in the newer groups (none of whom had developed third generations of any size when Hansen wrote in 1938), that the antagonistic and rejecting attitude of the second generation as well as the "return" of the third generation was most prominent. The voting blocs of Poles, Italians, and Jews were never so important as they were in the 1940's and 1950's.[15] In part, of course, this was because a greater number of them were voting; in part, because of the effects of World War II. But these groups would not have shown such strong, common reactions had they not main-

---

[15] See Lubell, *op. cit.*, throughout, for material on this point.

tained some common identity which made it possible for events to affect them, at least in some measure, as a group.

We have already pointed out that these later groups (except for the Jews) did not so much bring nationalistic ideologies from Europe as develop them while discovering their identity in America. To this extent, therefore, the "return" reaction of the third generation was already apparent in the first. But these original discoverers of their nationality had a difficult time keeping any sizable numbers of their children close to it. However, other factors soon came into play to bring the wandering children back to their past. For one thing, it is now more difficult to maintain ethnic anonymity than it was fifty years ago. When America's character as an Anglo-Saxon nation was most obvious, incoming immigrants formed no threat, for they were often in small enough numbers to be either invisible or exotic, and they did not reinforce a pre-existing mass of their compatriots. Thus, they often found it easy to assimilate, or hard to resist the conditions making it so easy. We find in many towns records of the existence of groups of Jews in the early part of the nineteenth century who had completely disappeared by the twentieth; in some cases, we can trace the details of their disappearance by intermarriage and conversion. If such a hardy element disappeared, it is easy to believe that the spearheads of other ethnic elements were also swallowed up in a different America.

But this was not very likely in twentieth-century America. A century of immigration had alerted the "native" population to the characteristics of immigrant groups; a century of agitation had made them exclusivist; a society in which large, bureaucratic, organizations played a greater role, in which the habits of the frontier were no longer even a memory, in which a hectic rate of growth and expansion had been succeeded by somewhat greater stability, led to a stronger emphasis upon a man's origins and his "type." In sum, "respectability" had become an important value in American life. Although it led, on the one hand, to a more complete effort by some individuals to deny their origins by name-changing and religion-changing in order to gain the advantages held by the "respectable" elements of the society, it also led many others to react by asserting their individuality more sharply.

It is this development in American society itself, as well as certain subsidiary factors (such as World War II, and the heightening of ethnic consciousness it brought) which has produced on a wide and important scale a "third-generation" reaction among the newer immigrants. This has happened even though the newer immigrants, for the most part, live in cities, where in the earlier days they were most easily assimilated. But today, the cities and towns are the chief seats of the new cult of respectability.

The third-generation reaction among the newer groups, it would seem, affects to some extent the earlier groups; it gives them a justification for asserting a common interest. The Germans, despite the loss of the culture which was their glory up to 1914, again re-establish themselves in the form of an underground common identity, scarcely acknowledged even to themselves. Yet the existence of a common reaction to events on the part of many of German descent made them almost as important in the election of 1940 as they were in that of 1860.

To return to the two concepts with which we began: The "melting pot" described the reality of assimilation which has characterized, to some extent, and in every period, each one of the ethnic groups migrating to this country. The "nation of nations" has described a different reality in different periods of our history. Until 1890 or 1900, homogeneous colonies were to be found, principally on the great plains but to some extent everywhere in the country, that maintained the ethnic language and religion, and were real fragments of nations in America. To some extent they exist today. But today the nations that make up America, and that Louis Adamic spoke of, are no longer of this type. They do not find justification in a separate language, religion, and culture, all of which have succumbed to the eroding process of American life. The descendants of European nations in America are now completely divorced from their origins: they speak English, participate in American culture, and observe Americanized forms of the ancestral religions. Their justification for existence might be called on one level nostalgia, on another ideology. And this ideology has no organic relation to their real individual pasts but is rather in large measure a reaction to the conditions of life in the twentieth-century United States and the twentieth-century world.

From the point of view of any classic or legitimate idea of "nation," the "nations" of Poles, Jews, Italians, and so on, that now and then show themselves in American politics and culture, are empty or ghost nations. This is not to say they do not perform some functions, and even valuable functions, in American life, although to describe and analyze them would take us into another discussion. Yet, there is no question that the American groups to which these classic national identifications are attached are characterized by a vague nostalgia and an undefined ideology, rather than by any of the normal attributes of the term "nation."

In this perspective, it is not easy to envisage the role of the ethnic groups in the American future. We know that the action of the melting pot will continue, at different rates for each group, and at different rates for the different elements of each group (the detailed variations are mostly unknown, for lack of research). We know that the fragments of real nations scattered about the country will be worn away. What is most questionable is the status and future prospects of the "empty" or "ghost" nations, built around ideologies of support of the home countries, and drawing their real strength, I believe, from experiences in America which make those who participate in them feel less than full Americans. Even the partial and subconscious re-establishment of the German nation in the form of "isolationism" and "nationalism" stems from experiences which make them feel more disadvantaged than other Americans—that is, the need to participate in two wars against their ancestral homeland. Whether these empty nations are only given the illusion of a relatively vigorous life by recent developments in Europe; whether they are not perhaps stimulated by politicians who are attracted to (and help create) any partial grouping that may support an appeal to special interest; or whether the conditions of American life are not such as to maintain and strengthen them for some time to come: these and many other questions remain. This writer tends, for many reasons, to hold to the last alternative.

But this chapter has already proceeded perilously far along the branches of generalization from a thin trunk of solid research, and we must simply have more facts before we can say more or even say as much as we already have with a satisfactory feeling of security.

THE STATE AND SOCIETY

8

INDIVIDUAL LIBERTY TODAY: CHALLENGE AND PROSPECT

THOMAS I. COOK

In the broadest sense, the search of the political philosopher in our day has been to provide an adequate theory for interpreting the direction of the open and experimental democratic society under conditions of industrialism, of sub-continental organization, and of world-wide interrelations of peoples. The United States, the first country to combine constitutional democracy, sub-continental organization, and highly developed industrial technology, provides a vast exhibition for the philosopher bent on such a task; and in the history of its institutions and ideas it reveals the problems and difficulties involved in such a combination. Europe, on the other hand, is the source of the generic ideals to be combined, the Greek concept of the cultured citizen and the Christian ideal of the ultimate moral person.

The American experience and attitude have begotten a pluralism in institutions and a pluralistic and individualistic outlook. They have also produced a pragmatic and instrumentalist philosophy whose secular protestantism makes closed monistic systems of thought irrelevant and renders statism abhorrent (but not impossible). Yet our way of life and thought tends to be inimical to societal unity and it tends, despite nobler aspiration and deeper insight, to undue stress on means and, consequently, to the unintended rejection of that ethical universalism without which libertarian diversity becomes destructive or is sacrificed at last to an imposed absolutism.

European philosophies, however, for all their concern with universalism, have themselves too frequently ended in absolutes, when they have not led to a negative skepticism through inability to create

177

or adequately to defend certainties initially sought. Absolutes, certainly, have been the norm of Idealist philosophy and political thought, even in so liberal and sensitive an Idealist as T. H. Green. Nor has English empiricism here fared better, at least on the political side. Rather, it has offered the concept of a legal and political sovereignty as the alternative to the German Idealist state or nation. Attempted revolt, as in the case of H. J. Laski, has led first to the near-anarchism of extreme pluralism (which is also an American danger) and then to a return to the monistic statism characteristic of a Europe of nation-states descended from royal absolutism, even though Marxist monism be in name anti-state.

The uncompleted quest, so vital in a period where the United States is by virtue of its power the leader of the democratic cause, is to combine a universalist insight which shall provide a moral basis for an integrated state-society, and for a wider order, with the pluralistic sense of variety, at once realistic and moral, which shall be insurance against the denial of personality.

That search, already begun but aborted in Europe, and particularly in England, before the period of American ascendancy, owes much to both utilitarian and neo-utilitarian empiricism and to British neo-Idealism. It came closest to solution, perhaps, in the teachings of L. T. Hobhouse, whose ideal of dynamic harmony rested precisely on an attempt to combine a liberal and humane empirical sense of variety with a metaphysician's longing for unity, not incompatible with a rejection of formal, and politically dangerous, Idealism.

But, for reasons already indicated, it is the United States which alone has hitherto provided the milieu for both the posing of this enduring problem and for its solution in our time—a solution, moreover, that gives promise of being more universal than has ever been possible until now.

Toward that solution various thinkers have already contributed. Here, too, the initial contributions have, without any planning, appeared to be at opposite poles. On the one side stand James, Mead, and Dewey, who, in emphasizing variety and openness, have yet in their succession sought to defend a hierarchy of values while avoiding and even rejecting system or dogma. In Dewey, at least, that search has ended in a combination of generous-minded nobility and imprecision in philosophy which, however inspiring and suggestive, is, at least on problems of state and citizen, lacking in the clarity needed for public policy and political ethics. On the other side are ranged Royce and Hocking. Both tended, in widely diverse ways, to an Idealist overemphasis, although both likewise endeavored to reconcile Idealism with, and render it serviceable to, the American tradition and practice of group life and individualism. Their success was, however, limited; and neither compounded effectively the needs of community, the reality of society, the necessity of state, the instrumentality of government, with the final claims of the person.

It is here that Robert MacIver has made his special contribution. Schooled at once in Scottish and British empiricism and in English neo-Idealism; sympathetic, like Ernest Barker, to pluralist criticism while aware of the necessity of an organizing and functioning state; at once a philosopher and a sociologist—even before coming to this country he had, in *Community* and in *The Modern State,* proposed and analyzed the central issue stated above. In later years he broadened and deepened a political theory, with its roots in good sense and temperamental moderation, by a further sociological awareness informed by philosophy and related to the American milieu. *The Web of Government* was a major step toward the reconciling of concepts of societal interest and the inescapable state through the mediation of instrumental government. *Leviathan and the People,* admittedly a *livre de circonstance,* tackled in the light of the established fundamentals the urgent issue indicated in its title and defended the rightful ultimacy of the person. In essence it has been MacIver's special task to restate the problem of individual, group, and state in such a way as to avoid the empirical-idealist alternative, and to provide foundations for a democratic philosophy which shall utilize the insights of both while avoiding their errors and biases. The full carrying out of that undertaking is the task he has bequeathed. It is also the great imperative of the Western, and more especially of the American, ethical and political tradition; it is the vital necessity for the security and progress of free society.

What follows is an attempt, after an initial statement of a view of liberty now widely accepted, largely as a result of the impact of MacIver's work, to pursue further the analysis and application of the root idea and to call attention to a particular distinction which seems urgently necessary, in the light of current problems.

Liberty and Responsibility. For the purpose at hand, liberty may be defined in the conventional way as absence of restraint on the wills and activities of persons. Given the social character of man, such absence of restraint cannot be absolute. So that the human being may function with any effectiveness, a knowable and widely known social and legal context, at once restraining and empowering, is necessary. Indeed, insofar as law and the fabric of social institutions do not provide a framework for the effective pursuit of human purposes, men dissipate their energies fruitlessly and suffer a sense of frustration. Nevertheless, that necessary limitation accepted, the absence of restraint is a good. Further limitation and abridgement are properly to be undertaken only when their advocates are able to prove that such action will at once strengthen the framework and contribute to, rather than diminish, the possibilities of effective pursuit of human goals.

The implication of the preceding definition of freedom is that men do have the capacity to will, that they are able to make choices between meaningful alternatives. Men may, indeed, act irrationally, yet man as a moral being possesses a certain degree of rationality. The very concept of responsibility rests on the possibility that alternatives are perceived, that meaningful choice is actually open, and that persons are answerable for the choices they make.

To tender consciences this doctrine of responsibility appears harsh. They have rightly stressed the imperfections of the social order within which choices are made, the collective responsibility of all for that order, and the real, though limited, sharing of guilt with those who make wrong choices. But whereas an earlier age took contrition and mercy to be the proper inferences from, and corollaries of, this situation, many moderns, turning the conditions of choice into conditioning, and conditioning into causation, utterly exculpate the actor. Hence, by rendering praise and blame equally irrelevant, they have, with misdirected pity and a false concept of determinism, made pity and sympathy themselves meaningless through making man amoral. By a curious illogic, such thinkers have often defended passionately the claims of their fellows to liberty, without confronting the implication for society of divorcing liberty from responsibility, or the irrelevance of liberty to the person if he is not a moral being.

Very different in its course, yet similar in its final amoralistic implication, is the exaggeration of the harshness of the doctrine of responsibility by stress on the tendency of men, left alone, to make wrong choices. This doctrine, stated with moderation, may properly note the value of social reforms and social-political controls as means to prevent constant and insistent temptation to wrongdoing or to moral corruption. That, broadly, was the position taken by the Oxford Idealist, T. H. Green. It was a true doctrine of moral risk-taking and denied at once human perfectability and any normally dominant tendency to viciousness. The extreme of this position, however, is that men, either evil or ignorant or both, will make wrong judgments unless continuously and forcibly prevented; and that, thereby destroying their own and others' security, they will end in total degradation. Hence, for the safety and well-being both of themselves and of their fellows, strong government must abridge, and even deny, liberty. That is, because men make wrong choices it is desirable, not simply to define carefully the range of choice open to them, but to prevent them from making any choices in realms deemed politically and socially significant. Hence, as a corollary, since no one advocates mere inactivity, it is desirable, and even necessary, through law and leadership backed by force and propaganda, to tell them what they are to do. This viewpoint, most characteristic of totalitarianism, tends also to be the practice of majoritarian democracy, particularly when reinforced by a confidence in the power of law to make men good, by lack of doubt as to what constitutes the good, and by survivals of the puritan and puritanical heritage.

The initial thesis here propounded is, then, that individual liberty and responsibility are complementary. Freedom without responsibility and responsibility without freedom are not consonant with human nature and need, nor with the lasting well-being of society. Under constitutional democracy alone can liberty and responsibility function in proper relation. Straight majoritarian democracy is morally inadequate and practically dangerous. Save in those areas where public choices have to be made between different and incompatible goods, including different liberties, decision by majorities is irrelevant, improper, and presumptuous. Majoritarian democracy, as many classical thinkers already realized, can readily become a form of tyranny. Nowadays it does so through a kind of suicide: an abdication to a strong, charismatic leader, who, though he may profess himself demophil, in practice is obviously inimical to democracy.

But the concepts of individual freedom with responsibility, and of constitutional democracy as limited government with protected individual rights, manifestly have as their corollary a doctrine of the necessity of moral risk-taking for the sake of development of the person, and therefore of a right to a protected realm of risk-taking. Doubt as to the necessity of such risk is nevertheless the reason that in our own day so many people are prepared to abandon judgment, to accent irresponsible leadership, and to see themselves and their fellows more constrained than is required from the point of view of the social compatability of different values and different liberties. The impersonality of modern society, the weakness of men in a complex world they scarcely understand, their resultant uncertainties and fears, and their consequent inadequacy and impotence, lead them to seek security at whatever costs. Men deem they can escape risk, thereby denying their essential humanity and destroying or abandoning the institutions necessary for its expression and growth.

In essence, however, the lot of man is a tragic one. The tragedy is not to be abolished by any acts of individuals or of rulers. The search for a security which will prescribe men's duties, render their responses automatic, and reduce them to satisfied organismic mechanisms is mere delusion. Just because human beings are at once individuated and social there are bound to be conflicts of desires, of aspirations, of obligations.

Yet, soon or late, selfish interests are transformed into rational interests of persons. Conflicts of diverse persons, engaged in divergent pursuits, and seeking varied satisfactions, lead to the reality and the integrity of conscience. Finally, just because the political order is external and instrumental, the enlightened conscience and the state come into conflict. Such conflicts are not to be genuinely solved by external power, by force alone. Neither supremacy of the majority nor the concept of the ethical ultimacy of positive man-made laws provide a lasting answer. But constitutional democracy at least avoids much frustration, leads to the maximum human dignity, and provides a basis and an ethos for reconsideration and redefinition of spheres in which, by reason of the imperfection of men and their institutions, such tragedies as occur are (even if inevitable) not forever insuperable.

The very condition of man's development is, then, the recognition of his finiteness: the fundamental basis at once of liberty and of responsibility. Such recognition implies an awareness that freedom may end in disaster. But that finiteness, although its corollary is freedom and risk-taking, does not imply a diminished or passive policeman-state. The role of government is precisely to insure conditions of fruitful, as against fruitless, risk-taking. Under different circumstances that role necessitates a broad or narrow role for government. The criterion is always the fulfillment of that all-inclusive function of governments. Hence, whatever its partial truth in its day, the concept of laissez faire was even then, as it is most clearly now, narrowing and misguided. Essentially it applied as a dogma what was at best a directive for the economic realm. As principle, the teaching is sound in what may properly be called the moral-intellectual realm. There the connection between risk, uncertainty, and profit is clear enough. The very cost of that cultural development, which is ultimately the development of individuals as persons, is the taking of risks, and the square confrontation of the tragedy implicit in the uncertainties following from men's finiteness, and implicit also in the very concepts of character-development and fulfillment.

The Impulse to Dominate. What are the implications of these principles, or of this attitude toward life, for individual liberty and for democracy in our time? The American tradition, upon which we must build, has been characterized by a very real belief in individualism, or in various types of individualisms. These have marked not less the agrarian than the industrial approach to, and way of, life. Combined with that individualism has been a profound and widespread activism, conscious or unconscious. That spirit has emphasized the need at once for individual and for group activity; and it has, especially when related to a genuine or simulated puritanism, inspired much of the ardor to do good to others, either by social pressure or through law. That ardor, however, has generally revealed rather little tender concern for personalities or for freedom. The activism which is deep in our flesh and bones has formed the basis of our psychological attachment to freedom and of our belief in that kind of public and cooperative action which may threaten the liberties of others. It may thereby hamper their very development and fulfillment as persons in the name of insuring their salvation.

The dangers to liberty from such activism are today rendered more serious by reason of our recognition of the nonrational element in man, the danger of its triumph, and of the possibility of its use for controlling him. In an earlier period, out of which came some of the greatest formal defenses of liberty, men believed in the essential rationality of man. They looked at man through the glasses of John Locke and his successors. Psychology, nominally empirical, and actually both introspective and associationist, was conceived on the basis of man as a being at rest, isolated and reasoning rather than acting. Even where, to coin a term, he was "passioning," he was doing so in a calm situation, by himself. His behavior in battle, in riot, in private quarrels, was indeed well known, but was regarded largely as aberration, as not the real self, and in any event as something to be overcome by reason. Activity was, or ought to be, the transformation into action, into public behavior and, where necessary, into institutional controls, of the insights of calm reason. Leadership was justified by possession in superior degree of that reason, or of those economic and familial heritages and endowments which presumably permitted its flowering.

The psychology and the doctrine of leadership were, no doubt, alike inadequate. So, too, were the vastly different, later, and romantic visions of energized democracy of Whitman and the independent, but ultimately upright, virtues of Bret Harte's miners. But the activism of the latter did not countenance disrespect for individual variety nor the intolerance of a facile perfectionism which forced men into a mold of goodness defined by the collective mass; while the former were favorable to those very liberties of calm privacy now so under attack.

Today we have become aware that man is equally a person whether in isolation, calm, rational, and contemplative, and in the smaller activities of the group where personality is not overwhelmed, or in his actions and responses as part of a crowd, or even of a mob. We are aware, indeed, that there is some degree of irrationality even in his most contemplative life, as well as in his mass responses. Leaders now learn how to play on his emotions, to organize the collectivity, and to evoke the latent desires in mass or in majority in order to impose their own moral standards. At best they may thereby endeavor to prevent socially deleterious risk-taking by the individual, as well as activities deemed to insult, if not to hurt, the majority. Unconvinced of the sure prevalence of reason in society, and uncertain of its dominance in the individual, they are ready, with widespread support, to impose standards as though risk could be eliminated.

Threats to the abridgement of liberties which are not simply traditional, but fundamental, arise from the conviction that it is impossible to permit men to go their own way without disaster to themselves and to society. Those threats are increased through the development of modern technology, which on the one hand creates an enormous social complexity, and on the other hand encourages confidence in the ability to control. Science itself is the means. Its triumphs readily lead to a scientistic conviction of the possibility of complete knowledge, of social prediction, and of potential overall social control. This conviction is reinforced by modern developments of personnel management and of techniques of public administration generally.

The conclusion that modern complexity and social interdependence necessitate radical redefinition of liberty is not in itself evil. Yet the psychic responses of men rendered insecure by complexity may lead, not to a genuinely liberating because functionally relevant redefinition, but to support of, and finally dominance by, those who, anxious to impose order for the sake of selfish power and prestige, exploit the very desire for security in a manner which leads to an unwillingness for moral risk-taking, and then to the abandonment or destruction of the institutional arrangements which alone make it effectively possible.

The Danger of the Drift to Statism. Such, then, are the new dangers to moral man and to liberal democratic society; and they are not lightly to be dismissed. Nevertheless, the congruence and the compatibility of limited democracy and industrial technology, the marks of the American adventure, make possible as never before in recorded history the full release of the energies of men, not only in instrumental functioning, but also in the pursuit of cultural fulfillment. For together these preconditions of full humanity make materially and spiritually available here, and elsewhere to a lesser degree, that leisure necessary for the effective risk-taking of the spirit which creates and promotes cultures. Such leisure will allow men to combine the essential insight that flows from Greek, and above all from Aristotelian, philosophy with the yet more essential insight of the Christian way of life. The former stresses the nature of citizenship as participation by men who have leisure and are delivered from arduous work in the realm of means only, while the latter proclaims that moral personality always constitutes a limit on the public order, on state and on government, and that men must enjoy the withdrawal from the market-place necessary to cultivation of personality.

The means to such realizations are already available. Modern industrial technology (itself so closely bound up with constitutional liberty) has provided that diversity of consumer goods which allow men of different temperaments the means more adequately to pursue their vocations and avocations. Its provision of adequacy of goods far beyond animal necessities, now reasonably secure short of devastating war, permits the leisure and rest necessary to a creative consumption. It permits liberty and effectiveness in the pursuit of varied whims and, more important, of cultural and spiritual callings. Such wants and such pursuits are without known limits. But, happily, in the realm of final goods diverse and divergent undertakings are generally possible without inevitable conflicts between persons—a condition not true of the functional and instrumental realm. Hence the promise implicit in constitutional freedom and in free enterprise can now be to a great extent fulfilled in the proper and enduring realm.

Yet, to insure that fulfillment requires increased limitations upon certain classical rights and liberties in the instrumental realm, precisely in order that industry may continuously and smoothly serve these higher purposes. Such limitations, the rationale of the welfare state, are nevertheless in practice a source of danger: regulation tends toward centralization, centralization tends toward statism. Popular demands for the use of power to control the instrumental realm tend imperceptibly to be transferred to the realm of ultimate goals, of personal fulfillment. The genuine liberty made possible through use and control of nature and through industrial organization tends to be frustrated by unnecessary extension of those interferences whose rationale is only the equitable distribution of the means of access to enduring personal satisfactions.

The irony of the situation is that consensus within the political order, necessary to a stable harmony and to an ever creative but never completed unification which will permit the flourishing of personal diversity, too readily becomes totalitarian. For the recognized necessity turns into a demand for total conformity. Consensus becomes the glorification of a mythical common end, secular in character, to which all must submit. In the name of a supposed collective necessity, every person is sacrificed. The confusion between needful consensus and totalitarian unity is the result, indeed, of a long history. The secular rationalism which reached puberty in the Renaissance and came of age in the seventeenth and eighteenth centuries, through the praise of power devoted to worldly ends, tended to leave man naked before his ruler rather than before his Creator. Similarly Protestantism, which, though not uniquely responsible, was so important alike in the genesis and development of modern capitalism and modern constitutionalism, led, through the dissidence of dissent itself, to threats of social disruption in the absence of a strong ruler and by reason of the fragmentation of spiritual authority. As a consequence, the moral conscience came to lack a common institutional embodiment or interpreter, just when the availability of material goods was inducing an amoral concern with the exercise of power. In due time, it is true, industrial technology, at least in these United States, produced the long-desired means to the good life in sufficient quantity to permit effective citizenship and genuine personality development to all. Up to that point, however, men's energies were consecrated to the development of means, of resources, and of skills. Their behavior, however self-interested, appears in retrospect sacrificial. But the outlook they developed in the course of their business had meanwhile become a threat to the achievement of those very ends their work made possible.

In our own time and place—by happy fortune—ethical insight and institutional tradition on the one hand, and practical knowledge and know-how on the other, now unite to offer hitherto unique opportunities for that classless society of friendly competition and diverse insight, free of want, creative, which Marx envisioned as possible only on a very different pattern. Yet here, too, men find themselves subtly driven toward the collective self-frustration of totalitarian power used for incredibly narrowed purposes. To defend and maintain liberty within particular states, and to extend it on a universal scale, which, for reasons indicated, ought to be easier than in earlier times, is today a task of heroic difficulty. The very varieties of belief and unbelief, which are presumably good in a world ever seeking but never fully finding enlightenment, combine with the necessities of political control to defeat freedom, and so to hinder their own survival. For today we lack, probably beyond any hope of creation, what the medieval order possessed: a spiritual power which may be the counterpoise of political order. We cannot, for better and for worse, call upon an agreed custodian, supernatural in character, of the liberty of the human spirit. We have escaped indeed the dangers of repressive orthodoxy from such a power. But we are at present in a situation of competing ideological orthodoxies actually or potentially far more oppressive, and far less spiritually enlightened, by reason of the narrowing of their devotion to things instrumental.

The Majority Threat to Liberty. The struggle for constitutionalism from the seventeenth century on, though devoted to the protection of liberty within the political order and against government, was (despite its religious inspiration and support) largely an endeavor to lift our social selves by our own bootstraps. In the post-Reformation world, absolute and increasingly arbitrary executive authority developed along with, and largely as a corollary of, the independent and this-worldly nation-state. In being made citizens, men were rendered subjects; and it was as citizens or as nationals within particular countries that they had to struggle for their liberation. Their objective was, on the one hand, participation in the making of the national destiny, and, on the other, withdrawal from the purview of government of a major and vital area of their lives, to be protected by guaranteed rights. But the consequence of their success was first identification with, and then subordination within, the particular nation. Subsequently, in the nineteenth century the struggle of various conscious nationalities for the right of self-determination actually reinforced rather than combatted this containment of man within the nation-state, itself originally a liberating force in the secular sphere. He became dependent on its internal pressures, even though he professedly helped create them as he sought to become a dignified citizen. Citizenship, envisioned as handmaiden to personality, too readily became a self-imposed imprisonment of the self.

Moreover, with the development of the Industrial Revolution constitutionalized power tended to be transformed into democratic power. With the growth of late nineteenth-century imperialism, emphasis on man as national led, through identification, toward democratic totalitarianism: the nation, as national people under representative institutions, was envisioned as collective master because it was the collective embodiment and source of common fulfillment. The nation was even depicted in organismic fashion, or in the image of the Idealist state. The very reduction of industrial and city man to mass man led toward denial of effective scope for cultural development by the individual as person, and to assertion of the psychic sufficiency of his sharing in national pride and power. Similarly, the very doctrine of economic liberty, especially in regions where sharing of products was conspicuously inadequate, encouraged a passionate identification of men with their nation, or, yet more sinister, with their supposed race. Constitutional liberty, difficult although not impossible to attain in opposition to the arbitrariness of absolute monarchy, has proved exceedingly difficult to maintain in the face of convinced majorities whose members lacked security and self-confidence and sought facile superiority through the imposition of collective power. People en masse suffered from that sense of anomy which is so oppressive a part of our civilization. In suffering, they tended to view a certain uniformity of manners and morals as necessary to demonstrate their collective superiority as nation or race, and to secure and reassert their stature and uprightness. They confused that demonstration with the possession of personal dignity and inner worth.

But that development is an abandonment of personal responsibility and an escape from freedom at the very time and under the very conditions which at last make freedom with responsibility a practicable adventure for all, rather than for a limited aristocratic class. Industrial production and advanced technology, the tradition and institution of democratic constitutionalism, and, in America, their happy combination and partial realization in a federal sub-continental state, give to the generality of men here the full opportunity to develop as free and diverse beings. To realize the potentialities of our fortune, it is necessary to preserve the institutional pluralism that has so long marked our ways. It is important to avoid undue political emphasis in our activities. For the consequence of such emphasis is increase in political and governmental activity at the center, even when its nominal objective is decentralization.

No doubt political overemphasis results in large part from the growth and impact of economic behemoths with interests to further and protect, and from the subsequent perception by the victims that politics is the way to relief. Yet the restoration of the primacy of the political, in itself a good as against a narrowed and man-eating individualism, tends, in counteracting Behemoth, to create Leviathan: the locus of battles between group interests, as well as of the imposition of peaceful solutions. The parties are opposed. Yet their unwitting common cause is the reduction of genuine personal freedom, and increasing inclusion of all affairs, not excluding religion, in the realm of politics; for men see political controls as their major hope for preserving freedom interstitially, between the margins of conflicting interests. Yet, in the event, the common interests becomes increasingly material and instrumental. The concept of freedom, divorced from the ultimacy of moral personality, is transformed into a search for victory or insurance of limitation or defeat, in group battle, without assurance of lasting peace, and indeed with fair assurance that peace will not last.

Institutional Pluralism. The foregoing criticisms are not an attack upon pluralism but only upon its corruption. Purely political pluralism, with its strife of pressure groups, tends to support and encourage rather than to combat statism, defined as the omni-competence of government or governments. It does so even where it professes to be in favor of states' rights and decentralization. Pleas for loyalty and for effective participation in public life, though conceived as defenses rather than as attacks on freedom, are too often devoted to the counterbalancing of other powers. They then tend to prove harmful to an ultimate freedom by forgetting that men are not participants or citizens only.

So to argue is not to deny the importance of participation in the political order, or in institutions partially oriented toward political action. Nor is it to reject the view that ethical enlightenment must generate and utilize power for its defense and furtherance. Indeed, an awareness of the necessity, as well as of the potentially corrupting character, of power is itself a mark of such enlightenment. But a healthy society requires an institutional, not less than a political, pluralism. Indeed, the former provides an effective basis for the latter, and constitutes insurance against purely political abuses and corruptions.

The institutional pluralism here envisaged is not simply the existence of only instrumental organizations. For such organizations are essentially pressure groups and mainly political. Almost any group may, indeed, become incidentally involved in the political process. For the pursuit of all purposes rests ultimately on a material basis, and most purposes require instrumentalities for their effectuation. They need, at the least, a local habitation and a name. But a healthy social-democratic society comprises groupings almost as numerous as the activities and concerns of men. In and through such groupings persons, as active and consuming personalities, may pursue their purposes and fulfill their wants directly. Religious, aesthetic, philanthropic, community improvement, and avocational groups, all have their proper role to play. Their essence is decentralization, localism, direct participation for fulfillment, rather than influence on an often distant and alien public politics.

Yet even such pluralism is not enough. Moreover, it is not secure against the theory and practice of instrumental pressures and materialistic objectives unless behind it there stands an informing and inspiriting sense of personal values. Such values are, indeed, at once expressed and inspired by such group life, even though they remain always an expression of the person as ultimate. What is more, the security and effectiveness of such pluralism rests ultimately on a nonparticipating privacy. Such aloneness, unlike anomy, at once recognizes and communicates with other independent spirits and cherishes and protects an inviolable core of independence and retreat. The right of privacy is among the most important of all rights, as it is the most neglected and the most attacked in our own time. Under modern conditions, too, it is the most readily vulnerable. The responsibility which accompanies its exercise is neither specific nor pre-determined. Indeed, it is by its very nature beyond definition. Yet the securing of that right is basic to morality and, thus, to responsibility. Societal pluralism gives support to that right; purely political pluralism, only less than totalitarian statism, is its enemy and destroyer.

Current insecurities of constitutional liberty and the attacks, in the name of crisis and the need for security, upon freedoms of speech and thought, result from a glib aspiration to get things done, to be active, to see good times in our world. The root ill which impels us to abandon or to reject the real goods now at last possible is an undue stress on instrumental means. Its essence is a false materialism which drives more and more toward immediate external satisfaction. Such materialism leads to atrophy of the spirit. It rejects as unreal or unimportant those diverse goods which are to be attained only by indirection and are to be enjoyed through the activity of contemplation and sensitive perception. For latterly we have perverted the concept of the questing, the seeking, man, which runs from Roger Williams through William James to John Dewey. That concept properly stresses the need for a principled trial and error in life. But perversion of the concepts of instrumentalism and of operational method lead to a reduction of life to means only, and to a denial of values, to be pursued and realized through living. The enemy of the open society is far more a false idealism predicated on a misunderstood instrumentalism than it is philosophic Idealism proper. But an effective defense of that society must, as indicated at the outset, embrace elements both of Pragmatism and Idealism and must reduce them to a coherent and logically consistent pattern. Robert MacIver himself has suggested the means and has provided the foundation and scaffolding. But the superstructure, the completion of the building, is a task which still lies ahead.

9

AMERICA'S CHANGING CAPITALISM: THE INTERPLAY OF POLITICS AND ECONOMICS

J. M. CLARK

Two Levels of Interpenetration of Politics and Economics. This chapter centers around the thesis—possibly obvious—that the march of historical fact has broken down the older conceptions of the boundaries between the fields of economics and government—government in both its political and its administrative aspects—and that each discipline, and practice, enters inevitably into the field of the other. I shall be trying to give this thesis content by examining some of the leading forms which this interpenetration takes. In the field of what may, for lack of a better term, be called "official" government, economic processes determine the structure of economic interests and forces which shape political issues and measures. The resulting economic tasks of government determine its administrative form. This in turn has cut us off from older and simpler forms and ideas of democracy, and puts new and difficult obstacles in the way of achieving and protecting the substance of popular government under any form. Government in turn increasingly shapes the course of economic affairs, leaving economics to face some problems as to what its "economic laws" are supposed to be and to do.

Less obvious, perhaps, but not less important, is the combination of political and economic characteristics in the nominally private bodies which carry on economic affairs. This dual nature turns out to be an indispensable key to an adequate understanding of their motivation and behavior.

Many of us would like Jeffersonian democracy—especially if we could combine it with the material conveniences of a mechanical age. But these conveniences spell industrialism, and industrialism is incompatible with the simple, agriculturally-based economy which was the most appropriate foundation for Jeffersonian democracy. This, perhaps, is our story in the proverbial nutshell. And so it comes about that we live in a society of organized pressure-groups, of commission-government, public utility regulation, anti-trust action, farm price supports, social security, supervision of collective bargaining, and the kind of regional planning involved in the Tennessee Valley Authority. We live in what is variously thought of as the welfare state, the transfer-payment state, the Santa Claus state, or the grab-bag state. The principles of government cannot be understood as independent of the economic tasks which the electorate assigns it to perfom. And while some of these tasks may be needless excrescences, many of them are not optional, given the modern economy and an educated electorate.

From the other side, an economist seeking to analyze the forces that determine economic action is more and more forced to recognize these governmental interventions as factors in the complex of determinants. Insofar as he studies conditions in some chosen field, he necessarily encounters regulatory laws and their execution. After examining their economic consequences, he may suggest modifications. This much contact with governmental matters he can hardly avoid. If he tries to avoid them, while engaging in pure theoretical analysis, he usually takes refuge in analyzing, or speculating about, what *would* happen if government were willing to keep its hands off. As to the relevance of such analyses, no short and simple statement can be adequate; but it clearly presents a problem in an interventionist society.

At the nominally private level, trade unions and large business corporations not only are affected by the actions of official government, they exhibit governmental qualities in their own structure and motivation. What are students to do about this? As to economists, if they can gain sufficient understanding for their purposes by simply assuming that these organizations follow their organizational self-interest (defined in some meaningful fashion), then they may perhaps be content to ask no questions about the internal arrangements that bring about this result. They would merely be debarred from representing their theoretical system as a deduction from the assumed pursuit of *individual* self-interest. They are instead assuming that individuals act as faithful representatives of the collective interests of an organized group. Actually, the assumption that organizations act as "economic men" needs to be supplemented before theory can fill certain gaps in its scheme of explanation of business behavior.

As to political scientists, it would seem that before they could conclude that there is no problem here for them, they would need to ask one further question—namely, Are these units constrained to act in their collective interest by outside pressures—whether of competition, supply and demand, or the power of bargaining adversaries —which leave them substantially no alternative? Or does their economic behavior depend on how well or how ill their internal quasi-political and administrative organization operates to make them represent the interests of their members? This last appears to be the case, besides which the organization introduces other material elements of motivation.

This second level of interpenetration—the quasi-political character of private economic units—may be fully as significant as the more obvious relations between private economic activities and formal or official government. It may also be more difficult for the existing disciplines to deal with—both for political science and for economics. So far as economics is concerned, the difficulty may be greatest in some of the theoretical sectors, which naturally tend to lag farthest behind the development of historical facts and institutions. The student in touch with collective bargaining can recognize the political character of unions more readily than the wage theorist can assimilate this into his theoretical models. It is no accident that wage theory is at present in a sort of doldrums.

The Older View: Distinct Fields of Government and Economics. We may take our point of departure in the period—now more than a century past—when "economic laws" were considered as something "independent of human institutions," representing supreme forces by which government action was limited and to which it was bound, in some sense, to conform. These laws were rooted in the basic and inevitable tendencies of individual behavior, including the tendency of population to multiply—regarded as a biological constant—and the drive for the pursuit of individual self-interest. These tendencies were most clearly seen in the behavior of markets that were left free; but they also took effect in resisting or thwarting the attempts of government to interfere, either evading or nullifying them or causing them to lead to unintended and self-defeating results.

Under this theory, the activities of government were kept within a simple and modest scope. First, and most fundamental for the economy, came the maintenance of the basic framework of personal freedom, property rights, enforcement of contracts, and maintenance of justice, on which the operation of the free market depended. Public defense was, of course, also rated as basic. The relation of church and state we may leave to one side, our concern being economic. Next came a rather limited range of fairly obvious public works and some further things for which, for various reasons, the market omitted to afford the necessary conditions and incentives. Public education may have been regarded in this light at first, but later came to be included as part of the basic framework. Later, also, the piecemeal control of particular abuses was added, each case bearing its own burden of proof in the face of the general *prima facie* presumption in favor of nonintervention. Finally, there were actions beyond these limits; and especially regulatory actions. These were invariably held to be mistakes, bound to bring their appropriate penalties, under the action of economic law. "Government," in this context, meant what has here been called official government. The more subtle forms of interpenetration, arising from governmental qualities in nominally private organizations, had not worked their way into the integral structure of the economy sufficiently to command recognition.

Actually, the recognized boundaries of governmental action were never as sharp as this stereotype represents them. There was progressive enlargement of the scope of governmental action approved by liberal economists: an enlargement that appears rapid in the light of historical hindsight, although at the time it might have appeared gradual and grudgingly reluctant. Piecemeal controls of particular abuses and shortcomings grew apace. Some of these have already been listed. But the main stream of economic life was not diverted.

More disturbing was a series of developments in the field of labor. Safety-appliance acts were easily assimilated; but employers' liability for industrial accidents, and the limiting of hours of labor, interfered with the free labor contract; and it was only after long resistance that judges accepted them, with the explanation that "the heart of the contract"—work and wages—was still intact and subject to free bargaining. The final transition to social insurance amounted to compulsory and socialized provision for a large range of personal needs, for which it had been supposed to be the individual's responsibility to make his own provision. The transition was resisted on this ground, as well as on account of being an importation from autocratic-militaristic Germany. The minimum wage was a further encroachment, but left bargaining free above the minimum, and was justified—following the Webbs' argument—as eliminating "parasitic" trades or employers. Even after its adoption, the main stream of production, purchase and sale, qualities and prices, was still subject to accustomed forces. The law that directly determined these matters was still economic, not political. But a change was coming.

Partial Reversal of Relation of Economic and Political Forces. At present, the "heart of the contract" has unmistakably been invaded. Not only provision for old age and unemployment, and minimum wages, but farm prices and production, rates of interest, and foreign exchange are subject to public action, along with (for example) the extraction of crude petroleum (with effects on its price). And contractual wages are—or were, before World War II— determined mainly by a process known as "free collective bargaining," the term "free" signifying mainly that official government forbears to interfere, and leaves the outcome to the informal quasi-governmental organs that have come into existence in this field. Of this, more later.

For present purposes, the essential point is that there has been, to a considerable extent, a reversal of the classical relation between "economic law" and political action. When Ricardian economics was at the height of its prestige, "economic law" was supposed, by economists and a good many others, to be an effective force determining the main features of the actual course of economic events, while political government (once a few questions like the corn laws were settled) made gestures, largely ineffectual, in the direction of its ideas of what was good and desirable. Economic law, to be thus effective, did not have to be understood by the agents who automatically fulfilled the destiny it appointed for them.

Now it may be, on the whole, nearer the (very complex) truth to say that there are large areas within which agencies of government, plus nominally private agencies of an essentially governmental character, determine what actually happens and are able within fairly wide margins to disregard or neutralize the forces of "supply and demand." The converse of this is that the economists' brand of economic law, no longer an all-pervasive and automatically effective force, is reduced to a body of normative theory, trying not too effectually to sit in judgment on the acts and policies of the agencies that wield the power, and to determine whether these acts and policies are sound, or what sound policy would be. To the extent that this is true, economic law does not become effective except as it is understood and deliberately followed by agencies that have the power, if they choose, to act otherwise.

This last seems clearly true of money wages, farm prices and other prices that are genuinely "administered"; and of trade practices, so far as they are controlled by unified action, either of public or private agencies. Of course, the general level of real wages may still be limited by overall productivity, beyond anything collective bargaining can do; and the effects of price changes on consumer demand are still not arbitrarily controllable. Discretionary power acts within some kind of limits which are difficult or impossible to determine with anything like precision. And these limits are not universally identical, but depend on the social and political temper of each people, which is far less uniform than the calculus of self-interest as economists have employed it.

This is, of course, only one side of the story. The other side, as noted at the beginning of this chapter, is the impact of economic interests and forces on government.

Government as Controller and Controlled. There is, of course, nothing new about the idea that the kind of government a country can have is a function of its economic and social system. Jefferson long ago stressed the importance of a simple and largely agricultural economy as a base for the kind of democracy he sought. And today Wilhelm Röpke ascribes the political sickness of modern civilization to "massism," and speaks in that connection of the "politicalization of economic processes." He wants a simple, small-scale, decentralized economy, and thinks of Switzerland as a satisfactory example.[1] But, given the modern urban mass-economy, this road to political salvation appears closed. Our government rests on a base of sharply differentiated economic groups, with urban labor far outnumbering the farm population and carrying corresponding weight. The business interest, outnumbered in voting strength, must try to maintain its political influence by other means. The government must strike some sort of balance among all these interests, according to a complex of criteria in which the prevalent sense of justice and the common interest plays some part in enabling minority groups to get the support they need from other groups, if measures in their interest are to go through. This element is probably at its strongest where nation-wide public opinion is brought to bear directly on a problem. In the kinds of deliberations that take place in the proverbial "smoke-filled rooms," minori-

---

[1] W. Röpke, *The Social Crisis of Our Time*, and review by Frank Munk, *American Economic Review*, December, 1951, pp. 962–964.

ties can buy support by the time-tried method of log-rolling. And always a solidly organized minority, which will vote more or less as a unit, carries more weight than more numerous but unorganized groups, whose votes will scatter.

The issues these groups raise for political action arise out of the way in which our economic life is organized, and the needs and inequities which each group feels. Many of these are rooted in the character of our complex mass-economy, which is only to a limited extent automatically self-adjusting. As these issues become more numerous and differentiated, government perforce becomes more specialized and complicated. And as the subject matter becomes more technical, administrative agencies proliferate, and popular control of government becomes more remote and more difficult. Here lies one of the most powerful ways in which the character of the economic base affects the structure and functioning of government.

To take one major example, one of the principles which we have accepted as an essential of representative government, as we conceive it, is the separation of powers. But the specialized and technical character of the subject-matter of the regulatory activities has made inevitable the growth of commissions, specialized to different subject-matter and acting under such indefinite mandates that they may be compelled to create the content of these mandates (a legislative function), put them into effect (executive), and settle disputed cases (judicial). Courts tend increasingly to accept a commission's verdict on the economic evidence as final, limiting review to more strictly legal matters. The Federal Trade Commission prosecutes cases before itself as a quasi-judicial tribunal, and has not wholly overcome the drawbacks arising from this dual personality.

More serious, however, is the inability of the public, or even Congress, to watch continuously and effectively all these various baskets in which the governmental eggs are distributed. The public can concentrate its attention on only a few things at a time; and after the original setting-up of a commission, or one of the rare major revisions of its mandate which arouses real interest, public attention turns elsewhere. A twofold danger results.[2] An original vigorous sense of public mission may decline, with time and changing personnel, into the morale of bureaucratic survival and routine operation. And while public attention is intermittent, the activities and pressures of the interested parties are continuous, and may wear down the purpose of the agencies while the public is looking

---

[2] This point has been forcibly developed in an unpublished manuscript by Walton H. Hamilton.

the other way. Thus the democratic character of government may be impaired as a result of the multitude and technical quality of the tasks imposed on it by the character of the modern mass-economy. This is one of the serious problems of the interaction of government and the economic subject matter with which it is forced to deal.

The Dilemma of Normative Economics. From the other side, what of the problems of an economics whose theories have become largely theories of what is sound and economically correct, rather than of the forces determining actual events? Economics, in the capacity of science, is not supposed to carry the full responsibility for policy recommendations—that is, for persons who must weigh both economic and political considerations. They must weigh the economists' testimony in the light of what the "people" want, and whether suggested measures are administrable. The next question is: Should economists take this into consideration in advance and accept the idea that it is poor advice that flies in the face of the political machinery through which policies will be reshaped and carried out? If so, would this amount to accepting political standards and resigning their proper special function as economists? Or if not, would this mean that their analysis, with its policy implications, would be doomed to impracticality and ineffectiveness? This is a real dilemma. In one form, under the Truman Administration it beset the operations of the President's Council of Economic Advisers—that important experiment in the utilization of expert economic diagnosis to guide the comprehensive economic policy which current economic conditions impose upon government.

Economists outside government can escape the obvious impact of this dilemma and should be free to let their analyses lead where they will. But difficulties remain. For example, concepts involved in the pure theory of perfect and imperfect competition, adopted for intellectual reasons, are imperfectly adapted to serve as guides to antitrust policy and other policies to which these theories may have relevance. Such theoretical analysis may point to so many defects in competitive practice that, if government were to attempt to deal with them all, both government and business would be overloaded —as indeed they may be already. Furthermore, some of these "imperfections" are really virtues, since theoretical "perfect competition" is defined with reference to a single objective—reducing prices to cost—and ignores the more important conditions of progress in methods and in products.

Economists need to retain a sense of the relative importance of the issues on which their analyses impinge and of the relative availability of official and unofficial ways of dealing with them. At less theoretical levels, their most essential service is rendered by unsparingly objective critical analysis both of conditions and of the economic effects of governmental policies. Some may have a talent for devising remedies. But when they do this, they become something more than economists, and assume a responsibility for considering political and administrative feasibility on their own account, or for collaborating with those who will bring these considerations to bear.

Collective Bargaining as a Quasi-Political Activity. So far, we have been looking at the relation between economics and official government. Turning to the second level of interpenetration—the governmental character of nominally private bodies—we may look first at collective bargaining, starting with its impact on wages. Economists naturally want a theory of the forces determining wages. Their inherited theory—that of marginal productivity—is a theory of competitive equilibrium; and its relevance is obviously called in question by modern forms of collective bargaining. And attempts to develop the so-called "bargain theory" into an adequate substitute have not so far had convincing success. I should like to explore the hypothesis that the source of the difficulty lies in the attempt to treat unions as economic bargaining units of the traditional sort, rather than recognizing their political character.

Theorists feel obliged to assume, as a basis for a theory, that a bargaining unit is trying to maximize something; but they have so far failed to identify just what it is that unions try to maximize, or ought to try to maximize. Increased money wage rates may be closer than any other single objective to the actual aim of most union bargaining about wages. But is that a rational objective, if pursued without regard to effects on prices or employment? As to prices, a union may concede that increased money wage rates, in excess of increased physical productivity, tend to be neutralized in the aggregate by increased prices. But a single union may still gain if it outstrips the others, or may lose if it falls behind them. And it may judge that its own self-restraint will not stop the general procession. A disregard for the effects on employment may be rationalized *via* the theory that higher wages make for increased employment, through increasing the diffused variety of purchasing power; or it may simply rest on recognition that no one really knows enough to generalize confidently about the effect of wages on employment, so they might as well concentrate on the thing they can see and measure. Or in cases in which it may appear fairly certain that employment would suffer from the level of money wage rates that is being demanded, the demands may still represent "economic rationality" for those workers whose seniority protects them from being laid off. They may also be the most influential group in determining union policy. But at this point we clearly enter into considerations that are matters of internal union politics.

Or if an annual wage is demanded in a given industry, is this done in the light of the probability that, if granted in this particular industry, it would be bound to be confined to workers who have been employed for a minimum term? If so, how many of the union members who are invited to support the demand do so with recognition of this probability? Again, this is a matter of internal union politics. Or is the demand a bargaining maneuver with an undisclosed purpose? If granted, would it perhaps make the industry adopt a more hospitable attitude toward efforts of government to stabilize employment? Once more, a question of political implications.

One pioneer theorist in this field has pictured a union balancing the probable cost of a strike against the probable wage-gain the union might hope to secure by striking, beyond what it could secure without a strike.[3] On the basis of such a weighing of probabilities it is determined whether the employer or the workers will "have to yield," or whether both are interested in concessions. Such a theory has a certain rationality, but it would appear to be different from the rationality displayed in the fairly numerous cases of long and costly strikes for a trifling wage gain above what was available without striking. It seems likely that there are imponderables here, presumably related to prestige or the demonstrating of power, or both, which cannot be summarily dismissed as irrational, but which do not possess the kind of rationality assumed in economists' theoretical models. On the whole, it appears to be rather a variety of political rationality, or political motivation, rational or otherwise.

It appears that one falls far short of understanding unions if one approaches them *via* the assumption that each is an economic bargaining unit, with a quantitatively defined objective which it pursues single-mindedly and undertakes to maximize, after the fashion familiar in the models of economic theory. As a key to the interpretation of union behavior, this leaves too much unexplained, and in some respects is too wide of the mark.

---

[3] See F. Zeuthen, *Problems of Monopoly and Economic Warfare*, 1930, Chapter IV, esp. pp. 111–121.

Suppose one tries instead the hypothesis that the union is primarily a political entity? At once, things that have baffled the economic model begin to fall into place. True, it is notably different from the more familiar kinds of political entities, but the main elements are there. Officers are elected, and to get elected they make promises or point to a past record; having made promises, they must deliver as much as possible and find scapegoats to blame for any shortages. They must claim credit for all gains made, whether or not these gains would have come if the union had not existed. It is not gains made, but gains won by union action, that constitute the record on the basis of which the union makes its appeal for new members, and for old members to continue their support, and on which the union official makes his appeal to his constituents. Employers who volunteered a wage increase have found that the increase the union would have demanded in any case has simply been added to their voluntary concession. If they made the increase unilaterally, without giving the union a chance to pass on it and to do some bargaining about it, they may be found guilty of an unfair labor practice.

Unions are considered less democratic than towns or states, as is natural for an entity which specializes in combative external relations; but by way of compensation, the divergences and conflicts of interest within the membership, while decidedly in evidence, are nowhere near so strongly marked as in the population of a city or a state. But the most notable distinguishing feature of the union as a political entity is the dominance of external relations in its scheme of activities and interests. With all its internal social, educational, civic, and benefit activities and interests, it is still like a state, whose economic revenue is determined by the terms of a trade treaty periodically negotiated with a powerful neighbor state. Its very subsistence centers in the arts of negotiation, normally peaceful but with the possibility of war always in the background.

It is, of course, a limited war. It is as if there were an international law, more powerful than actual international law has ever been, regulating the tactics of combat and protecting the rights of the parties to resume trading with one another, after one of their temporary stoppages of intercourse. This code does not, of course, prevent all violence. But if union and employer are pictured in the guise of sovereign states, negotiating with one another, they operate within a federal league or union which has effective judicial machinery for interpreting and enforcing the treaties that are made. And the best of these treaties are of constitution-making character, defining the rights of the parties, not only in money terms, but in terms of the human rights involved in the standing relationships entered into, in which the worker undertakes performance and subjects himself to discipline, but acquires protections against arbitrary action by foreman or boss. Such a development was needed, in place of older absolute rights of dismissal, and employers have adjusted themselves to it; but in the process many an employer must have felt as if he had been compelled by *force majeure* to grant rights of extraterritoriality in an area over which his sovereignty had previously been absolute.

In fact, it seems probable that it is in this realm, of human rights and the jurisprudence that centers around them, that the most important gains of unionism are found: more important even than wage gains. Much of the increase in real wages would presumably have come without the compelling force of unions—no one can tell how much. But this body of human rights pertaining to the employment relation, and of private jurisprudence to interpret and enforce it, is the peculiar creation of collective bargaining.

In the foregoing, we have seen the essential political factors at work, though in the distinctive forms peculiar to collective bargaining. Elections and appeals to the electorate, executive government or leadership, diplomacy and treaties, constitution-making and jurisprudence—all have played their part; and the resulting structure exercises, within its scope of action, a genuine authority over individual union members. The result, as far as it goes, tends to support the hypothesis that, to understand the motivations that take effect in collective bargaining, the character of unions as political bodies must be taken into account.

The Character of the Business Unit. The business unit does not present such a striking array of political characteristics as do trade unions, but it will repay a brief examination from this standpoint. It is possible for economic theory to proceed on the (deceptively) simple assumption that all business units seek to maximize their profits. This has considerable relevance. Also, as already noted, it by-passes the question how a large corporate organization comes to act as if it were a single unified personality, leaving this question to the students of management and industrial organization. They have dealt with it, both practically and theoretically, and have been known to express the view that in developing the principles of administrative organization, they were ahead of the political scientists. Economists, under the heading of the "theory of the firm," are making beginnings with analysis of how the different classes of members in a great corporate team go about the task of gearing their functions, perspectives, and activities together. In studies of corporate organization (but not in general economic theory) they have envisaged divergences of interest among management, directors, and stockholders.

A case could be made for further departures from the simple assumption of maximizing profit, on the ground that this is too limited a theory of motivation to account for all the significant facts of corporate behavior. Management may be conceived as hammering out an accommodation among the interests of investors, customers, workers, the government, and local communities. It may be shortsighted, or may look far ahead, or may adopt conceptions of sound practice which imply a long time-perspective to justify them. Survival, prestige, physical growth, and public relations all enter the picture; and at times the continuity of the business itself seems to become an impersonal end in its own right. For a struggling business unit, immediate necessities may dominate policy; it is the strong and well-established enterprises that have sufficient margin of discretion in policy to be able to give weight to considerations farther removed from immediate profit. But these stronger enterprises may be more important than the weaker, struggling units in determining the behavior of an industry as a whole.

Conclusion. We have been looking at a few of the ways in which government is determined by its economic setting and the economic tasks it is called on to perform, and at the dilemma of economics as government increasingly takes command as a determining force in the economic realm. And we have also looked at the ways in which economic bargaining units themselves present features and problems that pertain to the science of government. We have been raising problems rather than undertaking to settle them, but this cursory inspection points to certain conclusions as to the spheres of study of political science and economics.

Political scientists hardly need to be told that, as government becomes more frankly a vehicle through which groups may directly promote their particular economic interests, the strains on political and administrative machinery are enormously increased, and the democratic character of government seriously compromised. Economists may not be fully aware of the way in which they have, in their various fields, been making their adjustment, with more or less success, to the extension of government's controlling functions. In the Keynesian economics, theory has been in the van of this adjustment; in other areas it has lagged, especially in the theory of wages. And in unions and large business corporations we have seen a fruitful field for joint study by economics and political science, both being equally well advised to beware of trying to apply their ready-made models to this material, since it has its own unique qualities and requires fresh study and interpretation from both its political and its economic angles.   For better or for worse, the two aspects are interwoven.

10

THE DEMOGRAPHIC FOUNDATIONS
OF NATIONAL POWER

KINGSLEY DAVIS

Too often the course of history is ascribed to the astuteness of generals or the intentions of statesmen. Interpretations tend to be motive-centered, to find the "causes" of events in the ignorance or knowledge, in the goodness or badness, of the leading actors. The more fundamental causes, because they are slower and more impersonal in their operation, receive less popular and often less scholarly recognition. Yet economists, geographers, sociologists, and demographers have been showing for decades that it is the economic developments, the growth or decline of population, the changes of technology, the transformations of society that set the stage and write the script for the military and political actors. In politics, as on the stage, brilliant acting alone cannot bring success. A good setting and a good drama are also required. It is not so much what Wilson or Hitler *did* which affects history, but rather what they *could* do. The personal stature of Munoz Marin in Puerto Rico or of Aung San in Burma doubtless equals that of Churchill in England or Roosevelt in America, but the vehicles in which they appear are too inconspicuous for comparable recognition. Great opportunities breed great men.

One way of avoiding a superficial view of international relations is to seek the determinants of national power. Such a quest brings the nation to the fore as the unit of analysis, rather than its leaders or the words they speak. It also calls for an answer in long-run terms, because a nation's power vis-à-vis other nations rarely changes suddenly. Finally, the relative power of nations offers one of the main keys to international affairs. Just as the big trees control the ecological balance of all the organisms in a forest, so the powerful nations determine the pattern and the trend of relations among all countries. No wonder political science now considers the problem of power a fundamental one.

Reasoning in terms of power unfortunately conotes a "Machiavellian" view. It is taken to mean that a nation seeks naked power as the supreme end, by fair means or foul. But the present discussion does not make this assumption, nor does it make any judgment as to whether power is a desirable or an undesirable goal. Our interest lies solely in differences of power as one of the major facts of the international world, and in the role of demographic elements in those differences.[1] In addition, power is regarded simply as the ability of a nation to influence other nations. Thus conceived, it is not thought to be manifested solely in military might but also in economic, ideological, and cultural influence. In the last analysis power comes from no single means but from a judicious combination of several of them.

Although all countries can theoretically be ranked in terms of their power, this is hardly worthwhile. As with social classes, interest attaches to those at the top of the hierarchy. Yet one must get some idea of how the elements of power are distributed among all nations in order to understand the position of some. The following analysis deals, then, with all the independent nations—not in the sense of trying to rank them all but in the sense of trying to see what groups they fall into and why.

THE MEASUREMENT OF POWER

If some direct measure of a nation's international influence were available, any theory of the elements of power could then be tested in terms of this measure. Just as the relative performance of different airplanes may be measured in terms of, say, their speed and then the factors responsible for their differing speeds analyzed, so with nations—if there were a measure of their power. But since no such direct measure exists, the best that can be done is to analyze as logically and empirically as possible what seem to be the elements of power, and then to see if the results check with our impressionistic knowledge of international affairs. This procedure is something like analyzing the factors in the speed of planes without ever having any measure of that speed except the casual observations of people

---

[1] These and other aspects of this general question are given extended treatment in a volume, *Population and International Relations,* being prepared jointly by the writer and Katherine Fox Organski; this volume is one of a series of topical studies in international relations by various authors.

on the ground. The method is far from satisfactory, but it is better than none at all.

Lacking a direct measure of national power, one searches for some indirect measure, some index, which is an approximation to what one wants. One such index, and perhaps the best, is the total national income, which expresses the grand result of all the productive forces at a nation's command. As a matter of fact, the ten top nations in national income would come close to being what people generally regard as the ten top nations in terms of power, as reference to Table 1 will show.

This much granted, the next question concerns the elements that govern the national income. Table 1 demonstrates that one of the factors is the total population. The table not only gives in rank order the 20 countries with the highest national income, but also provides in the second column their rank in terms of *per capita income*. Comparison of the two columns makes it clear that a nation's total income may be high primarily because its population is large (for example, India and the Soviet Union) or because the per capita income is high (for example, Canada and Sweden). It is noteworthy, for example, that of the first ten countries in terms of total income, there are six which rank below the first 20 in terms of per capita income. These are countries which hold their high position in the world primarily because they have a great many inhabitants. Despite some anomalies in the figures (Western Gemany was still not recovered in 1949, nor was Japan), the data show not only that national income is a fair index of national power but that it results from radically different combinations of population and per capita income.

We therefore have a rationale for regarding the total population as an important determinant of national power, although by no means the only one. Accordingly we shall deal first with this factor as parallel in importance to per capita income. Later we shall take up per capita income itself insofar as it is influenced by demographic variables other than total numbers.

TOTAL POPULATION AND NATIONAL POWER

Although few deny the importance of total population in national strength, its influence has seldom been analyzed. Since populations do not double overnight or die off quickly, the course of world relations is not noticeably affected by demographic change over a brief interval. In contrast, an army or air force can strike

TABLE 1. THE TWENTY TOP NATIONS IN NATIONAL INCOME AND THEIR RANK
IN PER CAPITA INCOME

	National Income 1949 [a] (Million U. S. Dollars)	Rank in Per Capita Income [b]
United States............	216,831	1
Soviet Union.............	59,500	23
United Kingdom.........	38,922	6
France.................	19,857	13
India..................	19,572	55
Germany (Western Zone)..	15,300	22
China.................	12,384	69
Canada................	11,797	2
Italy..................	10,800	29
Japan.................	8,260	42
Poland................	7,344	24
Argentina..............	5,722	19
Brazil.................	5,530	40
Sweden................	5,426	5
Australia..............	5,374	8
Belgium...............	5,015	10
Netherlands............	5,000	12
Czechoslovakia..........	4,625	17
Switzerland............	3,940	4
Pakistan..............	3,760	57

[a] Statistical Office of the United Nations, *National and Per Capita Incomes, Seventy Countries*, 1949.

[b] It should be noted that the source gives the data for only 70 countries, whereas there are actually 80-odd independent countries as of 1949. Those not included, however, can be presumed to have a very low rank. Many dependent areas have higher national incomes, or higher per capita incomes, than many independent areas. Data for most of the underdeveloped countries are not reliable, and hence not much credence should be given to small differences.

suddenly, a foreign minister can announce a change of policy in minutes, a treaty can be concluded in days. These rapid changes tend to capture attention and become the main substance of international history. Yet, as already mentioned, national power is hardly a function of brief events. It is a function of slow changes which build up the possibility of a rapid development such as a Hitler or a Napoleon may launch. The fact that human beings cannot multiply much faster than 3 per cent per year does not mean

that differential population growth as between nations has no effect
on their relative power.

In a true appraisal of total population in relation to national
power, three points must be emphasized. First, population is one
of the major determinants of power, ranking with any other factor
that can be mentioned. Second, it resembles other factors in that it
alone is not sufficient to provide "great power" status. Third, it
differs more as between one country and another than most other
factors. The first and third points are interrelated; the second,
which is a denial of demographic determinism, is made clear in the
treatment of the other two.

Why Numbers Are Important. The significance of human numbers lies in the fact that nothing else can be entirely substituted for
them. Machines can be used in industry and weapons in warfare,
but behind these there must be human beings. In economic production human labor, whether of brawn or brain, will always be
a sizable factor. In the United States, for example, wages and sal-
aries of employees in manufacturing make up over 50 per cent of
the value added by manufacture. It can be maintained with truth
that the more advanced the technology, the less labor is required for
a given product—indeed, this is the definition of an advanced technology. But it is also true that an industrial system must produce a
much greater *total* product than an agrarian system; what is gained
in labor per unit of product is counterbalanced by what is required
in terms of more units produced. Furthermore, the very creation of
a modern economic system is much easier if there is a sizable population within the national borders to furnish manpower for all the
specialized pursuits required and to provide mass consumption for
the goods and services produced. This is why countries with ample
resources but small populations, such as Australia and Canada, despite their modern technology and efficient economic organization,
desire more people. It is why the United States and Russia have
an advantage in mass production over Switzerland or Sweden.

From a military standpoint the necessity for numbers is scarcely
less obvious. One of the leading objectives of any military cam-
paign is to capture or destroy the enemy's fighting personnel. Weapons and materiel are worthless without men to wield them; indeed,
they may be highly dangerous because undermanned weapons or
machines may be captured and used by the enemy. In their successful revolutionary war the Chinese Communists fought and won
many battles with captured materiel. The loss of fighting personnel

may be crucial. Since such personnel is drawn most heavily, and with most effectiveness, from limited age groups, losses that look small in relation to the total population are often huge in ratio to military manpower. Since it is not possible to have large military age-groups except insofar as the total population itself is large, the military strategist requires a huge number of citizens from which to draw his fighting personnel. He also needs, in modern warfare, a substantial population to back up his military effort with indispensable economic production.

One of the important causes of Germany's defeat in World War II was her staggering loss of military manpower. By the end of the conflict she had lost approximately four million men killed, missing, or captured, which was about one third of the German men of military age.[2] On the home front in 1944 she was having to use some eight million foreigners as slave labor in a desperate attempt to bolster her economic production,[3] and this labor was more inefficient and costly than a similar number of Germans would have been.

A war cannot be fought on stable and prearranged lines. Troops must be moved about, often halfway around the world. Weapons and equipment must be transported over oceans and over mountains, whether it is raining, snowing, or sweltering. This unpredictability requires that abnormal quantities of manpower be always ready, whether they are used ordinarily or not. In short, armies waste manpower, not simply because they are careless but because they must waste it.

Finally, the necessity of having adequate manpower to reap the harvest of military victory should not be overlooked. Again Germany is a case in point. Hitler's conquests were so widespread that German personnel was spread thin in supervising and controlling the captured areas. Had the German population been twice as numerous, a much more adequate production could have been obtained from the occupied countries and a much better control over the resistance movements. More than one nation has lost in peace what it won in war because its manpower was too short to exploit its victory. It is alleged with some truth that the military and civilian personnel of the United States is currently spread too thinly over the rest of the world to accomplish the purpose (the containment of communism) which this country supposedly wishes to accom-

---

[2] See U. S. Bureau of the Census, *Population of the Federal Republic of Germany and West Berlin* (Washington, D. C.: Government Printing Office, 1952), pp. 1, 6, 20, 66, 89.

[3] *Ibid.*, p. 6.

plish. If the United States, with its huge population, finds it hard to meet its manpower needs, we can see how much more difficult is the achievement of a powerful international position for a country such as France or Argentina.

It is possible, of course, to use somebody else's manpower to fight a war. This is the principle of the defensive or offensive alliance, of colonial troops, and of slave troops, mercenaries, and janissaries. But in the last analysis the nation must have the power to inspire allies with confidence and a willingness to go along and to secure, maintain, and to control any foreign soldiers under its immediate direction; and an element in this power is its own population. The Korean war has raised the serious question of whether the Soviet Union is finding a way to tap the inexhaustible manpower of Asia for its own military purposes. On the surface it appears that Russia, as an industrial nation, can simply manufacture arms, furnish military advisors, and provide the proper ideology while China draws upon its population of 400 to 500 million to furnish the soldiers. If such an arrangement were successfully engineered, it would certainly justify all the fears which the idea has already inspired among the free nations. But while such a plan might work for a while, the situation looks to be inherently unstable. Foreign armies are notoriously hard to control. When they are massive, made up of people from one culture and representing a supposedly sovereign nation, they cannot be long controlled by another power unless the latter has an even stronger army. One can say that, since an army is weak without modern weapons, the industrial nation can maintain its control simply through its ability to furnish the instruments of war. The trouble with this argument, however, is that there is not one industrial nation but several, so that all of them can play the game that Russia is supposedly playing. Russia may successfully use the manpower of her European satellites, because these are all small nations compared to Russia; but on reflection it would seem unlikely that she can long use the manpower of China, a nation twice as populous as Russia, to fight her battles for her. If she does she will have to maintain a stronger military establishment than China, and this is the cost that the whole plan of using Chinese manpower was designed to avoid. Foreign troops would seem to be more useful as supplements to a nation's own forces rather than as full substitutes, and more controllable if they come from many small nations rather than from one big one.

All told, it seems hard to escape the fact that a large population is an indispensable asset to a nation that would be powerful. There is no way in which a small nation can overcome the defects of its smallness, because there is no perfect substitute for human beings or for one's own nationals. This does not mean, obviously, that a large population is itself a guarantee of great national power, or that a nation is inevitably inferior in power to whatever nation has more people in it. Other conditions must also be present. In other words, population, like every other factor in national power, is a necessary but not a sufficient cause of greatness.

The Extreme Inequalities of Numerical Strength. A peculiarity of the population factor is its tremendous variation from one country to another. Leaving aside the freaks such as Liechtenstein and Monaco, we find startling contrasts like the following: India has something like 1190 times as many inhabitants as Bhutan; Russia has approximately 165 times as many as Albania; and the United States has more than 188 times as many as the Republic of Panama. Is it any wonder that in each of these cases the smaller is dominated by the larger nation?

Few determinants rival total population in variability. One of them is territory. Taking all of the sovereign nations as of 1950, we find that the coefficient of variation for the population frequency curve is 254 per cent, while for the territorial frequency curve it is 353 per cent.[4] But population is a more important determinant of power than its territory. Iceland has a territory a third as large as that of Italy, but its population of 143,000 is only $\frac{1}{325}$ as large as that of Italy, and its international influence compared to Italy's is negligible. Of course, Iceland's territory is not particularly rich, but New Zealand can be cited as a country whose rich territory is greater in extent than that of the United Kingdom but whose population is only $\frac{1}{26}$ as large and whose influence, compared to that of Britain, is nearer to $\frac{1}{26}$ than to equality.

Another important factor, as we have noted, is per capita economic production or income. But the differences between nations in per capita productivity are not so great as the differences in total population. The United Nations has estimated the per capita income for seventy nations in 1949, expressed in United States dollars. The highest figure for the United States ($1,453), and the lowest is that for Indonesia ($25).[5] The first is 363 times the latter.

---

[4] The coefficient of variation is the standard deviation divided by the mean. It is a measure of the degree of spread around the mean independent of the particular unit used.

[5] Statistical Office of the United Nations, *National and Per Capita Incomes, Seventy Countries, 1949* (New York: United Nations, 1950), pp. 14–16. The estimate for Indonesia may be too low. See the discussion of national income estimates for agrarian

This is certainly a great difference, but among these same seventy countries the most populous has, for the same year, 3,334 times the population of the least populous.[6] The coefficient of variation for the seventy countries is 104 per cent with respect to per capita income, as against 254 per cent with respect to population.

The Number of Large and Small Nations. Let us look more closely at the figures on total population. Omitting Andorra, Liechtenstein, Monaco, San Marino, and Vatican City (which together had a population of 55,000), we find that there were 82 independent countries in 1950 with a total population of 2,200 million.[7] Their average population was 26.8 million. Table 3 on page 219 shows the distribution of the countries by population. It will readily be seen that the distribution is heavily weighted toward the low population side. In fact, there are only 14 countries which are above the average, while there are 67 below it. Indeed, 35 countries, representing 43 per cent of all of them, had less than five million inhabitants. The average is clearly influenced unduly by the few countries with huge populations and is therefore virtually a meaningless figure. As of 1950, the median population—the number which divides the countries into two halves—is only 7.01 million. This is just slightly less than the population of Sweden.

This distribution of the world's independent countries by population raises an interesting question. Since at least 42 per cent of them are too small to defend themselves, how does it happen that they are independent? They do not defend one another. They are not united among themselves. If sheer force alone were involved in international relations, it seems likely that most of the tiny countries would not have this status. It appears that there are various reasons why the existence of small countries is tolerated by the big ones. For one thing, it is extremely difficult to govern, without excessive cost, a highly civilized and unified people who do not want to be governed by outsiders. For another, there are certain diplomatic and political advantages to be gained by the big nations. In some cases the price of taking over a small nation might be warfare

---

areas on p. 6 and the note on Indonesia on p. 21. See also, Statistical Office of the United Nations, *National Income Statistics, 1938–1948*, pp. 15–16.

6 The two countries are China, with 463 million, and Iceland with 139 thousand. Although China's population is estimated, the margin of error would not have much effect on the comparison with Iceland.

7 United Nations, *Demographic Yearbook 1951*, pp. 91–103. Germany is treated as a single unit, as are China and Korea. The United Nations definition of "independent" is followed here, although some of the countries, such as Bhutan and Albania, are not entirely so.

for the big nation that takes it over. The factors responsible for the numerous small countries can be better assessed if we look at their location.

Table 2 shows that most of the small nations are contained in only three regions of the world. These three are the Americas south of the Rio Grande (Latin America), the Near East, and Europe. Of the 41 countries of less than 7.01 million inhabitants in 1950, these areas contained 37; whereas, of the 40 countries of more than 7.01 million, these areas contained only 22. Europe, however, has a large share of moderately sized nations, and so does not have quite such a large proportion of small nations as do Latin America and the Near East. The latter two areas are pre-eminently the homes of the small countries.

In both Latin America and the Near East the explanation of the high proportion of small countries seems to be as follows. They represent the breakup of great empires, in the one case the Spanish Empire and in the other the Turkish Empire. This disintegration occurred during the nineteenth and early twentieth centuries— roughly from 1820 to 1920—which was ideologically and factually an era of local nationalism. Furthermore, in both cases there were political reasons leading the big powers to allow the formation of small nations rather than to encourage the formation of big ones. In the case of Latin America the Monroe Doctrine precluded inter- ference by great powers other than the United States; and the lat- ter, with its bias toward national self-determination, was not inclined to interfere with the formation of small states, although not objecting to the creation of such a big country as Brazil. In the case of the Near East the rivalry of the great powers of Europe made the formation of small states a convenient device for a division of spheres of influence. Furthermore, the Near Eastern states were formed late (in the period of World War I and after), when the whole world was under the spell of the American doctrine of national self-determination. In addition it should be noted that the Latin American territory, although huge, was sparsely settled; population growth had not been fast enough to give these countries numbers commensurate with their areas. In the Near East some of the territories are deserts or near-deserts, and they too were sparsely settled, although settled more fully in terms of resources than were the lands of Latin America. The Latin American terrain is divided by mountains, jungles, and deserts; also, in the first half of the nine- teenth century when these nations gained independence, transport was still primitive; consequently, the isolation of different regions led naturally to local solidarity.

TABLE 2. DISTRIBUTION OF SMALL NATIONS BY MAJOR WORLD AREAS, 1950

	Total Number of Countries	Average Population (Millions)	Countries of Less Than 7.01 Million
Africa..........................	4	12.4	1
America North of Rio Grande........	2	82.8	..
Asia Excluding the Near East ª......	14	83.3	3
Central America and Caribbean......	10	4.5	9
South America....................	10	11.1	6
Near East........................	14	4.5	12
Europe ᵇ.........................	25	15.7	9
Oceania.........	2	5.1	1
U.S.S.R........	1	193.0	..
Combined....................	82	27.1	41

ª Excluding the U.S.S.R. The Near East, as here defined, includes Iran but not Afghanistan.
ᵇ Excluding the U.S.S.R. and the European part of Turkey. The latter is included in the Near East.

Interestingly enough, in neither Latin America nor the Near East were cultural differences an important reason for the formation of small nations. Latin America was generally Iberian, and the Near East predominantly Moslem, in culture. In Europe, on the other hand, it was linguistic, religious and ethnic differences, persisting for centuries, which caused small nations to arise in abundance. That the nations of Europe, generally small in territory, are not correspondingly small in population, is due to their heavy density of settlement. In contrast to Latin America, Europe has been settled by people of advanced culture long enough to have a much higher ratio of population to territory, and thus does not have as large a proportion of demographically small nations as the other two regions.

The preponderance of large countries elsewhere seems also explicable in historical terms. In the temperate areas north of the Rio Grande and in the Pacific, settlers came from Western Europe, mainly from England. They therefore began with advanced agricultural and commercial arts and achieved industrialization rapidly. They had too the peculiar genius of English and Scandinavian culture for stable government. They could thus achieve political unity over large areas, especially since they had the added advantage of cultural uniformity. In the tropical areas of the Pacific, just as in the tropical Caribbean, the development of islands was not along the lines of European settlement but rather of European exploitation through plantation agriculture. They therefore became colonies, and when independence comes to them, as it has come in many cases in the Caribbean and Central America, it will probably be as small countries.

The size of Asiatic countries outside of the Near East seems to be accounted for in terms of the great population densities of those areas. To a great extent southern and southwest Asia was taken over in large chunks by European powers. The larger of these chunks, large especially in terms of population, have now gained their independence; whereas the smaller ones are still colonies and so do not figure in our list.

It must be kept in mind that the present chapter deals only with self-governing countries. Both Africa and Oceania contain many dependent political units which are small in terms of population. These may evolve into small nations. Indeed, it would appear that the normal evolution from colonialism to nationalism would make the average size of nation smaller in the future than at present, except that such a "normal" evolution is not guaranteed. If small nations are weak nations, forces may be afoot today which will compel them to yield their sovereignty again. Many of the independent countries today are sovereign more in law than in fact.

The Share of Population in Each Class of Country. We have just been discussing the number of small or large nations as a proportion of all nations. Now let us look at the figures to see how large a share of the world's population lives in each class of country.[8] The fact that there are more small nations than big ones does not mean that more people live in small nations. On the contrary, since "size" is the number of citizens, it follows that a larger percentage of the earth's inhabitants live in large countries than these countries constitute of all nations. In fact, the distribution (as exhibited in Table 3) looks a good deal like those familiar tables showing distribution of land in various sized holdings in countries with a rich land-owning class. Such tables show many more tiny holdings than big ones, but most of the land is in the big holdings.

---

[8] Strictly speaking our treatment does not include the world's total population, but only the total living in independent countries. This embraces approximately 92 per cent of the world's people, for the number living in colonies is now only about 200 million.

As previously noted, 41 nations, half the nations of the world, each had less than 7.01 million inhabitants in 1950. When the population in these countries is totaled, we find that they contained only 123 million inhabitants, or only 5.6 per cent of the total population in independent countries. On the other hand, the four giant nations each boasting over 150 million citizens (China, India, U.S.S.R., and the United States) contained 1,166 million people, or 53.1 per cent of the total population in self-governing countries. In other words, a majority of the people who live in independent countries live in one of the four great ones. If these four huge nations each had other aspects of power commensurate with their population, or if they were united, they could easily dominate and perhaps govern the rest of the world. As it is, the two with strong elements of power in addition to numbers (Russia and the United States) have probably more international influence than all the other countries combined.

Table 3 shows some interesting gaps in the distribution of population by size-class of country. As of 1950 there were no independent nations with 30 to 39 million inhabitants, and none in the broad range from 85 to 149 million. The proportion of the world population (independent) in the 69 countries of less than 30 million was 27.5 per cent; in the eight countries of 40 to 84 million, 22.6 per cent; in the two countries of 150 to 200 million, 15.7 per cent; and in the two countries of over 355 million, 37.4 per cent.

These figures all reveal one demographic clue to the impotency of little nations. Even if such nations found a way to combine their forces effectively, they would still be outnumbered in terms of people. In the analogous land-holding situation in a country with a wealthy proprietor class, the small holders have the advantage of numbers if anything like democracy is practiced; but among nations, the small ones do not even have the advantage of a human majority. If in some international body each nation has one vote, then the small nations do have a majority. But population is such an overriding factor in power, and so unequally distributed, that any international body in which all nations have an equal vote is a hollow sham of democracy rather than the real thing. It would be an odd circumstance if the 54 smallest countries, representing a two-thirds majority of the 82, should determine world policy—because these 54 countries contain only 13 per cent of all the people living in independent countries. It would hardly be democracy if 87 per cent of the people were commanded by the remaining 13 per cent.

TABLE 3.   DISTRIBUTION AND POPULATION IN INDEPENDENT COUNTRIES BY SIZE-CLASS, 1950 ᵃ

Size-Class (Millions)	Number of Countries	Percentage of Countries	Population in Class	Percentage of Total Population
0–4	35	42.7	67.3	3.1
5–9	15	18.3	109.1	5.0
10–14	6	7.3	72.0	3.3
15–19	8	9.8	139.7	6.4
20–29	6	7.3	149.5	6.8
30–39 ᵇ	..	....	.....	....
40–49	2	2.4	89.1	4.1
50–84	6	7.3	403.2	18.4
85–149 ᵇ	..	....	.....	....
150–194	2	2.4	344.7	15.7
194–354 ᵇ	..	....	.....	....
355–464	2	2.4	821.5	37.4
All Classes	82	100.0 ᵇ	2,196.1	100.0 ᶜ

ᵃ Computed from data in United Nations *Demographic Yearbook 1951*, pp. 91–103.
ᵇ No countries are found in these classes. They are given simply to show some of the major breaks in the distribution of countries by population.
ᶜ Totals do not add up to exactly 100.0 because of rounding.

DEMOGRAPHIC FACTORS IN NATIONAL EFFICIENCY

Although the case for population as a factor in power has been put strongly, the truth still remains that it is not the only factor. After all, despite the influence of the United States and Russia, the four most populous nations in the world are not the four most powerful. In fact, the two with the most people, China and India, can be regarded as weaker than Britain at the moment, and in a few years they may once again be weaker than Japan and Germany. Nor can it be said that all the less populous countries are powerless. Australia, with only eight million inhabitants (far below the mean for independent countries and barely above the median) is the most conspicuous example of the powerful but demographically small country. Other examples are Canada, Argentina, the Netherlands, and the Scandinavian countries. Clearly there must be other determinants of national power in addition to total population.

Mention has already been made of the fact that per capita productivity or income is a rough index of the other factors. Although it is obtained by dividing the national income by the population, this is a purely formal relationship. Per capita income varies independently of total population. As Table I illustrated, a country with a big population may have a high per capita income (for example, the United States) or a low one (India); and the same is true of a country with a small population. What per capita income really measures is (a) the adequacy of the resources and (b) the efficiency with which these resources are combined with technology, economic organization, social structure, and population. Two countries with the same efficiency may have a differing real income per head because of different resources; or two countries with the same resources may differ in real income per person because of differences in such things as their technical efficiency, their economic organization, or their population balance. For our purposes the main point to bear in mind is that demographic factors are involved in efficiency (which is partly measured by per capita income), and that this is a channel of influence on a nation's power different from that of sheer total population. The latter measures the sheer strength of the human material that a country has at its command—the raw manpower, so to speak—whereas the demographic factors in efficiency concern the ways in which this human material is produced, trained, and utilized in relation to resources and the social order.

In understanding the role of efficiency in national power, it will help if we group the countries of the world into four classes as follows:

(1) High per capita income and large national income;
(2) High per capita income and small national income;
(3) Low per capita income and large national income;
(4) Low per capita income and small national income.

Evidently class (3) countries are those that achieve their large national income by having a large population rather than by being economically efficient. Those in class (2) are the opposite, for they have a small national income despite their efficiency and therefore must have a small population. Class (1) countries, on the other hand, are those in which both factors are favorable, and class (4) those in which both are unfavorable.

If "large" or "high" is defined as being above the median value in the scale, and "small" or "low" as being below this value, then we can place the seventy countries for which 1949 income data exist exactly in the four classes. This is done in Table 4 where it can be seen that class (1) is a small and elite group of powerful countries and class (4) is a large group of poor countries. If our income data covered all the countries of the world, it is undoubtedly class (4) that would be expanded.

TABLE 4.   FOUR CLASSES OF COUNTRIES WITH RESPECT TO TOTAL AND PER CAPITA INCOME, 1949 [a]

	Number of Countries	Average National Income (Millions)	Average Per Capita Income (Dollars) [b]
Class (1) [b]............	26	16,841	606
Class (2)............	9	698	245
Class (3)............	9	6,545	50
Class (4)............	26	386	55
Median Values.....		1,453	126.5

[a] Countries embraced in each class are as follows:
  Class (1): Argentina, Australia, Austria, Belgium, Canada, Cuba, Colombia, Czechoslovakia, Denmark, France, Germany (West), Hungary, Italy, Netherlands, New Zealand, Norway, Poland, Portugal, Sweden, Switzerland, Union of South Africa, U.S.S.R., U.K., Venezuela, Yugoslavia.
  Class (2): Chile, Finland, Greece, Iceland, Ireland, Israel, Luxembourg, Panama, Uruguay.
  Class (3): Brazil, China, Egypt, India, Indonesia, Japan, Mexico, Pakistan, Turkey.
  Class (4): Afghanistan, Bolivia, Burma, Ceylon, Costa Rica, Dominican Republic, Ecuador, El Salvador, Ethiopia, Guatemala, Lebanon, Liberia, Haiti, Honduras, Iran, Iraq, Korea (South), Nicaragua, Paraguay, Peru, Philippines, Saudi Arabia, S. Rhodesia, Syria, Thailand, Yemen.
[b] Weighted average.

The data reveal an interesting fact. There are certain countries with large populations which nevertheless have not only a low per capita but also a small national income. Thus Brazil, with 49 million inhabitants in 1949, had a national income more than two billion lower than the median. Pakistan, with 79 million, had a national income only one fourth of the median. In other words, their per capita performance is so poor that even a population far above the median does not pull them above the median in national income.

Overpopulation as a Source of Weakness.   Such countries suggest the following question: Is the population so large in relation to resources that it affects adversely the efficiency of the economy?

Or, to put it differently, is the number of inhabitants so great in relation to resources *and the existing stage of efficiency, that gains in efficiency* are more difficult to achieve than they would otherwise be? The answer would seem to be yes in respect to many countries, although conclusive evidence is extraordinarily hard to find. Since the present chapter does not deal with resources directly, we cannot push the analysis far enough to answer the question. The theoretical basis for an affirmative answer is of course that as numbers are increased relative to other factors, a point of diminishing returns is reached and eventually an absolute loss in total income is experienced.

From the standpoint of national power, an additional aspect of the problem needs emphasizing. Not only does national income cease at some theoretical point to grow in proportion to the rise in population, but the ways in which the income is produced and distributed are altered—and they are altered in such a way as to weaken the nation. That a population must have subsistence is axiomatic. The arts of war, propaganda, and diplomatic negotiation, however, require something beyond subsistence. Insofar as a national economic system, because of the density and rapid increase of numbers, must devote most of its economic effort to gaining mere subsistence for its people, it is in no condition to enjoy a high degree of industrial production for purposes of foreign trade, military might, and assistance to allies. It has the manpower but cannot put it to effective use. As war has grown more dependent upon intricate weapons produced by advanced industry, the capitalization of each soldier has increased tremendously. A country bogged down by excessive manpower in relation to both its natural resources and its existing technology cannot secure the necessary capitalization. Nor can it afford the nonmilitary avenues to foreign influence; propaganda by short-wave radio in foreign languages is expensive, as is the dissemination of literature overseas or the maintenance of economic and military missions on foreign soil. A country with a huge population, or even a large national income, may therefore be forced by its overpopulation into a defensive position in international affairs. It may tend to become the object of propaganda rather than the disseminator of it; it may focus its military force on defense rather than offense; it may receive rather than give aid. It may thus be forced into a secondary role which, with a more appropriate population, it could eschew.

An excessive population in relation to productive factors has other disadvantages. One is that an equitable distribution of the national product, if it should occur, would mean virtually no opportunity for capital development.   Funds would be invested in immediate necessities rather than productive enterprise.   By a sort of functional adaptation, therefore, most of the societies with excess numbers have evolved a rigid social stratification whereby a small but wealthy elite runs the government and the economy, the bulk of the population being in great poverty.   The elite has surplus funds to invest; it does the investing and the managing, the rest of the population doing the hard physical work.   While such an arrangement worked well enough in the antique world, it has a hard time surviving now.   The state is today faced with the necessity of instituting basic reforms (thereby offending the rich and the powerful) or of doing nothing (thereby risking the pent-up and explosive resentment of the gradually awakening masses).   Few states in heavily overpopulated agrarian countries have shown themselves capable of steering smoothly and firmly past the two horns of this dilemma. The usual history has been one of vacillation in the face of mounting domestic problems, which has of course weakened the nation in international affairs.

There are other disadvantages accruing from a redundant population, but these can be dealt with later in connection with birth and death rates.   The main point to be stressed for the moment is that a country with a large population in relation to its resources is worse off, from an international point of view, than one with the same resources but with fewer people.   It does not follow, then, that the bigger the population, the more powerful the nation. Whether or not a nation has too many people is independent of the absolute size of its total population, but depends rather on the relationship of population to resources and existing economic efficiency.   Some small countries are overpopulated, some big ones are not.   Our view is that India would have a much better chance to be one of the great powers if it had 100 million fewer citizens than it has.   Egypt, Japan, Italy, China, Pakistan, Mexico, Haiti, Ceylon, and Israel would also be more powerful with fewer people.

A general principle can now be stated.   For top rank among the world's nations a country must have a large population—at least 60 million as of the midpoint of the twentieth century.   With less than this, it can still achieve major-power status if it has, in addition to 40 or 50 million at home, a substantial and well-controlled colonial population abroad.   But a large population does not guarantee great-power status.   Other factors, such as good natural resources, economic efficiency, governmental stability, and military discipline must also be present.   In fact, a population out of balance with the rest of the national economy may be a handicap rather than an advantage.

The Industrial Nation and Its Traits. Given the right number of inhabitants in relation to its resources and existing technology, a nation's claim to potential power rests largely on its economic and political efficiency. The key to efficiency lies in industrialization. The powerful nations are those that are both big and industrialized. The reason is simple. Industry means the use of machines and inanimate sources of power to secure greater production per man-hour of labor. The more industrialized the nation, therefore, the greater is its productive capacity in relation to its population. As a consequence, its competitive economic position vis-a-vis other nations is better and its surplus for military use is greater than if it were not industrialized. This explains why no nation can hope to be a major power without industry. It may be highly industrialized but not very powerful, as in the case of Belgium and Switzerland, but it cannot be powerful and not industrialized. Of course, a large nation which has a low per capita industrialization may nevertheless have a relatively large total industry. This is the sense in which a large population may compensate for inefficiency. Thus India is only slightly industrialized, and yet its total manufacturing production roughly equals that of Sweden, a highly industrialized country.

If industrialization is a key to efficiency, then our task is to examine those traits of a highly industrialized nation (in the per capita sense) which are either affected by demographic variables or measured in demographic terms. There are many such traits, but we shall single out five for special mention. An industrial population is one which has (1) the bulk of its people in nonagricultural pursuits, (2) a high proportion of its people in cities, (3) a sparsity of agriculturalists on its agricultural land, (4) a high proportion of educated people, and (5) a combination of low birth rates and low death rates. Some of these traits appear to be self-evident, but their implications are less so. Others run contrary to common-sense impression.

The Occupational Structure. An industrial economy generally has such an efficient agriculture that relatively few people are required to produce food and fibers, thus permitting the bulk of its labor force to be employed in manufacturing, trade, and services. Even a country which exports primarily agricultural products and therefore seemingly depends on agriculture as its basic pursuit will be found, if its economy is efficient, to have more people employed elsewhere than in farming. Thus Australia, which exports wheat and wool, had in 1947 only 498,000 engaged in agriculture, forestry, and fishing. This was only 15.6 per cent of the labor force, while manufacturing engaged 799,000, or 25.0 per cent; commerce employed 479,000, or 15.0 per cent; and services engaged 572,000, or 17.9 per cent. Similarly, New Zealand had in 1945 only 20 per cent of her labor force in primary production, and Denmark in 1940 had 29 per cent in agriculture. Colombia, on the other hand, had in 1938 no less than 72.7 per cent of her labor force in agriculture, forestry and fishing.

There is, as we should expect, almost a perfect negative correlation between the percentage of the labor force engaged in agricultural pursuits and the amount of per capita income. The occupational structure is therefore a good index of a nation's industrialization or economic efficiency. Taking our four classes of country, we find the average per cent of occupied males engaged in agriculture for each class to be as follows:

> Class (1)......... 36.6
> Class (2)......... 53.0
> Class (3)......... 69.4
> Class (4)......... 75.3

Since three-fourths of the world's population lives in peasant-agricultural countries—that is, countries with more than 50 per cent of their male labor force employed in agriculture—it is not surprising that only Class (1) countries are below this percentage. Class (2) countries are also above the median in per capita income, but they are below in total income. They are below in the latter because they have a small population. Class (3) countries, on the other hand, are those that get their high national income primarily from a large population, and it can be seen that in degree of industrialization they are not far different from those at the bottom of the scale on both counts.

Urbanization. Agriculture requires large land areas. Other economic pursuits use land merely as sites, and little of it is required. Accordingly, to the exent that an economy is mechanized and highly capitalized, its population abandons the countryside and lives in towns and cities. There is, in fact, a very close correlation between urbanization and per capita income. This can be seen in terms of our four classes of country:

Per Cent
in Cities
20,000-plus

Class (1)........	36.8
Class (2)........	30.2
Class (3)........	13.2
Class (4)........	12.4

In this case, even more clearly than in the case of agricultural employment, there is not much difference between classes (1) and (2), which are high per capita income countries, nor is there much difference between the two classes low in per capita income.

Agricultural Density. The overall, or average, population density in a country bears no particular relationship to its degree of industrialization. In fact, we find the highest average densities at either end of the economic scale. Java, Egypt, and Puerto Rico, for example, although they are agrarian countries, rank in general density of settlement with such highly industrial and heavily peopled countries as Belgium, Holland, and Britain. On the other hand, some of the most industrial countries are sparsely settled, as are some of the peasant-agricultural countries. The following figures illustrate the lack of correlation between overall density and degree of industrialism:

POPULATION PER SQUARE MILE, 1950

Urban-Industrial Countries		*Peasant-Agricultural Countries*	
The Netherlands.....	808	Formosa (Taiwan)....	575
Japan...............	583	Ceylon..............	298
United Kingdom.....	536	Haiti...............	290
France..............	197	Philippines..........	168
U.S.A...............	49	Thailand............	93
Sweden.............	41	Mexico..............	34
New Zealand........	18	Brazil..............	16
Australia...........	3	Venezuela...........	13

Clearly the ratio of total population to total land surface is a function of historical development, the kind of land involved, migration, etc., and not a function of economic development per se.

But the *distribution* of the population over the land is definitely a function of the degree of industrialization. In a peasant-agricultural economy the highest concentrations of population are found in those areas which, from the standpoint of climate and soil, are most suited for tillage. Since, however, agriculture requires a great amount of land per unit of production, these concentrations never reach an extreme degree. Something like 2,000 persons per square mile is about the highest density that can be found under purely agricultural conditions. An industrial society, on the other hand, with most of its people living in cities, can reach densities in particular areas as high as 100,000 per square mile. Moreover, as noted already, the agricultural activity of an urban-industrial society is so highly capitalized and so efficient that relatively little labor is required for production. Holdings tend to be large, machinery is substituted for manpower, and people leave the land. As a result, the industrializing society is one in which the rural population is either growing much more slowly than the rest of the population or is actually diminishing, and correspondingly the rural density declines noticeably in relation to overall, or average, density.

In the United States, for example, the rural farm population declined from about 23 per square mile of farm land in 1910 to 13 in 1950. Similarly, the population aged ten and over that is gainfully occupied in agriculture decreased from ten per square mile of farm land in 1890 to six in 1940. In contrast to the decline of rural density, overall density increased during the same period from 21 per square mile in 1890 to 31 in 1910 and 51 in 1950.

One of the best indices of rural density is the number of agriculturally occupied males per square mile of agricultural land. Although the data are hard to obtain and to standardize for all countries, we have attempted to assemble the material. The results show that the more industrialized or urbanized a country, the less its agricultural density. There are many exceptions to the rule (notably Japan), and the coefficient of correlation is only .343. In terms of our four classes of countries, the agricultural densities are as follows:

Class (1)........... 42
Class (2)........... 61
Class (3)........... 189
Class (4)........... 132

It can be seen that there is a pronounced break between the first two classes (countries with high per capita incomes) and the second two (countries with low per capita incomes). The reason why the figure is higher for Class (3) than for Class (4) is apparently that Class (3) countries include more of the densely settled countries with rich agricultural lands and huge populations, whereas Class (4) includes a number of countries whose territories are so poorly developed that they have sparse populations even on the agricultural land.

From a military standpoint the concentration of people in cities is a weakness. It means that the bulk of the population and the major economic activities are located at pin-points on the map, easily bombed and dislocated.   It is easier for a peasant-agricultural country to give up territory and count on guerrilla tactics and attrition of the enemy than it is for an urban-industrial country to do so.   On the other hand, an urban-industrial nation, other things equal, is a more powerful belligerent which can rely upon its striking power to carry the war to the enemy and to protect its large urban concentrations.   It has a greater economic surplus above subsistence which can be turned to war purposes.   In a peasant-agricultural country each region is nearly self-sufficient, but at a low standard of living.   Struggling constantly in peacetime to get simply enough to eat and wear, it has a hard time marshaling resources for the support and equipment of a large military force.   As noted already, if a high agricultural density has been built up, the poverty and rigidity of the economy may become extreme.   In short, we return to the point that military power is not necessarily proportional to total population.   India, China, and Egypt have nothing like the military power that their sheer numbers might imply. There is nothing that can completely substitute for economic efficiency, just as there is nothing that can completely substitute for population.   The price that an advanced nation pays in terms of the concentration of its people in cities is less than that which a peasant-agricultural country pays in terms of economic and social inefficiency.

Educational Achievement.   Education contributes to the power of a nation in several ways.   If diffused throughout the populace to at least an elementary level, it facilitates internal communication and national solidarity.   The schools can be used for indoctrinating the young with national sentiments.   Too much education, of course, may become a drawback to a nation if it leads to skepticism, political hair-splitting, and the excrescence of useless arts.   Yet technical education of a high caliber is absolutely essential to an urban-industrial system.

An agrarian economy can be carried on without benefit of formal education.   The simple techniques of cultivation, involving few tools and no science, can be transmitted by informal instruction and example.   The handicrafts can be learned by apprenticeship.   Even businessmen in backward regions show amazing capacities to keep accounts in their heads.   The number of literate persons may therefore be small indeed, even in areas where reading and writing have been known for centuries.   An urban-industrial economy, on the other hand, rests on a myriad of activities that require precise

knowledge, written communication, and formal education. Consequently, we find that the rise of widespread education (especially
public education provided by the state itself rather than by the
church or private initiative) has risen concurrently with industrialization and urbanization, and today among the countries of the
world there is a high correlation between educational attainment
and economic productivity.

For purposes of international comparison, no perfect measure of
educational achievement is available. Despite certain difficulties,
literacy comes nearer than any other index to being a standard
measure; but it has other defects that limit its usefulness. First, the
sheer ability to read and write gives no clue to the quality or
content of education. In the second place, the degree of literacy
fails to differ much among the advanced nations. It certainly sepa-
rates the advanced from the nonadvanced, but as between Germany,
Sweden, England, and Japan there is little to choose, for they are
all virtually 100 per cent literate above age ten. If the data were
available, one would prefer to go beyond literacy to such things as
the average level of schooling achieved, the ratio of high school and
college enrollment to primary enrollment, the proportion of scientific and technical training in the total educational effort, etc. But
since school systems vary markedly in different countries, information of this type cannot be standardized to even the same degree as
literacy.

Using literacy for what it is worth, we find it a good enough index
to be highly correlated with per capita income, urbanization, and
other measures of economic efficiency. Our four classes accordingly
come out as follows:

	Average Per Cent Illiterate Age 10-plus
Class (1).....	11.4
Class (2).....	20.6
Class (3).....	74.1
Class (4).....	72.0

Not only is the big break as usual between those with high and
those with low per capita income but, as with the previous measures,
a lesser break also occurs between Class (1) and Class (2). Somehow
it seems that a country with a large population gets more out of a
given level of per capita income than one with a small population,
but the cases are so few that it is dangerous to emphasize this interpretation.

It can be argued that widespread education is a consequence rather than a cause of economic efficiency. An examination of the requirements of a modern economy, however, will show that formal education is an indispensable ingredient. As agricultural pursuits shrink until they occupy only 10 to 20 per cent of the population, the rest of the people are engaged in occupations which either require or are enhanced by literacy. As agriculture itself becomes mechanized and scientific, as it undergoes higher capitalization and specialization, as it acquires greater sensitivity to marketing problems and taxation policies, the literate farmer gains an advantage. In the nonagricultural sector, a certain proportion of people must be trained in science, medicine, engineering, accounting, statistics, and other branches of advanced learning. The broader the base of those who get a primary and secondary education, the more easily can the selective mechanism turn up talented people for these learned pursuits. The better the selection, the more readily can the country continue its technological advance.

Low Birth and Death Rates. Few will question that a high standard of health contributes to the strength of a nation, but there are many who, for one reason or another, resist the idea that a high level of planned parenthood also does so. The two characteristics, however, are intimately related. In attempting to show that both are important for national power, we shall discuss the mortality side first and then fertility.

The Consequences of Mortality. National death rates, as we have seen, vary to a marked degree. The variation is probably greater than the figures show, because the backward countries have deficiencies in death registration which usually lead to an understatement of mortality. The following figures, however, give some idea of the approximate range in the expectation of life at birth.

India, 1931–41................... 31.7
Mauritius, 1942–46.............. 33.0
Egypt, 1936–38................. 38.6
Mexico, 1940................... 38.9
Thailand (Bangkok), 1937–38...... 40.0

Trinidad and Tobago, 1945–47..... 54.5
Japan, 1949–50................. 57.9
Ireland, 1940–42................ 60.0
France, 1946–48................ 65.2
Australia, 1946–48.............. 68.4

It can be seen that the force of mortality in underdeveloped countries is sometimes more than twice what it is in advanced countries.

Differences of this magnitude must surely have serious consequences. Among the ways in which good health and longevity favor national efficiency, the following deserve special mention.

(1) *Labor Productivity.* Good health directly enhances labor productivity, because people who are well can work longer, harder, more intelligently, and more effectively than those who are sick. A country with a regularly high death rate is one that has an astonishing amount of debilitating illnes, and, by virtue of this fact, a low output per worker. In a country such as Liberia, for example, the ordinary individual is infested with intestinal worms, subject to dysentery, afflicted with malaria, undernourished and malnourished, and burdened with one or two other diseases as well. The exceptional person in such a milieu is one who is reasonably well. It is little wonder that the average Liberian is poor and shiftless, showing little initiative, making more work for himself by his lack of foresight and his primitive methods, yet working as little as possible within the harsh conditions his very inefficiency has made for him. Nor is it surprising that Liberia has shown little local initiative in economic development. The exploitation of Liberian resources is left principally to outsiders, not because Liberia is a dependency (in fact it is a sovereign country) but because only a nation with a low mortality has enough energy to exploit its resources effectively. "There are instances in the tea gardens of Ceylon of the output of the Indian laboring forces having been increased as much as 25 per cent as the result of treatment of vermifuges, and . . . with a lessened prevalence of disease of all kinds." [9] Ghosh, having summarized the impact of disease in India, has this to say: "Those who survive the attack of the various cell diseases that are rampant in this country must continue to live on a low plane of initiative and working capacity. Death may be selective in the sense that it weeds out the weaker element first; but it does not necessarily improve the quality of those who escape it." [10]

(2) *Resource Exploitation.* In a country characterized by longevity and good health, all parts of the national domain are generally open to exploitation; but in other countries it sometimes happens that certain areas are not utilized because of high mortality. The so-called Dry Zone of Ceylon, for instance, which was once heavily

---

[9] *Report of the Indian Industrial Commission,* 1916–1918, Appendix L, p. 161. Cited in Daniel H. Buchanan, *The Development of Capitalist Enterprise in India* (New York: The Macmillan Co., 1934), p. 385.

[10] D. Ghosh, *Pressure of Population and Economic Efficiency in India* (Bombay: Oxford University Press, 1946), p. 23. See also pp. 57–60 for a summary of nutritional deficiencies in India.

settled, is now very sparsely populated. A 1935 report had this to say: "The people are in a continual state of ill-health through malarial infections and lack of food. Year by year, the deaths exceed the births, infant mortality in Mannar is over 300 per 1000 births, and the population is maintained only by immigration." [11]   The sparse settlement of tsetse fly areas in Africa is well known, as is also the fact that one of the measures for dealing with the disease is to remove people from the infected area (however suitable for agriculture and cattle raising these areas may otherwise be) and resettle them in cleared surroundings. [12]   The rich terai lands of northern Indian and Pakistan, benefiting from drainage from the Himalayas, have remained unexploited until recently because of malaria.   One of the major reasons for the inadequate exploitation of tropical areas, in fact, has been the difficulty of disease control.

(3) *Dependency.* Because of the crippling character of disease, an unhealthy nation, in contrast to a healthy one, suffers a huge burden of sickness-induced dependency. The blind, the bloated, the rotted, and the paralyzed may live on for years or decades before death claims them.   The actual labor force, already debilitated itself, is thus small in relation to the number of the ill that it must support.   This, plus the beggary, insecurity of health, fear of infection, and hand-to-mouth charity that go with it, has a demoralizing effect on the whole population.

(4) *Ill-health and Social Stratification.* Prevalence of ill-health tends to strengthen the rigid stratification usually present in a peasant-agricultural society and thus to weaken national solidarity.   Most diseases, for example, malaria and tuberculosis, are no respecters of persons, but the well-to-do generally have more and better food which builds up their resistance and becomes a master key to better health.   They also have much greater access to whatever medical facilities may exist.   As a result, high mortality in a country is not equally high in all classes.   The upper strata can survive only by tending to their own needs and being relatively indifferent to the claims of the lower strata.   Otherwise their wealth and their advantages would soon be dissipated.   The upper strata fear not only contamination from the poor and dirty, but also deprivation.   There is not enough of the means for good health to go around.   Somebody must take the brunt of the struggle for life, and it is necessarily the disadvantaged people.   The higher classes therefore seek to wall themselves off from the lower.

---

[11] Quoted in Stephen Taylor and Phyllis Gadsden, *Shadows in the Sun* (London: George G. Harrap & Co., Ltd., 1949), p. 42.

[12] *Ibid.,* pp. 152, 171–179.

(5) *Morbidity and the Army.* A generally high mortality also makes doubly difficult the maintenance of standing armies. Army life, with its camps in which thousands live close together under makeshift conditions, has always been especially liable to epidemic attacks. Furthermore, an army must be mobile. It not only draws its personnel from many regions, but it must travel into different areas, each with its own peculiar health hazards. It is only recently that even the most advanced countries have been able to give the soldier a reasonable prospect of good health, quite apart from battle risks. A country with a generally high mortality either is not able to keep its army healthy or must incur extra costs in doing so.

(6) *High Mortality and High Fertility.* Not the least of the disadvantages of a high mortality is that it necessitates a high fertility. The sentiment of nationalism is too strong in most countries to allow population decline to be viewed with equanimity or to permit immigration to make up for a deficiency in natural increase. France, for example, was worried about her excess of deaths over births in the 1930's, and was not at all happy to depend on the immigration of Poles, Italians, and Arabs to fill the gap. As long as a high mortality persists, the birth rate will tend also to be high. In fact, most of the cultures and civilizations evolved prior to the modern age had built into them the mechanisms and motivations yielding a high fertility. They had to have an ample ratio of births because, with a high mortality, they could not have survived otherwise.

THE CONSEQUENCES OF FERTILITY

Whereas a high death rate is virtually never encountered without an accompanying high birth rate, the reverse is not true. The rapid growth of population in the world today is the result of the tendency of mortality to decline ahead of fertility. Accordingly, more countries now suffer whatever disadvantages are brought by an elevated birth rate than suffer those brought by a high death toll. This is necessarily a temporary condition, because a high rate of natural increase, or population growth, cannot be maintained permanently. Birth rates eventually decline after this has happened to death rates earlier. But in the meantime we find a large number of countries with a greater harvest of children than they need.

The disadvantages of high birth rates are not generally admitted for two reasons. First, quite independently of the facts, there is an ideological prejudice against admitting that a high birth rate can in any way be harmful, and so an anti-natalist policy does not gen-

erally appeal to politicians. Second, there is a widespread belief
that an ever greater pool of manpower is a military and economic
asset to a nation. It therefore comes as a shock to many people to
hear it maintained that one of the demographic factors weakening a
nation's power is a high birth rate. No one can maintain that a
pre-industrial birth rate is always and in every way disadvantageous.
In certain instances it may be an asset. But an analysis of the effect
of birth rates on a nation's efficiency will show that in most cases
today the advantage lies with a low rather than a high rate. Among
the considerations, the following deserve particular attention:

(*1*) *Fertility and the Age Structure.* A birth rate as high as 30
to 50 per 1000 population causes the age structure to be heavily
loaded with children. This means that the nation has a burden of
young-age dependency much greater that it would have with a birth
rate, say, of 18 per 1000. For instance, Puerto Rico, which experienced during the period 1932–50 an average annual crude birth
rate of 39.7, had a population in 1950 over half of whom were
children—that is, 52.7 per cent were under 20 years of age. Contrast
with this the United Kingdom which, during the twenty years up to
and including 1950, had an average birth rate of 16.3 and in which
only 28.9 per cent of the population in 1950 was below 20 years of
age. In other words, Puerto Rico had to support almost twice the
proportion of children that the United Kingdom did.

If mortality has declined rapidly, the effect of a high birth rate in
giving a country a heavy child burden is most marked, because the
greatest lowering of the death rate occurs at ages zero to five. Also,
a heavy emigration has the same tendency. Both of these conditions
have prevailed in Puerto Rico and help account for its extraordinarily high proportion of children. Since there is probably an
underenumeration of children in the Puerto Rican census, the percentage cited above may be lower than it should be.

One hears the argument that such an abundance of children is in
the long run a good thing, since they will eventually be adults and
can then contribute economically. But as long as the birth rate
continues to be high, the age structure will continue to be weighted
heavily in favor of children. The next generation, greatly expanded, will have a correspondingly expanded mass of children to
support.

(*2*) *Fertility and the Labor Force.* Not only does a country with
a plethora of births have a child dependency burden, but it also
tends to have a lesser proportion of its *adults* in the industrial labor
force. The constant bearing and rearing of children take up the
time of most women. In industrial countries women with young

children are represented less in the labor force than women without any children or with only older children. In the United States in 1940, for instance, among women aged 18–64 who were married and living with their husband, 21.6 per cent of those with *no* children under ten years of age were in the labor force whereas only 6.5 per cent of those with two or more such children were in the labor force.[13] This fact explains why Hitler's early pro-natalist policy ran into difficulties. Originally he intended both to increase the birth rate and ease the unemployment problem in Germany by removing women from jobs and keeping them in the home. As the tempo of rearmament and army recruitment was intensified under the Third Reich, however, women were urgently needed in industry. The policy of keeping them at home was dropped in favor of other methods of stimulating the birth rate.[14]   In fact, the main factor in raising the birth rate was apparently not the disemployment of women, the giving of marriage loans, or the offering of bonuses, but the policy of full employment. Germany during the depression had had one of the highest rates of unemployment ever known. Under Hitler unemployment went down to almost nothing and labor became scarce. Kirk found that the fluctuations in the birth rate of the Third Reich were almost perfectly correlated with fluctuations in employment.[15] Germany's birth rate, however, never rose high enough to impede seriously the employment of women. The highest rate occurred in 1939, when it stood at 20.4 births per 1000 inhabitants. Compared to the nonindustrial nations, Hitler's Third Reich was clearly a low-birth rate country where the employment of women could be maximized.

If the average woman is giving birth to six children during her lifetime—a likely figure in a peasant-agricultural society—she will spend something like 23 years of her life caring for children under ten years of age,[16] assuming that the children live. Since her ex-

---

[13] John D. Durand, *The Labor Force in the United States, 1890–1960* (New York: Social Science Research Council, 1948), p. 77. The percentages quoted are based on the groups when standardized for age.

[14] D. V. Glass, *Population Policies and Movements in Europe* (Oxford: Clarendon Press, 1940), pp. 289–290; Clifford Kirkpatrick, *Nazi Germany: Its Women and Family Life* (New York: The Bobbs-Merrill Company, 1938).

[15] Dudley Kirk, "The Relation of Employment Levels to Births in Germany," Milbank Memorial Fund *Quarterly*, Vol. 20 (April, 1942), pp. 126–138.

[16] This assumes an average interval of 2.5 years between births. Peasant societies normally have rules that forbid cohabitation immediately after the birth of a child, advocate long periods of nursing, and tend toward reproductive pathology of the woman after the first two or three births. These factors all combine to make the interval between births fairly substantial, especially for the later births.

pectation of life is comparatively short after the reproductive age is reached, this means that the normal condition of the woman is that of being the mother of a child under ten. If, on the other hand, the average woman is giving birth to only 2.5 children during her life-time—a likely figure for an urban-industrial society—she will spend approximately fourteen years of her life caring for children under ten. Thus there is a saving of nearly ten years during the most active period of the woman's life, and since the expectation of life is comparatively long after her children are older and require little or no care, the industrial society has the enormous advantage of a great potential female labor force.

In any country special measures may be adopted to enable mothers of young children to enter the labor force. Under the stress of war, industrial countries have on occasion found it expedient to care for young children during working hours in groups, thus releasing most of the mothers for employment. In England, for example, the last war saw the development of government-aided nursery centers and neighborhood nurseries.[17] Such measures do not work very sat-isfactorily even in countries with a low birth rate. There seems to be an inherent conflict, never successfully overcome, between woman's role as mother and her role as an industrial employee. In a sense the peasant-agricultural nation has less difficulty, because the woman can contribute to agricultural or handicraft production in and around the home without having to be away from the chil-dren. Furthermore, in the large or joint household, the older folk who are less productive economically can care for the young children during the daytime and thus free the mother to work in the fields. But the kind of economy which can employ women in this way is an inefficient economy. As industry develops and hence per capita productivity rises, the burden of child-care increasingly interferes with female employment. The interference reflects itself both in the prejudice against employing women outside the home (because they supposedly *should* be at home caring for children) and in the sheer difficulty of finding suitable arrangements.

(3) *The Birth Rate and Human Waste.* If the high birth rate is linked with a high mortality—as it invariably is if it persists for much more than two generations—it is extremely wasteful of human effort. Under such conditions women are normally either pregnant or nursing, and their lives revolve mainly around children; yet all this effort, the effort of going through repeated gestation, of feeding,

---

[17] Royal Commission on Population, *Report* (London: Her Majesty's Stationery Office, Cmd. 7695, 1949), pp. 182–184.

clothing, and caring for the young, is largely wasted. It is wasted because a good share of those born never reach maturity. For instance, in India during the years from 1931 to 1941 the birth rate was excessive, being approximately 45 per 1000 population. The death rate was also high, averaging about 31.2 per 1000. The difference was large enough to give India a rapid growth in population during the decade, but still, of those born, only 55.6 per cent ever reached age twenty.[18] In New Zealand, on the other hand, the natural increase during the decade was almost as great (8.9 per 1000 per year), but it was achieved with a much lower birth rate (17.7 per year). New Zealand was able to have this natural increase with a low birth rate because its death rate was extraordinarily low, averaging 8.7 during the decade. In other words, New Zealand's demographic balance was very efficient. Of those born, 94.0 per cent reached age twenty. India was paying a terrific cost for a net result that New Zealand achieved at much less cost.[19]

The fact that, when a low mortality is achieved, the greatest reductions are made in infancy and early childhood, means that an improvement is made in the efficiency of reproduction greater than the drop in the *total* death rate would suggest.

(4) Fertility and Health. Excessive childbearing, like malnutrition or disease, is a cause of ill-health and death. For example, countries with high birth rates are also countries with high maternal mortality rates. In the Ceylon figures on cause of death, one finds that the average annual deaths per 1000 from puerperal infections were 7.7 during the three years 1947–49, and from other diseases of pregnancy, childbirth, and the puerperium, 26.1; whereas in New Zealand during the same period the average annual deaths per 1000 were only 0.8 from puerperal infections and 2.0 from diseases of pregnancy, childbirth and the puerperium. The danger to women of frequent reproduction is reflected also in the life tables. Whereas in virtually all of the low-fertility countries the survivorship of women is greater than that of men at all ages, the reverse is frequently true with respect to the reproductive ages in high-fertility countries. On the island of Mauritius, for instance, which has predominantly an Indian population and a high birth rate, the fe-

---

[18] Kingsley Davis, *The Population of India and Pakistan* (Princeton: Princeton University Press, 1951), pp. 36, 63, 69.

[19] The figures for New Zealand were computed from data in the United Nations, *Demographic Yearbook 1951.* We are aware that New Zealand's age structure, in contrast to that of India, caused the crude rates to exaggerate fertility and minimize mortality. But the fact remains that New Zealand was replacing its population with a very small effort expended on reproduction, as is characteristic of advanced nations.

male expectation of life at birth for the years 1942–46 exceeds the male expectation, being 33.8 years as against 32.2; but from age fifteen to age thirty-five the female survivorship for each five-year age interval is less than that for the male.

A high birth rate tends to increase mortality not only by its effect on women but also by its effect on children. The proper care of children becomes difficult when a family has a large number. If, in addition, the people are poor and undernourished, proper care becomes impossible. This is one of the reasons why countries with high birth rates are almost invariably countries with high infant and childhood mortality—a relationship that has been frequently noted. All told, excessive fertility can be regarded as one of the specific causes of a high death rate.

(5) *The Birth Rate and Education.* Children are of no value to a nation unless they are assimilated to the national culture, properly trained, and placed advantageously in the occupational structure. However, a huge increment of children every year in ratio to the total population interferes seriously with this process of "socializing" the young. Adequate educational facilities essential to the task are almost impossible to provide. Formal training is denied to many and is substandard in quality for those who receive it. There are, of course, other reasons why educational facilities are inadequate, but one reason is a high birth rate per se. It has been stated by Puerto Rican officials that the cost of education was "breaking the back" of the insular treasury. With 52 per cent of the population below twenty years of age, expenditure on education has represented one-fourth of the budget (in contrast to one-tenth in the continental United States), and yet only about half the children of school age were in school. It is not wholly accidental that the countries with high birth rates are those with much illiteracy.

(6) *Fertility and Employment.* Not only in formal education but also in the vocational placement of youth does an excessive birth rate impose obstacles. A poor country has difficulty finding the capital to put to work in efficient ways the evergrowing increments to the labor force. Instead the government is tempted to adopt means of full employment which are detrimental to efficiency. In India the writer frequently heard people raise the following objection to some suggested improvement in agricultural technique: "What would we do with the millions who would be thrown out of work?" Part of the specious rationale for dividing up the land in agrarian reform movements is not to increase efficiency (although that may happen under certain conditions) but to *make* more work. If jobs are not found or made for the myriads of new workers, there

is the likelihood that the unemployed will not only demand a dole but will be fruitful soil for the seeds of political agitation and revolt, thus weakening the solidarity of the nation. In agrarian countries the lack of economic opportunity outside agriculture often means, given an elevated birth rate and some control over mortality, that the population growth is backed up on the farms. The peasant's numerous progeny, trying to make a living on ever smaller plots, are underemployed; they have work only part of the time and when they are at work they work inefficiently, substituting labor for capital. Examples of agrarian regions surfeited with manpower are easy to find. Vance has analyzed this situation in detail for the southern states of the United States.[20]

In sum, a birth rate of 30 or more per 1000 inhabitants is a drag on any nation. It is certainly a drag from a short-run military point of view, because it loads the age structure with children who increase nonmilitary costs; it withdraws women from the industrial labor force; it increases ill-health and mortality; and it places a great burden on educational and other facilities which must be either expanded or allowed to deteriorate. Accordingly, both Hitler and Mussolini were mistaken in their policy of trying to increase the birth rate. Both of them knew that they would shortly be at war. They should have known that the main task of a nation at war is to win the war. Had their population policies succeeded as they hoped, the flood of births would have made their chances of winning even less than they were. As it turned out, Mussolini did not succeed in raising the birth rate at all in Italy, and Hitler succeeded only in getting a normal post-depression rise earlier than usual. Eventually other countries, which had no pro-natalist policy at all, such as the United States, had a greater rise in the birth rate than did the Third Reich. As it turned out, therefore, the pro-natalist policies of the Fascist nations did not interfere with their war effort because they did not succeed. The kind of birth rate that really impedes a war effort is the kind that an urban-industrial nation has never succeeded in inducing by any policy yet developed. It is the kind of birth rate which Russia had during all her wars and which was one of the factors making her a weaker nation than her total population and her resources would have otherwise made her. It is the kind of birth rate that peasant-agricultural nations always have. Even Japan, with its remarkably fast industrialization, was impeded in its militry effectiveness by a birth rate that hovered around 30 per 100 during the 1930's and 1940's.

---

[20] Rupert B. Vance, *All These People: The Nation's Human Resources in the South* (Chapel Hill: University of North Carolina Press, 1945), Parts I and II.

Although it be granted that a high birth rate is a short-run handicap, one may still argue that in the long run it is a good thing because it guarantees an adequate supply of manpower in the future. This was seemingly the sort of consideration which Hitler had in mind, made particularly real to him when he looked to the east and saw the rapid growth of the Russian masses. But the objection to this cannon-fodder point of view is that it ignores the importance of technology, of weapons and science, in the conduct of modern warfare. If a high birth rate carries a heavy penalty in terms of economic and social retardation, it is not worth the extra manpower that it gives. This consideration, of course, pushes the argument back to the question of population growth in relation to long-run military efficiency.

Let us grant at once that under certain conditions an increase in total population may be a source of long-range military strength. If the country has the resources to support a growing population at a rising standard of living, as the United States had, then a fertility high enough to yield such a growth is a definite advantage, provided of course the economy and political system are adequate to realize the potentialities of the situation. The issue, however, is not clear until mortality is brought into the picture. As we have seen already, a population may grow rapidly without a high birth rate, provided its mortality is very low. If this is the case, the growth in numbers is secured at a minimum cost. Additional growth can be secured cheaply by immigration, and this may be an advantage provided the immigrants can be culturally and economically assimilated. The combination of a really high fertility and a very low mortality is at best a temporary situation and a dubious asset. Today it results chiefly from an artificial reduction in the death rate by bringing modern public health measures to backward areas such as Ceylon, Formosa, Cyprus, and Puerto Rico. In such countries the birth rate must be speedily reduced or else the deleterious consequences of continued high fertility will be so damaging that the death rate will eventually be pushed up again. Finally, the countries with both a high birth rate and a high death rate are at a tremendous disadvantage, because they suffer heavy costs on both sides of the demographic ledger. Even when, in such cases, the death rate is sufficiently lower than the birth rate to yield a substantial growth in population—as is usually the situation today—the costs are far too great for military and economic efficiency. Indeed, under these conditions the growth of population itself may be a positive handicap, as the cases of India, Pakistan, Egypt, Indonesia, Mexico, and many other nations indicate.

It must be stressed that other conditions besides those cited also lead to national weakness. It is our business to discus the demographic factors, but not our intention to suggest that these factors alone are operative or that, in any given case, they are necessarily the most important. Poverty arising from economic and technological inadequacy is a major cause of national impotency. High birth and death rates are a consequence of poverty as well as a cause of it. Indeed, they are so closely tied up with the economic and social organization that, as we have seen, they are highly correlated with different stages of development. Yet it is true that despite this close association, the demographic variables have effects in their own right and are therefore factors in the total equilibrium of forces contributing to national strength or weakness.

CONCLUSION

We have now covered, from a demographic point of view, some of the traits of a powerful nation. Such a nation is one that has a large population, a rich and extensive territory, an industrial economy, a high proportion of its people in nonagricultural pursuits, a high degree of urbanization, a low agricultural density, a great amount of public education, and a balance of low fertility and low mortality. Few nations in the world have all of these attributes. Those that have them we call the Great Powers.

In a sense there is nothing new in this conclusion. We knew to begin with that it was true. But it is worth documenting general beliefs with more specific data and tracing out the causal connections. Furthermore, when it comes to deciding which of two or more roughly equal nations has the edge in power, the issue can be better decided in terms of ordered knowledge than in terms of intuition.

A complicating factor is that of colonies. Presumably a nation's strength is greatly enhanced by extensive possessions overseas, although the French case does not lend *prima facie* credence to this assumption. Essentially our view is that nations have colonies primarily because they are powerful, not vice versa. A weak nation either has no colonies or has such impecunious and backward ones (for example, Spain and Portugal) that they are of no material help. A nation losing its strength tends also to lose its colonies; a nation gaining strength tends to get them, if there are any to be had. Much depends on the period in question, for colonialism as such is on the decline. It may well be claimed that for awhile a nation's strength is maintained by colonies it was once strong enough to get, on the theory that it is easier to keep them than to get them; but such a prop to strength is at best a temporary one, because a weak nation cannot really hold important colonies. A nation's possession or nonpossession of colonies accordingly offers no very important qualification to our discussion of the demographic factors in national power.

We have also said little about another complicating factor—alliances of nations. Seldom does one nation fight a war alone or exercise its influence without aid. But an alliance relies for its strength upon two factors: first, the degree to which the different nations are really committed in one another's behalf, and second, the power of the individual nations which compose the alliance. The first factor lies outside our sphere. It is largely a function of cultural and political conditions as well as strategy. The fact that the English-speaking nations have supported one another in two world wars is no accident, nor is it a coincidence that the Balkan nations have mutually collaborated only when compelled to do so by force and then never completely. Our demographic indices may suggest some of the cultural and political bases for alliances, but they reveal better the strength of the nations that compose an alliance.

It happens that the major division in the world today is that between the Communist bloc on the one hand and the free world on the other. Although the strength of each bloc is largely the strength of its individual components, the fact cannot be ignored that the Communist world is much more tightly integrated than is the free world. Indeed, some of the nations of the nominally free world remain aloof and could better be described as neutral. If one bloc works together more completely and effectively than another, its total strength is greatly enhanced. The free nations of the world will have to live closely and harmoniously if they are to realize the potential strength to which their traits as individual nations entitle them. In both camps of course there are sharp conflicts of interest. Integration is not easy on either side. The attempt to achieve it is being tried by fundamentally different methods, and it remains to be seen which method will have the most success when the chips are down.

11

SOCIAL CHANGE IN SOVIET RUSSIA

ALEX INKELES

Even in the case of so imposing, rapid, and extensive a social revolution as that experienced in the Soviet Union, one discerns a host of changes which can be equated with the broader sweep of social change that affected Western society in the last century. In the realm of authority, for example, there has been a shift from traditionally legitimated authority to a system of formal rational-legal authority although with a large admixture of charismatic legitimation. In the economic sphere the transition has been from the predominantly agricultural to the heavily industrialized, with a concomitant change in agriculture from small-scale units and a limited if not primitive technology to large-scale units worked primarily by machine. Accompanying these alterations in the economic structure there has been a characteristic trend in the direction of urbanism, with the development of large-scale urban aggregates. The extended family has been largely broken up, to be replaced by more or less isolated conjugal family units, and women in enormous numbers have been drawn into the occupational system. In interpersonal relations the "familistic," or what Talcott Parsons calls the particularistic, patterns of an earlier era have been ever pushed into the background to be replaced increasingly by formal, impersonal or "universalistic" relationship patterns under the impact of increasing role specialization and spreading bureaucratization and technicization. A relatively stable system of social stratification, based largely on role ascription and traditional criteria for the assignment of prestige, has been replaced by extensive social mobility with status largely assigned on the basis of achievement in turn intimately linked with the attainment of education and technical skill.

In the realm of values and fundamental "life-ways," religion has lost ground to the progressive secularization of values; and distinctive national folk cultures, with their infusion of religious prescription, have in significant degree given way to a more or less uniform national culture with the predominance of rational legal norms for regulating individual behavior. The relaxed, nonstriving, undisciplined, personality type which was modal, if not actually favored, has fallen into official disfavor relative to the model of the disciplined, goal-oriented, striving, energetic, optimistic "new Soviet man." Even that respect in which social change in the Soviet Union is frequently taken to be most distinctive—namely, the presence of a conscious and centrally determined plan for change—can be said to have its historical parallels, to which Kroeber calls attention, in Russia in the person of Peter, elsewhere in the Meiji modernization of Japan, and more recently in the wholesale social change in Turkey effected by Kemal Ataturk.

Although it may be comforting to be able thus to reduce the discrete aspects of changes in Soviet society to relatively standard descriptive categories, our understanding of the total phenomenon of social change in the Soviet Union is thereby only slightly enhanced. For such an approach fails adequately to deal with the unique *combination* of those elements which the Soviet Revolution represents. No less than inventions in material culture, the social invention of the revolutionary process takes its character from the unique combination of elements already at hand rather than from the generation of entirely new patterns of social relations.

In the Soviet case we have the distinctive combination of planned social change instituted from above, centrally directed and executed by a body whose occupational role is that of effecting change, backed by the power and all the economic and political force which a totalitarian regime can muster, guided by a central theory or ideology, carried out at a relatively unprecedented rate, and extending into every dimension of social life. Even leaving aside the distinctive element of the Marxist orientation of the Soviet Revolution, it is most doubtful that any program of this type on such a scale and of such intensity can be found in recorded history. Yet this is not to be taken as an event never reasonably expected to recur. Indeed, its significance comes largely from the fact that its leaders see it as a model for programs of social change in time to encompass the major part, if not all, of the world's peoples and societies. Furthermore, in many areas of the world it is apparently perceived as a model by revolutionaries who are already in power or who are making a significant bid to gather power into their hands. Consequently, although unique for its early season, the Soviet Revolution may become a widespread standard for social change in the next half century. Thus, added to its intrinsic interest as a social phenomenon is its continuing political significance. We are under double incentive, therefore, to seek in the Soviet Revolution the reflection of those "principles of change" which Robert MacIver set as the hardest yet potentially the most illuminating task of the social scientist.

The Russian Revolution cannot properly be conceived of as merely an event of precisely limited duration in the same sense as the American Revolution. It is rather a process of substantial duration, and one which affected all the major institutional components of the society in which it occurred. Indeed, it is not one process, but a complex of processes operating at different levels and rates. For example, political authority has never really in any fundamental sense undergone a transformation in Soviet society. From the earliest days control has been exercised by a small group of tightly organized, highly conscious and purposeful ideologists with a marked drive for political power. Such change as did occur was in the direction of making explicit and concrete the basic implications and propensities of the Leninist position which Stalin carried to its logical conclusion.

In contrast, Soviet policy in regard to the family has undergone profound change during the course of the revolution. Stimulated by Engels' hostility to the "bourgeois" monogamous family and his prediction that many of its functions would wither away to be replaced by state care and raising of children, and spurred on by Lenin's assertion that to be a socialist one must believe in complete freedom of divorce, the Soviet regime initially subjected the family to a frontal attack including divorce by post card, and legal and free abortion. But today not only is abortion no longer free, it is a serious offense except under certain extreme circumstances, and divorce is at least as difficult and expensive to obtain as in the great majority of states in the United States. The family as an institution is reconstituted in the eyes of the regime, defined as a pillar on which the society rests. Parents are hailed as the partners of the state in the bringing up of healthy, patriotic, obedient citizens devoted to work.

In the rural areas of the Soviet Union we are treated to still another level and rate of change. For here is a vast and complex form of social organization for agricultural production built at untold cost by a process of forced change on an enormous scale, followed by years of experimentation and adjustment, and by the regime's testimony proved in the test of war as successful in meeting its social functions. Nevertheless, it is inherently unstable, is clearly viewed by the leadership as transitory, and is marked for further radical transformation.

To understand this complex, to discover the essential pattern, we must discern the elements which have entered into the process of social change in Soviet society. Three main elements may be analytically distinguished, which have been in interaction with varying degrees of intensity throughout the history of Soviet social development. The first of these we term Bolshevik ideology, the conceptual apparatus, the aspirations and objectives of the power elite. The second we may designate as the social structure which the new authority inherited, in a sense, when it seized power in revolutionary Russia. The third is constituted by the new institutional forms and social forces set in motion by the revolutionary upheaval itself, and particularly by the early efforts of the Bolshevik leadership to place its program in operation. From the interaction of these elements, from the changes wrought in and on each, has emerged the structure of Soviet society as we know it today.

Can we discern in the interaction of the elements we have distinguished any pattern that would have more general application to revolutionary programs committed to the radical transformation of society? Viewed in the perspective of more than thirty years of development, the Soviet revolution suggests the existence of a patterned sequence of revolutionary social transformation which may have general relevance. The major determinant of that sequence appears to be the differential adaptability of social organization to consciously directed social change. In a sense the problem is one of delineating the timetable of social revolution and the limits on its effect and extent. Essentially, we seek an answer to the question: What in the old social structure can the revolution sweep away almost at once, what basic social changes can it effect in a relatively short course of time, and what institutional forms and behavioral patterns are most persistent and may be changed by the revolutionary process only in the very long run, if at all?

The different levels of change are, of course, not restricted to completely discrete time periods, but rather overlap substantially. Nevertheless, some rough congruence can be established between the major processes of revolutionary development and certain broad time periods. In a double sense, therefore, we may speak of the revolutionary timetable, from which we can read both the place of departure and the destination (or direction) of change, and the approximate time of initiation and termination of the various processes of change. The following exploration of the levels of social change in Soviet society will, therefore, distinguish three major time periods of revolutionary development in the Soviet Union: an initial period, termed the period of the seizure of power, lasting until roughly 1924; an intermediate period, termed the period of the consolidation of power, running until 1936; and a third, or current period, called the period of the stabilization of social relations. Such a division of Soviet development into stages and time periods, however, must be clearly recognized as a construct we impose on the data. Least of all should it be taken as a "timetable" in the sense that it provided an advance schedule for the Communist Party. On the contrary, the stages of Soviet development were almost certainly not foreseen by the men who came to power in October, 1917. Indeed, it may be said that it is precisely the fact of their inability accurately to anticipate the long-range development of Soviet society that makes more comprehensible many acts of the Bolshevik leadership which subsequently required radical alteration and adjustment.

The initial period of revolutionary development, the period of the seizure of power, begins before the revolution with the emergence of the revolutionary party, and witnesses the formulation and elaboration of its ideology and program of action, with successive adjustments in both political organization and ideology to meet the exigencies of the local situation and to incorporate the lessons of experience. The period includes, of course, the actual revolutionary seizure of power, and continues until the formally proclaimed seizure of power is rendered truly factual by the destruction, or at least the neutralization, of effective organized opposition. In the Soviet case this period may be dated as beginning roughly in 1898 with the formation of the Russian Social Democratic Party, certainly no later than 1902–03 when the Bolshevik faction, under Lenin's leadership, split with the Menshevik group; and it extends through the October 1917 Revolution and the subsequent period of Civil War and foreign intervention. In its last phases this period saw the calculated and ruthless overthrow and supplanting of the independent emergent political entities on the periphery of the former Tsarist empire, climaxed by the bloody and arbitrary destruction of the Menshevik social-democratic government of Georgia. The end of the period may be symbolized by the adoption of the Constitution of the Union in 1924, which established the unquestioned hegemony of the central power in the federated structure of Soviet Russia.

In the broad social and economic realm this period is characterized by the destruction or radical transformation of many of the gross institutional features of the old social order, and the primarily proclamatory initiation of the revolutionary features of the new social order. Perhaps the most important, certainly the first, major change involved the structure of power relationships through the transfer of political authority from the Provisional Government to the Workers' and Peasants' Government of Russia, meaning, in effect, the Communist Party. Following closely on the transfer of formal governmental authority and intimately associated with it, came the basic shift in the structure of property relationships, beginning with the nationalization of all land and its expropriation without compensation and the abolition in perpetuity of the right of private property. The establishment of workers' control over industry and related establishments was in turn followed by confiscation and nationalization of most industry. Nationalization of the banks, the effective confiscation of important holdings of individuals therein, the elimination of the rights of inheritance, and the proscription on hiring the labor of others completed the radical transformation of property relationships. Similar structural changes were effected in the nation's legal system, with the outright abolition of "all existing general legal institutions," the repudiation of the existing legal codes, and their replacement with a new system of People's Courts and the rule of "revolutionary legal consciousness."

The changes in the locus of authority, the transfer of property, the dissolution of the old legal system, in effect meant the destruction of the old formal class system. But this was further advanced by a decree abolishing all classes, divisions, ranks, and distinctions save that of "citizen of the Russian republic," extending to the abolition of even military ranks and titles. Finally these transformations reached to the realm of thought, belief, and interpersonal relations with the separation of church and state and at least the formal declaration of freedom of conscience, the institution of civil marriage, virtually complete freedom of divorce, the legalization of abortion, and the declaration of absolute equality for women in all legal, political, and economic relations.

The second major period of revolutionary development, the period of the consolidation of power, beginning in 1924, extends through the latter part of the New Economic Policy and the massive programs of industrialization and forced collectivization, down to the formal declaration of the establishment of socialism embodied in the so-called Stalin Constitution of 1936. The revolution had been fought to a successful issue. The old society was a bombed out shell, with only here and there a torn wall still standing, although a certain subterranean structure or foundation stood relatively undamaged and firm, and represented a phenomenon yet to be dealt with by the regime.

The task of revolution shifted to that of building the new society on the ruins of the old. Lenin was not unaware that the revolution was only a surface phenomenon so long as it was restricted to the formal destruction of the old social order. Many a revolution before had seen the rapid restoration of the old order despite the most sweeping formal legal changes. Indeed, Lenin was wont to speak of what he termed a peculiar "Bolshevik conceit" implicit in the assumption that revolution could be effected by decree rather than by the systematic construction of new institutional forms and patterns of social organization and human relationship. It is in this period, therefore, that we find the extensive social experimentation and innovation which produced the main institutional forms that we recognize today as the characteristic features of Soviet society. Indeed this period may be regarded as the second Soviet revolution (the first having been the revolution in the structure of formal power and authority): the social revolution, the revolution in the forms and patterns of social and economic organization.

By the late 1920's, in the agricultural realm, for example, the land was nationalized and the landowner gone from the countryside. But in most essential respects the forms of rural social and economic organization remained much as they had been before the revolution. The old patterns of social differentiation were still much in evidence. In 1927 8 per cent of the peasants were still landless, 20 per cent were classified as semi-proletarians, and over a third of the households were still obliged to hire their animal power and farm implements from the rich peasant or "kulak." Only about 3 per cent of the peasant households were joined in state or co-operative farms. As Sir John Maynard has phrased it, ten years after the revolution "the countryside was back in pre-war days, minus the landlord."

It was into this situation that the regime moved with its astounding program of forced collectivization on a scale unprecedented in history and with a ferocity and intensity such that even Stalin had to draw back, call a temporary halt, and cry "dizzy with success." Some 25 million farm families, constituting more than 100 million souls, were forced in the span of a few short years radically to change the whole pattern of their lives. Five million of these people, those in the families designated as "kulak," were dispossessed outright of their land and property, and a large proportion forcibly transplanted to other parts of the country. The Russian countryside glowed red—the sky with flames of burning peasant huts and government buildings, the ground with the blood of cattle slaughtered by the peasants and peasants slaughtered by the militia and the flying squads of Communist workers and the agitated peasant "Committees of the Poor." Between 1928 and 1933 the cattle population fell from 70 to 38 million, sheep and goats from 147 to 50, and pigs from 26 to 12 million. Losses of this magnitude for a predominantly agricultural country are so staggering as to be very nearly beyond comprehension. They meant for the country at large a drastic and violent decline in the supply of animal food and industrial raw materials, and for the villages in addition a colossal loss of draught power and animal fertilizer. Once again famine stalked the land.

Yet out of this chaos and destruction there emerged a new form of social organization which constitutes one of the major institutional complexes of Soviet society, incorporating well over half the population. The *kolkhoz* or collective farm system is a distinctive form of social organization, with its *kolkhoz* chairman, general meeting, advisory council, and other administrative forms; its brigades and links for the organization of the work group; its labor day, piece rate, and bonus system of remuneration; its social insurance funds, communal buildings, peasant reading huts, radio loudspeaker nets, and other instrumentalities for the provision of social services and facilitation of communication by the regime; its complicated contracts with the machine tractor stations and state breeding farms, and with government agencies which control production and regulate delivery to the state of assigned quotas of produce; its *usadba* or private garden plot, and other forms for relating the private economy of the peasant to the collectivized, state-oriented segment of the agricultural economy. All these are examples of the diverse institutional arrangements which had to be devised to convert the idea of collective farming into an adequate form of social organization capable of effecting agricultural production in accord with the interests of the regime, which would yet have an essential minimum of congruence with the needs and expectations of the peasants. Thus we see in the agricultural realm the characteristic pattern of the second phase of revolutionary development—to meet newly created or perceived needs, new forms of social organization are devised, tested, re-formed and reshaped, and finally woven into some viable system of social institutions for relating men to men, to the machinery of production, and to the larger society.

Certainly less violent, but perhaps no less spectacular, was the industrial transformation of Soviet society effected by the Five Year Plans. In the course of the first Five Year Plan more than 20 billion rubles were invested in industrialization, above 80 per cent of that sum going to heavy industry alone. The gross product of large-scale industry as evaluated in fixed prices was by Soviet report more than doubled, and although there is much doubt as to the accuracy of the figure it does reflect the magnitude of development, which is also apparent in the fact that the industrial labor force doubled in size from 11 to 22 million workers and employees.

In contrast to the situation in agricultural production, the regime was faced with much less of a task of creating institutional forms *de novo*, for there was at hand both the model of industrial organization in pre-revolutionary Russia and throughout the Western world as well as Soviet experience gained in the years of state industrial administration since 1917. At the same time, the leaders' experience was largely limited to restoring to its former level an already established industrial structure, whereas they were now faced with the rather different task of building a new industrial system. The problem was intensified not only by the greater magnitude and complexity of the new industrial order, but also by the fact that many of the industries now introduced were new to the Russian scene. Consequently in this area as well there arose imposing problems of evolving new forms of social organization, and of integrating the new molecular institutions with the molar social system.

The result was a vast amount of experimentation, invention, revision, and readjustment in the social and organizational forms which constituted the structure of Soviet industry. For example, to find the most efficient formula for relating the discrete industrial enterprises to each other the regime abolished the chief administrations or *glavks* and replaced them with combines in May, 1929, only to abolish the combines in turn and replace them in 1934 with the previously abolished chief administrations now reconstituted in revised form. As might be expected, the greatest uncertainly centered on problems of managerial responsibility, with a constant strain manifested between the demands of efficient, authoritative management on the one hand, and on the other the requirement for central control by higher economic organs and for supervision and political surveillance by the local Party and trade union organizations. There was, consequently, a long history of experimentation and halting development before there emerged the current Soviet variant on the common pattern of responsible plant management, which they termed *edinonachalie*, or one-man management.

A comparable range of problems was met in the effort to establish measuring instruments and standards for evaluating progress and making investment decisions. In time the regime was forced to adopt elaborate indices of qualitative and quantitative production, to set and manipulate prices, and to evolve a system of cost accounting, although many of the devices adopted had been assumed by Marxian economics to be unnecessary in a socialist economy. Comparable experimentation occurred in the effort to integrate the worker into the requirements of the evolving system of factory production. This produced in time the elaboration of work norms and quotas, the extensive piece rate system, the bonuses, socialist competition, the labor book, and other characteristic features of labor organization in the Soviet factory. The trade unions did not escape the process of adaptation, and were forcibly reoriented from concentration on protecting the rights of workers and collective wage bargaining, to emphasis on maximizing production, inculcating labor discipline, etc.

By the mid 1930's the process of tearing down the old social structure was complete in virtually all its phases, and the main foundations of the new social order laid down. The factories were built, and the peasants organized in collective farms under firm state control. The first process, that of tearing down the old social structure, was particularly facilitated by the release of revolutionary energies and by the natural destructive forces set in motion with the loosening of social bonds characterizing revolutionary periods. The second process, that of laying the foundations for the new social order, was greatly facilitated by the devotion and extra human effort of a small minority—even though a minority of several millions—pushing on the rest of the population by example, persuasion, and where necessary by force. This was the "heroic" phase of the revolutionary process.

But neither revolutionary fervor nor extra human effort constitute a firm basis for the persistent day-to-day operation of a large-scale social system. The political and economic development of the revolution had now run far ahead of the more narrowly "social." In the haste of revolutionary experiment, no systematic attention had been given to the congruence of the newly established institutional forms with the motivational systems, the patterns of expectation and habitual behavior, of the population. Furthermore, as the new institutions began to function they produced social consequences neither planned nor anticipated by the regime. The leaders found themselves somehow compelled to bring these elements into line. For they found that it was one thing to build large factories and form collective farms, but quite another matter to get those institutions to function persistently at reasonable levels of efficiency. They came slowly to realize that it was one matter to enroll the peasants in collectives and to mobilize millions of workers in industry, but yet another matter to induce them to labor discipline and high productivity. This realization was symbolized in Stalin's declaration in 1935 that, whereas in the first years of the Plan it was technique that was decisive, in the new period "cadres [personnel] decide everything."

We enter therefore the current, but what is also in a sense the last, phase of revolutionary development in the Soviet Union, the period of the stabilization of social relationships. It is this period that answers in large part the question: What elements in the old social order tend to persist despite the revolution, and are changed, if at all, only in the long run? It appears that despite the massive destruction of the main formal elements of the old social structure and the extensive elaboration of new social forms, a large number of basic attitudes, values, and sentiments, and of traditional modes of orientation, expression, and reaction tend to be markedly persistent. Although the revolution effected a radical shift in the locus of power, the traditional attitudes of the population to authority and authority figures cannot be assumed to have undergone a comparable transformation. The change in the formal pattern of property relationships was equally fundamental, yet there is little evidence that the common man's "sense" of property, his attitude toward its accumulation, possession, and disposition, was altered in significant degree. In brief, we come in contact here with national character or better the modal personality patterns of the population, which show a marked propensity to be relatively enduring despite sweeping changes in the formal structure of society. Certain core or primary institutional forms, notably the kinship structure and the pattern of interpersonal relations within the family, show a comparable resistance and delayed reaction to change despite the revolutionary process.

Such persistent elements in the social system have a major impact on the revolutionary ideology and the new institutional patterns created under its imperative in the earlier phases of the revolution. The interaction of these forces of course changes both elements, but if we are to judge by Soviet experience the accommodations and adjustments come sooner and are more extensive in the new institutional forms than in the traditional primary institutions and their associated behavioral patterns. The really massive attack on the problem, the large-scale conscious adjustments to meet this situation, appear to be delayed until the later stages of revolutionary development. This delay occurs in part because realization of the need for such adjustments comes but slowly to practical men in the habit of effecting social change by decree, and in part because the initial focus is so heavily on the destruction of the old society and the institution of the major formal structure of the new social order. In the case of a Marxist-oriented revolution, furthermore, there is the added influence of an ideology which predisposes the leaders to assume that fundamental changes in the patterns of human relations, seen by them as part of the dependent "superstructure" of society, must follow naturally and inevitably from changes in the formal political and economic system.

In any event, from the early 1930's there began, in regard to a large number of Soviet institutions, a series of fundamental policy changes which many saw as the restitution of the old social order, others as the betrayal of the revolution. The "great retreat," as Timasheff has labeled it, represented the regime's effort to place social relations on a stable basis adequate to the demands of a large-scale industrialized, hierarchic, authoritarian society. In the last analysis it was designed to produce disciplined, compliant, obedient individuals with respect for authority, who yet had a strong sense of individual responsibility and were active, goal-oriented, optimistic, stable.

Appropriately, basic changes came earliest in the realm of education, which witnessed rapid abandonment of progressive education and its replacement by traditional subjects organized in standard curricula, a formal system of examinations and grades, and perhaps most important, the restoration of the authority of the teacher. History was rewritten to reconstitute the role of the individual as a historical force, the great national leaders of the past were restored and now glorified, and the inculcation of patriotism became a prime responsibility of the school. The family, as already indicated, was restored to grace and defined as a pillar of the state, the authority of parents emphasized and their role defined as partner of the state in the upbringing of disciplined, loyal, patriotic citizens devoted to hard work and exemplary social behavior. The law was fetched out of the discard heap of the revolution and given an honored place as an essential ingredient of the new social order. Social stratification emerged in an elaborate and refined system of gradation of income and status which gave rise to a full-blown system of social stratification on the classic model of Western industrial society. Accompanying these changes, and in a sense symbolizing the whole range of development, was the profound reorientation of Soviet psychology. The old determinist attitude toward human behavior was condemned and replaced wholesale by a psychology which emphasized individual responsibility and the ability of man to shape his own personality and behavior by the action of his will. The whole trend was perhaps climaxed by the startling accommodation with the Church which the regime made during the later years of World War II and in the postwar years.

Thus virtually all the novel and radical orientations of the regime to interpersonal relations and primary social groupings, which for many people were the distinguishing characteristics of the revolution, were replaced by traditional orientations of a distinctive conservative cast. There emerged by the time of World War II a definite and relatively stable social structure which was a distinctive mixture of the old social order and of the new institutional elements which had emerged out of the commitments of the revolutionary ideology. Both elements were, however, greatly transformed, adapted to the inherent demands of large-scale organization and the traditional motivational and behavioral patterns of the population. In significant degree the revolutionary process inside Russia had come to an end.

Although the pressure on the Soviet leaders to adapt the patterns of social relations better to suit them to the demands of the new industrial order is clearly evident, it is by no means equally clear why the course of action adopted involved so marked a restoration of previously scorned patterns of social organization. Their availability may perhaps be attributed to the inherent resistance of primary relationship patterns to social change. Since the regime shifted its policies after little more than two decades of rule, during part of which time its preoccupation with merely staying in power drew off much of its energy, it is hardly to be expected that radical transformations in popular values and attitudes should have occurred in anything but a small segment of the population. Furthermore, the widespread absence of enthusiasm, indeed the active hostility, of large segments of the population to the Bolsheviks and their program, undoubtedly acted to heighten allegiance to old values and ways of life as a kind of stubborn, mute resistance to the regime which could be expressed more or less safely because it was so covert. Finally, one should not neglect the fact that in times of rapid change and general social disorganization there is a widespread tendency to find a modicum of security in ritualistic adherence to familiar values and patterns of life.

The resistance offered, and consequent strain posed, by these persistent orientations undoubtedly forced some direct compromises on the regime. The granting to the collective farm peasant of the right to a private plot, and later the right to sell his surplus more or less freely in the peasant market, can both at least in large measure be explained as such forced compromises. But the changes in policy toward the family, the restoration of law, the reorientation of the school system, the reintroduction of ranks and distinctive uniforms in the military services can hardly be fully explained as the product of any inescapable compromise on the regime's part with the demands of the populace. The stimulus for most of the changes came directly from the central authorities; they were another manifestation of what Stalin has called "revolution from above." Indeed, in the case of the law making abortion illegal, the measure was forced through despite obvious widespread resistance on the part of major segments of at least the urban women.

The explanation of such changes must, therefore, be sought primarily in changed orientations of the Bolshevik leadership, changes in their conception of the nature of Soviet society and their role in it. Although Lenin was an exceedingly hard and ruthless politician, there were elements of radical "libertarian," indeed utopian, thought in his conception of the new society under socialism. These "libertarian" sentiments were given full expression by Lenin only during the brief period immediately preceding and following the revolution, particularly in his *The State and Revolution*. Yet we cannot dismiss them entirely. Although those thoughts represented a definitely minor mode in the total pattern of Lenin's thinking, they did constitute one facet of his intellectual make-up. Thus, alongside of Lenin's view of the mass man as inert, lacking in consciousness, and requiring stimulation and direction from without, another element of Lenin's view of human nature treated man as essentially spontaneously "good," and capable of tremendous works of creative social living once freed from the constraints, pressures, and distorting influences of capitalist society. He envisioned a relatively "free" society, in which the oppression of the state would be directed primarily against the former possessing classes, whereas the proletarian masses would enjoy a new birth of freedom. Lenin therefore assumed a high degree of direct mass participation in the processes of industry and government, epitomized in his statement that every toiler and cook could help run the government. He assumed that personal motivation would also undergo a transformation, and that men would work harder and better than ever before, because now they would be working "for themselves." Finally, the general problem of social control would diminish in importance, partly because of the new motivations of man under conditions of freedom, and partly because the community of men would take it directly into its own hands to deal with those who violated social norms.

The realities of maintaining power and governing the former Russian Empire under the conditions of civil war and general social disorganization assured that whatever the real weight of the views Lenin expressed in 1917, little was done to implement them on any significant scale. Nevertheless, Lenin apparently was clearly still motivated by some of this earlier thinking, as evidenced by his continued emphasis on mass participation, although in definitely more circumscribed and limited form than he had earlier envisioned. There is some evidence for believing, furthermore, that the apparent disillusion, the sense of doubt and perhaps defeat, which he experienced before his death in 1924, was related to his feeling that so far as the encouragement of man's free development was concerned, Soviet society was not going in the direction he had hoped.

Lenin's successors, Stalin and his coterie, at no time revealed a philosophic orientation to the problems of man's role in society which was at all comparable to that revealed, however briefly, by Lenin in 1917. They were hardly social radicals in the sense that Lenin was. They came to power by means of their talent for controlling and manipulating the Party apparatus, wielding traditional instruments of power. They effected their program by force, and came through further experience to rely on the efficacy of organization and discipline, and to respect rules, order, training, and duty. Their approach to institutional forms was exceedingly pragmatic, their faith being largely in institutions that "worked"—that is, accomplished the functions assigned them in the social realm—so long as those institutions were consonant with the general goal of maintaining the Communist Party in power, and facilitating the transformation of Soviet society into a large-scale industrial power, state-socialist in form.

This new leadership was faced, in the late 1920's and early 1930's, with a distinctive problem in Soviet development which heightened the probability that its basic propensities in the treatment of people would be maximally expressed. The rate of industrial expansion in the initial Plan period was much more intense than had been earlier expected or indeed planned. This rate of development, imposed as it was on a system already operating with a most meagre margin of popular consumption, created enormous, seemingly insatiable and self-perpetuating demands for the sacrifice of individual comfort and freedom of choice. Unless the pace of industrialization were to be significantly relaxed, a possibility the Stalin leadership apparently rejected outright, continued functioning of the system required absolute control of every resource including in the first instance human resources. The problem of social control became central to the Stalin group, and the answer it posed to the problem was consistent with the patterns it had manifested in its own ascent to power within the Communist Party. Thus, however limited their chances for survival even under continued Leninist rule, the radical libertarian aspects of the earlier stages of the revolution fell a certain victim to the combination of circumstances represented by the propensities of the Stalinist group and the demands of the forced pace of industrialization which that group set.

The type of authority which the Stalinist leadership represented, and the pattern of institutional relations it had forged in Soviet society, required obedience, loyalty, reliability, unquestioning fulfillment of orders, adherence to norms and rules, willingness to subordinate oneself to higher authority, and other personal qualities suitable to an authoritarian system. In fact, however, the supply of such people was exceedingly limited.

The Stalinist faction was obliged, rather, to deal with two main types. First, more limited in number but widely present in positions of responsibility and trust within the elite, were the goal-oriented idealists, who found it difficult to compromise principle and to accept the apparent sacrifice of basic revolutionary goals for short-run intermediate objectives. Although these people were most prominent amongst the older generation of Bolsheviks, the Soviet school and the Young Communist League continued to attract and develop such individuals in substantial numbers. Second, the great mass of the rank-and-file of the population posed a related but different problem. Here, the widespread traditional Russian characteristics of evasion and suspicion of authority, avoidance of responsibility, lack of discipline and striving, were not being systematically countered by Soviet education, nor discouraged by Soviet law and custom through rigorous sanctions. Indeed, the system of progressive education probably seemed to the Stalin leadership to reinforce many of these basic orientations, and the beleaguered family was hardly a model of "proper" authority relations.

The problem posed by the core of goal-oriented idealists was of course summarily resolved by the ruthless method of the great purge in the mid 1930's, and by the reorientation of Party and Komsomol selection and training. The problem posed by the rank-and-file of the population, and particularly by the growing generation of young people many of whom were expected to enter the Soviet elite, was not resolvable by such simple means. The Stalinist leaders recognized that marked changes would be required in both the initial training of young people and in the environment in which those individuals would live as adults. The restoration of law, the reintroduction of ideas of guilt and personal responsibility, the intensification of sanctions, the imposition of firmer discipline, were therefore largely rational selections of means for the given end.

The restitution of the family and the changes in educational policy may be understood in much the same way. The leadership was concerned with developing disciplined, orderly, hard-working, responsible individuals who respected and feared authority. The restoration of the teacher's authority along with the reintroduction of regular curricula, examinations, school uniforms, student "passports" and the rest was apparently a product of careful calculation relative to the attainment of the goals indicated.

In seeking to achieve those goals it is not surprising that Soviet leaders should have looked to the past for models which had proved that they could "work" and which might be expected to take more "naturally" with the people. It is not at all necessary to assume, as some have, that this tendency arose because the Bolshevik leaders had "mellowed" as their stay in power extended itself, and that they consequently came to value traditional Russian forms as ends in themselves. Indeed, it is perfectly clear from the marked selectivity in the choice of elements from the past to be reconstituted, that only those were chosen which could serve the current objectives of the regime. The Bolsheviks restored many old forms, but they were not restorationists. Although the forms utilized were conservative they were adopted to serve the radical end of remaking Soviet man in a new mold of subservience, and although tradition was emphasized the Soviet leaders sought to manipulate it and not to follow it.

There were, of course, other alternatives open. Particularly in the case of the family, the regime could conceivably have attempted to bring up all children in state institutions in an effort to develop precisely the type of human material it desired. Indeed, the development of such institutions on a limited scale in the postwar period, in the form of the Suvorov and Nakhimov military schools, reveals the probable attraction of this solution for the present Soviet leaders. But the cost and burden for the state would have been enormous, the alienation of the population extreme, and the effect on the birth rate severe. Since the family could therefore not easily be replaced, the leaders acted instead to convert it to their purpose of raising a work-loving, loyal, disciplined, authority fearing generation. Again, although the solution adopted may have been conservative, it hardly derived from any desire to return to the old way of life. Rather, it was an adaptation to the purposes of the regime of established and tested institutional forms. Indeed, it may be said that a characteristic of the last fifteen years of Soviet rule has been the increasing precision with which the leadership has come to manipulate institutions and juggle situations in order to harness private motivation for the purposes of the regime.

Marx was much more concerned with elaborating the developmental "laws" of capitalism than he was in outlining the institutional structure of socialist society. Indeed he tended to regard such efforts in a class with utopianism. Lenin, in his turn, was much more concerned with developing a model of the revolutionary political party, and with the strategy and tactics for the revolutionary seizure of power, than with detailing the pattern of social relations that should exist in the new society. Yet they left a sufficiently large number of explicit prescriptions and prognostications about the institutional forms of socialist society to permit a meaningful comparison between their expectations and the reality of Soviet social organization. Barrington Moore, attempting such an assessment in his *Soviet Politics,* has concluded that of all the aspects of Bolshevik doctrine the transfer of the means of production to the community as a whole represents the main instance of close congruence between pre-revolutionary anticipations and post-revolutionary facts. Although many might produce a more extended list, there certainly is no doubt that the expectations concerning the school, the family, the organization of industry, mass political participation, social equality, and even religion, are hardly met by contemporary social reality in the Soviet Union.

In the light of this fact, what remains of the characterization of Soviet society as the product of planned social change? Certainly little, if anything, if our measure be the congruence between the current social structure of the U.S.S.R. and the specific institutional patterns called for in the social blueprint of Marxist-Leninist doctrine to which Soviet leaders ostensibly adhered. Long-range planning in this sense in the Soviet Union has been largely limited to the pursuit of very general goals, which were themselves frequently subject to change. It is perhaps more appropriate, therefore, to describe the pattern of social change in the Soviet Union as one in which the forces which produced change were centrally planned, or better set in motion, rather than to speak of the precise resultant institutional patterns themselves as having been planned. Thus, Stalin decreed the forced collectivization, and in some degree he planned and controlled the stages of its execution. But apparently no one in the Soviet regime had a plan for the detailed, or even for the broad, structure of human relations within the collective farm. The collective farm system as the complex of social organization which we know today was planned by no one. It grew out of a continuous process of accommodation and adjustment between the regime's interest in production and its control, the requirements of efficient organization within the structure of large-scale farm units, and the persistent desires, needs, interests, and expectations of the people who worked the farms.

The relatively unplanned development of the internal organization of the collective farm, however, represents only one aspect of advance social planning in the U.S.S.R. In particular, this type of development was most characteristic of the middle period of Soviet history, which we have termed the period of the consolidation of power. In the more recent period, as the preceding discussion of the changes in family, education, law, etc., sought to emphasize, there has been a marked tendency for the "revolution from above" to become ever more precise in effecting change rationally designed to achieve specific social ends. Furthermore, evidence from both published Soviet sources and interviews with former Soviet citizens strongly supports the premise that the regime has been surprisingly successful in its attempt to build "stability" in social relations.

There remains, nevertheless, the striking basic change in policy concerning the role of certain institutional complexes in the larger society, such as the family, education, and the law, about which Marxist-Leninist doctrine had been relatively specific. The importance, for understanding this development, of the change in the composition and life situation of the Bolshevik leadership has already been indicated. That change in leadership is a necessary but not a sufficient explanation of the "great retreat" of the 1930's. One must in addition give proper weight to the distinctive historical phenomenon with which Soviet development confronts us.

It is possible to discuss here only two of the crucial historical factors. In the first place, we must recognize the exceedingly limited experience of the Bolshevik leaders in the administration of a large-scale government apparatus imposed on a highly heterogeneous society. The Communist Party was a training ground only for the revolutionary seizure of power and for the explosive destruction of the old social order, and its personnel was both attracted to and selected by it on those grounds rather than on grounds of actual experience in or potentialities for administration and social construction. In the second place, it must be recognized that in the eyes of most Marxists, indeed to some extent in the eyes of the Bolshevik leaders themselves, the Russian Revolution was an accident if not a mistake. Initially the Soviet leaders firmly believed that they could not stay in power and could hardly proceed to build socialism, unless revolution soon came to the advanced countries of

Western Europe which would aid and support the Soviet regime. Even the limited guidance Marxist doctrine offered as to the program to be applied after the proletariat came into power was intended for and assumed to be applicable only in an "advanced" capitalist country with widely developed industry, a well-trained and disciplined working class, an efficient and functioning administrative apparatus.   None of these requisites was available to be taken over by the Communist "vanguard of the proletariat" in Russia, and indeed what did exist was in a state of deterioration and disorganization at the time the Bolsheviks seized power.

The Bolshevik leaders, however, were perhaps understandably not prepared to relinquish power even though their own theory defined their position as an historical anomaly.   Indeed, after an initial period of about six months of relatively cautious activity, they launched that overzealous and rigid implementation of the main features of the Marxist revolutionary program of social change which characterized the years of "War Communism."   The personal qualities of the Bolshevik leaders and their experience in seeking to seize power had led them to raise to the level of principle the ideas of not compromising and of pushing ahead at all costs.   Further, the early radical policy was in part a response to the pressures created by the Civil War and the foreign intervention, which required absolute state controls.   It was also in part a response to the apparent wave of revolutionary sentiment in the mass of the population, which the Bolshevik leaders sensed and by which they were somewhat carried away.   In addition, however, one detects in the absolute quality of the policies of the War Communism period a desperate effort on the part of the Soviet leaders to prove both to themselves and to "history" the legitimacy of their revolution through great works of social transformation in the direction indicated by Marx.

In any event, whatever the potentialities of a Marxist program of revolutionary social change, it was certainly inappropriate to the conditions which existed in Russia in 1917.   This incongruity was magnified by the explosive and wholesale character of the Bolshevik destruction of the old social order, and by the intensity of the pace with which the program was put into effect.   It was perhaps inevitable, therefore, that social disorganization and a host of crises should have assailed the regime.   And when the unworkability under Soviet conditions of the initial program of social radicalism became unmistakable, the reaction against it and its wholesale replacement with new action programs displayed that same sweeping, explosive nature which characterized the action patterns of a leadership trained predominantly in the absolute use of force.

Yet beyond the specific historical circumstances which attended the Russian Revolution and the distinctive features of the Bolshevik leadership, one may discern the effects of a crucial lack of sensitivity and awareness of the salient characteristics of social organization which one need not expect to be limited to Communist social engineering. The Soviet leaders failed, for example, to give adequate consideration to the interrelatedness of the elements of the social system; that is, they failed to recognize the extent to which it was indeed a *system* such that basic changes in any major institution would have important implications for the functioning of other institutions and hence for the structure as a whole. Thus, they initially showed no real awareness of the implications of their family and educational policy for the rest of the system—in particular, the impact it would have on the fundamental attitudes toward authority which would be inculcated in youths raised in an atmosphere of distrust and suspicion of the earliest authority models, the parent and teacher. They neglected to weigh the influence of inherited motivational systems, and the culturally determined behavior patterns and expectations of the population. Thus, in their policy in regard to the remuneration of labor both in industry and agriculture they were faced with a prolonged struggle with apathy, lack of incentive, and consequent low productivity and high mobility of labor, which in significant measure resulted from the absence of any correspondence between the system of rewards which they had devised and the expectations of the population. They overestimated the ability of formal verbal pressures, of propaganda, significantly to affect behavior in the absence of legal sanctions and social norms, even when the behavior required ran counter to the existing personal motivation of individuals, and particularly when that motivation was lent support by pressures generated in the life situation of individuals. Hence, the failure of their propaganda efforts against abortion when it was legal and free, and when the individuals concerned had strong desires to avoid having children in the face of the pressures of inadequate income, housing, and other requirements of stable family life.

Perhaps least of all were they prepared to anticipate the possible diverse social consequences of any specific social action, or to recognize the imperatives which inhered in certain forms of social organization once they were instituted. Thus, they did not anticipate, and had no advance program to meet, the implications of the commitment to develop large-scale industry, with its inherent demands for hierarchical authority, technical competence, labor discipline, and the integration of complex tasks, and which therefore required the training of new personnel, inculcation of new habits of work, development of chains of command and channels of communication, of systems for allocating rewards, and other adjustments. From these commitments were to rise consequences, such as the rapid social stratification of the population, having far reaching implications both for the revolutionary ideology and for the structure of the old social system on which it was imposed.

These are but a few examples of what might be termed the "lessons" of centralized social planning as they emerge from Soviet experience, further discussion of which is beyond the scope of this chapter. They are stated here in relatively value-neutral terms and, therefore, do not express the political reality of Soviet society with its monopoly of power, its secret police and forced labor, its censorship and absence of personal liberty and freedom, and its sacrifice of human comfort and dignity to the demands of a totalitarian power group. Crucial as they may be, such features of Soviet totalitarianism do not exhaust the significance of Soviet society and its changes. Efforts at large-scale social planning will undoubtedly be made in different political and cultural environments. And those efforts will also be obliged to deal with the realities of social organization, of culture, and of human psychology. It is a political decision whether or not such programs are undertaken, but once they are an understanding of the dynamics of social systems can contribute to minimizing the resultant social disorganization and the consequent human travail. Certainly further study of Soviet efforts at planned social change can be expected to contribute to our understanding of the dynamics of social systems and the forces which must be reckoned with by those who seek consciously to change and direct such systems.

12

THE UTILITY OF POLITICAL SCIENCE

GEORGE CATLIN

Use and Misuse of Political Terminology. That the field of politics is an especial reserve for lawyers is something well recognized, although statistics show that landowners in the past and journalists today offer competition. One medical student, it is reported, was advised by Mr. Ramsay MacDonald to become a lawyer and acted on the advice. He very nearly became Foreign Secretary of Great Britain, thanks to the suggestion. Of recent years, the desirability of bringing trained economists into the affairs of government, where economic issues are involved, has come to be recognized, not indeed without grave distrust, even by politicians. They are tolerated provided they are "on tap but not on top." The economists, also, have thus become great men. Again, when a work of destruction is on hand, the physical scientists have shown that they are nationally indispensable. And, if one has to find oil for the navy, one has to employ a geologist. But the connection between the study of political science and the practice of politics remains vague, ill-defined, and unrecognized. However much he may cry his wares, like a veritable Confucius, no government feels compelled to employ the services of a political scientist or a sociologist as such, as it is compelled to employ economists, lawyers, and even anthropologists. Is there not something anomalous here; and, if so, what?

One of the earlier of the self-styled political scientists, Jeremy Bentham, had a quite clear conception of his duties: to define the terms, to analyze the functions, to reform the system, and to codify the law. But, ironically enough, the politicians could see little use in the proffered advice of the prophet of utility, and the eccentric Utilitarian was left to wage an unending war against "the sinister interests." The patient when sick turns to a physician. But, de-

265

spite Plato, the politicians regard themselves as being the physicians, well acquainted, as practical men (defined by Disraeli as "those who practice the errors of their forefathers"), with the means; and, as democrats and moreover elected representatives of the people, needing no instruction from busybodies as touching the ends. One man studies political science and the evolutionary movements of the century. Another sells hardware. When it comes to an issue, on which the national security depends, of applied political science, the politicians turn to the great executive in hardware or to the advertising man who sells his goods. The old aristocracies and especially the statesmen-churchmen did better.

At Chicago and Yale Professor H. D. Lasswell has used an admirable technique, adapted from the economists. It is a species of political logical positivism and involves a study of semantics. Its use and object are to instill into the student humility and a recognition that he does not know what he thought he knew all along. Unfortunately at present congressmen are not among the Yale students. In *My Three Years in Moscow,* General Bedell Smith records how he and General George Marshall found, in the Soviet Union, that they were confronted with statesmen and diplomats who used many political words, such as "democracy," in an almost precisely opposite sense to theirs. Indeed this is a task in dialectics upon which trained Marxists have been engaged for a century. Ruefully, General Bedell Smith writes that he and his colleagues, not having heard of Lasswell's method, had to sit down and draw up a document explaining what they themselves meant by democracy. This document is an excellent effort in a Jeffersonian statement of natural rights. As a definition of democracy, however, I doubt whether it would have stood up against Aristotle for five minutes or against Plekhanov for ten. But maybe they had not heard of Plekhanov. Oddly enough there was in Russia present before their eyes the consequences of tyranny that Aristotle had prophesied two millennia before as flowing from "democracy"—in the sense that both the Soviets and Aristotle understood the term. The difference between Aristotle and the Soviets was that Aristotle thought democracy a materialistic and perverted system of government, and the Soviets liked it. The United States is of course a republic but not a pure democracy—not only because it is a representative democracy, in which Senators and Congressmen stand between man and his god, the sovereign will, but because a majority even of the representatives cannot change the Constitution. Far from giving effect to the Gallup poll, the American system is riddled with individual, minority, and state rights which derive their justification from quite other quarters than plain majority rule. Rather it is a "mixed constitution," such as Polybius praised, containing democratic, aristocratic, and—yes, certainly—monarchical elements.

Any system which finds a constitutional place for "the wisdom of the Founding Fathers" has an aristocratic element. But it is a neat point whether—even supposing that a Soviet majority did (despite Lenin's purge of the Constituent Assembly of 1918) approve the Bolsheviks and the present close circle of rule; or the German majority approve Hitler or the Italian majority Mussolini—a democracy can, as such, use its majority right to terminate its own power, giving one man or a few a *tribunitia potestas* almost absolute. Aristotle thought democracy could, and would. So did Napoleon III. It is arguable that the Menshevik (or Girondin) system was authentically democratic and was bound to end, under Russian conditions (or under certain French ones), in a Bolshevik (or Jacobin-Bonapartist) tyranny. It will be recalled that, at the time of the Bourbon restoration, Jefferson regretfully decided that the French, unlike the Americans, were not politically mature enough for "freedom." [1]

All I am concerned to stress here is that misunderstandings, quarrels, and even wars can arise from the naïve use of market-place terms, "emotive" and ill-defined, as if they were (in Bentham's terminology) precisely "descriptive" and scientific. (Against this abuse of terms some writers have protested, from Sir George Cornewall Lewis to Mr. J. P. Plaminatz. Even eminent lawyers, such as John Chapman Gray, can be amazingly lax in their use of political terms.) There is, of course, another and perhaps more fruitful definition of democracy, at least as traditional—not as a mode of government but as a mood of social life with a highly equalitarian emphasis. Here America, even if capitalistic, measures up better to democratic standards than does the Russia of today, even if socialist. But this argument is not easily accepted by the Asiatic who, like the Roman proletarians, thinks of equality as equality in poverty under Caesar. The Americans and Westerners seem to him to be priviliged *en masse*. We have to face this fact and to admit that there are arguments both ways. The West aspires to human equality sometime. It does not at all propose to practice the abandonment of inherited advantage from China to Peru now. The essence of democracy today for the West lies in the right of each citizen to contribute, without intimidation, to set up or to overthrow peacefully the government he likes or dislikes, operating within a Con-

---

[1] D. Brogan, *The Price of Revolution* (London: H. Hamilton, 1951), p. 17.

stitution which permits these procedures and of which he in general approves. This "essence" connects with intuitions about the political dignity of man; it is a natural right doctrine semi-religious in character; and it corresponds with the form of government accurately called by Bentham "non-despotical."

It is improbable, and might even be regrettable, that all human beings should agree on one political philosophy of *ends,* even if they had the advantage, at present denied to them, of being able to define these ends for which they are doubtless prepared to fight to the death. This is true although some peoples' political philosophy is bad, can be shown to be bad, and is even contemptible. The study of *means,* that is of political science properly so called, is a more promising field for the aspirant who desires not only to offer his services to the government or industry but to see them inevitably accepted (thanks to technical and indispensable knowledge). How then shall we educate the young men for this?

Even here we must be careful to make clear what we mean. Many political scientists are not so much sociologists, authentically gathering data for scientific generalizations about how society will act, as historians of contemporary institutions. Broadly it is true in practical politics that, if somebody has the misfortune to be historically erudite, he will do well not to call attention to it. Nothing, I recall, moved politicians and journalists to more ill-concealed fury than to be told that, to understand the mind and hopes of the romantic Hitler of the Third Reich, it might be prudent to know something of the position and aspirations of Germany under the First Reich. Today the instinct of a politician, when he plays with the notion of engaging in the battle of ideas, is to turn for guidance to "practical folk" such as a journalist or an advertising man. Mr. George Kennan, a temporary academic who is far too modest about his own claims as a historical scholar, yet observes most sagely in his *American Diplomacy* as a warning to learned men:

If it would seem in an academic setting unscholarly, or perhaps not even useful, to examine this subject against such a [limited] background, I can only say that this is precisely what the policy-makers in Washington for the most part have to do. The heart of their problem lies—and will always lie—in the shaping and conduct of policy for areas about which they cannot be expert and learned.

It may indeed be said that the policy-makers take far less trouble, and the Treasury permits them to expend far less money in hiring available knowledge, in these high affairs of peace and war than they would dream of doing if the affair was one of armaments or business or domestic engineering. They expect to draw up blueprints "on the cheap." *Quantilla prudentia orbis regitur.* The wars, therefore, are won and the peaces lost. Nothing is more shocking to a balanced judgment than the radically casual and irresponsible, accidental nature of high politics. Anyone with experience can illustrate this. The issue of the Union of Europe, for example, tended in Britain to turn on a personal jealousy. If politics were conducted as it ideally should be, and not as to whether Conservatives or Socialists can best promise, if elected, to produce a utopia of plenty in Britain, attention would be given to the real issues of food supply, soil erosion, raw materials, conservation, and an analysis, accompanied by detailed case studies, of the causes of industrial and civil strife or *stasis* superior to the diagnosis made by Marx. But, on the other hand, we have to recognize that, as Sir William Temple said more than two centuries ago, politics is "a gross art." It is the art of power—"who rules whom?" What we do yet well to remember is that most great Revolutions, such as that of the Commonwealth in England and the American Revolution, turn on little more than an idea, an interpretation of history. If ever a man was an academic, library-using historian, employing history to demonstrate theory, that man was Karl Marx. By comparison, T. H. Green was a practical busybody.

On this topic of political science as mere contemporary history of institutions (since the days of Pietro Giannone of Naples called "civil history") one further comment is relevant. It will be noted that political theorists such as Marx and Spencer, and indeed the seventeenth century pamphleteers, made their theory an effective instrument to which politicians had to attend, not by the amassment of sociological and antiquarian detail, but by using history to illustrate and confirm their own hypotheses. I am not here concerned with whether this was a proper procedure. I am saying that, by beginning with a challenging hypothesis, they made it an effective one. Provided that it was psychologically sound and that the real basis of political theory lies, as Lord Bryce thought, in psychology, not history, then it may have been a valid method also. What I am concerned to do is to discourage those who think that a science of politics or of history will, self-prompted, leap out of the facts like a jack out of the box. This is no more true in the social than in the physical sciences.

It is quite true that a striking impact on opinion may be made, as was recently done by Mr. George Kennan in the work previously cited, by honestly demonstrating the historical connections of cause and effect. But the result is here achieved on the tacit hypothesis that those who operate the causes want a particular kind of effect, for example, peace or the advance of the national interest. If the events were regarded as merely cinematographically in flux, no lesson could be drawn. The lessons we can draw are about human nature and passions. There must be deliberate abstraction if there is to be a science. The comparative method is a partial recognition of this principle and of the need, not only to lay bare the sinews, but to proceed from anatomy to political physiology and to discover the function. A thousand studies of the American Senate or of the Constitution of Athens taken in isolation would not reveal whether, whatever their internal defects, anything better was practicable. Realistic political analysis demands more than merely considering one state at one period. It demands, not only precise definition of terms, but study of *the state* against the background of wider society and inclusive community—a task to which R. M. Mac-Iver has devoted many years—if we are to gain an intelligent and useful perspective of the social functions of this specific (and perhaps transient) political form.

Political Science and the Ideological Struggle. Moreover, if we are to discover the utility of political science, we had better do so empirically. For years we used to hear that political science was a subject that did not exist; that it was at best a *Wissenschaft* and not a science; that it was a field in which no controlled experiments were possible; and that it permitted of no exact measurement. These statements are, of course, quite false and could now only be maintained by some specialized scholar ignorant of the literature of the field. The error largely arose from a failure precisely to define the terms, to define what was the activity which politics studied, to wit, the relationship (necessarily social) of human wills as touching control or power. Such students as Professor Gosnell have conducted numerous controlled experiments and, partly because "labor relations" are an important part of the field, more controlled experiments in rules and social adjustments are being conducted daily. The most remarkable development, however, has perhaps been in the field of measurement—of which Lord Kelvin said: "when you can measure . . . you know something about it."

Here we must pay honor to Dr. Gallup who has indicated to us the contemporary possibilities of pure democracy, especially since broadcasting supplied "the voice of Stentor." To those of us who have long advocated measurement of politics as the science of power, it is not surprising that Dr. Gallup should hit a resounding target. His activities are precisely what a good political scientist would have

predicted should be his activities since, under all systems, opinion
and, under the democratic system, the vote constitute the index,
measurable by units, of the market of political power. A matter
for thought, however, is the alarmed interest that practical men in
politics are taking in these polls. This is naturally so, since the
polls are indications, like predictions of future consumption in industry, which show to politicians their future expectations in the
power of their parties and in their personal incomes and careers;
moreover, they may even influence—owing to the desire of many
voters to favor the winning side—these expectations. The Gallup
polls are the most important innovations of our day, more mobile
than plebiscites and more hostile to easy rhetoric about "what the
people think." If they could have been suppressed by the politicians, they undoubtedly would have been. As it is, even allowing
for the accidental factors which enter into the "interviewing"
method, the polls are a fact with which politicians have had to come
to terms. These polls have been the work of political scientists who
put a strangle-hold on the politicians and have thereby made one of
the most significant constitutional developments of the century in
the direction of pure democracy. Imagine the possibilities of Gallup polls in Russia. At present parties usually regard the opinion
poll as totally unreliable except when it favors them. Of course,
it registers an expectation, which may be changed; and only the
electoral poll registers the fact from which congressional power
derives.

If the politician knows the trend of public opinion, he then becomes concerned to accelerate or to change it. The old medium of
the personal speech, whether in a public hall or on the doorstep or
even at a whistle stop (as adopted by Messrs. Truman and Attlee),
is less important than it was, as is also the press. The issue was
fought out between Mr. Lloyd George and Lord Northcliffe, as
publisher of *The Times*. The new media of radio and television
win against the press. The foreign correspondent is indeed the
newest profession, self-claimed to be more important than that of
the diplomat. But there are also the technicians of the new techniques. Moreover, with the enlargement of the activities of government and, under socialism, its deep penetration into business, there
comes, not only the advertising man, but his important half-brother,
the public relations officer. It is doubtful whether any man can be
a good public relations officer who has not a knowledge, disciplined
or "instinctive," of the psychology of public opinion—a subject on
the border between politics and psychology—and indeed of what (as
I shall explain later) I choose to call "natural law." Too many

members of American and other agencies abroad do not have this basic knowledge.

We thus come to the field of political propaganda, which involves a knowledge of psychological techniques and an insight into the structure of society, and which can decisively affect the balance of power, international strategy, and national security. It is closely related to those techniques of change and revolution studied by Aristotle and to political morphology. Although partially determinant factors of geography (hence "geopolitics"), demography, economics, and strategy may enter into and shape the political structure, what has to be recognized is that "the state" is yet fundamentally a structure based upon choices, habitual or deliberate, upon will, but especially upon ideas. And by ideas, revolutionary or conservative, that structure can be changed. The material appartus of politics, or even the habitual and intellectually empty nature of so many of the choices made, must not blind us to this. So far as the data of psychology can be described as conditioned by physiology and yet are nonmaterial, so far is this aspect of politics nonmaterial—however much a field of quite gross desires for power. If the psychological side of political structure is recognized, then the extreme importance in politics of information, as presentation of ideas through description, and of propaganda, as presentation of ideas with a view to persuasion, will also be appreciated. Political science is in no small part concerned with the analysis of and interconnections between the material (as by Marxism) and the mental and ideational aspects (as also more covertly by Marxism) of the political structure with a view to throwing light, in applied science, upon effective controls.

One of the gravest difficulties of the West at the present time is that, after two world wars, its diplomats have shown themselves not to be as good as its soldiers, and that ground has been lost, thanks largely to successful propaganda by the other side, which ought to have been held. Hence, of this last World War, many are now disconsolately asking why in effect, we lost it to the Soviets? Was it due to Roosevelt? Was it due to Churchill? There is a most practical need, upon which even national survival may depend, for a systematic study of propaganda abroad, just as national security can depend upon such a dispassionate study at home. It cannot be done by dilettanti or amateurs. It is a field in which no one should be employed who is not a trained and qualified political science graduate. Here are the kind of matters in which, if not the Department of State, then, for example, the Ford Foundation should be deeply interested. The importance of such study has been stressed alike by General Eisenhower and by Mr. Paul Hoffman in *Peace Can Be Won* (1951). The task could usefully be begun with as systematic a study of Soviet techniques as Marxists themselves have made of the strategy of capitalism.[2]

Among the most explosive things in human history is a revolution. A revolution is usually an explosion of ideas. It has to be met by ideas. A great religious movement, such as Christianity or Islam, is of the same order. Soviet Communism or, more precisely, Bolshevism, is both: it is the doctrine of a revolutionary vanguard which for them also constitutes a "religion." So also was National Socialism although (and in despite of the Mussolini-Gentile *Dottrina*) it was less well-based doctrinally and more ready-made and "reach-me-down" as a theory. Mr. George Kennan, in his exceedingly able book *American Diplomacy,* to which I have referred more than once, holds that Soviet Communist propaganda has been less successful than I would judge, especially in Asia and Africa. Nevertheless Mr. Kennan acutely points out that, in contemporary politics, we have forces that cannot be caught or held by the mesh of the nets of lawyers or of military men—forces adequately important to change the mental climates of peoples, effect *coups d'état,* and establish "puppet" states and governments. Talk about international law and treaty obligations of sovereign states is simply "buckshot" that goes over the head of these subversive activities.

Little purpose will be served or actual loss may even result if America supplies money and munitions to countries whose peoples fulfill Lenin's classic conditions of successful revolution, and whose armed forces are permeated by the kind of religio-ideational motives which have never yet in history been beaten back by drum-head court martial. In contemporary Southeast Asia we see French forces beleaguered in Indo-China, and against them the uniting force of an idea—"Resistance to Colonisation." [3] It may, perhaps, be a quite inadequate idea. But the political scientists of the West have done a deplorably incompetent job in exposing it as such for it remains an effective idea.

---

2 Cf. my "Propaganda as a Function," in *Propaganda and Dictatorship* (Princeton: Princeton University Press, 1936); also the systematic *Materialismo dialettico Sovietico,* by G. A. Wetter (Turin, 1948).

3 Cf. Col. Arthur E. Young, "Defeating Communism in Malaya," *New York Herald Tribune,* 6 June 1953: "Let us not be mistaken about the kind of battle which is being fought not with guns but with ideas and ideals." Col. Young, sometime Commissioner of City of London Police, was in charge of anti-Communist operations, under General Templar, in Malaya. Such a comment from a policeman is encouraging.

The American concept of world law ignores those means of international offence—those means of the projection of power and coercion over other peoples—which by-pass institutional forms entirely or even exploit them against themselves: such things as ideological attack. . . .[4]

Kennan continues, on this vital theme of the battle of ideas:

Where your objectives are moral and ideological ones and run to changing the attitudes and traditions of an entire people or the personality of a regime, then victory is probably something not to be achieved entirely by military means. . . . This is why the destructive process of war must always be accompanied by, or made subsidiary to, a different sort of undertaking aimed at widening the horizons and changing the motives of men. . . . In a sense, there is not total victory short of genocide, unless it be a victory over the minds of men. But the total military victories are rarely victories over the minds of men.[5]

It is not my business to assess here how much should be done in the way of dynamic presentation of the Western case, if, in contrast to the authors of *Defence in the Cold War*,[6] we can agree that any common case exists. Nor is it my business to assess how much should be done by way of attack on, or even psychological warfare against, the Bolshevik-Soviet case. Nor should I try to estimate how much should be by way of radical self-criticism as something requisite for any faith that is authentically worthwhile; if the faith is intellectually contemptible—since all the people *in the long run* cannot be deceived—it is sure, in the long run, to be defeated. It is only my business to point out to politicians and to citizens the solid, practical importance of these tasks being undertaken. This "Fourth Arm" is as fully and precisely important in the waging of war and in the maintaining of peace as any of the other, very costly Three Arms. The Fourth Arm need not be bellicose or negative. And it is infinitely more creative. It is far, far cheaper. Such a program is avoided and neglected because a complacent civilization, unused to being attacked at the level of its head, finds it unfamiliar and, this side of a renaissance, will continue to find it awkward and unfamiliar.

Although it may well be that many ideational factors—not only Marx-Leninism but also Asiatic Nationalism—are operative in contemporary China, nevertheless it remains true that the United Nations' Armies in Korea have not confronted an aggressive Russian Red Army marching into battle; Russian soldiers were rarities. They

---

[4] George Kennan, *American Diplomacy, 1900–1950* (Chicago: University of Chicago Press, 1951), p. 98.

[5] *Ibid.*, pp. 102, 89, 101.

[6] Published by the Royal Institute of International Affairs, 1950.

confronted Korea and Chinese forces which were there for reasons exceedingly acceptable to Moscow and which were held there by certain ideas to which they or their leaders, unlike Chiang's men, had been converted. With the ending of the Korean war, the propaganda war in an epoch of good will can start in full earnest, unless indeed there is a Russian Thermidor and Georgi Malenkov proves to be the Tito and "normalizer" of Russia. As Burke said truly of the French Revolution, "we face armed ideas." Only those with better ideas, whether they be the product of political science (the "how") or of political philosophy (the "why") are likely to be able to make headway for long against them. Otherwise, beaten down in one place the sparks will spurt up in another, as Bacon foretold.

There is one way of meeting ideas. And one does not have to accept the full Hegelian philosophy of thesis and antithesis to perceive what it is. An idea which can attract and master men's minds and wills is a force as powerful as arms; and men armed to fight for one cause but inspired by the other, as Lenin knew, will desert. But every idea, short of some superhuman pure truth, is fissionable. It carries a contradiction within itself, to wit, the implication of the truths which it omits or distorts. The more the idea is "false," the more unstable and highly explosive the mixture. The French Revolutionary idea, distorted by Napoleon's imperialism, exploded in his face.

The Marxist idea, certainly as false, is also unstable and fissionable. It preaches the brotherhood of man but also the hate of his neighbor. It is held together by a pessimistic philosophy of history —such as, for example, Professor Laski expounded—a philosophy of domination, which expects violence and sees no way of dealing with those of other views except to liquidate them and to deny their humanity—or, admitting their humanity, to declare that "reason of state" and success in the social war require that their human rights be ignored. This pessimism rests upon the egoistic psychology of Hobbes, of the French hedonists, and of classical economists of the Manchester school, whose psychology Marx took over uncritically. This psychlogy is out-of-date and is today regarded as "unscientific" in studies of human relations. The task today in the projection of ideas is to substitute the positive and religious notion of human cooperation among men of good will, ready to cooperate for human development, rather than the negative, defeatist, and war-producing notion of inevitable social conflict. But of course these notions, like those of Jefferson, have certain practical coefficients in race relations which some people find too inconvenient, even if opposite ideas are now arming Asia and Africa for Marxism.

The "Moralistic" and "Scientific" Approaches. Profiting by Professor MacIver's *Modern State,* I long ago discarded the notion that political science is the analysis (or maybe the description with anecdotes) of an immoble form, possessing certain sovereign or godlike attributes, called the State or even the Nation, which in some miraculous fashion superseded the erstwhile generally prevalent City-state or feudal barony, but which itself will never be superseded. I gave up such a view, even though this thesis still seems to be prevalent especially in the backwaters of Great Britain, and maintained in 1926, in my *Science and Method,* that politics, like economics, was concerned with the study of a *market*—in this case not the market of wealth as goods but the market of power. I lay claim to no patent. I note that, in his recent work (1951), Sir Ernest Barker [7] makes use of the same thesis, construed especially by way of interesting analogy. It is, however, much more than analogy and flows from the fundamental power analysis—which is not at all to be confounded with a "domination" analysis, although many writers, such as Simonds, Spykman, Schwarzschild, and Morgenthau (and Niebuhr in a different fashion), tend to this tacit assumption. If we accept this thesis that much of political activity is a form of higgling of the market, then we shall be the more willing to sympathize with Mr. Kennan's view that much of what, in international (or domestic) politics, makes honest citizens grow hot under the collar and inclined to take leave of their judgments—and their humanity—in fact can be explained as a normal readjustment to tensions. If, for example, by totally destroying the balancing power of Germany and Japan, Messrs. Roosevelt and Churchill in their wisdom created a power vacuum, some other force will rush in to control, when unopposed by the virtuously inert or by the comfortably unarmed.

If we choose we can refer to this thesis, along with Professor Herbert Butterfield,[8] as "the scientific approach" as distinct from "the moralistic." Let us add that this does not mean that "the moralistic approach" should be bowed out as a rationalistic simplification of the sad "human predicament," tragically comprehended by the latest school of Protestant Existentialists. That is not my view. And, deep as is my admiration for the wisdom of my friend Mr. George Kennan, I can only regret that he has committed himself to an unexpected idealism, the "moralistic" immoralism, in the

---

[7] *Principles of Political and Social Theory* (Oxford: Clarendon Press, 1951), p. 246. Also *Reflections on Government* (London: Oxford University Press, 1942), p. 227.

[8] Herbert Butterfield, "The Scientific Approach *versus* the Moralistic," *International Affairs,* October, 1951.

name of science—thus his remark that "the pursuit of our national interest can never fail to be conducive to a better world." This is pure Pangloss. Whatever the defects of his anti-liberal arguments elsewhere, Professor E. H. Carr is at least justified in pointing out that the assumption is vicious that "there is some solution or plan" of pre-established harmony which, "by a judicious balancing of interests, will be equally favorable to all and prejudicial to none." [9] I am well aware that Mr. Kennan qualifies with important reservations his assertion, which perhaps is a caution to the American people against making unarmed crusading interventions, with ill-informed moral recommendations, where the angels fear to tread. He demands, for example, as precondition of this pursuit of national interest—or, as the Premier of Canada recently unhappily said, our own "self-interest"—decency of purpose, "unsullied by arrogance." But when has a sovereign people been prepared to admit, save under a *Diktat,* that its purposes were indecent and sullied?

To revert to a domestic illustration of the operation of the market, contemplation of which could cause us to be cooler and less partisan in political matters: Since the beginning of this century a re-pricing has been taking place of political goods which is neither more moral nor less than other re-pricings of what people want in accordance with demand. The industrial worker who has come into increasing power since the beginning of the century—has, as it were, political money in his pocket in the shape of the vote and the intention to use it—and sets much store by security [10] or full employment and much less than of old by the traditional Liberal prizes of liberty of the press and of writing. He is not a lawyer or a journalist and doesn't want to write a political pamphlet, even if he knew how or could get a publisher. In free England he is quite content with a monopoly British Broadcasting Company, which accepts G. B. Shaw's dictum that "culture has always been imposed from above," to exclude what is bad from him and to give him what is untarnished by vulgar advertisements such as sustain the free press. Even eminent Liberals arise to insist on the virtue of a national mental monopoly in television, most powerful instrument in the shaping of thought and expression and determining their freedom. The rising peoples of Asia are influenced by security and have never known Benthamite liberty of assembly; and they have the rifles, which give them elementary power. It is said that the

---

[9] E. H. Carr, *The Twenty Years' Crisis* (London: Macmillan & Co., Ltd., 1939), p. 71.
[10] Cf. Erich Fromm, *Escape from Freedom* (New York: Farrar & Rinehart, 1942).

bourgeois masses today prefer peace to liberty, at least until they have lost it; and indeed that the American-invented atomic bomb, ironically enough, has damaged the prospect of ready military support for America from those most likely now to be bombed. If this growing pacifism be indeed occurring, it is vitally important to choose *now* and *rightly* the constitutional form for a future ever more adverse to defend freedom by force and war.

As a practical affair, if the United States of America is to carry through a transfer of power such as has never been carried through before without war and, under its hegemony and lead, is to produce lasting peace by the maintenance of the rule of law, it becomes essential that those led—who with clipped sovereign wings are likely to be most resentful of this benefaction—shall be persuaded by the *idea* that this transfer of power is going to be of highly prized advantage, not to America only or to its "national interest," but to themselves; and that it will not result merely in newly-bombed citizens, atomized children, and the joys of military "liberation" for the sake of freedom of assembly and the press. This persuasion can probably be carried through only under the heat of impassioned belief in some new ideas, at present lacking—ideas beyond price or of higher price maybe than life. It will not be carried through in a mood of defeatism, diplomatic trifling with chauvinism, or official skepticism about the value of ideas. Be it noted that I am not saying that a great war can be launched only by a moralistic crusade reciting conventional ideas and slogans. I am saying that one war will follow another, hostility to dominant Germany or Russia will be followed by hostility to dominant America or X, *unless* an intellectually respectable faith and commitment can be produced. The faith must be in and the commitment to what, as a traditional humanist, I hesitate to call, with Professor Carr, a "New Society," but would prefer to name a deeper understanding of the human spirit and of its Natural Law.

Political Science in the Service of Man. By Natural Law, which is the basis of our science, I here understand the empirical laws of human psychology *insita in natura* and detected by reason in the individual man and in his society. They are the laws of the constants of human behavior and the conditions of full psychological and social health. If morality is spiritual health, then they constitute the canons of human morals. If man's *psyche* is more than physical and is also rational, they indicate the norms of sagacity or models of rational behavior. But they are not themselves the norms. They lie in the nature of the facts and brook no breach with impunity. If health can properly be called the norm at which good medicine aims, then political science can empirically discover those rules which circumscribe the norms of those who would live in society *secundum naturam,* in the sense here used. So long as human nature remains based on any psychological constants (and Pavlov held that the demand for freedom itself was fundamentally a conditioned muscular reflex) we cannot alter these rules. We can of course, in the final analysis decide whether to live healthily in society or unhealthily in the discontent of frustration.

It would be quite contrary to my purpose and would fail to do honor to the best sociological teaching of the present, if I left the impression that a political science of power had no need to be completed by a political philosophy of man. One of the utilities of political science, apart from those of which governments in quest of survival can detect the need, is to convince students that no plethora of engineers can themselves arrange the just society for us, and that even the technocrats and engineers of power can become very pestiferous fascists, red or black, unless they can recognize the need for considering the ends of power, as of wealth. These issues obviously raise questions about the more fundamental nature of man. We cannot prove the answers. We can but present the conclusions, reinforced by the accumulation of experience in the Grand Tradition of history, about which I have written at length elsewhere.

In any political philosophy, indeed, there is a certain submerged clericalism. Matthew Arnold recognizes this implicit tendency in his *Culture and Anarchy.* We are putting forward something that we allege to be more than ordinary opinion. Our *clercs* who must, as M. Benda suggested in *The Treason of the Intellectuals,* not be traitors to their insight may, for all I know, be Confucian Mandarins or James Mill's "educated class" upon which the Liberals counted to redeem society—or they may be true red Marxists. In any event they claim a knowledge about the right ordering of society for human happiness or about the nature of enduring happiness which repudiates the view that here all opinions are born free and equal, although democracy has tended to this view since the days of Cleon of Athens.

What we are entitled to say is that, if the ends and traditional values in political philosophy determine the means, the means studied in political science reciprocally limit and condition the ends. It is, for example, improbable that the Marxist-alleged ends of the withering away of the state and of the fraternal society can most easily emerge from the Marxist means of dictatorship and terror in waging the class war. We can go beyond this. We have to be exceedingly clear about our ultimate ends if we do not wish the customary means of politics, deeply ingrained in human nature, to defeat in the long run those wishes which we entertain in the short run.

Let us illustrate this. It was said, in 1914: "And if you defeat the Germans what do you do with Russia?" But most people could not be bothered with such a problem. Two avoidable wars have been fought and we have come up against this question, which should have been asked at the beginning before the balance of power was so gravely disturbed by *la guerre totale* (a French phrase of World War I). If the power theory of political means is right, there will always be the tendency of an all-powerful state to dominate, since it will see no reason to restrict the freedom of its self-will and "good intentions"; and the smaller states will enter into coalition to defeat this hegemony. In his article to which I have already referred, Professor Butterfield writes:

It was the principle of balance which enabled them to endure without being mere satellites in a world of power-politics. We might describe the whole Eighteenth-Century system as the science of how to maintain the existence and autonomy of small States in a world of power-politics —that is to say in a world where the natural operation of force would be towards the accumulation of one or two giant systems of power.

The destruction of Germany and Japan has destroyed the European and Asiatic balances of power. Let us now assume that the United States is slightly stronger than the U.S.S.R.—the argument works in reverse if the contrary is true. Then three courses in power politics are possible: to break up the United States, as one might Germany in Europe, and then to bring it into coalition with a poly-archic Europe to check Russia; to strengthen the U.S.S.R. in order that a United Europe, as Third Force (ironically built up by the United States), may hold the United States in balance; or to reconstruct the entire political system so that, under a supra-national organization, power is in such decisive *un*balance that resistance is impracticable —this organization itself either being one, as Hobbes would say, "by contract" where no constituent member desires to dominate, or by "domination," where one state is in a position to knock down any opposition so that there will be no chance of bringing in a balancing force from the outside.

There is a contemporary tendency, in the writings of Messrs. E. H. Carr, Herbert Butterfield, and even George Kennan, to eschew "ideology" and to think of eighteenth-century power politics as cleaner and saner. I agree in the sense that the power analysis is so far true that it can warn us of our danger. I deliberately choose certain rather shocking consequences of uniting Europe and of the power activities of an America, favoring a United Europe, which does not realize precisely what she is doing, so that we may be warned. But we must not be hypnotized by this power in means. There is the highest conceivable utility in a political science that can give us these warnings—such as that small powers always have allied to maintain their independence against an over-powerful power and that, by all analogies, America, with or without the defeat of Russia, could be "the next for it" *unless* the entire archaic political structure is changed.

Let me make clear my own position. The National-State system is as outdated as the City-State system. Whether or not we agree with Lord Acton that it was always a menace, at least the National-State is now an anachronism and a dangerous anachronism. We must accept, if the series of atomically-explosive world wars is to be terminated, the establishment of a supra-national authority, *precisely because* the power-theory is true—whether as we hope under contract or, as may be, under domination by conquest by the United States or the U.S.S.R. Those who have adopted, at last, the power theory of political science have hitherto failed to examine what they mean by power. Power can "work" either by domination or, more stably if more delicately, by cooperation. The psychology of cooperation —for example, ceasing to talk about "our" pattern of living and trying scientifically and empirically to discover the most healthful, or even the traditional, and most human pattern—is a subject hitherto neglected except perhaps in educational psychology.

There seems to me to be a great deal of muddleheadedness here in the arguments against "ideologies." It is at the moment—perhaps from disillusionment with the United Nations and in a frantic endeavor to meet the Soviet Union by some weapons other than her own—fashionable to talk as if an "ideology" was the deplorable opposite of the "scientific" approach; and as if recent "ideologists" and "fanatics" were responsible for the concept of "total war." As I have pointed out, this concept emerged from patriotic and even French chauvinist passion—mob passion, if one likes—in World War I. The notion of "total war" is filled with the demagogic emotionalism which Mr. Kennan deplores. But it had nothing to do with any "ideology," which was singularly lacking at that time, when Foreign Office diplomats and the old "secret diplomacy" of Sir Edward Grey—so secret that only Asquith was informed of Sir Edward's commitments—were in charge, save when deflected by popular outcries for vengeance. Just what was lacking, as Pope Benedict XV and Woodrow Wilson insisted, was an "ideology" or clear statement of aims. I am not prepared to talk existentialist jargon about "the human predicament," when what we mean is the casual unwillingness of statesmen to foresee a situation or to clear their minds on awkward and unpopular issues. What is needed is clear thinking. Marxists, whose thinking on the whole is clear and successful but which few Western officials trouble to study, do not make the blunder of putting "ideology" into opposition to "the scientific." On the contrary, if we are to shape means and the power thereto, we need an exceedingly clear ideology of ends. As Lincoln said, if we knew where we were going, we could the more readily get there.

An "ideology" is not to be confounded with the moralizing rhetoric, let us say, of some U. S. Senators under criticism in Mr. Kennan's book, or of British statesmen talking about the Middle East. Nor is "moralizing" the same thing as "morality" but, as irresponsible, is sometimes its opposite. Unlike Mr. Kennan, I would not put forward, as "scientific" or morality or the better ideology, the restated theory of a political pre-established harmony whereby "the pursuit of our national interest" (even if "decent" and "unsullied") "can never fail to be conducive to a better world." I prognosticate that it can lead to nothing but very dangerous complacencies. In brief, what we require is not "no ideology" but a better ideology and one very carefully considered—at least as much so as Marxism, the product of a century of brain work. We need a political logical positivism, a new political scholasticism, for a new world. Our disasters spring from the Anglo-Saxon popular contempt for ideas, so that year by year we live on the century-old capital of Locke and Jefferson. It won't do. After all, such men as Mao Tse-tung are not yokels but (as Dr. Hu Shih testifies) scholars.

One of the results of the uncritical identification of "power" with "domination," is the common identification of "ideology" with "fanaticism." Gandhi and others are witnesses that an ideology can be, almost excessively, an ideology of cooperation and peace. (I do not, of course, mean that the Gandhian ideology was one of nonresistance. It was one of resistance.) Moreover, the tolerance of the eighteenth century and the mutual tolerance of Christian, Hindu and Moslem, came because insurgent Protestantism and insurgent Islam discovered that, neither on the grounds of force nor of ideas, was it going to have "a walk-over." Men became fatigued and bored with an equal fight and turned to more polite ways of persuasion. Tolerance certainly did not come from the moral and intellectual collapse of one party. What is required is a confident but scrupulous ideological resistance, in touch with the objective facts and with a deeper, more imaginative insight into natural law and the nature of man than its opponents possess. Diplomats, however, will find that they are able to achieve little when they confront superiority of force and arrogance of ideas, while backed only by a culture in which the leaders themselves have lost confidence.[11]

The vital idea which has recently moved dynamically an exhausted Europe is that of European Union. It is, as a rival, with its political rather than an economic priority, one of the few ideas which Marx-Leninism fears. But it is local. The new idea beyond is that of the pooling of sovereignty over a yet wider area as the best method of avoiding war—of indeed avoiding that Eur-American war which can come when the Russian problem is disposed of. No rearrangement of the old sovereign countries will help. Such a union, let us be clear, will involve the payment of painful costs, not least by the manual workers of the more privileged countries: many Socialists will discover they are National Socialists with an interest in "imperial exploitation." The balance of power went when, with the French Revolution, new nonlegal forces such as equalitarianism, nationalism, communism took charge—movements (as Mr. Kennan points out) of which international law and balances take no cognizance. We cannot turn back on this change. Not even Mr. Eden, with his British-Soviet treaties, can ignore it. Nor do these forces end the utility of "cabinet diplomacy." But with what Ortega y Gasset disapprovingly calls "the revolt of the masses," they set limits to its functioning. The limitation of what can be done by balance of state powers (which involves the state concept as much as any thesis of international law [12]) in no wise invalidates the theory of power as such, as studied by political science. We merely confront the newer forms of power which require vast regional or world frameworks if they are to be controlled.

What we require today is an overall strategy of the democratic idea. At this point we transcend the boundaries of the political science of means. The world is quite unlikely to adopt, as I said at the beginning, any one philosophy so long as there remains, as valuable, so great a diversity of personalities. Nevertheless some philosophies are probably always bad or cheap and there are others which, before they have fulfilled their mission, dominate a whole age. I

---

[11] Brogan, *op. cit.*, p. 82.
[12] Kennan, *op. cit.*, p. 98.

can only make the suggestion that the philosophy which we need will be a restated Humanism and, in substance, a Christian Humanism of cooperation. We need to return to the affirmation of certain simple intuitions and to arouse ourselves morally to the full significance of the strange fact that our age, "the Twentieth Century of Peace, Progress and Prosperity," is an enormously barbaric and cruel age, an age when we care little if millions lose their lives by political persecution and when atrocious vandalism is readily excused as in the national interest or to speed the latest "war for civilization." We have indeed lost respect for civilization, which sobers us, in our passion for the intoxication of immediate success. It may be that democracy, undisciplined by education, has debauched our moral values. It may be that it is the tyrannies, which Aristotle thought would flow from it, that have done this. It may be that we no longer know what we mean by "a liberal education" when we adopt what Mr. Joseph Wood Krutch called the explosive and nonteleological "Modern Temper," the existentialist denial of objective values, superior to ourselves, which set a bound to the Babel realm of our caprice. Or it may be that "all will turn out right."

For myself I do not think this. The first requirement of man is the sense of personal significance: to find himself worthwhile, wanted by his community and not an outcast. A few men have the strength to be content to join the community of the future. The criminal seeks the warmth of his thieves' kitchen or longs to be readmitted as respectable. Likewise there are natures that feel themselves dispossessed, excluded from the favored circle, discriminated against. The need of today is to transfer the lessons which we have learned and accepted about individuals in, for example, child psychology, the lessons, for example, about the technique and discipline of cooperation, over to the field of politics and to the theory of organized political cooperation.

When I consider this theory of power I end by rejecting Dr. Reinhold Niebuhr's dangerous distinction of "Moral Man and Immoral Society." The cure for immoral society, as Lord Russell truly says, is to be found inside man and by study of his constant tendencies. The sound community is but the healthy *psyche* writ large. The utility of political science comes back, then, to the therapeutic utility of psychology and to the cure of souls. A new humanist movement can produce the widespread recognition of this fact.

The errors of the present include an uneasy desire, too characteristic of decadence, to push ideas on one side because we have not the answers; the refusal of officials to recognize that ideas constitute a Fourth Arm of warfare; an apathy in stating positively, constructively, and pacifically the Western democratic case; and an incapacity for carrying the discussion to a level sufficiently profound to detect the fallacy of Marxist psychology—itself rooted in "bourgeois" thinking. Ideas will be met only by ideas and bad ideas will be defeated only by better.

By no means always do I agree with Lord Russell's book called *Power* (1938). But there is therefore the better reason for me to state my entire agreement with certain conclusions of his more recent *New Hopes of a Changing World* (1951). We all agree that wars are evil things. And it is therefore odd that wars continue. Does another element in ourselves disagree with the agreement and find civilization a detested source of unfreedom and discontents?

What is mistakenly called "human nature" likes somebody to hate. . . . The real obstacles to world-wide social cohesion are in individual souls. They are the pleasure that we derive from hatred, malice, and cruelty. If mankind is to survive, it will be necessary to find a way of living which does not involve indulgence in these pleasures . . . the real war is within. For these reasons the war of man with himself is that which at the end of human evolution assumes supreme importance.

The political philosopher for this needed discipline will turn to the political scientist and he, in turn, should know where to look for his empirical studies. It may, indeed, be that men will find the development of their individualist personalities and the harmony of their powers in the sense of significance in sharing in an ideal Community of more value in their own eyes than themselves —maybe in some such pious and pacific culture as that which Dr. Ruth Benedict tells us characterizes the happy and religious Pueblo. —Or maybe the devil will continue to walk swiftly to and fro on the earth seeking fissionable material, physical and spiritual. But these speculations carry us beyond our present subject.

13

Robert M. MacIver's Contributions to Sociological Theory

HARRY ALPERT

Lincoln Steffens reports that he once asked Einstein in Berlin how he had been able to make great discoveries. "How did you ever do it, I exclaimed, and he, understanding and smiling gave the answer. 'By challenging an axiom.' " [1] If a latter-day Lincoln Steffens were to ask Robert MacIver how he has been able to make his contributions to sociology, an appropriate reply would be: *by drawing a distinction.* The like and the common, state and society, community and association, interest and attitudes, corporate class consciousness and competitive class consciousness, the inner and the outer, culture and civilization, the modes of the question why, the varieties of social causation (precipitant, incentive, responsible agent, etc.), the two types of prejudice (socially rooted and personality rooted), balances and circles, evolution and progress—this is but a partial listing of the numerous conceptual clarifications for which sociologists are deeply indebted to Robert MacIver. Add to this list such conceptual tools as social image, dynamic assessment, and multi-group society, and one has, indeed, an impressive array of solid ideas upon which to erect a systematic sociology.

MacIver's contributions to sociology may be viewed as fourfold. First, as just indicated, he has systematically developed and fruitfully explored an impressive network of fundamental sociological concepts. Secondly, he has helped stem the tide of excessive positiv-

---

[1] Lincoln Steffens, *The Autobiography of Lincoln Steffens* (New York: Harcourt, Brace & Co., 1931), Vol. II, p. 816.

ism and raw empiricism. Thirdly, he has reaffirmed the view of man as a creative human being with subjective hopes, feelings, aspirations, motives, and values. Finally, he has positively demonstrated that sociological writing can be beautiful, clear, artistic and literate.

MacIver has properly evaluated his own work as new only to the extent that it is an interpretation and re-integration, within a consistent framework, of things already known. Historical sources can undoubtedly be found for most of the concepts he has developed. This should not detract, however, from the originality either of perspective, or expression, or exploration of implications. The concepts themselves are important; equally significant is the analytical uses to which they are put.

Enemy of fuzzy, confused thinking, champion of clarity and preciseness, Robert MacIver has guided sociology to an appreciation of the need to begin with organizing concepts. Space limitations forbid discussion of all the major concepts developed by MacIver. Our comments will be confined to four important areas: the classification of social interests, the distinction between community and society, the concept of social evolution, and the harmony theory of the relation between society and individuality.

The classification of social interests, and especially the distinction between like and common interests, has proved of immense value in clarifying the nature of interindividual relationships, the bases of group organization, and the nature of the social bond. Along with Giddings, Spencer, Durkheim, Toennies, and other sociological theorists, MacIver has demonstrated the fruitfulness of analyzing the social implications of the various types of interests.[2]

The distinction between community as the matrix of social organization and associations as specific organizations which grow and develop within that matrix has likewise been extremely fruitful. The implications for political theory of the view of the state as an association of and within the community are treated elsewhere by Dr. Spitz. To sociologists the distinction between community and association has proved significant in permitting a more precise definition of the problem of social solidarity and in providing a framework for a deeper understanding of the nature of a pluralistic or multi-group society. Without community, in MacIver's sense of the term, there can be no organized society. Society, without community, is reduced to a congeries of competing, interrelated, but

---

2 It is significant that Calverton chose the classes of social interest as the subject with which to represent MacIver in his anthology of sociological literature. *The Making of Society*, edited by V. F. Calverton (New York: The Modern Library, 1937).

not necessarily interconnected, groups: there are only associational ties, no communal bonds. It is difficult to reconcile such a picture with the observed facts of common interests, common understandings, and common symbols. The bond of community is indeed a real one, albeit difficult to identify in a mass society. MacIver's concept of community is an indispensable analytical tool.

MacIver's reaffirmation of the validity of the concept of social evolution, in the face of the bitter attacks upon it by anthropologists such as Goldenweiser, anticipated by many years the recent resurgence of interest in and defense of the concept by Julian Steward and other American anthropologists. Numerous insights have stemmed from MacIver's tracing of a pattern of social change from the primitive type of functionally undifferentiated society wherein social life is of a communal nature, to the more evolved, functionally diverse, and institutionally and associationally differentiated social group wherein the basis of individual relationships is less communal and more associational and wherein personality becomes more developed and more expressive.

Brief mention may also be made of MacIver's brilliant resolution of the time-worn controversy of the relationship between the individual and society. Rejecting both social contract theories and organismic theories, he stressed the fundamental harmony between individuality and society, recognizing, at the same time, that this harmony is far from perfect. Sociality and individuality, he asserted in one of his most successful formulations, develop *pari passu*.

MacIver came upon the American scene in the early 1920's. American sociology could then be characterized as a nonphilosophical and even anti-philosophical creature content to wallow in the big heap of factual garbage which it had been busily piling up in its own raw-empirical trough. Under the influence of behaviorism, pragmatism, bigger-and-betterism, we-don't-know-where-we're-going-but-we're-getting-there-fastism, by-all-means-measure-even-if-you-don't-know-what-you're-measuringism, and other manifestations of our general extravertism, American sociologists of the 20's were devoting their efforts, with that ebullience of energy and vigor for which this country is noted, to concrete, specific, delimited problems of social investigation. In the mad, voracious hunt for facts sight was lost of the need to ask, as Robert S. Lynd did somewhat later, knowledge for what? At this juncture in the history of American sociology there came from Robert MacIver, among others, the warning that sociology stood in danger of becoming "too scientific," of ignoring the art of interpretation "which is the soul of the sciences of man," of jettisoning its true subject matter for the sake of a spurious objectivity, and of thus rejecting both that which in a scientific system is system and that which in social facts is social. In his eagerness to combat the preposterousness and the conceit of the behavioristic standpoint in sociology, MacIver may have overstated his case. One may accept his statement that "the understanding of society *begins* from our personal experience as members of society," if, as we have done, one underscores "begins" and keeps in mind that beginning is not ending. The science of sociology should stand ready to utilize knowledge from all sources, but its end-product is not all knowledge however derived, but only that knowledge which can be, and is, scientifically sifted, treated, and tested. Such knowledge must be organized in terms of a systematic conceptual framework, and, to be sociological, must deal with the *social* aspects of reality.

By insisting on this, MacIver did much to stem the tide of atomistic raw empiricism. He urged that sociological research be guided by a theoretical framework and rescued the "inner" as a legitimate object of sociological inquiry. MacIver is properly listed by Barnes and Becker as among those who insist on a little "armchair" work, without which research is doomed to sterility. "It is notorious," these authors comment, "that men will go to any amount of trouble rather than think; they flock after any prophet who relieves them of responsibility by saying soothingly, 'Let your Comptometer be your guide.' " [3]

If American sociology today is less characterized by the crude empiricism of the 1920's, if, indeed, there is more theory-oriented research and research-oriented theory, MacIver's efforts have not been in vain. Both by his own example and by encouraging his students to undertake critical reviews of theoretical sociological systems (Sewny on Baldwin, Page on class concepts among American sociology's founding fathers, Alpert on Durkheim, etc.), to re-examine the basic concepts and presuppositions of empirical research activities (Robison on delinquency, Alihan on social ecology, etc.), and to bring meaning to social facts in terms of systematic theory (Tomars on the sociology of art, etc.), MacIver fought valiantly against the excesses and wastes of the raw empiricistic position. The battle is by no means over, if we can accept Harry Elmer Barnes' characterization of American sociology in 1951. Barnes describes much of the social theory of today as "comprehensible only to the theorist himself, if indeed, he knows what he is saying" and is concerned over the continued prevalence of trends toward "quanti-

---

[3] H. E. Barnes and H. Becker, *Social Thought from Lore to Science* (Boston: D. C. Heath and Company, 1938), Vol. II, p. 998.

tative mysticism." "The research topics," he states, "are not less esoteric and minute and the results of research are becoming even more obscure to all save the initiated." [4] MacIver's leadership in combating these trends is still needed, it seems, as much as ever.

In much of the strictly positivistic writing in sociology there emerges an image of man as essentially a passive, mechanical creature responding automatically to external stimuli which have no particular meaning to him. In MacIver's humanistic and "verstehende" sociology there emerges, in contrast, the image of man as an idealistic, goal-seeking, value-creating being who is especially distinguished by his capacity to impute meanings to events, objects, and people. In a characteristic passage which has been severely attacked by Lundberg and others, MacIver asserted that "there is an essential difference, from the standpoint of causation, between a paper flying before the wind and a man flying from a pursuing crowd. The paper knows no fear and the wind no hate, but without fear and hate the man would not fly nor the crowd pursue." [5] Here, in essence, is MacIver's conception of social science as a humanistic discipline. This viewpoint was perhaps most forcefully presented in his essay on the social sciences contributed to the volume "On Going to College." [6] There he stated that if he were compelled to run a college he would institute one fundamental rule—namely, that there would be two broad divisions of the curriculum. The first Division would consist of "the area of the calculable, the ungainsayable, the absolute. It is the whole world that science seeks to envisage *sub specie aeternitatis.*" This Division would not include history. To the historian MacIver would say,

It is true that Caesar crossed the Rubicon, but that mere act of locomotion is not history. What you are interested in is Caesar's imperial ambition and the tangle of conditions that gave it play and its impact on the further course of human life. These things are not in the objective record. You cannot photograph Caesar's ambition on a sensitive plate. You cannot see it or interpret it except in the light of your own discernment.

So the historian is invited over to the second Division, the one which includes the humanities, "all the changing systems of human values, all the institutions, and all the creative works of man." In this Division Two, one is also seeking indubitable facts but recognizes

---

[4] H. E. Barnes in *American Sociological Review*, Vol. 16, December, 1951, p. 875.

[5] R. M. MacIver and C. H. Page, *Society: An Introductory Analysis* (New York: Rinehart & Company, 1949), p. 628.

[6] *On Going to College: A Symposium* (New York: Oxford University Press, 1938), pp. 121–140.

that the interpretation of them, or in other words the more inclusive and meaningful fact, is always relative and never finally attained.

A basic corollary to his fundamental rule, MacIver insisted,

. . . would be that no one shall teach any subject in Division Two as though it belonged to Division One. No one shall teach as though he had the whole truth or the final formula about anything. No one shall offer precise formulae for human equations, capable of being worked out to the *n*th decimal point. No teacher shall divest the "facts" of meaning or treat meanings in detachment from situations. For this is the negative condition on which alone he can attain the proximate, the relative truth, and save himself and his students from the dogma that blinds understanding.

In the sciences of man we cannot ignore the inner life.

Social facts are all in the last resort *intelligible* facts. When we know why a government falls or how a price is determined or why a strike takes place or how a primitive tribe worships or why the birth-rate declines, our knowledge is different in one vital respect from the knowledge of why a meteor falls or how the moon keeps its distance from the earth or why liquids freeze or how plants utilize nitrogen. Facts of the second kind we know only from the outside; facts of the first kind we know, in some degree at least, from the inside. Why did the citizens turn against the government? Why did the union call a strike? To answer these questions we must project ourselves into the situations we are investigating. We must learn the values and the aims and the hopes of human beings as they operate within a particular situation. There is no inside story of why a meteor falls or why a liquid freezes. We comprehend it as a datum, as the expression of a law and nothing more. It is because on the other hand there is always an inside story, or in other words a meaning, in human affairs that we never attain more than partial or relative truth. Here is the paradox of knowledge. The only things we know as immutable truths are the things we do not understand. The only things we understand are mutable and never fully known.

The essential task of sociology, then, is the search for meanings. "In all his social studies," MacIver wrote, "the student is occupied in translating fact indices into meanings." We must, I believe, accept the legitimacy, even the necessity, of *verstehen* analysis in sociology. Our knowledge is indeed meager if we fail to seek out the *becauses* of human action as they affect social processes and situations, if we ignore the effective valuations in terms of which the human agents in a social situation behave.[7] As social scientists, therefore, we are faced with the problem of developing objective methods for dealing with data of inner experience. We cannot, as

---

[7] Cf. H. Alpert, *Emile Durkheim and His Sociology* (New York: Columbia University Press, 1939), pp. 108–111.

scientists, dispense with controls, standardization of procedures, verification and validation. Where we cannot observe directly we must devise techniques of indirect observation such as Durkheim's method of indexes.[8] We are obliged, as MacIver himself recognized, to make full use of statistical and observational data, but we cannot abjure the responsibility of treating such quantitative data as guideposts to understanding rather than as ultimate goals of sociological inquiry.

Not the least of MacIver's contributions is the clear demonstration that good English, literary style, clarity of expression and systematic presentation are not incompatible with sociological writing. Unfortunately American sociology merits the charge that many of its products are atrociously written. There are, however, some glaring exceptions, among which we must assign a prominent place to the sociological writings of Robert MacIver. To an area of confusion and literary and intellectual chaos MacIver has brought both clarity of thought and felicity of expression.

Despite these positive achievements MacIver's work has not been uniformly appreciated by his American colleagues. In fact, his contributions as a sociologist have been far better appreciated abroad than in the United States. MacIver's sociology, nevertheless, is still vigorous, useful, and certainly pertinent for the present generation. It is true that MacIver may not have contributed much to sociology in the way of new data or new facts or new techniques and methods. There is no MacIver Neurotic Inventory, no MacIver Index of Morale, no MacIver Hidden Attitude Analysis; nay, not even a MacIver Scale. What, then, did he contribute? The most precious things of all—understanding, and the example of clear thinking and expression.[9]

---

[8] *Ibid.*, pp. 119–127.

[9] Daniel Bell, Robert Bierstedt, Michael E. Choukas, Elizabeth K. Nottingham, Charles H. Page, Vahan D. Sewny, Sophia M. Robinson, and Adolph S. Tomars, former students of MacIver, present their evaluations in H. Alpert, ed., *Robert M. MacIver: Teacher and Sociologist* (Northampton, Mass.: Metcalf Printing and Publishing Co., Inc., 1953).

14

Robert M. MacIver's Contributions to Political Theory

DAVID SPITZ

POLITICAL FORMS AND HUMAN GOALS

Ever since Machiavelli, political theorists have understood, even if they have not always observed, the necessary distinction between political behavior in the positivistic sense and the ethical values by which such behavior is judged. It is the strength of Robert M. Mac-Iver as a political thinker that he has utilized still another dimension in the study of politics; he has shown, along with Max Weber, that men's conceptions of what they ought to do are themselves determinants of what they actually do, and that, in turn, what men do or can do tends effectively to limit the range of their ethical obligations.[1]

---

[1] Where, as in the first two sections of this paper, I have largely limited myself to an exposition of MacIver's ideas, I have made liberal use of his own language, unburdened, however, by the apparatus of quotation marks and page references. For his social philosophy, I have relied most heavily on *Community* (3d ed., London: Macmillan & Co., Ltd., 1924) and *The Elements of Social Science* (9th ed., London: Methuen & Co., Ltd., 1949), and to a lesser degree on *Society: A Textbook of Sociology* (New York: Rinehart & Company, Inc., 1937). His political theory is systematically developed in *The Modern State* (London: Oxford University Press, 1926) and *The Web of Government* (New York: The Macmillan Co., 1947); but I have also found useful "The Meaning of Liberty and Its Perversions," in *Freedom: Its Meaning* (ed. Anshen, New York: Harper & Brothers, 1940), pp. 278–287, *Leviathan and the People* (Baton Rouge: Louisiana State University Press, 1939), *Towards an Abiding Peace* (New York: The Macmillan Co., 1945), and *The Ramparts We Guard* (New York: The Macmillan Co., 1950). For his methodology, the major item is *Social Causation* (Boston: Ginn & Com-

So understood, political behavior and ethical values are neither divorced nor unilaterally related. Ideals move men even as men move toward the realization of their goals. Values thus become motives that govern as well as principles that explain human behavior. Yet in politics as in other areas of social action, MacIver has reminded us, the actual range of historical possibilities places outer limits on what may be allowed as the attainable moral desiderata of political behavior. Hence, theories of what government should or should not do must properly be rooted in the objective realties of the social situation.

If the political theorist, then, is to apprehend the nature and direction of the state—that is, the state in its historical activity, sociological relationships, and ultimate purposes—he must avoid, so far as he can, those arbitrary and subjective interpretations which accord with his own ethical tradition. But he ought not on that account—as in fact he cannot—rule out considerations of human ideals; he must enter imaginatively into the realm of values and relate social institutions to human intentions and their consequences. For the state is an agency of human purpose, and if it is true that its character changes as its purpose changes, it is no less true that its purpose tends to be revealed and linked to the possible as human intelligence and human will mold or influence the structure itself. We are thus enabled to see the importance of MacIver's insistence that, while an "objective" understanding of the character of the state is the necessary foundation for an appreciation of its ethical value, the latter is equally necessary to give meaning to the political structure.

In this respect, the business of the political theorist is not, in MacIver's view, to validate an ethical philosophy, for an ethic cannot possibly carry its own authentication and those who reject it can offer no *proof* that it is wrong. Instead, his task is to take the entire complex of incoporated values that we call culture as a datum of his study and relate it to the utilitarian or instrumental systems that sustain the culture. The latter—comprising the political, economic, and technological systems—make up the huge apparatus known as civilization; they constitute a complex of means, not ends. And from this point of view the state or the political

pany, 1942), but I have gained much illumination from two articles—"Sociology," in *A Quarter Century of Learning, 1904–1929* (New York: Columbia University Press, 1931), pp. 62–91, and "The Historical Pattern of Social Change," in *Authority and the Individual* (Cambridge: Harvard Tercentenary Publications, 1937), pp. 126–153—and from his book, *The Contribution of Sociology to Social Work* (New York: Columbia University Press, 1931).

system is essentially a mechanism for the manipulation of means, differing from the economic system (which also controls means) in that it is the authoritative ordainment for the social regulation of the basic technology. The state is of course more. It is an association established by the community for the regulation of the universal external conditions of social order—for example, codes of behavior. But it is not coterminous with the social order; nor is it, as the Hegelians insist, the embodiment of a transcendant purpose which the social order exists to fulfill. Consequently a theory of the state is a theory of an association within a more inclusive unity; it is a theory about means, not ends, and it takes account of ends only insofar as they determine the character and uses of the means.

This implies that political theory is social theory brought to bear on one agency of social existence, the state; and that to understand the state as it is and as it changes, one must first grasp the meaning of community and of the structures and processes of society. Accordingly MacIver as political theorist has been concerned with general sociology as well as with its application to the life of the state. He has sought to classify the types of political situations, seeking an understandable order of things out of the vast complexity and variety of political patterns. He has not been unaware of the risk of the "ideal type" approach—as evidenced, for example, in Max Weber's treatment of the Protestant ethic—in discounting or ignoring the tendencies to change already present in the situation. But even though the "ideal type" does not fully correspond with reality it remains, in MacIver's view, an indispensable instrument of understanding. For it enables us to grasp the political situation, the historical moment, the social system, as something coherent, as somehow a unity of elements. And, although individuals and groups only approximate these typical ways of behaving, these generally accepted norms of action, they tend in the main to act in accordance with them.

Consider, in these terms, his classification of the forms of government.[2] Traditionally, such classifications have accepted the tripartite division into monarchy, aristocracy, and democracy, and have been based on political factors alone. But a moment's reflection will make clear that this distinction is more a formal than a substantial one, resting on much too narrow a ground to encompass

---

2 Generally MacIver has been careful to distinguish the state as an abiding association from its temporary administrative agent, the government. In *The Web of Government,* however, he reverses the usual order of definitions and employs the term "government" more broadly to refer to the organization of men under authority. On this basis the state becomes a form of government.

a full measure of reality.   No government is ever a mere monarchy, for the one who titularly rules is nearly always the representative or symbol of an associated class, clique, party, or group of some kind. And in the strict sense the many, or the people, never *rule;* for the actual business of ruling is always in the hands of the few.   Hence, the real as well as constitutional question concerns the relation of the few who rule to the many who are ruled.   If the few are responsible to the many, the system is democratic; if they are not responsible, it is oligarchic.   Aristocracy, MacIver argues, is a question-begging expression since no method has ever been devised to assure that the best qualified persons preside over the state, or indeed to determine who are the persons best qualified for that role.   Consequently the constitutional basis of classification must be a bipartite one, its major categories being democracy and oligarchy. MacIver's classification takes account of the variations within each of these categories—subsuming monarchy, dictatorship, theocracy, and plural rulership under oligarchy, and limited monarchy and republic under democracy.   But no less significant is his extension of the bases for the classification of governments to include economic and communal differences and the sovereignty structure.   Thus the various types of government can be separated according to their feudal or capitalistic or socialistic economy, or with respect to their tribal or national basis, or as they form a unitary or federal state or empire.   By means of criteria other than that supplied by the traditional constitutional taxonomy, a more adequate classification of political forms becomes possible.[3]

But government is not to be understood if it is confined to a study of political forms alone.   What is required is a more comprehensive analysis of social power, of the graduated orders of command and obedience, of the characteristic and distinctive pyramids of power that exist in every type of society and weigh heavily or lightly upon men in varying stations of life.   From among the wealth of types and their endless variations, MacIver has outlined three broadly differentiated types of the pyramid of power.   One is the caste pyramid, characterized by virtually impenetrable barriers separating the different levels of the pyramid and a marked inverse relation between the power and the size of each stratum.   This "ideal type"—of which the Indian caste system is an illustration—is approximated only under conditions of primitive technology, the vast masses of the population being both illiterate and poverty-

---

[3] I have followed here the conspectus given in *The Web of Government*, p. 151; cf. also the conspectus in *The Modern State*, p. 363.

stricken. The second broad type—the oligarchical pyramid—differs from the first in that, although the main classes of the population are still anchored to their assigned social status and are still clearly demarcated by cultural differences as well as by the ranges of opportunity and of power at their disposal, individuals nevertheless have some chance to rise from one level to another, there being somewhat greater differentiation within each level, and a less distinct differentiation between levels. The slope of the pyramid is less abrupt and the middle class is proportionately greater than it is in the first type. The later stages of feudalism and the oligarchical centralized states that have emerged out of feudalism approximate to this type. The third broad type—to which Canada, the United States of America, and the Scandinavian countries, among others, belong—is the democratic pyramid, characterized by a breakdown of the corporate character of the class structure and a greater mobility within and between the various levels of the pyramid. Status position and power no longer coincide, and groups disadvantaged by class or wealth may accordingly move to power through organization.

MacIver does not, of course, advance these power pyramids as categories into which political or power systems are to be forced; they are rather analytical tools, instruments that enable us to comprehend the nature of a system and, within that system, to relate social institutions to human values. For what the political theorist must seek as the basis for his formulations is the order within society, the nature of the species as well as of the individual members of a species. Without such perception, without insight into the character and types of structures and processes, the theorist cannot hope to understand, or to contribute to an understanding of, the causal nexus itself. He cannot interpret the dependence of one phenomenon on another, and that greater interdependence of them all which constitutes at each moment the changing social and political equilibrium; he cannot see how in the intricate complex of conditions every change that is introduced reacts, or might react, upon a whole situation. He cannot, in a word, construct a valid political theory.

SOME CONCEPTS AND METHODS

Although the political theorist must use a correct methodology, methodology alone cannot produce a political philosophy. For methodology remains incidental to the formulation of doctrine; it is useful only as it aids or confirms insight, only as it contributes to our knowledge of the principles that govern, or ought to govern, political and social systems.⁴ What makes MacIver's work so significant is that he has understood and kept constantly in mind the proper relation of analysis to doctrine. His search for and discovery of political facts—that is, the myths or value-systems that men live by or live for, and the techniques or ways of knowing that enable them to control objects, including persons as objects—has led to the revision of old and, because imperfectly understood, partly erroneous concepts so as to vest them with a new meaning and a new validity. His perception of the unity of community and of the relations of institutions to values has enabled him to reintegrate into a new theoretical unity a body of doctrine that explains not only what the state *is* but what it ought or ought not to do. MacIver's reinterpretation of the general will may serve to illustrate the former of these contributions. His theories of federalism and democracy, and within democracy of freedom, power, and political obligation, will be used to indicate his sense of the community and his scheme of values.

MacIver's use of the general will derives, of course, from Rousseau. It is a principle that builds on the recognition that society is an integral unity and that the consciousness of unity emerges out of the sense of common interest or welfare. And to the extent that Rousseau affirms the general will to be the true sovereign and ultimate authority in a state he shares, with MacIver, the democratic thesis that the people are politically sovereign. But when Rousseau goes on to argue that the general will is not to be equated with the will *of* the people but is the will *for* the general good, and that the necessary political sovereignty of the people is identical with a moral sovereignty, he creates insuperable difficulties. Although it may be insisted that the sovereign cannot err, this is only an expression of a legal truth. Legality cannot transcend law but morality obviously can. To hold otherwise is to confound the actual with the ideal; it is also to deny the necessary distinction between the state and the community, between the bonds of law and the moral sanctions that keep a society together. And while it may be to the general interest

---

⁴ This point would be too obvious to mention were it not for the fact that the bulk of what is called social science research in this country—not least in sociology and in politics—has shifted from the quest for knowledge to the proliferation of measurements, forgetting that measurement alone is not knowledge and that the things most knowable—the nature and purposes of man, movements of thought, social relations and social institutions, and the like—are the data which are least amenable to quantification. Indeed, as MacIver has argued, since what can be measured is only the external, only that which lies outside the grasp of the imagination, men can measure only what they cannot understand. This may help to explain why American social scientists generally avoid causal analysis and take refuge in correlations.

or good that the general will should be fulfilled, it does not follow, as MacIver has shown, that the general will is the will for the general good; for what is general in Rousseau's sense is the interest, not the will; and this may be willed by one or by a few, in which case the will is not that of the body of the people but of only a fraction of the population. But which will is it that wills the general will? Clearly there is no positive standard in Rousseau's theory according to which this can be determined. When Rousseau therefore turns to a majority will determined through a balance or cancellation of pluses and minuses, he accepts a political principle that is useful and perhaps alone practical, but one that nevertheless bears no necessary relation to the general will as he understands it.

By avoiding Rousseau's identification of the political with the social order, MacIver has given the general will a new and more realistic application. In his construction, the general will is not the will *of* the state but the will *for* the state, that is, the will to maintain it. It is not the will that directs or determines policy, that, as Rousseau believed, continuously and directly legislates; it is rather the will that sustains the community in the face of differences among men and groups as to what that policy shall be. It is the will of the person to be a citizen, to accept the decision of a majority or of a constituted government even if it does not win his approval. It is the will for political unity and is therefore logically prior to and more universal than the will of the political association, which is never more than a partial and evanescent will. This latter will, conceived of as the will *of* the state, is the majority or policy-directing will. It is, in MacIver's theory, the true ultimate sovereign which sets up and pulls down governments and which dictates the contours of their policy. In no state, least of all in a democratic state, is the active government the choice of all the citizens; the "will of the people" is rarely, if ever, the will of all the people. The government in power is at most sustained by the will of a fluctuating majority, a sovereign neither one and indivisible but elusive and inconstant. But it is a sovereign that, through its incessant rejection of alternatives, can alone give direction, can alone move through difference to the policy of the hour. Since, however, common action cannot proceed simultaneously from a great number of autonomous wills, however common their interest, the political as every other association must have a center or focus of action. Here MacIver finds his third kind or stage of common will, which he terms the government or legislative sovereign. The majority will or ultimate sovereign makes (and unmakes) the government, but it is the government or legislative sovereign that has the exclusive right, during the term assigned to it by the ultimate sovereign, to make laws of universal validity within its own sphere, together with the right to the exercise of force in the maintenance of such laws and of the machinery for their enforcement. But this right accrues to the government only because it is the guardian of the constitution, the executor of the laws—laws which it enforces but which it too must obey. The government does not have this power in its own right; its power is not legitimate outside the realm of law.

Thus the will of the community is revealed in the maintenance of the state; and the will of the state is manifested in its laws. This explains why the law is obeyed by those who oppose as well as by those who support it. Political theorists who ascribe obedience to the fact that the majority has also the greater force fail to perceive that there is a will more ultimate than the will of the state, and that is the will to maintain it. Consequently, states in which the general will is not active must be regarded as imperfect forms; and the state *qua* state—the state as an organ of the community— must be a democracy, understanding by democracy not necessarily the rule of the many but the active functioning of the general will, giving direct support, and not merely passive acquiescence, to a government chosen by itself.[5] More explicitly, MacIver means by democracy a form of state in which (*a*) the distinction between the state and the community is constitutionally drawn, and (*b*) both the composition and the policies of government are determined through the free operation of conflicting opinions. The first of these criteria implies, among other things, the existence of constitutional guarantees and civil rights which the government is not empowered to abrogate. It is a way of making power responsible by confirming and strengthening the distinction between government as an agent and the people as the principal who holds it to account; it is a way of establishing the formal superiority of the community over the state. The second criterion implies, among other things, a system

---

[5] Reasoning along these lines, MacIver arrived at the conclusion in *The Modern State,* pp. 339–340, that the historical trend of political evolution, in spite of reversions, was in the direction of democracy. It is to be noted, however, that *The Modern State* was published in 1926, when prevailing conditions were charitable to such a view. It is at least questionable, in the light of subsequent developments, whether history can sustain the argument. MacIver's conclusion would be more plausible were it based solely on logical rather than historical considerations, for then the state as he defines it most truly approximates itself—that is, its true nature or end in the Aristotelian sense—as it moves toward democracy. But unless one is prepared to deny that dictatorships and other forms of oligarchy are states—and MacIver does not of course entertain such a notion—there are limitations even to the logical argument. MacIver's inference from history is attacked, though crudely and without the necessary analysis, in E. M. Sait, *Democracy* (New York: The Century Co., 1929), pp. 16–18.

under which any major trend or change of public opinion can constitutionally register itself in the character and policies of government.   It is not a way of governing, whether by majority or otherwise, but primarily a way of determining who shall govern and, broadly, to what ends.   It is consequently the meaning of democracy that the political system is one form of the organization of the community, limited to the ends that meet with major approval of that community, and that force is never directed against opinion as such.

In these terms, federalism becomes the necessary principle for the coordination of community, and democracy the necessary principle for the control of power and the protection of freedom.   MacIver here employs the term federalism in its wider meaning to refer to the general relation of local to national autonomy; it is the attempt to reconcile the nearer specialized claim with the more universal claim, to transcend the multiplicity of allegiances rather than to reduce all allegiances to one.   As a pluralist, MacIver seeks to retain not only the numerous likenesses but also the differences among social groups; he respects and wants to preserve the diversity of interests within the wider community.   He argues, indeed, that the small community need not and should not be completely absorbed within the great community, since the small community fulfills a unique and valuable service—the realization of intimate loyalties and personal relationships, and of the specific traditions and memories of everyday life.   On the other hand, the growth of common interests has made the institution of war between nations both irrational and vain; hence the coordination of community into some permanent form of international federation with appropriate sanctions is indicated.   The principle, if not the application, of federalism thus becomes clear: so far as common interest extends, so far ought a federation also to extend, with narrower and wider circles of community duly corresponding to narrower and wider needs.

What sustains a federation, in MacIver's conception, is the general will; and what distinguishes a federation from, say, an empire, is that the general will is as broad as the federation (except, of course, in a time of civil war), whereas empire rests on a far narrower basis of will.   A federal state thus presents an important problem of reconciling sovereignty with the requirements of coordination.   For in a true federation each of the constituent units has a certain autonomy, a partial sovereignty, recognized in the articles of union through a definition of the respective powers of the federal state and of its constituent states.   It would then seem to follow that no change in the relation of the unit to the whole can legitimately be forced upon the constituent unit by a majority outside itself, that, apart from the conditions it has accepted in entering the federation or at any later time, the constituent unit remains in the position of a free state.

Its jurisdiction and power thus limited, the federal state should not, in MacIver's view, attempt to exercise compulsion over the communities organized into constituent states. It is rather the latter which should prevail as against the federation, when on some issue they are overwhelmingly and bitterly opposed to a principle of policy accepted by the rest. The alternative is to risk disruption of the federation. In this way, MacIver believes, the coordination of the community, once achieved, is maintained; and the general will is able to override, though not to remove, the interests that divide men.[6]

Federalism is the form a state must take if it is to act as a unifying agent, but it can act in this way only if it has itself undergone evolution toward democracy. Although no institutions are secure, those which rest on the sustaining power of the conscious cooperation and participation of the community are, in MacIver's judgment, the strongest. The institutions are then not alien to the people but are the people's own. A people can overthrow any form of government, but what reasonable alternative is there to overthrowing one that is uniquely its own? Clearly democracy would be foolish to restore the class-ruled state—a state historically identified with the interests of a ruler or ruling caste, military or landed or financial oligarchy— as against a state directed toward the interests of the whole. The democratic state, even when only partially realized, reveals in striking form the transition from a power-system to a welfare-system. In an oligarchy the holders of power may profess the general welfare, but they are rarely, if ever, committed to it; nor are they constitutionally responsible for their failure to move from verbal profession to actual deed. But if power is an instrument and welfare a goal, the ultimate and crucial distinction is between a system maintained for the welfare of a class and one maintained for the welfare of the whole. Since democracy alone makes the state responsive to the dominant desires of the people, since indeed it is the only kind of government that explicitly rests on the constitutional exercise of the will of the people, it is of all political systems the least likely to deny the welfare of the whole. And it is by the same token the system most likely to realize the general will.

---

6 This special problem of federalism is treated most directly in *Community*, pp. 264–266, and *The Modern State*, pp. 378–381.

It is true, of course, that citizens in a democracy do not always set the common welfare above their special interests. This gives greater urgency to the task of the state, which is to strengthen the sense of common interest by promoting the common good. By providing equality of citizenship and of opportunity, and by extending power and assuring certain primary liberties to all the people, the democratic state can emerge as the guardian of the whole. Thus only can the regard for personality—which is in MacIver's political theory the only intrinsic value, the highest end—be secured, and only then can freedom and power be so reconciled as to achieve this value for all men.

By freedom MacIver means an ordered system of liberties and restraints. By power he means the capacity to control the behavior of others, whether directly by fiat or indirectly by the manipulation of available instrumentalities. Since power is social and not merely political, the determination of what freedoms shall exist is made by those who have economic, religious, military, and other forms of power as well as by those who control the state. This produces unending conflict between, and in a multi-group society within, the various power centers; for each of the power groups, in seeking to advance its own interests, attempts to restrain the activities of those that impede it. Since, however, political power remains under all conditions the final lever of control of the social order, most a-political power groups have generally sought to attach to themselves the power of the state. At all times the state has been a primary object of the ceaseless struggle for power.

To make the state the instrument of the whole and to prevent abuse of the power of the state by special groups, the community must set limits to the power of the state—even a democratic state. Fundamentally, these limits are set by certain civil and political liberties which the state may not transgress. Such liberties, MacIver is aware, do not cover all the liberties that men prize, and there are other things besides their liberties that men prize, most notably economic security. This suggests to MacIver that the state may properly assume the additional function of supervising the economic order. In the interests of the community, the state should, among other things, control the restraints imposed by power organizations such as business corporations and labor unions, ensure a basic standard of well-being, assure to the worker a social position as a partner in enterprise rather than as a mere item of cost, and sustain, where the system itself proves incapable of doing so, the economic equilibrium.⁷ Another task of the state is defined by the area of culture. There are certain functions—in particular those which sustain and equip the arts of living (for example, museums, libraries, and public parks) and which provide opportunities for the citizen to share the cultural heritage of mankind (such as education)—that properly, although not exclusively, fall within the domain of the state. But where one group of people can practice its particular code without entailing outward consequences that directly impede or prevent other groups from practicing in equal liberty their own ways, the state should not attempt to invoke coercive sanctions against the group code. What, in these terms, the state can properly do and what it should or must leave to others cannot be settled merely by the establishment of broad principles. There remains always a large debatable area, where experience alone can be an adequate guide and where the lines of interference should be adjusted to the needs of the time, changing standards of private and public morality, and advances in the art of government itself.

Through such transformations and expansions of its functions, the state fulfills and increasingly reveals its true nature as the guardian of the community, wielding its power in the interests of the general welfare. And this is achieved, MacIver maintains, precisely because the state is a democratic state; for only in democracy is government rooted in the active and freely expressed will of the people.

But the will of the people, as we noted earlier, is seldom, and perhaps never, the will of all the people. Almost always dissenters will oppose the policy of the government. Almost always there will be those who do not *will* the law. Why, then, should they obey? Traditionally, MacIver observes, the obligation to obey has been justified on two main grounds. One is the legitimacy of the source from which law emanates, that is, the right ascribed to the law-making authority. The other is the rationality of content, the intrinsic merit of the law itself. Whether these are conjoined or distinguished, the answers thus far given remain, in MacIver's judgment, inadequate; for, even if the legitimacy of the source is acknowledged, there are other authorities and other obligations, with whose demands the law of the state may be in conflict. To which shall we yield the prior obligation—state or church, state or

⁷ For MacIver's ideas on the relation between the state and the economic order, see his *Labor in the Changing World* (New York: E. P. Dutton & Co., Inc., 1919); *The Modern State*, Chapter IX; *The Web of Government*, pp. 125–143, 331–359; and *Democracy and the Economic Challenge* (New York: Alfred A. Knopf, Inc., 1952).

labor union, state or political party, state or family? On a question such as this, MacIver is convinced, there is no hope of consensus; the answers given will differ with the kind of government under contemplation as well as with the value-system of the respondent. In general, however, MacIver holds that obedience is obligatory except when, in the considered judgment of the citizen, disobedience promotes the greater welfare of the whole society in which he lives. Where the law of the state denies or overrides other claims, it has no sure foundations; the firmament of order is not likely to be sustained. Hence a wise state will not seek unnecessarily to impose laws that clash with the customs, beliefs, or traditions of any important sector of the people. It will endeavor instead to recognize and, so far as is possible, to accommodate within its legal framework the various loyalties of men. Thus only, in MacIver's view, can we approach a truly universal general will.

EVALUATION

A political theory can be criticized on a variety of grounds, and MacIver's effort—like any comprehensive system of theory—has already been subjected to a critical scrutiny of some of its first principles of methodology and value.[8] In what follows, I shall confine myself to the terms of the system itself, accepting (for the moment) its values and presuppositions, and seek instead to explore some of the difficulties which follow from their application. This will make it possible to focus on the two difficulties that attend all formulations of theory and bedevil all political philosophers irrespective of the "truth" of their values or the "rightness" of their principles. One is the reduction of right principles to right conduct. The other and more serious difficulty involves the reconciliation of conflicting principles. In all such conflicts one of three solutions is open. If one principle takes precedence over the other, we sacrifice the lesser, in which case no real problem can be said to exist. If the conflicting principles are relatively equal in value, we may look to a standard or value transcending either of them in terms of which the resolution can be made. Or if the conflicting principles are relatively equal but no consensus can be reached concerning a greater or

---

8 See, for example, Morris Ginsberg, *Reason and Unreason in Society* (London: Longmans, Green & Co., Ltd., 1947), pp. 115–121; J. D. Mabbott, *The State and the Citizen* (London: Hutchinson's University Library, c. 1948), pp. 79–85; P. A. Sorokin, *Society, Culture, and Personality* (New York: Harper & Brothers, 1947), pp. 116–118; D. B. Truman, *The Governmental Process* (New York: Alfred A. Knopf, Inc., 1951), pp. 49–52, 351; and the article by J. H. Muirhead in *Mind*, Vol. XXXVII, 1928, pp. 82–87.

more comprehensive principle, we may look to a method such as democracy and the principle of majority rule—in place, say, of force or divine intervention—as a necessary expedient rather than an eternally "true" solution.

These difficulties, and MacIver's resolution of them, can best be demonstrated as they emerge from his applications of his broad principles. I shall restrict my examination here to two instances in which MacIver's reduction and reconciliation of conflicting principles do not, in terms of his own theory, exhaust the possible alternatives—where, indeed, the political and moral elements of that theory suggest a contrary solution. These are, first, the clash between the principles of federalism and of political obligation; and second, the conflict between the values of freedom, order, and political obligation with respect to the treatment of those who advocate the overthrow of democratic government by force.

(1) **Federalism and Political Obligation.** It is easy to see how these principles may come into conflict. Federalism urges, as a necessary principle of unity, that the greater power abstain from coercing the constituent states on matters concerning which the latter feel deeply and uncompromisingly. But federalism does not limit, any more than does any other political arrangement, the action of the greater state to instances where it obtains unanimous agreement. It is the first axiom of political obligation, as MacIver understands it, that the minority must, for the sake of the common good realized through the association, accept and carry out the decision of the majority. This, for him, is the established rule of all associations; it is part of the sociality of the civilized man. He admits, however, that the policy of the majority may on occasion seem to the minority to be destructive of the general good. In this event, he argues, the minority *must* secede and form a new association. And where, because of the thoroughgoing character of state power, secession is impossible, disobedience is the remaining and proper alternative. The individual and the group must choose what seems to them the greater loyalty; and since the act of disobedience depends on the same sense of obligation which alone justifies enforcement of the law, it cannot be condemned.[9] In the interests of the community, therefore, MacIver contends that "in spite of the verdict of the American Civil War, it may be generally better for the federation as a whole to suffer the inconveniences and hindrances result-

---

[9] The argument is concisely put in *The Elements of Social Science*, p. 166. See also note 6 above.

ing from the concomitant operation of contrary principles than to enforce its majority-rule against the determinate opposition of a real community." [10]

Now it is by no means clear that MacIver's conclusion follows from the terms of his argument. Where a constituent state represents a fairly homogeneous set of interests motivating the great bulk of its population, his case for pure or extreme federalism is readily sustained. For under such conditions, a conflict of values between the constituent state and the federal government would involve distinct sets of interests clearly opposed and embodied in the respective political units: the constituent state would stand for one set of interests, the federal state for another. But if, as is quite generally the case, there are divisions or conflicts within the constituent state no less strong or important than those that applied in the first illustration, then pure federalism, pushed to an extreme, merely serves to promote the special interests of the group that happens to be in power, that controls the government of the constituent state. MacIver's principle would thus lead to the defense of a fictional geographic interest and the sacrifice of a real and perhaps overriding economic or social interest of the bulk of the total population.

How can secession in the latter case be held to promote MacIver's greater principle, the general good? And if a resolution of the conflict is not to be made in terms of a superior standard or value, how can one reconcile secession with the alternative principle of majority rule? How reconcile the ensuing state with the principle of the general will; for if the basis of the state is the general will, whose will is it that in this circumstance wills the withdrawal of the constituent state? These considerations are all the more relevant when a cleavage within the constituent state follows the lines of rigid stratification, as in the American South before the Civil War. For then, in the face of a dual community, the free adjustment of differences is clearly precluded.

The conflicts of principle are thus multiple and weave bewildering patterns. On the one hand, a dissenting constituent state is, in MacIver's theory, entitled to disobey the will of the greater majority. But a minority within the constituent state is also entitled to disobey. Now, however, disobedience by the latter against the majority-will of the dominant group involves, or might involve, obedience to the majority-will of the total community. Thus the disruption of the greater community does not assure the unity of

---

[10] *Community*, p. 265.

the lesser community; while compulsion of the constituent state may make possible the creation of a new unity between the minority within the constituent state and the national majority. Which community shall the federal state seek to serve? Which obligation shall it recognize? If we take personality as the ultimate value, the standard against which we shall measure these conflicting claims, can we legitimately say, as MacIver seems to imply, that the personalities of the rulers within the constituent state have a greater claim to fulfillment than the personalities of the dissenters? If we adopt the alternative method of resolution, the majority process as it operates in democracy, shall we say that this shall prevail only at the level of the constituent state but not at the level of the federal state? The principle of federalism is but one of many values, and I am unable to see why, in MacIver's own terms, it carries an inherently superior claim, why it necessarily compels the conclusion to which MacIver was led.

(2) **Freedom, Order, and Political Obligation.** "To establish order and to respect personality—these are the essential tasks positive and negative of the state." [11] This is the central principle by which MacIver seeks to delineate the limits of state action. What, however, does it mean to establish order? Obviously MacIver does not have in mind the order of a concentration camp. He means a particular kind of order, an order conducive to the general welfare which, in his view, is not only a proper aim but the sole justification of government. It is an order that establishes certain liberties and concomitant restraints which make for the development of the free personality. And foremost among such liberties MacIver puts freedom of opinion. Whatever else the state may or may not do, it should not, MacIver argues, seek to control opinion, *no matter what the opinion may be.* But to this underscored principle a crucial exception is immediately entered: the state may take cognizance of incitements to break its laws or defy its authority. MacIver does not imply by this that the citizen in a democracy may not voice his belief that an existing law is pernicious, or that an act of authority is illegitimate, or even that the constitution is misguided; the citizen can, indeed, go further and seek by peaceful persuasion and all constitutional methods to change the law and the constitution. But to urge law-breaking is to attack the fundamental order, the establishment and maintenance of which is the first business of the state. Here, MacIver insists, the state must have the right to take what-

---

[11] *The Modern State,* p. 150.

ever steps it deems necessary to assure the very object of its existence. Particularly is this true where the incitement is itself an attempt to subvert the rule of free opinion, where an individual or group advocates the overthrow of government by force.

But if, as MacIver also contends, opinion can be fought only by opinion, if force is pitifully irrelevant in the control of ideas, why should not the advocacy—as against the utilization—of force be countered by opinion? Why resort in this instance to force? To suppress the advocacy of force by force does not make what is advocated untrue. Indeed, as MacIver recognizes, to use force is to snatch from truth its only means of victory. It is itself a blasphemy against truth.

What is at issue, among other things, is the distinction between the word and the deed, between what men say and what men do. "Order" can tolerate many things that men might say, for even the strongest words become virtually impotent in certain situations—a truth to which Hyde Park and Columbus Circle orators will readily attest. It is the context in which the word is uttered that is most relevant, and here I must still follow the "clear and present danger" precept of Justice Holmes. MacIver himself seems to share this position when he remarks that the state has authority over action but not authority over thought and opinion, and again when he asserts that a democratic system does not, in principle, deny the right of the citizens to advocate anti-democratic ideas or even the complete abandonment of democracy.[12] But he remains fundamentally committed to the broader restraint. Repeatedly he returns to the principle that when an individual in a democratic system approves the resort to force for the furtherance of any cause, or when, in pleading this cause, he identifies himself with any group or party that accepts this method, he rules himself out from the sufferance of democracy.[13]

MacIver thus takes the position that the free play of ideas is, in effect, a principle that does not apply to its own domain. Unlike ideas per se, the free play of ideas is but a method through which ideas are judged; it is pre-eminently the rule by which the political game

---

12 *Ibid.*, p. 219; *The Web of Government*, pp. 200–201.

13 So concerned is MacIver with the security of the social order that at one point he even defends the right of the state to forbid the teaching of certain religious doctrines that are calculated to undermine the social order, provided the state is right in its conception of the social danger and commits no counterbalancing evil by interfering. *Community*, p. 40. Apart from the ambiguities (e.g., the definition of a "counterbalancing evil") and the dangers (e.g., granting to the state the responsibility for determining the rightness of its own judgment) in this doctrine, MacIver has himself, in his later books, shifted the emphasis to the democratic principle of religious liberty.

shall be played. But one can affirm the instrumental superiority of this method only if he is prepared to accept whatever policy decisions may emerge from it. It does not, *as a method,* carry an intrinsic value that is beyond attack. For those whose sense of personality forbids acceptance of a method that might lead the state to adopt what is in their view a wrong policy, democracy commends itself but poorly. For such men the supreme value is another ethic or principle; and democracy is valid to them only as it conduces to the achievement of that value. It is easy enough for one who believes in democracy to say—and to say truly—that the method permits of self-correction; but what if the necessary corrections are not made? What if men of rigid conscience, what if revolutionaries, of whatever orthodoxy, find that they cannot achieve their objectives through the democratic framework, and further, that there is no hope of winning popular support for a constitutional change in the structure itself? Then clearly their only alternative, as MacIver recognized in another connection, is secession or rebellion. But if MacIver admits the right of political disobedience and rebellion when the citizen is convinced that by such action he is promoting the general welfare, why should he repudiate that principle when the citizen merely seeks greater support for his cause by the oral or written expression of his ideas?

Once again we are confronted by a conflict of principles—the claims of order *versus* the claims of civil disobedience. If MacIver's philosophy of political obligation has merit, I cannot see why the individual must in principle accept as final the state's denial of his freedom to advocate the revolutionary overthrow of the government. No state, it is true, can as a matter of policy admit this right; but neither can a state admit any claim to disobedience. This, however, is a legal and not an ethical principle; and in point of fact states do concede the right of men to refuse obedience in certain instances, as in the case of those who profess a conscientious objection to military service. From the point of view of the individual, the moral issue is not essentially different. In both cases he is confronted by a law he cannot accept; in both cases he disobeys, knowing full well that certain consequences will attend his refusal to abide by the law. If MacIver vindicates an act of disobedience in the one case, it is difficult to grasp the principle that precludes vindication in the other.

It may even be argued that in this respect the cause of order is advanced rather than obstructed by the recognition of such a freedom; for it is easier for a state to protect itself against those who openly urge its destruction than it is to guard itself against those

who disobey.   What, for example, would the state do if, in the face
of the Taft-Hartley Law which the labor unions vehemently oppose, labor were to put down its tools in a general stoppage of work?
Would it be easier for the democratic state to sustain the social
order under such conditions than it would be to protect it from
the constantly known, because openly affirmed, advocates of revolutionary overthrow?   "In the last resort," MacIver once said, "character needs to employ force only against the stupidity which relies
on force." [14]   It does not appear to me that the democratic state
must operate as if it were *always* driven to the last resort.   The faith
and intelligence of men committed to a right principle, when conjoined with a fundamental respect for personality—of all men, not
merely of themselves—can maintain a social order even in the face
of violent dissents.   The general will is not destroyed by the extreme
pleadings of a recalcitrant few.

MAC IVER'S CONTRIBUTION IN SUMMARY

These reflections articulate certain difficulties in MacIver's political theory, but they are the difficulties inherent in all philosophies
that do not rest on closed systems.   In the absence of absolute truth,
of the kind of conviction that is indistinguishable from dogma, men
cannot "solve" what MacIver knows to be an irreducible ethical
conflict, the conflict of principles.   MacIver has failed to reconcile
these conflicts not because he has been unaware of them, but because, as a democrat, he respects personality and recognizes that
men will always differ in their sense of right and wrong.   Enlightenment, no matter how close it may lead men to the abandonment of
their innumerable petty difference-breeding bigotries, will always
vary from person to person; conflicting interests are in any case always powerful in shaping ethical judgments.   Thus the conflict
can never cease.

The political problem is then to resolve the conflict in ways that
will not disrupt the community.   It is to discover not a solution but
a means to a solution, a means at once consistent with the ultimate
value of personality and with the maintenance of the social order.
This is the central principle of democracy.   In this principle alone,
MacIver is convinced, can such a resolution be secured.   For no
other principle builds on the diversity in man.   No other system
respects man's individuality and seeks to bind him to the social
order not by demanding a total and exclusive loyalty but by an al-

14 *The Modern State,* p. 228.

legiance that transcends, and therefore absorbs, the multiplicity of loyalties intrinsic to his nature.

In the elaboration of this principle, MacIver has made his primary contribution. He has grasped the meaning of democracy and related it to human values and the sense of community. He has analyzed the structures and processes of human action to show how democracy can employ its utilitarian or instrumental systems to achieve and sustain the values that constitute culture. If his approach has been at times a pragmatic one, it is because the very nature of social life does not admit of mathematical reduction; always there are vast areas in which experience is the only guide, in which the establishment of broad principles cannot settle concrete problems. What democracy can do is to supply the form of solution, but the application of it is a task that has no end.

Much may be said to dispute some of MacIver's concepts, such as the theory of the general will, and to point to certain shortcomings or inadequacies of analysis, such as his failure to treat the nature and problems of horizontal mobility in the same systematic fashion that he examined vertical mobility in the pyramids of power. Nor is his system without certain difficulties when his principles are applied and at times come into conflict, as I have tried to indicate above.

But when all this has been said, it remains clear that MacIver has contributed an important and searching body of doctrine to political theory. His influence has already been manifested in the works of contemporary theorists, not least that of G. D. H. Cole, although MacIver would not, I think, subscribe to the conclusions to which Cole was led. His elucidation of terms such as community, association, institution, state, and the like, has made for greater clarity in political and sociological analysis. His own incisive and systematic analysis of social causation and social controls, of the state as an association of community, of theory as a methodological tool, and of the relations between political structures and processes on the one hand, and human values on the other, between the actual and the ideal—these are contributions that have profoundly affected the course of political thought. MacIver owes much, of course, to the thinkers who have preceded him, particularly to such German sociologists as Tönnies and Alfred and Max Weber. But in the depth and richness of his own formulations, and in the lines of exploration he has suggestively advanced, he has laid a groundwork on which future theorists can in turn firmly stand.

INDEX